OBSCURITY AND CLARITY IN THE LAW

Obscurity and Clarity in the Law
Prospects and Challenges

Edited by

ANNE WAGNER
Université du Littoral Côte d'Opale, France

SOPHIE CACCIAGUIDI-FAHY
National University of Ireland, Galway

ASHGATE

Published by
Ashgate Publishing Limited
Gower House
Croft Road
Aldershot
Hampshire GU11 3HR
England

Ashgate Publishing Company
Suite 420
101 Cherry Street
Burlington, VT 05401-4405
USA

www.ashgate.com

British Library Cataloguing in Publication Data
Obscurity and clarity in the law : prospects and challenges
    1. Law - Language 2. Semantics (Law) 3. Legal composition
    I. Wagner, Anne, 1968- II. Cacciaguidi-Fahy, Sophie
    340.1'4

Library of Congress Cataloging-in-Publication Data
Wagner, Anne, 1968-
Obscurity and clarity in the law : prospects and challenges / by Anne Wagner and Sophie Cacciaguidi-Fahy.
    p. cm.
    Includes bibliographical references and index.
    ISBN 978-0-7546-7143-5 (alk. paper)
    1. Law--Language. 2. Semantics (Law) 3. Legal composition. I. Cacciaguidi-Fahy, Sophie. II. Title.

    K213.W34 2008
    340'.14--dc22

2008003565

ISBN 978-0-7546-7143-5

Mixed Sources
Product group from well-managed forests and other controlled sources
www.fsc.org Cert no. SA-COC-1565
© 1996 Forest Stewardship Council
FSC

Printed and bound in Great Britain by
MPG Books Ltd, Bodmin, Cornwall.

Contents

PART 1: CROSSROADS BETWEEN LAW AND LANGUAGE

PART 2: AN INTERNATIONAL PERSPECTIVE

List of Figures and Tables

Notes on Contributors

M. Douglass Bellis hold a BA in Greek and Latin Classics and in Government from Cornell, 1968 and a JD Duke, 1971. He was admitted to the North Carolina State Bar in 1971 and has been an Attorney in the Office of Legislative Counsel to the U.S. House of Representatives since 1971. He is currently Deputy Legislative Counsel. He is the author of numerous journal articles on matters of interest to legislative drafters.

Sophie Cacciaguidi-Fahy is a Lecturer in Law at the National University of Ireland, Galway. She has published in the area of legal discourse, law and culture, law and semiotics, intercultural legal and business communication and human rights law.

Deborah Cao is affiliated to the Socio-Legal Research Centre of the Law School, Griffith University, Australia. She has published in the areas of legal language, legal translation, pragmatics, court interpreting, legal theory, semiotics, philosophical, linguistic analysis of Chinese law and legal culture. She also teaches and writes about animal law and animal rights, and is a Fellow of the Oxford Centre for Animal Ethics. She is currently the deputy editor of the *International Journal for the Semiotics of Law*. Her books include *Chinese Law: A Language Perspective* (2004, Ashgate), *Interpretation, Law and the Construction of Meaning* (2007, jointly edited with Anne Wagner and Wouter Werner, Springer), *Translating Law* (2007, Foreword by Justice Michael Kirby, Multilingual Matters), and *Animals are not Things: Animal Law in the West* (2007, Preface by Peter Singer, China Law Press).

Anne-Françoise Debruche holds a PhD in comparative law from the University of Liège (Belgium). She teaches property law and comparative law at the University of Ottawa, civil law section. She has been a researcher (*aspirant*) for the Fonds National de la Recherche Scientifique (Belgium) and at the Quebec Research Center of Private and Comparative Law of McGill University. She is co-author, with Professor Donald Poirier, of the third edition of the *Introduction générale à la common law* (Bruxelles: Bruylant and Cowansville (Qc): Yvon Blais, 2005).

Barbro Ehrenberg-Sundin coordinates the linguistic draft revision of Swedish legislation in the Government Offices. She is also a member of the Government's Plain Swedish Group (Klarspråksgruppen), which since 1994 has encouraged Swedish authorities to start their own plain language projects. Since 2002, she has helped establish an EU language service, promoting clear drafting in EU institutions and supporting the Swedish translators in the EU. She is chairman of the group Klarspråksgruppen, an informal co-operation between Swedish cultural organisations, such as the Swedish Academy, the Swedish Language Council and the

Centre of Terminology, TNC. She is also the Swedish representative for Clarity. She has written extensively in the area of Plain Language.

Alexandre Flückiger is a Professor of constitutional law at the University of Geneva, Switzerland. He obtained his PhD in 1996. He then undertook various research projects at the Postgraduate School for Administrative Sciences in Speyer (Germany). He has written extensively in the field of public law. After having been Chief of the Legislative Method Service at the Federal Department of Justice and Police in Bern, he then became a member of the Federal Commission of Data Protection from 2004 to 2007. Since 2005, he has been a member of the Geneva Evaluation Committee of Public Policies.

Maurizio Gotti is Professor of English Linguistics at the University of Bergamo. He is Director of CERLIS, the research centre for specialised languages based at the University of Bergamo. From 1999 to 2001, he was President of the Italian Association of English Studies. From 2000 to 2004, he was President of the European Confederation of University Language Centres. His main research areas are English syntax and lexicography, and the features and origins of specialised discourse. He is a member of the Editorial Board of national and international journals, and edits the *Linguistic Insights* series for Peter Lang.

James Kessler QC is in practice at the English Revenue bar. He is the author of *Drafting Trusts and Will Trusts*, 8th Edition (2006), now part of a series of books dealing with drafting in the jurisdictions of Northern Ireland, Canada, the Cayman Islands, the Channel Islands, Singapore and Australia. He is also the author of *Taxation of Foreign Domiciliaries*, 6th Edition (2007) and *Taxation of Charities* 6th Edition (2007). He is a founder member of STEP and founder of the Trusts Discussion Forum.

Andreas Lötscher, obtained a PhD in German Literature and Linguistics from the University of Zurich and a MA in Linguistics from the University of Chicago. From 1981 to 1991, he was an Assistant Professor of German Linguistics at the University of Basel. Since 1991, he is a committee member of the federal administration of law revision for the Central Linguistic Services of the Swiss Federal Chancery (Berne). His main research interests are legal language, diachronic syntax, and dialectology.

Tunde Opeibi, PhD teaches English Linguistics in the Department of English, University of Lagos, Nigeria. His areas of research are in Applied Linguistics, Sociolinguistics, Discourse Analysis, Political Communication, Pragmatics, Forensic Linguistics (Legal Discourse) and Multimodal Discourse Analysis. He has published in various journals in the areas of Political Discourse, Legal Discourse, Second Language Teaching and Learning. He belongs to many International Academic Associations among which are: Clarity International, International Pragmatics Association (IPrA), International Association of Forensic Linguists (IAFL) etc. He is presently the Senior Special Assistant (Speech and Communication) to the Governor of Lagos State, Lagos, Nigeria.

Aino Piehl works as a researcher and EU language specialist in the Research Institute for the Languages of Finland. Her research interests include the comprehensibility of administrative texts and the influence of EU legislation on Finnish administrative language. She is the co-author of two handbooks for writers of official texts and a guidebook for officials producing texts and speeches.

Ben Piper (OAM, B.Com., LLB., LLM. (Melb)) was a legislative drafter in the Office of the Chief Parliamentary Counsel, Victoria (Australia). Since early 2006, he has been the Chief Legislative Drafter of the National Transport Commission (Australia). Ben Piper is committed to the use of plain legal language and has presented at various conferences internationally mostly relating to the use of plain language in legislative drafting.

Anne Wagner is a Senior Lecturer in LSP at the Université du Littoral Côte d'Opale (France). She is President of the International Roundtable for the Semiotics of Law (www.semioticsoflaw.com). She is the Editor-in-Chief of the *International Journal for the Semiotics of Law* (www.springer.com). She is also a member of the Editorial Board of international journals, and edits the *Legal Semiotics Monographs* series for Deborah Charles Publication (www.legaltheory.demon.co.uk). She has published extensively in the area of law and semiotics, legal discourse, law and culture, and legal translation.

Louis E. Wolcher is the Charles I. Stone Professor of Law at the University of Washington School of Law, in Seattle, Washington (U.S.A.). Holding degrees from both Stanford University and Harvard Law School, he has written extensively in various fields of philosophy and law, including philosophy of language, philosophy of law and human rights. One of his essays, 'Time's Language', was awarded Second Prize by the final jury of the Millennial International Essay Competition in 2000, and his book *Beyond Transcendence in Law and Philosophy* was published in 2005 by Routledge-Cavendish (Birkbeck Law Press). He has also given and published numerous lectures abroad, including at the European Court of Human Rights in Strasbourg (France), at the Institute of Political Science in Tashkent (Uzbekistan), at the Faculty of Law, University of Ljubljana in Ljubljana (Slovenia), at Kobe University and Osaka University in Japan, and at Mofid University in Iran.

Foreword

Clarity at law, specifically in legislative drafting or legal writing, continues to captivate the attention of legal scholars and practitioners alike; and more recently linguists. Not only do obscurity, ambiguity, indeterminacy and vagueness at law give rise to complex questions about the essence of the interpretation of the law, the social and political function of the law and the practical role of the legal profession, but it also challenges the very conception of the role that law plays in our daily lives.

It is important to note that the concept of clarity has progressively moved to the mainstream of legal scholarship. Within the last decade, issues related to clarity and obscurity have become the subject matter of a newly shaped and quite significant academic discipline and professional practice. This development has surfaced questions, challenges and new prospects which have yet to receive, in some part of the world, a fitting conceptualisation and subsequent articulation.

The origins of this book lie in the 2nd International Clarity Conference held in Boulogne-sur-Mer (France) in July 2005. The conference had four major aims. The first was to evaluate the status of clarity and plain language in the legal space. The second was to achieve a critical nexus between law and language with regards to the debates on clarity, obscurity and plain language relating to legislative drafting, legal writing and legal interpretation. The third aim was to offer an international perspective on these issues, drawing from various national legal cultures. The fourth was to bring together practitioners to debate the ever growing challenges legal drafters face in an increasingly complex legal world.

Obscurity and Clarity in the Law: Prospects and Challenges differs from other books on clarity, obscurity and plain legal language as it is (i) an attempt to tap the views of the actors from a wide range of settings: legal and language academics, legal practitioners, legislative drafters, legal writers, jurilinguists and legal interpreters, and linguists; and (ii) it endeavours to take a broader more holistic view of the intricate nature of obscurity and clarity in the law. With the non specialist in mind, and embracing the multi-dimensional conception of clarity and obscurity in the law, this book explores how these different groups view and address the issue of clarity and obscurity in legal language.

For these reasons, we have included authors who examine the issues in both a civil law and a common law context. We have also attempted to broaden the scope of this study by extending its content to bi-legal (Canada) and multicultural and multilingual settings (Switzerland). We have also ventured to China where the inherent vagueness and ambiguity of Chinese renders legal language more opaque than most Indo-European languages; to Africa where clarity faces the challenges of multilingualism and access to justice; and finally onto the international stage with commercial arbitration legal language where the plurality of languages used in the arbitration process anchors clarity in different cultures. Above all this book seeks to promote a constructive interdisciplinary debate on clarity, law and language.

Within this brief foreword, we would like to express our sincere appreciation to the contributors who agreed to participate in this project, specifically those practitioners who honed their crystal writing style against that of the required academic publishing style; and more so to 'those' who agreed to obliterate 'the footie in the footies'. We are grateful towards all who patiently and speedily, and sometimes … wittily responded to a stream of revisions and justifications. As always, words cannot express Sophie's thanks to Martin for his reliable support and to Meadhbh and Emeline for their enduring patience with 'mum's work'. Anne wishes also to convey her appreciation to her family for their unfailing support as well as to two demanding and active small brigands, Adrien and Aline, who gave her time to reflect in a quiet and peaceful home.

Thirroul / Boulogne-sur-Mer, December 2007

Table of Cases

Court of Justice of the European Communities

France

Switzerland

Eidgenössische Steuerverwaltung v. AG, Federal Court 2A.542/2002 (Arrêt du Tribunal Fédéral du 6 janvier 2004)

X. v. Stadt Chur, Federal Court 129 I 161 (Arrêt du Tribunal Fédéral du 19 mars 2003)

United Kingdom and Northern Ireland

Aspden v. Seddon (1875) LR 10 Ch. App. 394

BCCI v. Ali [2002] 1 AC 251

Charter Reinsurance Co. Ltd v. Fagan [1997] AC 313

Deeny v. Gooda WalkerLtd [1996] STC 299

Deutsche Morgan Grenfell v. HMRC [2006] UKHL 49

Doe v. Gwilum (1833) 5 B. and Ad. 122

Equity and Law Life Assurance v. Bodfield (1987) 281 EG 1448

Heydon's Case (1584) 76 English Reports 637

Investors Compensation Scheme v. West Bromwich Building Society [1998] 1 WLR 896

IRC v. Raphael [1935] AC 96

London Borough of Harrow v. Donoghue [1995] 1 Estates Gazette Law Reports 257

Mannai Investment Co v. Eagle Star Life Assurance Society [1997] AC 749

Maunsell v. Olins [1975] Law Reports – Appeal Cases 373 [House of Lords]

Miller v. Farmer (1815) 1 Merrivale 55

Milner v. Milner (1748) Ves. Sen. 1

Pedlar v. Road Block Gold Mines of India Ltd [1905] 2 Ch 427

Pepper v. Hart [1993] AC 593

Perrin v. Morgan [1943] AC 399

Philpots (Woking) Ltd. v. Surrey Conveyancers Ltd. [1986] 1 EGLR 97

Prenn v. Simmonds [1971] 1 WLR 1381

Raffles v. Wichelhaus 2 Hurl. and C. 906, 159 Eng. Rep. 375 (Ex. 1864)

Re Doland [1970] Ch 267

Re Toal Application for Judicial Review [2006] NIQB 44

Rickman v. Carstairs (1833) 5 B. and Ad. 663

Schuler v. Wickman Machine Tool Sales [1974] AC 235

US

Frigaliment Importing Co. v. B.N.S. International Sales Corp., 190 F.Supp. 116 (S.D.N.Y. 1960)

R.M. Investment and Trading Co. Pvt. Ltd. v. Boeing Co. A.I.R. 1994 SC 1136

Lists of Conventions, Legislations and Rules

Arbitration Rules

Rules of Arbitration of the International Chamber of Commerce, 2004
Rules of the Arbitration Institute of the Stockholm Chamber of Commerce, 2004
Rules of the London Court of International Arbitration, 1998

Australia

Accident Compensation Act 1985 (Vic)
Accident Compensation and Transport Accident Acts (Amendment) Act 2003 (Vic)
Acts Interpretation Act 1901(Cth)
Acts Interpretation Act 1954 (Qld)
Dangerous Goods Act 1985 (Vic)
Dangerous Goods and Equipment (Public Safety) Acts (Amendment) Act 2005(Vic)
Estate Agents and Sale of Land Acts (Amendment) Bill 2002 (Vic)
Estate Agents and Sale of Land Acts (Amendment) Bill 2003(Vic)
Equipment (Public Safety) Act 1994 (Vic)
Interpretation Act 1987 (NSW)
Interpretation Act 1978 (NT)
Interpretation of Legislation Act 1984 (Vic)
Legislations Act 2001 (NT)
Liquor Control Reform Act 1998 (Vic)
Liquor Control Reform (Underage Drinking and Enhanced Enforcement) Act 2004 (Vic)
Occupational Health and Safety Act 2005 (Vic)
Road Safety Act 1986 (Vic)
Sale of Land Act 1962 (Vic)
Social Security Act 1991 (NSW)
Subordinate Legislation Act 1994 (Vic)
Transport Accident Act 1986 (Vic)
Transport Legislation (Amendment) Act 2004 (Vic)

France

Code Civil (Articles 5-6; 544-577)

Canada

Act Respecting Improvements under Mistake of Title, Revised Statutes of Saskatchewan 1978, c. I-1
C.C.L.C. (Articles 11; 406-441)
Code Civil Québec (Articles 653; 947-948; 954-975)
Conveyancing and Law of Property Act, Revised Statutes of Ontario 1990, c. C. 34, s. 37
Education Act, R.S.O. 1990, c.E.2
Interpretation Act, L.R.Q., c. I-16, s. 41.2
Law of Property Act 1931, Revised Statutes of Manitoba 1987, c. L.90, s. 28
Law of Property Act, Continuing Consolidation of the Statutes of Manitoba, c. L.90, s. 27
Law of Property Act, Revised Statutes of Alberta 2000, c. L-7
Land Registration Act, Statutes of Nova Scotia 2001, c. 6, s. 76(2) and (3)
Municipal Act 2001, S.O. 2001, c.25
Supreme Court Act, Revised Statutes of Canada (1985), c. S-26, s. 4 and 6

China

The Criminal Code
Decision on Interpretation of Law (1995)
Environmental Protection Law of the People's Republic of China (1989)
The Interpretation of the Supreme People's Court and the Supreme People's Procuratorate Concerning Certain Issues Related to the Specific Application of Law in Handling Criminal Cases Involving Gambling (2005)
The Interpretation of the Supreme People's Court Concerning Certain Issues Related to the Specific Application of Law in Hearing Criminal Cases Involving Environmental Pollution (2006)
The Interpretation of the Supreme People's Court Concerning Certain Issues Related to the Specific Application of Law in Handling Criminal Cases Involving Undermining Production Safety in Mines (2007)
Organic Law of People's Court of the People's Republic of China (1979)

EU legislation

Directive 95/16/EC on the approximation of the laws of the Member States relating to lifts (OJ L 213, 7.9.1995, p.1-31)
Directive 2002/3/EC relating to ozone in ambient air (OJ L 67, 9.3.2002, pp.14-30)
Directive 20/2002/EC on the authorisation of electronic communications networks and services (OJ L 108, 24/4/2002 0021 - 0032)
European Convention on Human Rights and Fundamental Freedom ETS No 5, 213 UNTS 222 (1950)
Inter-institutional Agreement on common guidelines for the quality of drafting of Community legislation (OJ C 073 , 17/3/1999 0001 - 0004)

Regulation No 852/2004 (EC) on the hygiene of food stuff (OJ No. L226, 25.6.2004, p.3)

Finland

Hallintolaki 6.6.2003/434
Valtioneuvoston päätös toimenpiteistä valtion viranomaisten kielenkäytön parantamiseksi 23.6.1982/497

India

Indian Evidence Act 1872

New Zealand

Personal Property Securities Act 1999

Sweden

Constitutional Act Tryckfrihetsförordning (1949:105) [Freedom of the Press Act].
Förordning (1996:1515) med instruktion för Regeringskansliet [Ordinance on the Duties of the Government Offices].
Förvaltningslagen (1986:223) [Administrative Procedure Act]
Inkomstskattelagen (1999:1229) [Income Tax Act]
Vallagen (2005:837) [Elections Act]
Verksförordning (1995:1322) [Government Authorities and Agencies Ordinance]

Switzerland

Loi fédérale régissant la taxe sur la valeur ajoutée (RS 641.20)
Loi fédérale sur l'assurance-maladie (RS 832.1)
Loi fédérale sur l'assurance-vieillesse et survivants (RS 831.10)
Federal Council, Message à l'Assemblée fédérale concernant le projet de code civil suisse, *Feuille fédérale*, vol. IV, No. 24 (1904)
Feuille fédérale [FF] 1995 IV 1340
Feuille fédérale [FF] 1997 III 669
Feuille fédérale [FF] 2000 942
Feuille fédérale [FF] 2000 942, 947

UNCITRAL Enactments

UNCITRAL Model Law on International Commercial Arbitration, 1985
UNCITRAL Rules of Arbitration, 1976

United Kingdom

Animal Welfare Act 2006 (c.45)
Interpretation Act 1978
Jobseekers Act 1995 (c.18)
Occupier's Liability Act 1957
Timeshare Act 1992

USA

The Clean Water Act (CWA) 33 U.S.C. ss/1251 et seq. (1977)

Introduction

The *Chiaroscuro* of Legal Language

Sophie Cacciaguidi-Fahy and Anne Wagner

As argued by Holland and Webb (2003, 108-110 citing Hanson 1959 and O'Barr 1982) the relationship between law and language is based on power: 'the extent to which the law relies upon its own language is a very basic indication of the closed nature of legal argument'. They contend that the purpose of 'legalese' is to conceal rather than to enhance our understanding of a legal system (2003, 108); a process which Grossfeld (1990, 47 as cited in Holland and Webb 2003, 108) described as 'camouflage'.

The Gordian relationship between law and language is a 'neverending story'. The language of the law is, for the most part, a language of traditions that is a language whose function is primarily to transmit a set of immemorial traditions (Goodrich 1990). Legal language is thus inscribed in history. Yet it is capable of renewing itself for the reason that the specialist nature of its lexicon is closely intertwined with the evolving social function of the law (Mattila 2006). In that sense, legal language is plurifunctional and pluridimensional.

Both obscurity and clarity are multifaceted concepts (Cacciaguidi and Wagner 2006, 29). The former often assumes the notions of lexical or semantic or syntactic ambiguity (Holland and Webb 2003, 111-113; Solan 2004; Schane 2007, 12-53); vagueness in legal texts (Endicott 2000) or vagueness of categorisation (Lupu 2003; Bhatia, Engberg, Gotti and Heller 2005); indeterminacy (Solan 1993; Tiersma 1999) or more pointedly referential indeterminacy (Schane 2007, 35); fuzziness in normative texts (Wagner 2005a). Clarity, on the other hand, has become an umbrella term for semantic certainty, lexical precision, often linked to the intelligibility and readability of a normative text leading to greater access to the content of what is mostly regarded by the non legal professional as complex and often turgid syntax and language (Solan 2004; Butt and Castle 2006). In essence, clarity and obscurity are intrinsic to the law: a *chiaroscuro*. They are an inherent part of the construction of meaning within language. At law, they affect the two stages of the legal process: drafting and interpreting (Stratman 2004).

In the ongoing clarity versus obscurity debate (see Barnes 2006), plain language has become the dominant 'paradigm' embraced by clarity advocates. Proponents of clarity have thus devoted a large amount of effort to stressing the variety of techniques available to render a legal text clearer and thus more accessible to the average public (Cutts and Wagner 2002); specifically with regards to laws that directly affect them such as criminal laws. There is now a plethora of guidance on how to draft in better legalese, obliterating the many superfluous archaic words, Latinate expressions and pompous syntax (Macdonald 2006a; Mattila 2006).

While the clarity debate to date largely reflects an Anglophone centric perspective, the literature has progressively emphasised that obscurity and clarity are not restricted to a few isolated countries, but is increasingly an international phenomenon (Bekink and Botha 2007). The enlargement of the European Union, the emergence of the so called 'BRIC' economies and the growth of international trade have given rise to new challenges with respect to clarity. As a result, the poverty and limitations of the largely asymmetric contributions of the plain language movement to resolving the issues at hand have become more apparent.

Books written on plain language and the law address the problems of legal language and legal writing from a single perspective that is writing in a plainer language for the purpose of better comprehension and/or better interpretation. This book however takes a more holistic approach to clarity in the law by exploring simultaneously the various disciplines of law, linguistics and policies-making not only to understand the nature of legal language, how it might be improved and clarified; but also for what purposes and who are the beneficiaries of clarity in the law. It also examines solutions proposed by practitioners to solve ambiguity outside the courtroom and in the government policy arena.

This monograph is a collection of twelve essays exploring the current status, challenges and future prospects for obscurity and clarity in the legal space. This overall mix reflects and highlights the complexity that obscurity in legal language creates. Taken as a whole, it considers the rapidly changing environment experienced by the legal profession since the timid appearance of clarity in the early nineties (see for example Adler 1990). It emphasises the contingency and fluidity of legal concepts and stresses the existence of overlapping, competing and coexisting legal discourses. In response to new problems, changing power structures, societal norms and new sources of injustice, established approaches of writing the law are reconsidered, reformulated and partly challenged by alternative approaches.

It is not possible in an introduction to exhaustively review and critique each chapter submitted to the reader. What follows is a broad synopsis of the contributions along with a specific focus on the author's particular area of interest. The essays collected in Part 1, 'Crossroads Between Law and Language' address a cluster of closely related aspects concerning the interplay of clarity and obscurity in legislative drafting and interpretation. As such they emphasise the central role which the normative text in all its clarity and obscurity plays as the tangible point of articulation between the policy makers' intention in drafting legislation and its subsequent interpretation.

Flückiger begins with exposing the ambiguity of clarity in legislative drafting. From the outset, he judiciously assesses the outcomes clarity can realistically achieve and as the introductory chapter aims to provoke the reader into thinking critically about the realistic achievements of clarity. His central argument is that the ideal of legislative clarity stems from its intrinsic ambiguity. Following a review of the history and the legal sources of clarity as a principle of legislative quality in the European Union, France and Switzerland, he points out that clarity is a plural concept which relies on a plurality of legal and political institutions. He posits two features of the principle of clarity, namely readability – based on the linguistic simplicity and conciseness of a text – and its concrete legal applicability. He then goes on to review the conflict between those two concepts arguing that a clear readable text may trigger further incidence of ambiguity. He concludes that Clarity is at the centre point of the never ending conflict between extreme readability and the concrete application of a normative text.

Kessler examines the merits and shortcomings of different approaches to interpretation, specifically the hazards associated with 'the objective principle' which sought to trump subjective intention with objective meaning as a foundation for legal interpretation. He argues that the more modern approach to interpretation has seen an extension of the reliance on background fact; rejection of the 'old intellectual baggage' of precedents and rules of construction and ultimately the embracing of less literal readings. In this, he sees a turning away from the 'false god of objective meaning' towards a search for the author's more subjective intention. While rejecting the extremes of both objective meaning/subjective intention, Kessler suggests that courts should increasingly aspire to find the subjective intention from the limited facts available and thus seek to construe a legal document sympathetically.

Wolcher's contribution may require numerous readings from the neophyte to gain a decent grasp of the intricacy of his view of the obscurity-clarity dichotomy. He suggests that from the beginning we need to recognise that clarity or obscurity of a legal text is inevitably clarity or obscurity within a given speech community. As such for lay people to fully understand and use a legal statement or document requires them not merely to find the 'clear meaning' in the text but rather to enter explicitly into the lawyers speech community and thus to understand legal language in the same way that lawyers do is to use it as they do. To fully achieve this understanding is to agree in one's behaviour and speech with the legal 'form of life' (Wittgenstein 1958, 8e) and not merely to take notice of something called a 'meaning'. For Wolcher the demands for clarity in legal language is as much a demand for admission into the form of life inhabited by lawyers, judges and legislators and the associated power as it is a search for meaning. In the intriguing quest for clarity the lay person, in Wolcher's view, leaves himself open to the Faustian bargain where complete clarity in legal thought equates with everyone becoming a lawyer.

Debruche has successfully woven a tapestry of the complex and different conceptions of 'clarity' in the civil and common law systems in a manageable text. Her argument rests on a comparative approach which evidence that one of the reasons legal language appears complex, lays in the duality of legal actors called upon to design and apply a certain rule to a specific case.

Gotti moves on to a wider field by analysing the linguistic quality of the *UNICTRAL Model Law on International Commercial Arbitration* including its explanatory note and the related arbitration rules. He deftly highlights instances of linguistic indeterminacy and imprecise language in these texts which he believes are mostly due to the drafters' intentions to provide maximum flexibility for State parties to implement the rules within their own national legal systems. He further argues that these indeterminacies are then clarified and improved when the texts are subsequently adopted into the various national environments, thus emphasising the impact of socio-cultural and legal national norms and behaviours. In this respect, Gotti concurs with Várady (2006, 10) by stressing that there is a 'need for more precision and conceptual clarity' in arbitral language.

Cao provides the reader with an insightful analysis of the inherent vagueness and ambiguity of legal Chinese which she argues is a direct cause of the intrinsic indeterminacy of the Chinese language. Drawing on previous research, she reviews the linguistic features of the Chinese language which contribute to the uncertainty of the law. She reflects specifically on the semantic nature of Chinese ideograms which she explains is both culturally and context bound. She further notes the additional problem of increased ambiguity when translating into another target language as Chinese, for example, does not use linguistic markers for plural nouns and verbal tense categories; and more pointedly often omits grammatically parts of the language which creates structural ambiguity in a text. She concludes by discussing the possible reasons for legislative uncertainty and the legal consequences of an unstable legal language; namely an incoherent and inconsistent legal narrative which she fears is a consequence of the lack of an independent judiciary.

Part 2, 'An International Perspective', concentrates on the conceptualisation of specific solutions to respond to the problems raised by obscurity in different legal cultures. Lötscher argues that legal texts can only fulfil to a degree the requirements of linguistic clarity such as precision and simplicity because such requirements are often contradictory; and also because legal texts are often subject to textual restrictions. To solve this, he proposes to examine what he coins the visual transparency of a text: that is the iconic qualities of a text, namely its structural content and form. This technique will be familiar to those from the civil law system where most legislative provisions are structurally codified in the Codes to provide quick access and facilitate access to the text's content. At common law, the technique was first used in US tax law to facilitate better comprehensibility (see Thuronyi 1996). Here, the logical organisation of a statute not only renders the texts visually clearer (that is more legible) but aids a better comprehension.

Piehl and Ehrenberg-Sundin explore similar concepts of clarity in Finland and Sweden, based primarily on the concept of general intelligibility and accessibility to the public at large. They both describe the history and development of a plain language policy at government level and best clarity practices in legislative drafting. Piehl provides a comprehensive exploration of Finland's quest for greater clarity as one of the early pioneers of clarity in the European context. Indeed since the 1950's, Finland has persistently campaigned for a uniform, clear and concise style of legislative drafting seeking lucid intelligibility as opposed to conformity of expression. Clarifying official documents, as Piehl explains, is part of a larger movement in achieving democracy and social equality and has been consecrated in several legal instruments as well as the setting up of government's appointed committees responsible for the clarification of the language of administrative and statutory instruments. What is interesting is her assessment of the negative impact that conventional European legislative drafting style has had on Finnish legislation; and in a very realistic manner her consideration for the practical resources allocations which allow for the persistence of textual obscurity in many Finnish legal documents.

Ehrenberg-Sundin's analysis of clarity follows a similar vein, yet goes beyond Piehl's assessment by providing a sharp critique of the comprise position espoused by the European Union vis-à-vis plain language drafting to suit the various aspirations of the Member States. Indeed, European drafting rules for legal texts merely accommodate European meaning with regards to texts pertinent to European institutions; often at the expense of national legislations and more importantly national meanings. Yet the reverse is also true in so far as when a particular legal word comes from a national language into EU 'jargon', its meaning no longer rooted in its original legal culture will often become obscure simply because little consideration is paid to national clarity legislation. Ehrenberg-Sundin's contribution is a practical assessment of Sweden clarity legislation and practices in so far as she acknowledges that linguistic quality does not necessarily guarantee lucid laws and advocates firmly to broaden the network of Clarity proponents with a view to cooperate and share best practices (see also Baedecke and Sundin 2002). More importantly, she unequivocally calls for the EU to take positive steps in modelling existing Members States clarity legislations to improve EU drafting practices.

Piper's chapter highlights the degree to which the State has a duty to ensure that legislation is carefully composed and clearly expressed to ensure greater clarity in the concept the law is trying to express. Bringing us behind the parliamentary scene, he offers first hand insights in the realms of legislative drafting by recounting the challenges he encountered as a parliamentary drafter and how he solved these by inserting narrative examples and notes within legislative provisions to provide greater clarity to a particular piece of legislation; a practice which he notes is already in use in jurisdictions such as New Zealand and Canada. His contribution is exceptionally valuable for the reader attempting to come to terms with the protean nature of avoiding obscurity and ambiguity in legislative drafting but also satisfying for the reader in search of practical examples and real illustrations on how to clarify a legal text with potential obscurity.

Bellis follows Piper's path to map the labyrinth of legislative drafting practices in the US. As an experienced legislative drafter, he contends that the search for the 'holy grail of clarity', that is perfect clarity in legal writing is illusory and that only a relative clarity may be achieved through 'sufficient sensitivity to the assumptions of the cultural context in which the writing takes place' and the intended audience. Obfuscation in the law, he argues, is due to a number of factors among which are haste, politics, amateurism, etc. He concludes like others (see for example Charnock 2006) that 'clarity is a creature of its time and place, and so relative and not absolute.'

Opeibi's concluding chapter considers those aspects of plain language drafting which are relevant to the social and legal activities of the average person. His views resonate that of Barnes (2006) and Bekink and Botha (2007) who argue that clarity must be analysed within the paradigm of law reform to enable the transformation of a legal system and enhance its development. In Nigeria, the demands for greater clarity, specifically in texts such as deeds of assignments, wills, court summons, and charge sheets, must be met by plain language drafting legislative reform like in South Africa, simply because they directly impact not only on the daily life of the average citizen, but also because they impact on the process of law-making, accessibility of the law, democracy and the rule of law. In this chapter, Opeibi examines those legal documents, drafted in legal English, he collected from a Magistrate court and legal firms to demonstrate how Nigerian legal texts – who are modelled on post colonial common law texts – continue to exhibit syntactic and semantic 'traditional' features of 'obfuscation' that have now been for the most part eliminated from similar documents in today's common law countries. He concludes that the need for the use of plain legal English in Nigeria is hinged primarily on the fact that English is not the first native language of many Nigerians and that a reform-based approach to clarity forms part of the solution upon which readability and accessibility are a part of which legal reforms are built.

The chapters in this book reflect an array of different perspectives on the current practises and continuing challenges. In assessing the chapters that follow, the reader will find that different contributors have focused on similar aspects of the debate, all be it, in different settings. A number of the contributors view clarity as a right, a necessity, where comprehensibility is the cornerstone of equality before the law (for example Opeibi). Others have chosen to examine well-established clarity themes in new settings or using new research approaches (for example Gotti, Lötscher).

While clarity and obscurity has proved a fertile ground for legal and linguistic scholars and practitioners alike, the resulting research outputs are open to criticism. When compared with the longer standing fields within the social sciences, the clarity obscurity debate has been characterised by a distinct lack of cumulative research progress and confusion regarding epistemology. The issue of how we acquire knowledge in the clarity field remains vexed and needs to be moved to the centre stage if the discipline is to progress. For many in the cognate disciplines which make up the loosely defined field of clarity, it remains a pseudo-science impoverished by the absence of an informing conceptual framework where few agreed conventions and testable hypotheses have emerged.

While the richness of individual once off jurisdictional-country or thematic case studies make a valuable contribution, the point is rapidly approaching where clarity needs to emerge from the pre-science stage and begin to embrace the more longitudinal and large sample research approaches which have helped advance our understanding in more established social science fields. The time has come therefore to look at how we can move the research focus of clarity beyond the "contrived rational study of lexical and grammatical features, syntax and layout" (Cacciaguidi-Fahy and Wagner 2006, 29) to clarity as a social process embedded in the on going power struggle between competing groups which make up legal exchanges. At the centre of this social process lies the communicative act between the policy makers, drafters, judicial interpreters and citizens.

PART 1
Crossroads Between
Law and Language

Chapter 1

The Ambiguous Principle of
The Clarity of Law

Alexandre Flückiger[1]

The ambiguous principle of clarity

A proponent of plain language legislative drafting has admitted to entertaining a dream:

> Like a poor man's Martin Luther King, I have a dream. It is that every person of reasonable intelligence and literacy may sit at their kitchen table and open a small book or CD-ROM in which the most important laws that govern them are clearly and simply written in their original, unabridged form. I have that dream. But we stand a long, long way from making it reality. Indeed, I sometimes think the prospect is daily receding (Cutts 2000, 11).

Is such a vision realistic? An historical review shows that the requirement to draft clear legislation is more than a contemporary legistics issue (Mertens 2004, 354ff, 380ff). Its continual resurgence over the centuries stands as evidence that legislative clarity has never been achieved definitively.

In this chapter, I will defend the thesis that the impossibility of achieving the ideal of clarity stems from its intrinsic ambiguity. Clarity can in fact be understood, as the above quotation suggests, from the linguistic perspective of readability, simplicity and conciseness. Yet it can also be seen from a more legal perspective: that of concrete applicability, with emphasis on precision of wording. Under this second meaning, a text is clear if it provides the reader, immediately and unequivocally, with a precise solution in a concrete case. Thus the conclusion is that, paradoxically, the principle of clarity is not as clear as it would first appear, since the two above-mentioned perspectives conflict: in pursuing one, the legislative drafter will necessarily overlook the other. The text will be clear in one sense, but obscure in the other, and vice versa. To illustrate this ambiguity, after examining the extent to which the principle of clarity is imposed on the legislator, I will examine successively the linguistic aspect and the legal aspect of the clarity requirement, followed by the resulting conflict.

---

1 An adapted French version of this article was first published in Flückiger (2006, 74-78).

Legislative clarity: a principle of legislative quality

The requirement to draft clear laws stands in counterpoint to a long tradition of criticism with respect to legislative production, whose evolution in quality, some claim, is inversely proportional to its quantitative development. Referring to a golden age of legislation, which has likely never existed given the persistent criticism of legislation over the centuries, numerous authors find a deterioration in contemporary law, citing such concepts as a pathology (Mathieu 2004, 71ff), a decline (Capitant 1917, 305ff),[2] a crisis (Viandier 1986),[3] and a sickness (Lasserre-Kiesow 2005) of law. This criticism is not easily summarised, as it concerns points as diverse as the unintelligibility and obscurity of norms (see Green 1993; Knaack 1993; Endicott 2005; Wagner 2005b), legislative proliferation or inflation (see Mathieu 2004, 76; Bergeal 2006),[4] and the ineffectiveness of law (see Berriat-Saint-Prix 1835; Gény 1922; Solan 2004; Cortese 2005), to mention only the most prominent.[5]

However, two reservations must be mentioned regarding these invectives. The first is the fact that the criticism may have been considered, politically, as associated with liberal doctrine (Courvoisier 2000 as cited in Mathieu 2004, 73). Here, the role of law as an instrument of public policy management has in fact been challenged (Papadopoulos 1995; Willke 1997; Arnaud 1998; Morand 1999a; Ost and Van de Kerchove 2002; Chevallier 2003, 89ff) in favour of various attempts at deregulation and privatisation,[6] which thus far have not led to the anticipated results.[7] The second

---

2 'L'art de faire les lois est en pleine décadence' [The art of lawmaking is characterised by complete decadence (my translation) (Capitant 1917, 305ff cited in Duprat 2005, 10).

3 Viandier (1986, 75 cited in Duprat 2005, 11) also points out the decline of legislative technique.

4 For a more general historic perspective on legislative inflation, see Mertens (2004, 17, 406ff); for a current bibliography, see Drago (2005, 38).

5 For a more detailed list, see for example Mathieu (2004, 75ff, note 1): proliferation of laws, legislation that is unstable, transient or too technical, unintelligible laws, parliamentary weak laws (for example, laws that give too great a role to government in legislative procedure), inclusion of regulatory or non-normative provisions in legislation, competition by other supra or infra-state norms, semi-public or private norms, unapplied legislation.

6 For example, in 1995 in Switzerland, a popular initiative proposed to add a general expiration for laws to the transitional provisions of the Federal Constitution in order to require the legislator to 'reduce the responsibilities of the State and to ensure true deregulation and reprivatisation of those responsibilities' (Müller, G. 2003, 579) (my translation). Any federal laws whose validity would not have been confirmed during that time by the Federal Chambers would be abrogated within five years (*Feuille fédérale* [FF] 1995 IV 1340). The initiative failed to pass due to an insufficient number of signatures (*Feuille fédérale* [FF] 1997 III 669). In 1999, the Federal Council published a report on deregulation and government reduction measures (*Feuille fédérale* [FF] 2000 942).

7 In its report on deregulation and government reduction measures, the Federal Council acknowledged a paradoxal effect leading to an increase in the quantity of norms: 'abandonment of State monopolies through privatisation and openness of markets often results in an inflation of the Classified Compilation of the Federal Law. This is due in particular to the fact that the State must from then on act as arbiter for markets that it previously regulated by internal administrative directives' (*Feuille fédérale* [FF] 2000 942, 947) (my translation). See also

reservation relates to the evolution of society, which has become more technical, complex and fragmented yet increasingly globalised. Such a society can no longer be run in an hierarchical, authoritarian and unitarian manner by 'laws' whose obligatory, general and abstract nature conflicts with a new order that more resembles a network than a pyramid (Papadopoulos 1995; Willke 1997; Arnaud 1998; Morand 1999a; Ost and Van de Kerchove 2002; Chevallier 2003, 89ff). The complexity of law is but a reflection of our complex world.

These critiques stress, in contrast, what a good law should be. However, the wide range of criticism complicates this task. As a result, legislative quality is inevitably a plural concept managed by a plurality of organisations.

The Organisation for Economic Co-operation and Development (OECD) insists on the improvement of law as an instrument of public policy management by proposing regulatory quality management, a new concept intended to lead to deregulation:

> Early notions of "deregulation" or "cutting red tape" quickly gave way to ideas of regulatory reform, involving a mixture of de-regulation, re-regulation and improving the effectiveness of regulations. However, these conceptions of reform also assumed that reform was episodic in nature, and aimed to restore the regulatory structure to some optimum state through a one-off set of interventions. Experience soon demonstrated that such views were untenable. Thus, they gave way in turn to the concept of regulatory quality management (OECD 2002, 16).

The European Union, for its part, succinctly summarises the facets of the issue in two agreements: the *Interinstitutional Agreement on Better Law-Making* (European Union 2003) and, concerning drafting in particular, the *Interinstitutional Agreement of 22 December 1998 on Common Guidelines for the Quality of Drafting of Community Legislation* (European Union 1999 [*the Agreement on the Quality of Drafting*]). Both texts state that quality of legislation is measurable based on criteria that can be described as legal, factual, or drafting-related:

- The legal criteria for quality legislation are democratic legitimacy, subsidiarity and proportionality, and legal certainty [...] and the utmost transparency of the legislative process (European Union 2003, articles 2, 10, 11).
- The factual criteria, for example. criteria for assessing the law's capacity to influence facts, are effectiveness, measured by evaluation (European Union 2003, articles 15, 27-30), and simplicity of action (European Union 2003, article 12).
- The criteria for quality of drafting are clarity, simplicity and consistency (European Union 2003, articles 2, 25, 31, 35; European Union 1998, articles

---

the position of the Organisation for Economic Co-operation and Development (OECD) in a report showing that deregulation has not led to the anticipated results: 'The first efforts at "deregulation" were driven by economic downturn and were based on the view that a too great quantity of regulation was impeding the economy by strangling innovation and entrepreneurialism. However, these early attempts at "deregulation" were, at best, only partially successful' (OECD 2002, 20).

1, 5, 6), as well as conciseness (European Union 2003, article 35; European Union 1998, article 4), precision,[8] and a reduced volume of legislation (European Union 2003 article 35).

A reading of the above criteria shows that these principles are interrelated, and thus cannot be considered in isolation. Although some principles support others – such as precision, which contributes to legal certainty, or a reduced volume of legislation, which can also be viewed as an expression of subsidiarity – other principles conflict, as we will see later for conciseness and precision.[9]

This chapter will focus on a single aspect: clarity of law, or legislative clarity. An examination of this requirement – an ambiguous one, as we will attempt to show – leads to an understanding of why it is so difficult to master the drafting of legislation.

Sources of the principle of legislative clarity

A jurilinguistic requirement of formal legistics   The requirement of legislative clarity is a precept of formal legistics, that is the branch of legistics that focuses on principles for improving the communication and understanding of laws (Morand 1999b, 18), subjects of jurilinguistics (Gémar and Kasirer 2005). Over time, the clarity requirement has also become a legal principle essential to the legislator in varying degrees, through either legistical directives published by public authorities or the development of national and international case-law.

Legistical directives: European Union, Switzerland, France   In Community law, the *Interinstitutional Agreement on Better Law-Making* states that the three institutions of the European Union (the European Parliament, the Council of the European Union, and the European Commission) 'further agree to promote simplicity, clarity and consistency in the drafting of laws' (European Union 2003, article 2) and 'will ensure that legislation is of good quality, namely that it is clear, simple and effective' (European Union 2003, article 25). The clarity requirement had been set out earlier in the *Interinstitutional Agreement of 22 December 1998 on Common Guidelines for the Quality of Drafting of Community Legislation* (European Union 1999). The requirement of clarity goes hand in hand with the requirement of simplicity and precision: 'Community legislative acts shall be drafted clearly, simply and precisely' (European Union 1998, article 1).

In its preamble, the *Agreement on the Quality of Drafting* states the *ratio legis* for this triple requirement of clarity, simplicity and precision, which aims to help

---

8 The 'precision' criterion is mentioned only in *The Quality of Drafting of Community Legislation* (European Union 1998, article 1) and not in the *Interinstitutional Agreement on Better Law-Making* (European Union 2003).

9 More specifically, the conflict between readability (which encompasses conciseness) and clarity within the meaning of concrete applicability (see infra, section on '*The conflict between readability and concrete applicability*').

the general public better understand laws, as well as to make the application of legislation more consistent and to improve its implementation:

> Clear, simple and precise drafting of Community legislative acts is essential if they are to be transparent and readily understandable by the public and economic operators. It is also a prerequisite for the proper implementation and uniform application of Community legislation in the Member States (European Union 1998, preamble (1)).

The *Agreement on the Quality of Drafting* directly links the requirement of legislative clarity to that of the foreseeability of law:

> According to the case-law of the Court of Justice, the principle of legal certainty, which is part of the Community legal order, requires that Community legislation must be clear and precise and its application foreseeable by individuals. That requirement must be observed all the more strictly in the case of an act liable to have financial consequences and imposing obligations on individuals in order that those concerned may know precisely the extent of the obligations which it imposes on them (European Union 1998, preamble (2)).

In Swiss law, the *Guide pour l'élaboration de la législation fédérale* [*Guide de législation*] lays down similar principles. It states that

> the language of law, as opposed to that of poetry, for example, must be clearer, less vague, and as direct as possible. Its characteristics are therefore: the need for a good prior grasp of the normative matter; consistency; clarity; conciseness; respect for any pre-existing terminology framework (Switzerland, Federal Office of Justice 2002, 365) (my translation).

and specifies that clarity 'is the chief quality of a normative text' (Switzerland, Federal Office of Justice 2002, 367) (my translation).

In French law, the *Guide français pour l'élaboration des textes législatifs et réglementaires* (2005) was drafted jointly by members of the Conseil d'Etat and officials of the Secrétariat Général du Gouvernement. It mainly brings together the circulars of the Prime Minister, notably the *Circulaire du 30 septembre 2003 relative à la maîtrise de l'inflation normative et à l'amélioration de la qualité de la réglementation* [circular of September 30, 2003, respecting control of legislative inflation and improvements to regulatory quality] as well as case-law and the reports of the Conseil d'Etat and the Conseil Constitutionnel. In the chapter on legislative drafting, the guide states that

> the drafting of a bill and its accompanying document (preamble or presentation report) must be clear, simple, and grammatically correct (France, Secrétariat général du Gouvernement and Conseil d'Etat 2005, record 3.3.1, 189).

The requirements of case-law: Switzerland, European Union, Council of Europe, France) The principle of legislative clarity has been recognised in case-law mainly in terms of concrete applicability: the law must be precise enough for the accused to understand his or her rights and obligations in a concrete case. The Swiss Federal Supreme Court deduced this from the principle of legality (article 5 of the Federal Constitution). For example, in the area of public contributions, it requires that the purpose of the income tax be identified in the law with 'appropriate clarity and precision' (*Eidgenössische Steuerverwaltung v. AG*, Federal Court 2A.542/2002, consid. 3.4.1).[10] More generally, the Federal Supreme Court has stated that the greater the severity of an offence, the more precise the legal basis must be (*X. v. Stadt Chur*, Federal Court 129 I 161, consid. 2.2, 163).

The Court of Justice of the European Communities (CJEC) deduced the clarity requirement from the principle of legal certainty:

> The principle of legal certainty requires that rules imposing charges on the taxpayer must be clear and precise so that he may know without ambiguity what are his rights and obligations and may take steps accordingly (*Administration des Douanes v. Gondrand Frères and Garancini* [1981] ECR 1931, para 17).[11]

For the European Court of Human Rights (ECHR), the foreseeability of a rule of law supposes that

> [...] a norm cannot be regarded as a "law" unless it is formulated with sufficient precision to enable the citizen to regulate his conduct: he must be able – if need be with appropriate advice – to foresee, to a degree that is reasonable in the circumstances, the consequences which a given action may entail (*The Sunday Times v. The United Kingdom* [1979] ECHR 1, para 49).

The French Conseil Constitutionnel also recognised the clarity requirement, which in its view ensued from article 34 of the Constitution:[12] The Conseil went on to formally sanction this requirement as 'the objective of the constitutional value of accessibility and intelligibility of law' (my translation) based on articles 4, 5, 6 and 16 of the *Declaration of 1789*[13] (for a further analysis see Champeil-Desplats 44-47). The purpose is to

> protect subjects of law against an interpretation contrary to the Constitution or against the risk of arbitrariness, without giving administrative or judicial authorities the power to set rules which, under the Constitution, can only be determined by law' (my translation).[14]

---

10 Regarding practice of the legality principle in Swiss law, see Moor (1994, 338ff).

11 See also Joined Cases 205/82 to 215/82 *Deutsche Milchkontor and Others v. Germany* [1983] ECR 2633, para 30; Joined Cases 92/87 and 93/87 *Commission v. France and United Kingdom* [1989] ECR 405, para 22.

12 CC DC 98-401 (Loi d'orientation et d'incitation relative à la réduction du temps de travail), 10 June 1998, 258.

13 CC DC 99-421421 (Loi portant habilitation du Gouvernement à procéder par ordonnances, à l'adoption de la partie législative de certains codes), 16 December 1999, 136.

14 CC DC 2005-514 (Loi relative à la création du registre international français), 28 April 2005, para 14. For further commentaries on this case-law, see Montalivet (2005, 103ff).

The two facets of the principle of clarity

Clarity presents two facets: a linguistic facet I will describe as readability and a more legal facet I will describe as concrete applicability.[15] The former stems from the adage that no one is deemed to be ignorant of the law (*nemo legem ignorare censetur*) while the latter stems from the principle of foreseeability and legal certainty, as well as the principle of separation of powers and protection against arbitrariness, since the judge's powers broaden to the detriment of the legislator's where vague wording is concerned.

Readability

A readable text is an intelligible text, that is, one that is easy to understand. It is generally simple (see infra, section on '*Simplicity*'), without archaisms or overly specialised expressions, and must be concise (see infra, section on '*Conciseness*'). Although readability is sometimes used in the typographic sense (Fernbach 2005, 161ff), here we refer to it as meaning 'understandability'.

The tradition of readability in Swiss law The readability requirement is a legacy of antiquity (Bentham 1830, 424ff; Mertens 2004, 380ff). The law must be understood by all (*leges intellegi ab omnibus debent*) as Roman law instructs (*Corpus iuris civilis*, 1.14.9).

In Switzerland, the tradition of legislative drafting in easily readable language is at least secular. Semi-direct democratic institutions (legislative referendum in particular) encourage the drafting of laws in a simple, understandable style since citizens may be asked to express their opinion on the acceptance or rejection of legislation in particular.[16] The bases of legislative drafting in plain language were set out over a century ago by the father of the Swiss Civil Code, Eugène Huber, who believed that the Civil Code should be a popular law written not only for judges but for all citizens.

> Modern laws are not drafted for the sole purpose of teaching judges how to proceed, where necessary. The law concerns everyone to whom it applies. The legislator's instructions must therefore, insofar as compatible with the subject at hand, be intelligible to everyone or at least to persons who, by virtue of their profession, are required to be familiar with the law. The rules established must have meaning even for the layman, which shall not prevent the specialist from discovering in them a broader or deeper meaning than the layman. That is what is meant by the words popular law (Huber 1901, 10) (my translation).

---

15 The French Conseil Constitutionnel formally distinguishes the requirement of legislative clarity from the intelligibility of law without it being possible, from a reading of case-law, to understand the distinction as both requirements appear to call for precision in law (Montalivet 2005, 126ff). The clarity requirement is decidedly unclear; Montalivet in fact requests that the Conseil Constitutionnel 'clarify' the distinction between the two requirements (Montalivet 2005, 127).

16 For more information about Switzerland's constitutional system, see Fleiner et al. (2005).

To achieve an intelligible Swiss Civil Code, Huber recommended a number of readability principles that he applied.

His first precepts were intended to produce a concise text: each article must have no more than three paragraphs; paragraphs must consist of a single sentence; sentences must be brief and subdivisions, rare:

> Other than lists [...], we were almost always able to limit articles to three paragraphs at the most. Paragraphs generally consist of a single sentence; they must always be fairly brief, so that a person, even one not used to consulting laws, may realise their content at first sight. Subdivisions are rare, and nowhere has an article been divided into subparagraphs. The law is thus easy to consult and easy to quote (Huber 1901, 12) (my translation).

Writers must not hesitate to re-use the same terms to designate the same concepts and must avoid synonyms, even if the outcome is somewhat monotonous:

> As long as it appeared compatible with the requirements of language, we always used the same terms to designate concepts that would repeat [...] The application of existing laws has more than shown the degree to which a simple discrepancy of wording, due to oversight by the legislator, can create confusion for the judge (Huber 1901, 14) (my translation).

Beyond its application to the text as a whole, the readability requirement applies to each article taken in isolation. This means avoiding cross-references whenever possible. Where necessary, the cross-reference must be made using a sentence that reflects the content rather than by referencing the number of an article:

> Secondly, the goal was to make each article intelligible or at least readable when taken in isolation. It was thus necessary to avoid cross-references whenever possible. Where these seemed inevitable, they were provided not by indicating the number of an article, but by a clear sentence, stating the content of the cross-reference. [...] It is our experience that in practice cross-references using article numbers indicated in parentheses often results in problems, as they can easily present omissions or errors embarrassing to judges. See for example Arrêts du Tribunal Fédéral Suisse [Judgments of the Swiss Federal Court] Vol. XXII, p. 342 (Huber 1901, 13) (my translation).

Huber also believed that a clearly planned structure improved the intelligibility of the text:

> The order used in the series of articles referring to a given subject is generally as follows: General rules are set out first, followed by prescriptions concerning the constitution and the extinction of a legal relationship, and finally, prescriptions governing their effects. This method [...] gives the draft a clear, easy layout (Huber 1901, 13) (my translation).

and

> The legislator did more than space out some of the essential content; every element is arranged according to a plan that is easy to scan with the eyes (Huber 1901, 17) (my translation).

These principles are repeated in current instructions for legislative technique in Swiss law, which writers of federal normative texts must follow.[17] In practice, due to the technical nature of certain subjects, Swiss federal legislation is now drafted to be accessible to the intended audience, not necessarily to the general public (Bertagnollo and Laurent 2005, 123ff).[18] In Community law, the *Interinstitutional Agreement of 22 December 1998 on Common Guidelines for the Quality of Drafting of Community Legislation* states along the same lines that Acts are to be drafted so as to take into account the intended audience:

> The drafting of acts shall take account of the persons to whom they are intended to apply, with a view to enabling them to identify their rights and obligations unambiguously, and of the persons responsible for putting the acts into effect (European Union 1998, article 3).

Simplicity Laws can be made intelligible by using simple expressions. In this regard we can again refer to the Swiss writing tradition as explained by Huber (1901):

> With respect to language, the main idea is that the project, as mentioned earlier, should be intelligible to all; we have sought to achieve this goal by choosing simple and clear expressions (Huber 1901, 12) (my translation).

and

> The most effective way to simplify legislation is the art of condensing legal precepts into clear principles (Huber 1901, 8) (my translation).

The Age of Enlightenment had popularised this requirement earlier. Montesquieu, in particular,[19] believed that laws should be simple so that every citizen might easily understand them:

> The style should also be plain and simple, a direct expression being better understood than an indirect one. There is no majesty at all in the laws of the lower empire; princes are made to speak like rhetoricians. When the style of laws is inflated, they are looked upon only as a work of parade and ostentation [...].

> The laws ought not to be subtle; they are designed for people of common understanding, not as an art of logic, but as the plain reason of a father of a family (Montesquieu 1914).

Since then, laws have not become simpler. The complexification of modern society is certainly a contributing factor (Bergeal 2006). The legislator must govern

---

17 Regarding concision, cross-references, and general principles of structure, see respectively the *Guide de législation* (2002, 349, 353, 345ff).

18 However, I cannot agree with Bertagnollo and Laurent (2005, 123) when they claim that 'hardly anyone continues to suggest that laws should be drafted so as to be accessible to the public' (my translation) as the accessibility of legislation, in their view, is increasingly a utopic ideal.

19 For references to other authors, in particular to Jeremy Bentham, see Mertens (2004, 380ff).

a growing number of ever more complex areas. In these circumstances, there is a question as to whether law can be made simpler without becoming simplistic.

Awareness has grown in recent years, as the interinstitutional agreements of the European Union cited in the introduction show. These texts provide that acts 'shall be drafted clearly' (European Union 1998, article 1; European Union 2003, articles 2, 25) and that 'acts and provisions which are too unwieldy and too complex to be applied' must be amended (European Union 2003, article 35). In practice, this goal is difficult to achieve. Such wording can read like empty political slogans. The European Constitution, which could have been a concrete test for application of these new principles, encountered the same stumbling block. Yet Valery Giscard d'Estaing had set out to draft the wording of the European Constitution in such a way as to avoid

> adverbs that dilute the force of the wording while intending to strengthen it, and parenthetical clauses that aim to say one thing and the contrary! (my translation).[20]

It is not certain that he was able to do so.[21]

Conciseness Conciseness of content is a crucial requirement of readability. As the Swiss federal government stated in 1904, it is the ideal of every popular law:

> We also had to ensure that the law would respect the ideal of conciseness, the ideal of every popular law, and we hope to have been successful in this regard (Switzerland, Federal Council 1904, 10) (my translation).

It is a matter of saying everything, but briefly, as the father of the Swiss Civil Code explained (Huber 1901, 17) and sacrificing the accessory to the essential (ibid, 9). Details lead to details for Portalis (1988, 26) as well as Montesquieu (1914),[22] whose model was the Twelve Tables:

> The style ought to be concise. The laws of the Twelve Tables are a model of conciseness; the very children used to learn them by heart (Montesquieu 1914).

Other authors warn against the exaggerated expectations placed on overly simple and overly brief legislation drafted to resemble a best-selling page turner (see in particular Gottlieb Svarez 1788; Schlosser 1789; Reitemeir 1800 as cited in Mertens 2004, 383, note 417). Francis Bacon had shown the dangers of excessive brevity as early as the 17th century. According to the English philosopher, law should not resemble the architect's Lesbian rule, a flexible ruler of lead for measuring both flat and curved surfaces:

---

20 Valéry Giscard d'Estaing had in the past supported the need to draft laws understandable to all (Giscard d'Estaing (1975) as cited in Fernbach 2005, 170, note 27).

21 'The Constitution is hardly anybody's ideal bedtime reading. It's long, turgid and complicated. That's why MPs should have to read it first, debate it and then explain' (Stuart 2004).

22 'When there is no necessity for exceptions and limitations in a law, it is much better to omit them: details of that kind throw people into new details' (Montesquieu 1914).

Not that I therefore approve of a too concise and affected brevity, as being the style of majesty and command, especially in these times; lest by chance the law should become like a Lesbian rule. We must therefore aim at a mean, and look out for a well-defined generality of words; which though it does not attempt to express all the cases comprehended, yet excludes with sufficient clearness the cases not comprehended (Bacon 1877, 102, aphorism 67).

Various authors criticised the Swiss Civil Code in this regard early on. They claimed its rubber-like provisions (for example Gmür 1965, 41), resulting from excessive conciseness, left too much latitude to doctrine and case-law (Merz 1962, 588; Gény 1904, 1034ff as cited in Gmür 1965, 42). Others, on the contrary, lauded the Civil Code precisely because it would allow for more changes over time (Saleilles 1904, 103; Gaudemet 1904, 969; Planiol 1904, 960).

The debate concerning the degree of conciseness highlights the second aspect of the principle of clarity: the concrete applicability of a normative text. When a law is too simple, too concise, its reader can no longer foresee how it will be applied to a concrete case.

Concrete Applicability

A normative text is clear, within the second meaning of the principle, when a judge ruling on a particular case finds it easy to apply concretely. Such a text is more precise and more detailed than a text that is difficult to apply to a concrete case. Its concrete application should in principle be more certain and more foreseeable.

We will again quote Montesquieu, so as not to limit his view to the necessity of simple laws (see infra, section on '*Simplicity*'), as this author of the Enlightenment also warned against oversimplification by demonstrating the need to avoid vague expressions:

When the law has once fixed the idea of things, it should never return to vague expressions [...].

The law of Honorius punished with death any person that purchased a freedman as a slave, or that gave him molestation. He should not have made use of so vague an expression; the molestation given a man depends entirely on the degree of his sensibility (Montesquieu 1914).

This requirement of precision is justified by the principle of certainty and foreseeability in law, as well as by that of protection against arbitrariness and the separation of powers, by limiting the judge's latitude. These legal arguments, found in positive law (see infra, section on '*The requirements of case-law: Switzerland, European Union, Council of Europe, France*'), were raised in the 17th century by Francis Bacon, Jeremy Bentham, Catherine II of Russia and Frederic II of Prussia (as cited in Mertens 2004, 359ff), to name only the most illustrious authors. In fact, reducing an Act's normative density arising from vague wording limits the legislator's ability to precisely orient the behaviour of its intended audience (Moor 2005, 54ff). In doing so the legislator gives judges and other enforcement authorities a freedom that it relinquishes, creating a degree of legal uncertainty until a verdict is given in concrete cases.

In many cases, however, a text that lacks clarity and is difficult to apply concretely – for example, a loose, vague, imprecise or indeterminate text – is in fact inevitable and sometimes even desirable (see Endicott 2000 on this particular issue; Bhatia et al. 2005). Aristotle showed 2500 years ago that law is intrinsically unable to settle all concrete cases due to its very generality.[23] The 'nature of the thing' prevents it from doing so; there are concrete cases for which a law cannot be made:

> The reason is that all law is universal but about some things it is not possible to make a universal statement which shall be correct. In those cases, then, in which it is necessary to speak universally, but not possible to do so correctly, the law takes the usual case, though it is not ignorant of the possibility of error. And it is none the less correct; for the error is in the law nor in the legislator but in the nature of the thing, since the matter of practical affairs is of this kind from the start. When the law speaks universally, then, and a case arises on it which is not covered by the universal statement, then it is right, where the legislator fails us and has erred by over simplicity, to correct the omission – to say what the legislator himself would have said had he been present, and would have put into his law if he had known […]

> In fact this is the reason why all things are not determined by law; that about some things it is impossible to lay down a law, so that a decree is needed (Aristotle, Book 5, chapter 10).[24]

It is naïve to think that legislation can be drafted clearly enough to eliminate uncertainty or simply enough to be understood by all. Yet François I of France, in his edict ordering the use of French in official and legal instruments, believed such a thing possible:

> And to ensure there shall be no cause to doubt the intelligence of the aforesaid decrees, we wish and order that they be made and written so clearly as to eliminate any ambiguity or uncertainty, or possibility thereof, and any grounds for seeking an interpretation of those decrees (François I of France 1539) (my translation).

It is an illusion to believe there can really be a clear meaning of the norm. According to the classical rule of legal interpretation, there is no need to propose an interpretation when a rule is clearly intelligible (*claris non fit interpretatio*). This statement, a stance of legal positivism, is open to criticism (see Moor 1994, 169; Papaux 2003, 102ff, 216). It is in fact a matter of degree: so-called 'clear' rules are not free from interpretation; there is simply no controversy regarding their interpretation in a concrete case, in any event for a given period (Moor 2005, 170). This opinion likely arises from the too frequent confusion, at least in continental law, between

---

23 Regarding the history of this issue during the era of the great private law consolidations, see Mertens (2004, 375ff), who notes that theorization concerning general clauses and indeterminate legal concepts dates back only to the early 20th century.

24 Available at <http://www.constitution.org/ari/ethic_00.htm>; see also Papaux (2003, 215).

the wording of a norm and the norm. Law is more than just the wording of law, and it is not an error on the part of the legislative drafter if he or she cannot follow the commandments of François I! The wording of law cannot contain all the law; the wording of the norm is not the norm itself (Moor 1994, 64, 165ff; Müller 1996, 168; Papaux 2003, 126ff), but one element among others – certainly an important one – used by the judge as material to create the norm each time it must be applied concretely to a specific case (Müller1996, 348ff).

Yet case-law has recognised that, in some cases, imprecision and a degree of vagueness is inevitable. In such a case examining this legal practice is tantamount to probing the breadth of the Aristotelian 'nature of the thing', which prevents the rule from foreseeing every imaginable case. The European Court of Human Rights [the ECHR] has developed in this regard an exemplary casuistry by interpreting clauses under which interference in the exercise of freedoms must be 'in accordance with the law' or 'prescribed by law' (paragraph 2 of respectively, article 8 and articles 9 to 11 of the *European Convention for the Protection of Human Rights and Fundamental Freedoms*).

As indicated earlier, the Court poses the principle that an individual 'must be able [...] to foresee [...] the consequences which a given action may entail' (see infra, section on *'The requirements of case-law: Switzerland, European Union, Council of Europe, France'*). However, it allows vague wording to avoid excessive rigidity in a concrete case and to allow the law to adapt to a range of circumstances,[25] to the evolution of social conceptions[26] as well as to evolving situations:

> [...] whilst certainty is highly desirable, it may bring in its train excessive rigidity and the law must be able to keep pace with changing circumstances. Accordingly, many laws are inevitably couched in terms which, to a greater or lesser extent, are vague and whose interpretation and application are questions of practice (*The Sunday Times v. The United Kingdom* [1979] ECHR 1, para 49).

In this respect the Court agrees with Francis Bacon, who three centuries ago warned against the illusion of certainty resulting from excessive precision (Bacon

---

25 See *Olivieira v. The Netherlands* [2002] ECHR 479: 'The circumstances which call the Burgomaster to issue the orders which he deems to be necessary for the maintenance of public order are so diverse that it would scarcely be possible to formulate a law to cover every eventuality' (para 54).

26 See *Barthold v. Germany* [1985] ECHR 3, para 47 concerning the imprecise term 'honest practices'. Huber (1991, 14) referred to the evolution of ideas to justify the use of indeterminate legal clauses in the Swiss Civil Code: '[...] and it would be an error to draft the law in a manner that would make it impossible for the courts to follow evolving ideas without review of the legal text' (my translation).

1877, aphorism 66).[27] More generally in *Malone v. UK*,[28] the ECHR deems that the law must be as precise as the interference is serious:

> [...] the law must be sufficiently clear in its terms to give citizens an adequate indication as to the circumstances in which and the conditions on which public authorities are empowered to resort to this secret and potentially dangerous interference with the right to respect for private life and correspondence (para 67).

In assessing the clarity and precision of the law, consideration should also be given to the technical and professional competences of the law's intended audience:

> [...] the scope of the concepts of foreseeability and accessibility depends to a considerable degree on the content of the instrument in issue, the field it is designed to cover and the number and status of those to whom it is addressed (*Groppera Radio AG and Others v. Switzerland* [1990] ECHR 7, para 68).

Highly pragmatic, the Court first recognised in *The Sunday Times v. The United Kingdom* 'the impossibility of attaining absolute precision in the framing of laws' (para 49) which it later reiterated in *Barthold v. Germany* when attempting to define the imprecise terms 'honest practices'(para 47); and subsequently in *R. v. The United Kingdom* when it stated that such precision may not necessarily be desirable.[29]

There are also institutional reasons for drafting imprecise laws that leave greater freedom in matters concerning the respect for constitutional distribution of competences within a federal State, for example. Political considerations may further be a factor when ambiguously drafted provisions – even differences in translations (Flückiger 2005, 346) – are accepted to forge an agreement between protagonists. In this case vague wording can contribute to a diplomatic resolution of highly conflicting interests (see Kuner 1991). In 1992, the French Conseil d'Etat observed that one characteristic of Community law was precisely its nature as a 'diplomatic' law:

> Where jurists seek precision, diplomats practice non-speak and are not averse to ambiguity. It happens more often than one might think that they fail to agree on a word simply because it does not have the same meaning for everyone. [...] They likewise encourage

---

27 'I must now speak of the obscurity of laws which arises from their being ill drawn up. The loquacity and prolixity used in the drawing up of laws I do not approve. For it does not at all secure its intention and purpose; but rather the reverse. For while it tries to enumerate and express every particular case in apposite and appropriate words, expecting greater certainty thereby; it does in fact raise a number of questions about words; so that, by reason of the noise and strife of words, the interpretation which proceeds according to the meaning of the law (which is the juster and sounder kind of interpretation) is rendered more difficult' (Bacon 1877, 102, aphorism 66).

28 *Malone v. UK* [1984] ECHR 10.

29 In this case the court rules that a law should not, under the pretext of less vague wording, subordinate the removal of children to evidence of actual harm rather than giving the authorities enough latitude to evaluate the grounds for seizure of custody from parents in each case (*R. v. The United Kingdom* [1987] ECHR 16, para 67).

writing techniques that here and there allow for perpetuating interesting – and promising - contradictions (France, Conseil d'Etat 1992 cited in Gallas 2001, 117ff) (my translation).

The Conflict between Readability and Concrete Applicability

The two aspects of the clarity requirement conflict (Mertens 2004, 356): a clear text- one that is readable – is often simple, while a clear text – one that can be applied concretely – is often long and complex, because it is more precise and detailed.

A text can be clear, meaning readable, yet difficult to apply concretely to a case. The rule according to which 'man and woman are equal' is admittedly easy to read and understand. The style is concise, the sentence is constructed simply around a single verb, and plain language is used. Yet this provision is not very clear, in the second sense of the word, because it is difficult to apply to a concrete case: should teachers of needlework earn the same wages as teachers of manual labour? Are nurses entitled to the same pay as police officers? To answer these questions, or clarify the norm, the provision should be drafted so as to be easier to apply concretely, but more complex:

> The following are members of Class C (gross annual salary of 40,000 €):
> a) teachers of needlework;
> b) teachers of manual labour.

This short list is destined to grow rapidly as judges rule on a variety of cases, obscuring the apparent clarity of the basic rule.

From this opposition one might also deduce that a text drafted with little normative content, apparently simple and readable, may result indirectly in even more complex regulations and case-law. What is bred in the bone will come out in the flesh.

Conclusion

The concept of clear legislation, at once readable and precise, is an ideal – an ideal ever desired yet never achieved, simply because it cannot be. A law that is perfectly precise and foreseeable would be excessively ponderous and complicated. A law that is light and simple would quickly become bound by reality, with all the avoided complexity carried over directly into regulations, case-law, and practice.

There is no definitive solution to this problem. The two facets of clarity are destined to conflict. To avoid becoming caught between Scylla and Charybdes, the legislator has no alternative but to opt for the middle path and balance the two ideals.[30] Clarity is thus the product of an equilibrium between the two facets, rather than the naïve and blind pursuit of extreme readability or extreme precision.

---

30 In Community law, the *Interinstitutional Agreement on Better Law-Making* describes the middle path as follows to the attention of the Commission regarding proposed directives: 'The Commission will ensure that a proper balance is struck between general principles and detailed provisions, in a manner that avoids excessive use of Community implementing measures' (European Union 2003, article 13).

Francis Bacon had reached this conclusion himself, concisely and precisely, some three centuries ago:

Obscure drawing up of laws arises either from their loquacity and verbosity, or on the other hand from an excess of conciseness [...] (Bacon 1877, 101, aphorism 65).

Chapter 2

Objectivity and Subjectivity in Interpretation

James Kessler QC[1]

Introduction

Interpretation is a difficult subject and it is helpful at the outset to explain why. The problems lie partly in the topic and partly in the case law.

There is no single principle of interpretation, or what purports to be the single statement of principle immediately needs explanation and qualification. Interpretation issues which arise in practice are generally complex and cases cannot be briefly summarised or neatly categorised. The principles upon which cases are decided are often assumed or not clearly expressed. Cases are not consistent: different judges have applied different principles, or the same principles in different ways; or any principle available as an ad hoc rationalisation to justify a fair result on the facts of the case. When judges wish to change the law, precedent and the declaratory theory of law encourage them to deny that they are doing so. The total case law relating to interpretation of documents or statutes is so vast that no-one can draw it all together into a coherent body of law. The only thing worse than too little data is too much data. As this chapter will show, some important aspects are hotly debated.

In short, as Voltaire observed, 'language is very difficult to put into words.' Nevertheless it is worth persevering. This chapter will outline the correct legal approach to interpretation, and consider and reject some rival approaches.

General principle

The starting point is Lord Hoffmann's much cited speech in *Investors Compensation Scheme v. West Bromwich Building Society.*[2]

Lord Hoffmann posits:

I think I should preface my explanation of my reasons with some general remarks about the principles by which contractual documents are nowadays construed. I do not think that the

---

1 This chapter is derived from Kessler (2006).

2 [1998] 1 WLR 896, 912–3 affirmed *BCCI v. Ali* [2002] 1 AC 251, para 8, see McKendrick (2003, 139).

fundamental change[3] which has overtaken this branch of the law [...] is always sufficiently appreciated. The result has been, subject to one important exception, to assimilate the way in which such documents are interpreted by judges to the common sense principles by which any serious utterance would be interpreted in ordinary life. Almost all the old intellectual baggage of "legal" interpretation has been discarded.

(1) Interpretation is the ascertainment of the meaning which the document would convey to a reasonable person having all the background knowledge which would reasonably have been available to the parties in the situation in which they were at the time of the contract. [4]

Factual background/previous negotiations/declarations of intent

Lord Hoffmann continues:

(2) The background was famously referred to by Lord Wilberforce as the "matrix of fact", but this phrase is, if anything, an understated description of what the background may include. Subject to the requirement that it should have been reasonably available to the parties and to the exception to be mentioned next, it includes absolutely anything which would have affected the way in which the language of the document would have been understood by a reasonable man.

(3) The law excludes from the admissible background

[a] the previous negotiations of the parties and

[b] their declarations of subjective intent.

They are admissible only in an action for rectification. The law makes this distinction for reasons of practical policy and, in this respect only, legal interpretation differs from the way we would interpret utterances in ordinary life.[5] The boundaries of this exception are in some respects unclear. But this is not the occasion on which to explore them.

---

3 It is not possible to identify a precise date or single author of this 'fundamental change.' Of the two cases which Lord Hoffmann cites, *Prenn v. Simmonds* [1971] 1 WLR 1381, 1384–1386 does contain a strongly worded passage ('The time has long passed when agreements [...] were isolated from the matrix of facts in which they were set and interpreted purely on internal linguistic considerations'). But like many (perhaps most?) important changes, its roots can be traced much earlier: 'It is difficult to measure what success the courts have achieved in attempting to give effect to the intentions of testators. One Chancery judge is reputed to have said "I shudder to think that in the hereafter I shall have to meet those testators whose wishes on earth have been frustrated by my judgments."' [Attributed to Eve J., (1941) 60 *Law Notes* 26]. This dictum seems to have been in the mind of Lord Atkin when, in a case which did much to free the courts from some rather technical rules of construction, he said 'I anticipate with satisfaction that henceforth the group of ghosts of dissatisfied testators who, according to a late Chancery judge, wait on the other bank of the Styx to receive the judicial personages who have misconstrued their wills, may be considerably diminished.' See Megarry (1955, 162) citing *Perrin v. Morgan* [1943] AC 399, 415. *Pepper v. Hart* [1993] AC 593 can be understood as reflecting the trend to search slightly harder for intention at the cost of convenience.

4 [1998] 1 WLR 912.

5 Literary critics (or at least some of them) adopt the same approach. See Wimsatt and Beardsley's essay *The Intentional Fallacy* (1954) [reprinted in *The Verbal Icon* (1970)]: 'The intention of the author is neither available nor desirable as a standard for judging the success

We have here one rule of inclusion: the Court must consider what Lord Hoffmann terms 'background'; and two exclusions – the Court will not consider previous negotiations or declarations of subjective intent. There are (as Lord Hoffmann suggests) a number of tensions in these principles. Some commentators advocate extending admissibility to include previous negotiations; others wish to restrict admissibility of evidence relating to background.[6]

Separate from the question of what background the Court must 'consider' is the question of what effect this considering should have on interpretation.[7] This takes us back to the problem of meaning.

Meaning of words versus meaning of document

Continuing Lord Hoffmann's speech in *Investors Compensation Scheme*:

> (4) The meaning which a document (or any other utterance) would convey to a reasonable man is not the same thing as the meaning of its words. The meaning of words is a matter of dictionaries[8] and grammars; the meaning of the document is what the parties using those words against the relevant background would reasonably have been understood to mean. The background may not merely enable the reasonable man to choose between the possible meanings of words which are ambiguous but even (as occasionally happens in ordinary life) to conclude that the parties must, for whatever reason, have used the wrong words or syntax [...]
>
> (5) The 'rule' that words should be given their 'natural and ordinary meaning' reflects the common sense proposition that we do not easily accept that people have made linguistic mistakes, particularly in formal documents. On the other hand, if one would nevertheless conclude from the background that something must have gone wrong with the language, the law does not require judges to attribute to the parties an intention which they plainly could not have had.
>
> [...] Leggatt LJ said that the judge's construction was not an "available meaning" of the words. If this means that judges cannot, short of rectification, decide that the parties must have made mistakes of meaning or syntax, I respectfully think he was wrong.

Lord Hoffmann draws a distinction between:

(1) the meaning of words[9] and

---

of a work of literary art [...]. Critical enquiries are not settled by consulting the oracle [the author].' But interpretation of legal and literary documents is in this respect quite unlike the interpretation of less formal communications, and that is what Lord Hoffmann means by 'utterances in ordinary life'.

6 See *Mannai Investment Co v. Eagle Star Life Assurance Society* [1997] AC 749.

7 The questions overlap of course because it can only be right to consider background which may have an effect on the construction of a document.

8 Lawyers are not the only ones who may misuse dictionaries. See the definition of 'Dictionary' in Bierce (2001): 'A malevolent literary device for cramping the growth of a language and making it hard and inelastic.'

9 Of course this begs the question of how one ascertains the meaning of words (isolated from background or context). The conceptual problem is not clarified but rather made even

(2) the meaning which a document conveys.[10]

It is obvious that such a conflict may exist. It may arise in three different circumstances:

1. The conflict may arise having regard only to the words of the document ('document context'). No-one has ever doubted that words must be construed with regard to document context[11] and in this sense the meaning of a document overrides the meaning of words in it.

2. The conflict may arise having regard to background knowledge not stated in the document but which would be known to the parties and known to any reasonably well-informed reader (including a judge) without need for evidence. We refer to this as 'intuitive context'. In extreme cases no-one has ever doubted that words must be construed with regard to intuitive context, and in this sense too the meaning of a document (if one can find it) may override the meaning of its words. Even the most ardent literalist would agree that, say, a gift expressed to be to the National Society for the Promotion of Cruelty to Children should take effect as a gift to the National Society for the *Prevention* of Cruelty to Children. Why is this? Because we know the background facts that the NSPCC exists and testators commonly make gifts to it; a National Society for the promotion of cruelty to children does not exist and no one would make a gift to it. But as soon as that is conceded, the extreme position that interpretation should *only* have regard to the plain meaning of words is lost. Lord Hoffmann is only expressing with more enthusiasm a principle

---

more obscure, by adding the epithet 'natural', and seeking a 'natural' meaning. Lord Hoffmann again: 'I think that in some cases the notion of words having a natural meaning is not a very helpful one. Because the meaning of words is so sensitive to syntax and context, the natural meaning of words in one sentence may be quite unnatural in another. Thus a statement that words have a particular natural meaning may mean no more than that in many contexts they will have that meaning. In other contexts their meaning will be different but no less natural.' *Charter Reinsurance Co. Ltd v. Fagan* [1997] AC 313, 391. One sees how philosophers are drawn to the (non-intuitive) view that a word out of context has no meaning. If an exaggeration, this is at least a healthy reaction against over-emphasis on dictionary meaning.

10 Of course this begs the question of how one ascertains 'the meaning which a document conveys.'

11 See for example Lord Hardwicke, *Milner v. Milner* (1748) Ves. Sen. 1, 105, citing Roman law.

which has for some time been observed by lawyers[12] and others.[13] It is in this particular area of conflict that the distinction is drawn between a literal (or semantic) as opposed to a less literal (or purposive)[14] approach. The difference between the two is a matter of degree.

3. The conflict may arise only when one has regard to evidence of background fact that would be known to the parties but not known to a judge (or others) unless additional evidence was provided. Lord Hoffmann's position (that this kind of background should be used to a greater degree than before in deciding issues of interpretation) is controversial.

The hard question in cases (1) and (2) and (if the evidence is admitted) in case (3) is not *whether* either kind of context can overturn the meaning of words but how easily or in what circumstances. In other words, how *does* one ascertain the meaning of a document?

The objective principle

The old style of legal interpretation had an answer to this problem. It drew a sharp distinction between:

1. subjective intention, for example the intention[15] in the mind of the author(s), the psychological data; and
2. objective meaning, the objective[16] meaning of the words used.

---

12 For example, see *Re Doland* [1970] Ch 267, 272: 'The point may be reached at which apparent caprice does become a warning signal that something may have gone awry with the testator's true expression of his intention. An error in drafting is sometimes clearly apparent from a grammatical defect, when for instance some word or words have been obviously omitted by accident. Or it may be manifest from the context that a testator has at a particular point used a mistaken word or a wrong name. In such cases if the court is clear about the true intention, it will, as an exercise of interpretation, give effect to that intention and for that purpose will remould the testator's language. Similarly, if the consequence of the language used by a testator, read in its primary and natural sense, is to produce a disposition or a series of dispositions which is so capricious as to be really irrational, the court may, in my judgment, be justified in concluding that the testator has failed to express himself adequately, and in such a case if, but only if, it can discern the true intention of the testator, it will give effect to it.'

13 For example, C.S. Lewis (1960, Chap 1, Pt. IV) distinguishes 'word's meaning' and 'speaker's (or writer's) meaning'; see also Wittgenstein (1974, 5.4732): 'we cannot give a sign a wrong sense'. The battle between words and documents extends to biblical interpretation, see Barr (1961).

14 *Hawkins on the Construction of Wills* uses the term 'intentionalist' (Kerridge 2000).

15 This begs the question of what we mean by 'intention', but although there is much that could be said on the topic, 'intention' is sufficiently clear to use for the purposes of this article without further analysis.

16 'Objective meaning' is objective in the sense that it is independent of the mind of the individual *author(s)*. It is nevertheless often subjective in the sense that it will often depend on

Having drawn this distinction, the solution to the problem of interpretation was seen to lie in ignoring the subjective intention in favour of the objective meaning. This is here called 'the objective principle'.[17]

There are three ways that this principle has been expressed'

1. The court seeks to find the intention of the parties but the expression 'intention' actually *means* 'the meaning of the document'.
2. The court seeks to find the intention of the parties but the meaning of the document is *deemed* to be the intention.
3. The court seeks to find the meaning of the words and intention of the parties is irrelevant.

Identification of 'intention' with 'meaning'

Lewison (2004) enthusiastically supports the first view:

> For the purpose of the construction of contracts, the intention of the parties is the meaning of the words they have used. There is no intention independent of that meaning [...]. In other words "intention" is equivalent to "meaning" (para 2.03).[18]

He cites *IRC v. Raphael*:[19]

> The fact is that the narrative [recitals] and operative parts of a deed perform quite different functions, and "intention" in reference to the narrative and the same word in reference to the operative parts respectively bear quite different significations. As appearing in the narrative part it means "purpose". In considering the intention of the operative part the word means significance or import— "the way in which anything is to be understood" (*Oxford English Dictionary*) supported by the illustration: "The intention of the passage was sufficiently clear".

This linguistic usage is to be utterly rejected for the following reasons:

---

the mind of the *reader*, for the same text may convey different meanings to different minds. (It is submitted that meaning of a text may properly be called objective if all readers of the text in context would agree on the meaning even though the meaning is of course dependent on the minds of the readers as a community).

17 This expression is capable of various meanings and should not be used undefined. It has not been used in the law reports. The objective principle of interpretation is distinct from the objective principle of contract formation. Among other differences, the principle of interpretation extends beyond contracts and applies to other legal documents.

18 Some non-lawyers adopt the same approach, see Fish (1989, 116).

19 [1935] AC 96, 135.

1. That is not the way the word 'intention' is normally used.
2. This usage is a sleight of hand giving the comforting impression that the reader or judge is seeking to find the true subjective intention; which is at best only partly the case.
3. This usage makes a discussion of the subjective/objective aspects of construction impossible.

In short, this usage highjacks the meaning of 'intention' in an Orwellian manner: contrast use of the word 'democratic' in the *German Democratic Republic* or 'trust' in *National Health Trust*.

Deemed intention

The second and more usual analysis is not to define (or misdefine) the word 'intention' to mean 'meaning' but to use the language of presumption or deeming:

> The question is not so much what was the intention, as what, in the contemplation of the law, must be presumed to have been the intention.[20]

This view is taken in *Norton on Deeds*:[21]

> [...] the question to be answered always is, "What is the meaning of what the parties have said?" not "What did the parties mean to say?" [...] it being a presumption *juris et de jure* [...] that the parties intended to say that which they have said.

This is distinct from the first approach, since it recognises that a distinction exists between the intention and that which is merely deemed (presumed) to be the intention; this is stressed because many cases and textbooks adopt both approaches in the same paragraph. The two are incompatible. The second approach is better than the first, but it is still to be rejected. The deeming is a fiction; all fictions are lies, and while they may have their purposes, the fiction is not needed here.

Intention irrelevant

The third and honest analysis is to forego the word 'intention' altogether. Here are some examples from 19th Century case law:

> The question in this and other cases of construction of written instruments, is, not what was the intention of the parties; but what is the meaning of the words they have used.[22]
> In expounding a will, the court is to ascertain, not what the testator actually intended, as contradistinguished from what his words express, but what is the meaning of the words he has used. I consider it doubtful what the testator actually meant should be done. But I have no doubt as to the meaning of the words used by him.[23]

---

20 *Miller v. Farmer* (1815) 1 Merrivale 55, 80 (per Lord Eldon).
21 Norton (1928, 50) approved *Schuler v. Wickman Machine Tool Sales* [1974] AC 235.
22 *Rickman v. Carstairs* (1833) 5 B. and Ad. 663 (per Lord Denman).
23 *Doe v. Gwilum* (1833) 5 B. and Ad. 122, 129 (per Lord Wensleydale).

Oliver Wendell Holmes, writing off the record, put the point more bluntly:

> We don't care a damn for the meaning of the writer, the only question is the meaning of the words.[24]

Relationship between objective principle and inadmissibility rules

The rule of inadmissibility of statements of intent/pre-contract negotiations is sometimes said to be founded on the objective principle.[25] This reasoning is not just fallacious but pernicious. The reason for the inadmissibility rules is that they offer practical, pragmatic advantages. In particular:

1. Cost saving: the cost of reviewing the additional evidence must be set against the number of occasions where it is significant. This applies not only to litigation but to every occasion where advice is given on construction. Some say that the cost/benefit ratio is very high.
2. Admissibility is unfair to assignees and other third parties who may not be aware of this material.[26]

Where the balance of advantage lies is at present actively debated. Those who think the cost/benefit ratio is low (or can be reduced by case management) would favour a relaxation of the exclusory rules. Those who think the cost/benefit ratio is high will favour retention of strict inadmissibility rules. This debate cannot be carried out (and so a well grounded rule of law cannot be achieved) if the inadmissibility rules are said to be necessary consequences of an 'objective principle' which is not open for debate. There is no reasoning with that and no arguing with it; it suppresses the policy debate which ought to be taking place.

In this debate the rules of inadmissibility of statements of intent and pre-contract negotiations should be considered separately. Everyone agrees that the rule

---

24 Holmes–Pollock letters, 9th December 1898 (DeWolfe 1961).

25 'The exclusion of the parties' subjective declarations of intent from the admissible material is a reflection of the principle that a contract must be interpreted objectively' (Lewison 2004, para 5.11.).

26 There is obviously some strength in this objection but a workable solution is to restrict admissibility in the case of assets (such as leases) whose assignment is a substantial possibility. In these cases rectification is a better tool as it is a discretionary remedy which can be refused if necessary to protect third parties. In *Prenn v. Simmonds* [1971] 1 WLR 1381, 1384, Lord Wilberforce offers a different reason: '[...] such evidence is unhelpful. By the nature of things, where negotiations are difficult, the parties' positions, with each passing letter, are changing and until the final agreement, though converging, still divergent. It is only the final document which records a consensus.' Unfortunately this is not true: a consensus will usually be reached on some points well before the final agreement; otherwise the evidence would be equally unhelpful in rectification cases (which is not the case).

excluding statements of intent is a sound rule.[27] The merit of the rule excluding prior negotiations is more marginal, and hotly contested.[28]

Relationship between objective principle and literal construction

The approach of seeking objective meaning (as opposed to subjective intention) is often taken to be synonymous with a literal or semantic (as opposed to a less literal or purposive) approach. But this does not follow at all. It is true that a literal approach to construction is not consistent with a search for the subjective intention of the author. However, a less literal and more background-sensitive reading of the kind advocated by Lord Hoffmann can properly be described as a search for the author's subjective meaning. Lord Hoffmann said:

> It is of course true that the law is not concerned with the speaker's subjective intentions. But the notion that the law's concern is therefore with the "meaning of his words" conceals an important ambiguity. The ambiguity lies in a failure to distinguish between the meanings of words and the question of what would be understood as the meaning of a person who uses words. The meaning of words, as they would appear in the dictionary, and the effect of their syntactical arrangement, as it would appear in a grammar, is part of the material which we use to understand a speaker's utterance. But it is only a part; another part is our knowledge of the background against which the utterance was made. It is that background which enables us, not only to choose the intended meaning when a word has more than one dictionary meaning but also, in the ways I have expressed, to understand a speaker's meaning, often without ambiguity, when he has used the wrong words.
>
> When, therefore, lawyers say that they are concerned, not with subjective meaning but with the meaning of the language which the speaker has used, what they mean is that they are concerned with what he would objectively have been understood to mean. This involves examining not only the words and the grammar but the background as well. [29]

This takes us back to Lord Hoffmann's statement of general principle set out above. He refers to 'meaning which a document would convey to a reasonable person'. However, a reasonable person looks for subjective intention of the author where possible, so it comes to the same thing. There is no practical difference

---

27 *Deutsche Morgan Grenfell v. HMRC* [2006] UKHL 49 para 14: 'Once a judgment has been published, its interpretation belongs to posterity and its author and those who agreed with him at the time have no better claim to be able to declare its meaning than anyone else'.

28 McMeel (2003, 139) advocates extending admissibility of prior negotiations. Lord Nicholls agrees (2005, 577). Sir Christopher Staughton (1999, 307) calls for restrictions: 'It is hard to imagine a ruling more calculated to perpetuate the vast cost of commercial litigation'. Few advocate admissibility of simple declarations of intent by the parties (but even if officially excluded they may slip in under the guise of background fact). The current distinction between background (admissible) and previous negotiations (inadmissible) is also troublesome since previous negotiations will contain factual background. For the use of earlier agreements/ trust documents to ascertain construction, see Newman (2006). Subsequent conduct raises similar problems: the traditional view is that it should not be relevant to construction but some advocate that it should be.

29 *Mannai Investment Co v. Eagle Star Life Assurance Society* [1997] AC 749, 775.

between Lord Hoffman's approach and an approach expressly looking for subjective intention. They are two buses to the same destination. But the latter is to be preferred as it more accurately expresses the destination. Lord Steyn makes this point:

> In determining the meaning of the language of a commercial contract, and unilateral contractual notices, the law therefore generally favours a commercially sensible construction. The reason for this approach is that *a commercial construction is more likely to give effect to the intention of the parties*. Words are therefore interpreted in the way in which a reasonable commercial person would construe them. And the standard of the reasonable commercial person is hostile to technical interpretations and undue emphasis on niceties of language.[30]

Arguments for and against the objective principle

We can and should distinguish between the objective principle[31] and the rules of inadmissibility of pre-contract negotiations and declarations of intent. They are completely separate rules and we can have one without the other. Having done so we can consider the merits of the objective principle.

The case against the objective principle is obvious and hardly needs to be stated. Those who sign legal documents have specific intentions in their mind and in principle they want *those* intentions to be acted on if possible and not any other.

The point is not theoretical. There is a good reason why a court should acknowledge that it is seeking to find the subjective intention of the parties. Disdain for subjective intention has pernicious consequences. It leads away from subjective intention where such intention does exist and can be found. Construction disassociated from the fetter of seeking subjective intention easily becomes very distant from it. Lewison (2004, 23) quotes with approval the approach of Nourse L.J. (reversing the trial judge on the construction of a rent review clause):

> I think it very probable that, in accepting the landlord's construction, the learned judge has correctly assessed what the parties did indeed believe and desire to be the effect of [the clause]. But a court of construction can only hold that they intended it to have that effect if the intention appears from a fair interpretation of the words which they have used against the factual background known to them at or before the date of the lease [...].[32]

Lewison defends this since:

> In the case of a lease there are potential successors in title of each party. Hence the court is right to insist that the intention must be made clear on the face of the contract (para 2.05.).

---

30 Ibid. at 771 (emphasis added).

31 By which is meant the principle that interpretation is the search for the objective meaning of the document and not the search for the intention in the mind of the writer.

32 *Philpots (Woking) Ltd. v. Surrey Conveyancers Ltd.* [1986] 1 EGLR 97. The decision of mainstream law reports not to report this case reflects tacit disapproval.

But if a judge can ascertain from the lease and intuitive context the 'very probable' intention of the parties, so too can any other reasonably well informed reader of the lease.

What then is the argument for the objective principle?

The objective principle is said to be a logical consequence of the rule of inadmissibility of pre-contract negotiations and declarations of intent.[33] This reasoning is fallacious. There is a distinction between the aim of interpretation and the materials the Court uses to achieve that aim. It is consistent to say that the law *does* seek subjective intention where possible but for good reason imposes certain restraints on how it sets about its task (and so sometimes will fail to find the subjective intention correctly).[34]

The objective principle is said to be a logical consequence of those situations where a Court cannot find a subjective intention because none exists. There are circumstances where no subjective intention exists. One case is where the issue to be decided never came to the mind of the author. This can happen with wills and trusts, though it is more common in wider ranging documents (typically statutes). A related case is where one person adopts with minimal consideration a standard form drafted by another; for example, an employee may pay money to a pension scheme without even seeing the trust deed. In this case the drafter may have subjective intentions where the employee has none. A second case is in a multilateral document where different parties may have agreed a form of words with different subjective intentions. An extreme example of this is a statute, where so many minds are involved (or half involved) that the concept 'the intention of Parliament' might be regarded as a metaphor or legal fiction which may fall more distant from the subjective intentions of any of those who took a part in the process of passing the statute (Bell and Engle 1995, Chap. 2). But even behind a statute there are human minds with subjective intentions, and it is usually reasonable to regard interpretation as the search for them.[35] However, although we cannot always find a subjective intention, it does not follow that we cannot or should not seek subjective intention *at all*.

Lewison (2004) says:

> The primary reason for adopting an objective approach to the interpretation of contracts is the promotion of certainty (para 2.05.).

If this were true it would be a powerful argument. Unfortunately, it is not true. It is based on the wishful thinking of Hawkins (1860, 583):

---

33 'If actual intent were the criterion, no reason can be given against admitting proof that the testator used every word in the language in a non-natural sense peculiar to himself. Short of that, we can only fall back on the objectively reasonable meaning of what the testator has said (Holmes–Pollock letters, 22 February 1899 (DeWolfe 1961)). 'The exclusion of the parties' subjective declarations of intent from the admissible material is a reflection of the principle that a contract must be interpreted objectively' (Lewison 2004, para 5.11.).

34 Contrast a trial which is generally and rightly regarded as a search for truth even though relevant evidence is excluded (so sometimes the court will reach a wrong conclusion).

35 The justification for regarding white papers, Law Commission reports and even *Hansard* as relevant background material is that it sheds light on those intentions.

The meaning of the words is, in theory at all events, a fixed one; it is independent of the writer, and capable of being known by the interpreter, not, like the writer's intent, with a greater or less degree of probability, but with certainty.[36]

This is fantasy. How one ascertains objective meaning (as distinct from seeking the subjective intention of the author) is more problematic (and more subjective, i.e. dependant on the mind of the reader) than proponents of the objective principle may realise.[37]

Admittedly, even when a subjective intention does exist, one cannot always expect to ascertain it from the materials available to the Court. But one can generally aim to find it, and in practice reach near it *if one tries*.

Moreover, in cases where a party had no specific subjective intention, his or her general intention would be that the matter should be decided in the manner most consistent with the documentation construed in its context. In this case the search for objective meaning *is* the subjective intention of the writer.

Precedent not the solution

Precedent does not offer a solution to problems of construction. It has been tried and failed as it was bound to:

> I think it is the duty of a Judge to ascertain the construction of the instrument before him, and not to refer to the construction put by another judge upon an instrument, perhaps similar, but not the same. The only result of referring to authorities for that purpose is confusion and error, in this way, that if you look at a similar instrument, and say that a certain construction was put upon it, and that it differs only to such a slight degree from the document before you, that you do not think the difference sufficient to alter the construction, you miss the real point of the case, which is to ascertain the meaning of the instrument before you. It may be quite true that in your opinion the difference between the two instruments is not sufficient to alter the construction, but at the same time the Judge who decided on that other instrument may have thought that that very difference would be sufficient to alter the interpretation of that instrument. You have in fact no guide whatever, and the result especially in some cases of wills has been remarkable. There is, first document A, and a Judge formed an opinion as to its construction. Then came document B, and some other Judge has said that it differs very little from document A – not sufficiently to alter the construction – therefore he construes it in the same way. Then comes document C, and the Judge there compares it with document B, and says it differs very little, and therefore he shall construe it in the same way. And so the construction has gone on until we find a document which is in totally different terms from the first, and which no human being would think of construing in the same manner, but which has by this process come to be construed in the same manner.[38]

---

36 Note that Hawkins himself resiles from this position later in his essay.

37 Hence construction is often described by judges as 'a matter of impression.'

38 *Aspden v. Seddon* (1875) LR 10 Ch. App. 394, 398 (Jessel MR), approved by the Court of Appeal in *Equity and Law Life Assurance v. Bodfield* (1987) 281 EG 1448. Likewise *Pedlar v. Road Block Gold Mines of India Ltd* [1905] 2 Ch 427: 'I remember hearing Sir George Jessel say that he should not regard himself as bound by the decision of a previous

We set this out at length (it deserves to be set out in stone) because it has not always been observed by judges. The use of precedent is part of the old legal baggage: it is inconsistent with the 'common sense principles by which any serious utterance would be interpreted in ordinary life.' The point is summed up succinctly by Lord Hoffmann:

> No case on the construction of one document is the authority on the construction of another, even if the words are very similar.[39]

Precedent may however be relevant if parties use a word or phrase in what appears to have been a technical legal sense. [40]

Similar points apply to rules of construction such as

1. *ejusdem generis*
2. *noscitur a sociis*
(the Latin tags themselves redolent of a past age).

These rules are useful in their spheres indeed they arise out of 'common sense principles': it is their rigid or insensitive application (or misapplication) which Lord Hoffmann intended to reject. They mean us to use them as signposts and are not to blame if, in our weakness, we mistake the signpost for the destination.[41]

Conclusion

This chapter has discussed a range of approaches to interpretation, and considered and rejected an objective principle. The modern approach to interpretation involves an extension of reliance on (and admissibility of) background fact; rejection of 'old intellectual baggage' of precedents and rules of construction; and recognition of less literal readings. These are large steps away from the false god of objective meaning and towards seeking the author's subjective intention: they require the Court to try harder to put itself in the position of the author(s) [42] and the result is that the Court is more likely to find the subjective intention.

In summary, the correct answer to the objective meaning/subjective intention debate lies between the two extremes. It is not the case (or it is considerable oversimplification to say) that the aim of interpretation is to find the subjective intention or the objective meaning. In interpretation, the court should aspire to find

---

judge on the construction of the identical document and the identical passage of the document which he had to construe.' (Warrington J.). The authorities are discussed in Lewison (2004, para 4.09.).

39 *Deeny v. Gooda WalkerLtd* [1996] STC 299, 306.

40 *BCCI v. Ali* [2002] 1 AC 251 para 51; McKendrick *supra* note 2, 152.

41 Lord Hoffmann is more blunt in *BCCI v. Ali* [2002] 1 AC 251, para 55: 'Books like *Jarman on Wills* are monuments to the rules of construction and a melancholy record of the occasions on which they have defeated the intentions of testators.'

42 The metaphor often used is being in the shoes or armchair of the author(s); if that means anything it means a search for subjective intentions.

the subjective intention, where possible, doing as best it can from limited information available. In the exceptional cases where there is (or appears to be) no subjective intention one should try to construe the document sympathetically, as if there were one (and of course one will not normally know that there is no subjective intention, that too requires one to look into the mind of the author). That is exactly what the modern law requires, and, surely, what the law ought to be.[43]

---

43 Article 5.101 of the Principles of European Contract Law provides that 'a contract is to be interpreted according to the common intention of the parties even if this differs from the literal meaning of the words [...].' The approach of this article therefore offers a reconciliation of the EU and the common law approach to construction, which is another recommendation for it. For the background of linguistics and philosophy of language see Kramer (2003).

Chapter 3

Rules and Statements

Louis E. Wolcher

Nam omnia praeclara tam difficilia quam rara sunt[1]

Clarity about the problem of Clarity

In this chapter we will attempt to achieve something as rare and excellent as it is difficult: philosophical clarity about how it is possible for legal texts (constitutions, statutes, common law decisions, written contracts and so forth) to be received and used by lawyers, judges and laypersons on the basis of the conceptual dualism 'clear versus obscure'. Although most of us know how to use the words 'clear' and 'obscure' in daily life, thinking about what makes a given legal text clear or obscure in the first place is something we hardly ever do. Seen from the point of view of the legal technician and the consumer of legal language, clarity of expression is instrumental for achieving certain goals. Indeed, even obscurity of expression can be used as a tool, as Jeremy Bentham noticed when he attacked the opacity and complexity of the old English common law for its tendency to serve ruling class interests (Kayman 2004, 214–19). But despite the many uses (and misuses) of legal language, getting clear about the problem of how it is possible for legal language to present itself as either clear or obscure is a different kind of enterprise than trying to craft it so that its audience will unreflectively receive it as clear or obscure. The second task is but an exercise in instrumental reason – a mere calculation of means and ends; the first requires genuine *thinking*.

Thinking, as I use the term here, is also not the same as theory-mongering, for trying to explain or account for something must be distinguished from thinking aimed at acquiring perspicuity on a theme. Like legal language itself, most philosophical theories of legal language are instrumental: they suppress differences in the interest of explaining and controlling their subject matter. This kind of fetish for control is absent here. If we do make what look like theoretical moves in the course of these investigations (for example, by using the soon-to-be-explained concepts of 'nonsense' and 'bipolarity'), this will only be because the moves in question open up the complexities of language rather than closing them down in the form of an

---

1 'For all that is excellent and eminent is as difficult as it is rare'. This is the English translation of the last sentence in Spinoza's great treatise, the *Ethics* (1955, 280). The original Latin is quoted by Schopenhauer (1969, vol. I, 384).

comprehensive explanation.[2] In this chapter we will share the indifferent attitude towards explanatory theories that Wittgenstein expresses in the following passage from one of his lectures on philosophical psychology during the late 1940s:

> We are not looking for a theory. [...] [For example] Freud's theory of dreams as wish fulfilment is explained with reference to primitive dreams. But it is a theory, and we can justly object by saying: "Oh, but there are other dreams". This is not the case with us. We are not giving a theory. I am only giving a type: only describing a field of varying examples by means of centres of variation. Any other example is not a contradiction; it is only a contribution (1988, 142).

Wittgenstein believed (as I do) that philosophical clarity is an end in itself: that it amounts to the kind of perspicuous overview of its theme that is or should be the ultimate goal of any philosophical enquiry that aspires to be non-dogmatic. What we do afterwards with our hard-won perspicuity about legal language is not so much a matter of critical reflection as it is a matter of concrete (and often tragic) action in the spheres of politics and morality. A philosophy that tries to 'help' the pre-existing projects of law and politics achieve their aims is never the result of genuine *philosophising*, for such a method takes for granted what is actually most question-worthy in this context: namely, how it is possible for any kind of language (including philosophical language) to 'achieve' anything whatsoever. That this critique of utility-minded philosophising is a debatable point of view on the philosophy of philosophy almost goes without saying. Be that as it may, however, one does not have to accept Wittgenstein's philosophy of philosophy in order to use his methods to achieve significant insights into the problem of clarity and obscurity in legal language. In a nutshell: getting clear about that problem as such is what really matters to us in this chapter – not arriving at a 'correct' (or useful) theoretical explanation of it.

In our quest for clarity about clarity we will make use of an important distinction that was first drawn by Wittgenstein during his early-to-middle period (roughly, from 1913 to around 1940), and that in one way or another stuck with him throughout his life. With Wittgenstein, we will distinguish between the *rules* that make up a system of language and the *statements* that are made, by means of the rules, within the system. The word 'rule' in this context does not refer to the same kind of thing that the term 'legal rule' (hereinafter 'legal norm') refers to. We think of the primary legal norms that are expressed in authoritative legal texts as normatively binding in the sense that we ought to obey them. Judges can even feel normatively bound to apply certain secondary norms for construing primary legal norms – familiar canons of construction like 'finding the original intent', 'reading the plain meaning' and 'determining the purpose of the law'. But the *implicit* linguistic rules that allow people to understand and use legal norms of both sorts are not legally binding in any normal sense of the term. To say that language is rule-bound in Wittgenstein's sense thus does not mean that there is a book of rules somewhere that determines whether speakers are or are not in compliance. Rather, *we* are the ones who find and articulate

---

2 'People who are constantly asking "why" are like tourists who stand in front of a building reading Baedeker and are so busy reading the history of its construction, and so on, that they are prevented from *seeing* the building' (Wittgenstein 1980, 40e).

the rules while we are thinking philosophically: we study the way various groups of people live and talk, and we report honestly about the regularities in linguistic usage that we observe. Indeed, the word 'rule' in this context is merely shorthand for the observation that a linguistic usage *is* regular. People do not follow these rules so much as exhibit them in their behaviour. The later Wittgenstein famously calls this kind of regularity in people's linguistic behaviour a *language game* [*Sprachspiel*, in German], which he defines as 'language and the actions into which it is woven' (1958, 5e).

As this definition of 'language game' suggests, regularities in the use of language hang together with what Wittgenstein calls *forms of life*. 'To imagine a language means to imagine a form of life', he says (1958, 8e), by which he means a shifting pattern of communal interaction in all of its aspects. For example, the primitive language-game of the builders that Wittgenstein imagines at the beginning of the *Philosophical Investigations* is connected intimately to their radically simple way of living: calling out the names of building materials is all the language they need in order to get the job done (1958, 3e–10e). Since our own forms of life are hugely more complex than theirs, the example of the builders is meant to show that one-size-fits-all philosophical theories of language are *a priori* inadequate to the task of understanding the many different language games that people play. The concept 'form of life' is therefore a helpful reminder that the actual speaking and writing of language is never isolated from the non-linguistic aspects of people's lives; on the contrary, every linguistic practice is woven into the fabric of the particular human activity that gives it its *raison d'être* (1958, 11e).

Six ideas on the differences between rules and statements

Having made the foregoing preliminary points as well as I can, permit me to summarise certain distinctions between *rules*, *propositions*, and *legal norms* in the form of six interrelated ideas or themes. These will serve to launch and pre-orient our investigation into the problem of how legal language 'means' what it is taken to mean. In describing the six ideas I will generally adhere to the following basic definitions: a 'sign' is that part of language that can be perceived by the senses; a 'statement' includes both propositions and legal norms, and consists in a sign that has a use in some language game; an 'expression' is a statement considered together with the particular human behaviour of which it is an element; a 'proposition' is the representation of a state of affairs that could be otherwise, and that can be compared with reality according to some method of comparison; and a 'legal norm' is a generally accepted legal thought-statement[3] for which there is a method of application.

---

3 Since it is not my intention here to develop a theory of what is and is not 'law', the chapter's rather loose (and admittedly circular) definition of a legal norm as a generally accepted legal thought-statement should not be read to advocate a position in the debate within legal positivism about the proper criterion for 'law', or to take a stand in the age-old controversy between positivism and natural law theory. Instead, what is most important about this definition is that it distinguishes legal norms, which no one doubts are statements of what ought to be, from propositions, which make assertions about that which is (states of affairs).

Here are the six ideas:

1) One of the most important functions of the implicit rules of language pertains to representation. The rules show what can be said, with sense, about the way things are (or are not) in the world – about *logically* possible states of affairs, in other words.

2) To speak of a 'way' that things are implies that there are *other* ways for them to be, for as Wittgenstein says, 'there is no sense in talking of a way if there is only one end and a different end is precluded' (1979, 73). For example, while there are many ways to get from Seattle to London, it makes no sense to talk about a 'way' of getting from Seattle to Seattle. Consequently, to say that a state of affairs is logically possible is to say that we can imagine it to be different. The sentences 'It is raining' and 'Elephants can fly' both depict logically possible states of affairs, but the expression '1 + 1 = 2', at least as a typical Western mathematician might use it, does not. In the first two cases we can imagine an antithesis to what is said (a sunny day or a flightless elephant), whereas in the latter case we cannot: there is no imaginable state of affairs that corresponds to the sentence '1 + 1 ≠ 2' in this context. Although it may sound shocking (or just plain ridiculous) to say it, a mathematician cannot sensibly say either that '1 + 1 = 2' is true or that '1 + 1 ≠ 2' is false. If an outraged mathematician were now to rejoin 'But the statement '1 + 1 = 2 really is true!' (as most undoubtedly would), the best *philosophical* response would be simply to observe that what he asserts is the equivalent of saying that the statement '1 + 1 = 2' has been *proven*. In short, the word 'true', as he uses it in this context, is synonymous with the phrase 'mathematically proven'. But a proven statement in mathematics is not true in the very precise sense that we are using the term here: that is, it does not exclude an imaginable antithesis.[4] To put this point in technical terms, a statement makes (or has) sense if it is bipolar – if it asserts a state of affairs that could be otherwise. Only bipolar statements are propositions, and only propositions have a sense. As Wittgenstein said to Russell, in 1913, 'What I mean to say [by the word "bipolar"] is that we *only* then understand a proposition if we know both what would be the case

---

In this respect the distinction between methods of comparison and methods of application is critical: the former compare propositions *with* reality, while the latter apply norms *to* reality.

4 For example, an impossibility proof in mathematics does not prove that a thing is impossible in fact. Suppose I spend years mucking about with a very precise ruler and compass and manage to divide a sixty degree angle into three parts which, when measured by the finest instruments we humans have available to us, yield measurements of exactly twenty degrees each. Does this mean that I have proven that the trisection of an angle *in the mathematical sense* is possible after all? No, it does not. When Courant and Robbins say (correctly) that it has been proven that 'the trisection of the angle by ruler and compass alone is in general impossible', their use of the word 'impossible' is terribly misleading (1996, 137-38). If trisection in the mathematical sense is impossible (which indeed it is), then trisection is not impossible in the same sense as my being able to fly to the moon by flapping my arms is impossible. The latter impossibility is physical, and can be demonstrated experimentally: that is, by comparing the flight-proposition with reality. But the sense of a mathematical sentence is never determined by comparing it with reality; rather, its proof simply *shows* what it means, without the need for comparing it with anything else.

if it was *false and* what if it was *true*' (1995, 47). Non-bipolar statements are neither true nor false: they are *nonsense* [*Unsinn*, in German].

The word 'nonsense', it bears noting, is not to be taken in the pejorative sense of being rubbish, for many nonsensical (non-bipolar) statements can and do have their uses. For example, absolute religious and ethical expressions – such as 'Everything whatsoever happens according to God's will' – have a use despite the fact that they are not bipolar. The example is not bipolar because the paradigmatic speaker of such a statement is stipulating in advance that he will *a priori* receive any horrible fact that one might offer to shake his confidence – the cold-blooded murder of children, for instance – as just another manifestation of God's will rather than as a counterargument. Although the statements that are the linguistic element of absolute religious and ethical expressions such as this one tell us nothing that could be otherwise, the expressions themselves frequently play the role of demonstrating the speaker's general attitude towards life (Phillips and von der Ruhr 2005, 91). Thus, if someone were to say with conviction that everything whatsoever happens according to God's will – again, a statement that admits of no antithesis – we could read his words as essentially the equivalent of the cry 'Hallelujah!' In other words, although this expression *says* nothing that could be otherwise, it nonetheless *shows* the religious faith of the speaker to anyone who cares to observe it: *that* is its use – its role in the religious language game.

Likewise, it is obvious that legal norms can have their uses even though they are not, strictly speaking, propositions 'about' the world. Although both legal norms and propositions are statements, only propositions are bipolar. Consider the *proposition* 'On January 1, 2006, Joe drove a car into the park': it is bipolar because we can imagine what it would look like if Joe did *not* drive a car into the park on that day. But a statute such as 'No vehicles in the park', although it appears to state something, does not purport to describe, as a proposition does, any particular state of affairs. Despite the fact that it is not a proposition, however, this statute *qua* legal norm can be the basis of an act of legal enforcement, and this is its primary use in the legal form of life. How a legal norm can be the 'basis' of an act of enforcement will be discussed later. For now, let me say that legal norms are applied according to some *method or methods of application*, and not according to their 'contents'; the latter way of conceiving of how legal norms operate is what we will have occasion to call the 'magical' (as opposed to the 'logical') point of view on language.

3) Logical possibility is not the same as empirical possibility, but consists in our ability to imagine and represent a hypothetical or actual state of affairs. For example, the proposition 'Unicorns exist' makes sense (even though it is and probably always has been false) because it is possible to imagine the existence of beings that look more or less like this:

Figure 3.1 Unicorn

In the *Wiener Ausgabe*, Wittgenstein sums up his entire philosophical method as a transition from the question of truth to the question of sense (1994, 177). This means that nonsensical statements have not earned the right, as it were, to be called true because they are not understood to represent anything of which it could be said, 'This is what it would be like if the sentence were false; but that's not what it is like, and therefore the sentence is true'. The best way to understand what someone who asserts a statement of the form 'X is true' or 'X is false' is getting at is to ask him to give a representation of *what it is* that is true or false. In the case of the assertion 'It is true that unicorns do not exist', for example, the speaker can give a description or draw a picture of the thing that he would call a unicorn if it *did* exist. His representation could then in principle be compared with reality as a means of deciding the *question* 'Do unicorns exist?', and hence of determining whether the *answer* 'Unicorns do not exist' is true or false. This example shows what it means to assert, as I did in the previous section, that absolute statements are never true, for as Wittgenstein says, 'in order for a proposition to be capable of being true it must also be capable of being false' (1984, 55e). Someone who says that the law of non-contradiction is 'necessarily true', for example, is not claiming that there is some imaginable state of affairs that is described by the statement 'p and not-p', such that just *this* state of affairs is not the case. What would it look like, for example, for a ball simultaneously to be coloured red all over and blue (not-red) all over? Of course, this does not imply that the statement 'The law of non-contradiction is necessarily true' has no use at all. The speaker may be expressing, by means of this nonsensical statement, that the law of non-contradiction – 'not (p and not-p)' – is a grammatical rule that she has decided to follow in constructing her sentences, and *this* possibility would give her statement a use.[5]

---

5 'The laws of logic, for example, excluded middle and contradiction, are arbitrary. This statement is a bit repulsive but nevertheless true' (Wittgenstein 1979, 71).

Wittgenstein makes the same point this way: 'all propositions which seem to be statements about the essences of things are grammatical propositions' (2003, 385), which is to say that they make the utterance of sensible propositions possible and do not themselves stand for any 'content' that one could contradict by negating them. It is easy to see that one does not contradict or disprove an explicit grammatical rule such as 'Do not split infinitives' by showing that sometimes people actually do split infinitives – at most this proves that the rule is sometimes violated. It is less obvious, but nonetheless equally true, that a statement such as 'The cardinal numbers are infinite', which seems to be about the essence of cardinal numbers, is really a disguised rule of grammar. This can be demonstrated by taking account of certain 'primitive tribes', as Wittgenstein puts it, that employ or have employed the number system '1, 2, 3, 4, 5, many': for in the arithmetical language game of these people there *is* a last number – namely, the numeral 'many' (Wittgenstein and Waismann 2003, 353). This example shows that the statement 'The cardinal numbers are infinite', although it appears to be saying something about the essence of cardinal numbers, is really no more than a grammatical rule. The rule says, in substance, that it makes no sense, in *our* system of arithmetic, to speak of a 'last' cardinal number.

(4) The propositions that we utter and write according to the implicit rules of the language-game in which we are participating, having a sense, can be compared with reality according to some method of comparison that allows us to ascertain whether they are true or false. A legal norm, although it does not represent something in the way that a proposition does, also requires a method in order to be of use: a method of application. A method of comparison is to a proposition what a method of application is to a legal norm. The first compares a proposition with reality; the second applies a norm to reality. For instance, the proposition 'There are unicorns in Seattle' might be *compared with reality* by holding a picture of a unicorn, such as the one shown above, next to every living being in the city, and then looking to see whether any of them exhibits the salient characteristics of the creature that is shown in the picture: this would be one possible method for comparing the proposition with reality. On the other hand, the hypothetical legal norm 'No unicorns are allowed in Seattle' might be *applied to reality* according to a legal fiction that takes horses to be unicorns, and requires the testimony of two witnesses to prove that a 'unicorn' (horse) is in the city: this would be one possible method for applying the legal norm to reality.[6] As these examples suggest, propositions can be compared (in theory if not in fact) with something that they are understood to be about, whereas bare legal norms, considered apart from their application to a concrete or hypothetical case, are never compared with something they are 'about'.

To be sure, legal norms can become the basis for forming propositions such as 'Louis illegally brought a unicorn into Seattle on 14 April 2006', but the legal norm

---

6 This example illustrates that the method of application of a legal norm is seldom *exclusively* a function of the implicit rules that inform a purely legal language game. Very often legal terms are applied according to implicit rules that are drawn from ordinary life. In other words, the legal and non-legal forms of life in any given society are never wholly autonomous from one another.

'No unicorns are allowed in Seattle', is not itself 'about' this (or any) particular event. Its role in the legal language game is non-propositional: the legal norm can be applied to Louis in the sense that it can be the basis of a proposition that, if true, would make him into a lawbreaker who is worthy of legal sanction; but standing alone the norm as such does not 'refer' to *any* state of affairs. This comes out of the fact that there is a category difference between the concept 'the meaning of a legal norm' and the concept 'the application of a legal norm'. The example noted above also suggests that concept-words like 'unicorn' that are used in legal propositions also have one or more methods of application, and this is true. The method of application that is used to apply a legal norm to reality will be the same method of application that is used to formulate a legal proposition that enforces that norm. Since a legal proposition is the linguistic product of the event of applying a legal norm, this is hardly surprising. Nevertheless, once such a legal proposition is expressed and understood as bipolar, it brings with it a method of comparison that the legal norm as such lacks – one that allows us to decide whether the proposition is true or false. For example, although the proposition 'Louis illegally brought a unicorn into Seattle on April 14, 2006' might be judged false if credible eyewitnesses testify that Louis was lying comatose in a hospital bed on that day, no amount of testimony can prove (or disprove) the 'truth' of the legal norm 'No unicorns are allowed in Seattle'.

The meaning of a statement – whether it is a proposition or a legal norm – cannot be determined by just staring at the signs of which it is comprised; instead, a philosophical description (in the sense of observing and reporting linguistic regularities within a form of life) of the methods of comparison or application that are associated with the statement shows what it means to the people involved. To illustrate this point, consider the apparently contradictory statement '1 = .9'. The Pirahã people, a group of hunter-gatherers who live along the banks of the Maici River in Brazil, use a system of counting called 'one-two-many', in which the word for one translates to 'roughly one', the word for two means 'a slightly larger amount than one', and the word 'many' means 'a much larger amount' (Anon. 2004, 66-67). It is obvious that the mathematics of the Pirahãs will not take them to the moon or allow them to invent workable computers and automobiles. But so what? They simply do not care that their mathematics produces what we would call contradictions, for they are perfectly content to count one apple as the equivalent of what we would call nine-tenths of an apple. They get along fine with this method of applying the numerals of their language, and it is not the job of a philosopher to deny that this just happens to be their form of life. Indeed, it ought to be a philosopher's job to notice this fact.

(5) It is senseless to say that the implicit rules of language themselves are true or false, for although the rules could be different, they themselves are not statements 'about' anything. As Arendt puts it, when people judge things 'only the individual case is judged, not the standard [of judgment] itself or whether it is an appropriate measure of what it is used to measure' (2005, 102). For example, most of the time our statements implicitly follow the laws of logic, such as excluded middle and non-contradiction. These logical rules themselves do not mean something that is capable of being true or false – they are not bipolar – but rather constitute grammatical

rules that 'determine a meaning and are not answerable to any meaning they could contradict' (Wittgenstein 1978, 29).[7] Whatever meaning there is in a law of logic is already included in specific statements that follow its form, and does not pop out as something 'extra' that the naked signs that make up the law itself 'represent'.

As I have already mentioned, this same principle applies to legal norms, for they, too, are not bipolar statements about the world. One can imagine the provisions of the European Convention on Human Rights being replaced by another set of legal norms, but what else would it mean to say that one could imagine the ECHR 'being otherwise'? Compare this example: although one can imagine a game just like chess, but with one of the official rules changed to permit the bishop to move as the knight does from the tenth move on, only a fool would say 'I can imagine a game just like chess, having all the same rules, but with those rules being otherwise'. A legal norm can exist; it can be in force; but as our previous investigations have shown, it does not have *being true* as one of its properties. On the contrary, a legal norm plays the role of a binding grammatical rule for the construction of propositions according to some method of application (more on this later). That is, this is how the legal norm is actually used by lawyers and judges, even though they might not describe the matter this way were they to step out of the legal language game and engage in the task of philosophizing about legal language. The norm plus its method of application comprise a kind of measuring device (quite literally a 'rule') that allows lawyers and judges to say of this or that particular action 'This is an instance of 'X' within the meaning of the legal norm that says 'Do not do X'.

(6) A legal norm does not have to take any particular form, at least in a common law system. This fact sometimes can make the distinction between norms and propositions difficult to draw. By way of illustration, consider the following series of mathematical statements:

E_1: $4 = 2 + 2$.
E_2: $2 = 1 + 1$.
E_3: $4 = (1 + 1) + (1 + 1)$.

Is the transformation from E_1 to E_3 accomplished by means of E_2, seen as a norm (of substitution)? Or does E_3 follow as merely the next step from the first two equations seen as co-equal configurations in the game? That is, do I go, step by step, from E_1 to E_2 to E_3 by means of an inference according to *other* norms, or does E_2 amount to the norm that I apply to E_1 in order to produce E_3? One might argue (erroneously)

---

7 Grammatical rules in this sense are like stipulations concerning units of length: we can use a stipulated length (a bar we call 'one metre', for example) to measure with, but it is hard to see what the point would be of saying that the bar we have chosen as our standard of measurement is *itself* one standard unit long. Consider Wittgenstein's remark about what was then the standard metre-bar in Paris: 'There is *one* thing of which one can say neither that it is one metre long, nor that it is not one metre long, and that is the standard metre in Paris. But this is, of course, not to ascribe any extraordinary property to it, but only to mark its peculiar role in the language-game of measuring with a metre-rule' (1958, 25e).

that E_2 is insufficiently general in its form as a matter of logical necessity, and that logic (as opposed to mere convention) requires us to have a substitution-norm of the appropriate 'generality of expression' in order to get E_3 from E_1 and E_2.[8] However, the statement of any such norm would consist in signs, just as E_2 does, and there is nothing to prevent us from reading (or failing to read) the appropriate level of generality in either of them. The appropriate level of generality that is required of a norm is usually decided on the basis of regularity of usage, and sometimes on the basis of the idiosyncratic choices of individuals. In either case an induction is what *human beings* (not norms) do, and no additional norm can save them this inductive step. As Wittgenstein puts it:

> The essential thing about [a rule], its generality, is inexpressible. Generality shows itself in application. I have to *read* this generality *into* the configuration. [...] A rule is not like the mortar between two bricks. We cannot lay down a rule for the application of another rule. We cannot apply one rule by means of another rule (Waismann 1979, 154-55).

In this passage Wittgenstein does not mean to deny that one can construct canons for construing norms; rather, he means that there is no such thing as a norm (including a canon) that can read itself *as* a norm. Thus, for example, we would not say of the interpretive legal norm of applying the 'plain meaning' of a statute that it itself has a plain meaning, for it is this very norm (together with its method of application) that establishes the possibility of saying that this or that statute has a 'plain meaning' in the first place. In short, the norm-like quality of a statement does not depend on its having a particular and preordained level of generality of expression. This is a point that was well-known to the American Legal Realists, who delighted in showing that the holding (the statement of a legal norm) of a common law precedent is always a function of the level of generality at which subsequent courts decide to characterise the precedent court's decision (see Stone 1964, 268-74). What one judge thinks of as the *holding* of a precedent case another judge might think of as a mere description of the *facts* of that case; the difference is that the second judge would read the sentences that make up the previous decision as standing for a legal norm which he expresses at a higher level of generality than the level expressed by the first judge: 'a gasoline-powered vehicle in the park' versus 'an automobile in the park', for example. The main point is that *any* set of signs can show itself as a norm. It all depends on how the signs are actually used by people.

Although an explicit norm dealing with signs is a stipulation about the use of signs, people constantly confuse statements of this type with a proposition because 'at first blush a rule dealing with signs looks just like a proposition' (Waismann 1979, 242). The statement 'Red is a colour', for example, looks similar to the proposition 'My sweater is red'. However, the latter tells us something about a state of affairs that could be otherwise (my sweater could be coloured blue, for instance), whereas the former tells us nothing of the sort; it is at best a reminder that the word 'red' belongs to the linguistic practice of describing things by their colour. To overlook this distinction is to confuse the grammatical with the factual. Thus, to say that the concept 'law' is itself lawful is like saying that the concept 'red' is coloured red.

---

8 For example: for the sign '2', wherever it occurs, '1 + 1' may be substituted.

Both ways of thinking and talking are confused. More generally, a great deal of philosophical confusion – especially confusion about the problem of clarity and obscurity in legal language – stems from a failure to understand and appreciate the differences between rules, propositions, and norms.

The hermeneutic circle

Now trying to get clear, in a philosophical sense, about the problem of clarity in the use of legal language is a bit like trying to sing a song about how to sing. Despite our best intentions to investigate the theme of clarity (or singing, for that matter) thoroughly and critically – from the ground up, as it were – we always begin the investigation by bringing certain pre-critical and unthought understandings of the theme to that very theme. Wittgenstein pithily summarises one aspect of this insight in remarking that 'to understand a question is to know what kind of proposition the answer will be' (Waismann 1979, 227). To generalise Wittgenstein's point, the project of investigation needs to have *some* idea of its object, however vague and un-thematic that idea may be, in order to care about the object in the first place and to isolate it for subsequent investigation within its 'proper' field.

Heidegger (1962) famously calls the reciprocal relationship between our implicit pre-understandings of a thing and our subsequent explicit understandings of that thing *the hermeneutic circle*, which can be described in general terms as a kind of circuit of intelligibility that runs from what is taken for granted about X (including its very identity *as* X) to X itself, and then back again.[9] The world helps us to understand it only on the basis of how the world is already understood, as if nature offered herself to be grasped only in measures that fit into the palms of human hands that are always already outstretched to receive what nature has to offer. Notice that the implicit grammatical rules that allow the production of understanding to proceed do not relate to some nameable or describable pre-hermeneutical reality that cannot be understood apart from these rules. In other words, it would be misleading to think that the sign 'X' and its method of application *refer* to some otherwise ineffable X, for to say that 'X is the ineffable thing in itself' (the *noumenal*, in Kant's terminology) already directs and shapes our intentions in advance in accordance with the sign 'X' and the method of application that we have learned for it. Thus, we do not grasp existing entities as the appearance of some pre-linguistic *thing* (X); rather, in the event of grasping X *as* 'X' there transpires an uncovering of what is already pre-connected to us by virtue of our cares and concerns. No matter how far your run, you will never succeed in catching your shadow by chasing it: understanding X *as* 'X' is all there is to understand.

It is important to realise that the hermeneutic circle is not a process that people can choose to enter into or leave. Rather, this concept expresses what has become almost a truism, at least in postmodern thought, concerning the manner of being of the human being: namely, that 'we are *permanently* set in motion and caught in the

---

9 I should indicate that as far as I know Wittgenstein knew nothing of the hermeneutic circle, although it is obvious that I find this concept to be a helpful complement to his philosophy.

hermeneutic circle', from the cradle to the grave (Heidegger and Fink 1993, 16–17). Heidegger's own discussion of the hermeneutic circle indicates both the limits that it puts on human understanding and the interpretive possibilities that it creates:

> It is not to be reduced to the level of a vicious circle, or even a circle that is merely tolerated. In the circle is hidden a positive possibility of the most primordial kind of knowing. To be sure, we genuinely take hold of this possibility only when, in our interpretation, we have understood that our first, last and constant task is never to allow our fore-having, fore-sight and fore-conception to be presented to us by fancies and popular conceptions, but rather to make the scientific theme secure by working out these fore-structures in terms of the things themselves (1962, 195).

As this passage suggests, far from being something negative, the concept of the hermeneutic circle is actually good news for philosophy and science, because without some sort of 'idealizing presuppositions', as Habermas puts it (2003, 85), we would not know where or how to look for phenomena such as 'clarity in legal language' in the first place. Kant famously expresses this same point in terms of the necessary interdependence of intuition and understanding: 'Thoughts without content are empty, intuitions without concepts are blind' (1998, 193–94). As the theologian I.U. Dalferth recently said, the postmodern version of Kant's insight radicalises the latter's critique of reason by resituating philosophy from a 'subject-centered to a language-centered approach' (Phillips and von der Ruhr 2005, 277). A language-centered approach lets go of attachment to the idea of a transcendental subject – roughly, Kant's view that mankind possesses a unitary mental architecture comprised of universally distributed 'faculties' and 'categories' that precede and enable all experience – in favour of the idea that human beings speak and think by means of heterogeneous conventions that are founded in history, culture, experience and, well, *forms of life*.

There is no need to accept any of this on faith. *Just look*. To put the facts of the matter bluntly, we just understand, in an intuitive and pre-reflective sort of way, what to do with and how to react to certain expressions, and this means that in our daily lives no question about whether these expressions are either clear *or* obscure ever even arises. But this does not mean that we 'know' what it is that we do not doubt in this way, or even that we frequently and easily 'interpret' language in standard ways. Interpretation is an act of will, and it may or may not accompany our reactions to language (indeed, usually it does not). The thought experiment that Wittgenstein proposes in this passage on following orders from the *Blue Book* demonstrates why this is so:

> If I give someone the order 'fetch me a red flower from that meadow', how is he to know what sort of flower to bring, as I have only given him a word? Now the answer one might suggest first is that he went to look for a red flower carrying a red image in his mind, and comparing it with the flowers to see which of them had the color of the image. Now there is such a way of searching, and it is not at all essential that the image we use be a mental one. In fact the process may be this: I carry a chart coordinating names and colored squares. When I hear the order 'fetch me etc.' I draw my finger across the chart from the word 'red' to a certain square, and I go and look for a flower that has the same color as the square. But this is not the only way of searching and it isn't the usual way. We go, look

about us, walk up to a flower and pick it, without comparing it to anything. To see that the process of obeying the order can be of this kind, consider the order 'imagine a red patch'. You are not tempted in this case to think that before obeying you must have imagined a red patch to serve you as a pattern for the red patch which you were ordered to imagine. Now you might ask: do we interpret the words before we obey the order? And in some cases you will find that you do something which might be called interpreting before obeying, in some cases not (1960, 3).

Everyday life is full of cases in which we do not explicitly interpret linguistic signs such as 'fetch me a red flower', but nonetheless manage to react to them in pretty much the same way that everyone else does. It would be a grievous mistake, however, to assume that all similarities in people's reactions to signs are caused by or grounded in the clarity of the signs themselves. This is because linguistic clarity cannot become what is called 'clarity' unless it is recognised *as* such; whereas in the kind of case that Wittgenstein discusses, although we certainly notice the signs themselves, we do not *take notice* of anything explicit *about* them, such as whether or not they are 'clear'. We simply react to the signs without question or hesitation, almost as if we were Pavlov's dogs salivating at the sound of a bell. To put the matter less pejoratively, regularities in the use of language do not prove that the language itself is 'clear' – they merely show that there is a consensus of behaviour within a form of life.

The phenomenological experiment that Wittgenstein performs with the order 'fetch me a red flower' decisively refutes Hume's 'private object' thesis, according to which the meaning of language is always taken to be a state of mind (an 'idea' or 'impression') that accompanies its production (Burtt 1939, 592-97). The experiment shows that in many, if not most, cases of speaking and hearing there is no fact 'in' the world (including mental facts 'inside' the subject) that constitutes the *meaning* of the expression. Please understand that this is not a denial that people *think* as they produce language, or that they *believe* things about the language they have produced, or that a wide variety of mental phenomena accompany the production, understanding and learning of texts. It is merely an observation that whatever role is played by these psychological phenomena in connection with the use of language, that role does *not* consist in the psychological phenomena being what the language means.

It is that damnable word 'meaning' that gets us all bollixed up. We wrongly think that unless a legal norm has something called a 'meaning' it must be a meaningless set of ink stains that cannot be of any use. Hence, some of us decide to invent a real or ideal 'state of mind' that we call the norm's true meaning, thinking that this move will save the rule of law from the abyss. But the phenomenal facts of the case simply do not bear us out on this score, for in most instances of people using words there simply is no state of mind that could reasonably be called the words' meaning. If you still harbour any doubts about this, perform the following experiment: (1) consider the fact that the statement 'I have one apple' means exactly the same as the statement 'I have the same number of apples as the root of the equation $x^2 + 2x - 3 = 0$'; (2) inwardly observe the different states of mind that correspond to the uses of these two sentences; and (3) then ask yourself whether you still want to believe, against the evidence, that the meaning of a statement is always (or even ever) what we would call someone's state of mind.

Wittgenstein once remarked that 'what the eye doesn't see the heart doesn't grieve over' (1983, 205). Given that the absence of any questioning in 'easy' cases like the order 'fetch me a red flower' also implies the absence of any answers, it is possible to construe Wittgenstein's poignant aphorism as a kind of philosophical warning. It warns us that it is dangerous to import our pre-critical interpretations of our everyday understandings of linguistic signs into our philosophizing by adhering unreflectively to the belief that the so-called 'easy case' is *ipso facto* always an example of clarity in legal language. Following this path would prevent us from surveying the complexity of the facts, including especially the fact that language can and often does play the role of a trigger for what H.L.A. Hart calls an 'automatic' response, unmediated by any interpretation, on the part of those who encounter and apply it (1961, 123).

Take, for example, just about the best illustration of legal clarity that I can think of: a traffic detour sign on which an arrow like this is painted: →. As I mentioned earlier, in the philosophy of language a 'sign' is defined as that element of the events of speaking and writing that can be perceived by the senses: the sound waves that we generate when we speak and the ink characters that appear on this page, for example. A *sign* in this sense is not yet a *symbol*. Thus, the string of letters 'Xfrcbbbnz' is just as much a linguistic sign as the string of letters that make up the word 'Stop', and this means that something *more* than their sheer materiality alone is required to make them into a word or statement. If this is so, what does it mean to say that just *this* linguistic sign, →, 'clearly' indicates (or symbolises) that drivers should go to the right? Couldn't someone interpret this sign as mandating a left turn? After all, the so-called 'head' of the arrow-sign → *can* be seen as a tail or base from which a left-pointing straight line emerges. Please notice that to imagine such a non-standard (but nonetheless rational) interpretation of an allegedly 'clear' sign is also to prove its logical possibility, for even a child can see that there is nothing 'inside' the material sign → *as such* that contradicts this interpretation. Kripke expresses what he calls the 'Wittgensteinian paradox' this way, with reference to the analogous problem of how to add numbers in accordance with the mathematical sign '+':

> The infinitely many cases of the table [of numbers] are not in my mind for my future self to consult. To say that there is a general rule in my mind that tells me how to add in the future is only to throw the problem back on to other rules that also seem to be given only in terms of finitely many cases. What can there be in my mind that I make use of when I act in the future? It seems that the entire idea of meaning vanishes into thin air (Kripke 1982, 22).

The key phrase in this quotation is 'it seems'. For signs such as 'meaning', '+' and '→' as we actually *use* them do not vanish into thin air despite the fact that we do not always hold something called their 'meaning' in our heads. And this is the real point that Kripke is making by taking radical rule-scepticism to its limit. Among other things, this example tends to confirm Shanker's observation that 'it is not the rule which compels me, but rather, I who compel myself to use the rule in a certain way' (1987, 17).

The philosophical puzzlement that can arise in connection with allegedly 'clear' legal rule-signs like → is similar to the kind of problem that can bedevil us in thinking about certain mathematical expressions. I refer to a feeling one sometimes gets in responding to questions such as 'What is the meaning of the expression "There is an infinite class of numbers, x, of which n is a member, and $3 + n = 7$"?' Just as *go to the right* seems to be 'there already' as the meaning of the legal sign →, it seems that *the number 4* is 'there already' in the infinite set of numbers x as the only correct solution to the equation $3 + n = 7$. In both cases it seems that it requires no further interpretation or calculation to recognise that the signs in question always already mean their right applications, before and apart from all human recognition. But on the other hand (and here comes the perplexity) how can we be sure of this, given that we have not run through *all* the possible interpretations of → or values of x? Wittgenstein observes that the root cause of the perplexity that philosophers feel in response to questions such as this is a confusion between *physical* impossibility and *logical* impossibility (1978, 451). It is physically impossible to count all the grains of sand on a beach inside of two hours because we do not have sufficient time to do so; nevertheless, we have some idea of what *trying* to count them would look like. But logical impossibility is altogether different: since it is logically impossible to 'check' an infinite number of propositions (infinity is not a quantity) it is also impossible to *try* to do so. The feeling that our solution or interpretation is somehow insecure because we have not yet tried to ascertain and consider every possible value of x or interpretation of → therefore rests on our inability to distinguish between these two forms of impossibility. But we *can* check (and prove) our intuition that 4 solves the equation $3 + n = 7$, and this method of applying the signs that comprise the problem is perfectly sufficient for our purposes. By the same token, a judge can check whether someone has driven to the left in violation of his widely shared automatic understanding of the meaning of the legal rule-sign →, and that too would be sufficient both for his purposes and the purposes of the legal system as a whole. Indeed, many a motorist has paid a fine or gone to jail on the basis of far less than this.

The fact of the matter is quite simple: since a linguistic sign *qua* perceivable entity does not in fact 'contain' anything, the concepts of clarity and obscurity simply do not apply to it. The bare sign →, for instance, is not comprised of the property of clearly-pointing-to-the-right amongst all of its other material properties, such as its dimensions, its blackness and its linearity. At best the sign simply displays its sense to those who perceive it in a certain way. As Wittgenstein puts it in the *Tractatus*, 'no proposition can make a statement about itself, because a propositional sign cannot be contained in itself' (1974, 16). To put Wittgenstein's point a bit more prosaically, there is no room 'in' → for anything other than →, and if this sign is taken to symbolise something in a clear (or even very clear) manner, this is only because we happen to receive it in a way that we call 'clear' because we do not doubt the correctness of our reception. To quote S.G. Shanker again: 'The impression of necessity is an illusion; the apparent inexorability of a rule reflects our inexorability in applying it' (1987, 17).

The truth to which Shanker refers should not be interpreted as bad news, for our inexorability in applying certain norms is no small thing: in fact it is a necessary condition of our form of life. One might even say that a description of how people actually apply legal signs like → is *pro tanto* a description of the rule of law. This is because such a description would tell us what *really happens* when we allow ourselves to be governed by legal norms. And the point of giving such a description would not be to advance the sceptical thesis that that there is no such thing as the rule of law. No, the point would be to show, by means of the description, what actually is called the 'rule of law' in our form of life. The contrary point of view – that signs like → clearly do or can mean only one thing, and that this single meaning is somehow currently present in the world as a kind of shadow that is cast by the sign itself, independently of any particular or general human reception of it – is based on a confusion that D.Z. Phillips, following Wittgenstein, calls *the magical view of signs* (Phillips and van der Ruhr 2005, 173).

The magical view of signs

The previous example of the arrow-sign → provides a clue about why our philosophical prejudices concerning the nature of linguistic clarity and obscurity are so hard to shake. We observe and recall that in everyday experience everyone we have ever known and seen always reacts to the sign → in the same way: *they just all go to the right*. But it must also be noted that if just about everybody does in fact go to the right in response to the arrow-sign, they also manifest a kind of indifference with regard to the *manner* of their experiencing the sign's command. As Heidegger puts it, 'the peculiarity of factical life experience consists in the fact that 'how I stand with regard to things', the manner of experiencing, is not co-experienced' (2004, 9). To be sure, when we are driving we undoubtedly do experience the event of our going-to-the-right upon encountering the sign →, but as I tried to make clear in the previous section, this does not mean that we also necessarily experience some sort of mental act or state that could reasonably be called 'the meaning of →' or even 'knowing what → means'.

Our everyday indifference to the underlying nature of our responses to language can be profitably compared to the phenomenon of seeing only one aspect of an ambiguous figure. In the context of a well-known gestalt drawing called the duck-rabbit, for example, it is possible to see what the picture represents in at least two different aspects. If you look at it one way, it appears to be a rabbit; but if you look at it another way, it appears to be a duck:

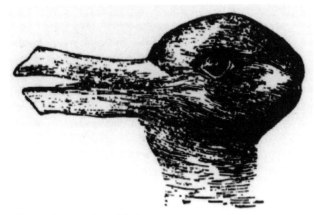

Figure 3.2 Duck-rabbit

In the *Philosophical Investigations*, Wittgenstein notes that there may be certain people who have always seen this figure as, say, a rabbit, and have never seen it in any other way (1958, 194e). For them the figure would 'clearly' be the picture of a rabbit and only a rabbit. Indeed, Wittgenstein also observes that there could even be people who are 'blind' to the possibility of seeing the figure as a duck despite having the figure's ambiguity pointed out to them in no uncertain terms. The twin phenomena of 'seeing-as' and 'aspect blindness' are perfect metaphors for why the problem of clarity and obscurity in legal language is so difficult to think about.

Consider, for example, Stanley Fish's description of legal formalism:

> Formalism is the thesis that it is possible to put down marks so self-sufficiently perspicuous that they repel interpretation; it is the thesis that one can write sentences of such precision and simplicity that their meanings leap off the page in a way no one – no matter what his or her situation or point of view – can ignore (D'Amato 1996, 134).

A dogmatic legal formalist of the type that Fish describes is like someone who is capable of seeing the figure of the duck-rabbit in only one of its aspects, and who goes on to insist that it 'clearly means' only this one thing. Such a formalist would suffer from an almost congenital failure of imagination that is analogous to aspect blindness. He would tend to judge non-standard interpretations of what he calls 'clear' signs like duck-rabbits and arrows as plainly wrong and irrational rather than as just plain different. In doing so, however, the formalist would render himself incapable of thinking perspicuously about the problem of how language can be *received* as being 'clear'.

The legal formalist takes *as* clear what he immediately receives as the sign's meaning and he does not pause to consider or think about what makes this very phenomenon of taking-as-clear possible. To borrow Catherine MacKinnon's wonderful phraseology, formalists of this type unthinkingly transform their own point of view into the standard for point-of-viewlessness (1983, 639). MacKinnon's way of putting it underscores an aspect of legal formalism that we have not yet mentioned:

it is intimately connected to the phenomenon of political power. Formalists think literally in a very precise sense of the word 'literally': they take signs such as → to 'literally mean' what they unquestioningly *receive* them to mean. Indeed, that is how the phrase 'literal meaning' is used in law: it elevates to the level of unquestioned dogma a particular reception of a legal sign that the receiver and others who are like-minded do not doubt. It is very important to understand that the phenomenon of reception is not a form of interpretation. Interpretation is a self-conscious process of reflecting on the meaning of signs which culminates in a transformation of the original signs into other signs; whereas reception names what does *not* happen and what is *not* doubted in the event of noticing language and then reacting to it without any reflection as to its 'meaning'.

As for the fact that other people *do* doubt the way they receive the legal sign that the formalist receives as unproblematic, well, what the formalist's eye doesn't see his heart doesn't grieve over. The paradigmatic legal formalists prefers not to think metaphorically, for as the poet Wallace Stevens says, 'metaphor creates a new reality from which the original appears to be unreal' (1997, 908), and there is nothing more threatening to the instinct for power than the feeling that the expressions of one's most cherished certainties are in fact ambiguous. 'Language is a part of our organism, and no less complicated than it', wrote Wittgenstein during the First World War, adding later that 'words are like the film on deep water' (1984, 48e, 52e). For the dogmatic formalist, however, words are but simple tools, and legal texts are never deeper than a wading pool.

Do our previous observations, including the examples of the arrow-sign and the duck-rabbit, suggest that philosophy ought to declare that there is no such thing as clarity in legal language and therefore that everything is up for grabs? Should we say that the very possibility of non-standard interpretations of signs like → and the duck-rabbit prove that legal clarity is a chimera? We should not. To understand why we should not, consider the following passage from the *Blue Book*, in which Wittgenstein reflects on the philosophical importance of just the kind of case that we have been considering:

Suppose we give someone an order to walk in a certain direction by pointing or by drawing an arrow which points in the direction. Suppose drawing arrows is the language in which generally we give such an order. Couldn't such an order be interpreted to mean that the man who gets it is to walk in the direction opposite to that of the arrow? This could obviously be done by adding to our arrow some symbols which we might call 'an interpretation'. [...] The symbol which adds the interpretation to our original arrow could, for instance, be another arrow. Whenever we interpret a symbol in one way or another, interpretation is a new symbol added to the old one. Now we might say that whenever we give someone an order by showing him an arrow, and don't do it 'mechanically' (without thinking), we mean the arrow one way or another [...].

Is it then correct to say that no arrow could be the meaning, as every arrow could be meant the opposite way? Suppose we write down the scheme of saying and meaning by a column of arrows one below the other.

$$\rightarrow$$
$$\leftarrow$$
$$\rightarrow$$

Then if this scheme is to serve our purpose at all, it must show us which of the three levels is the level of meaning. I can, e.g., make a scheme with three levels, the bottom level always being the level of meaning. But adopt whatever model or scheme you may, it will have a bottom level, and there will be no such thing as an interpretation of that. To say in this case that every arrow can still be interpreted would only mean that I could always make a different model of saying and meaning which had one more level than the one I am using (1960, 33–4).

Surprisingly enough, the most important aspect of this passage is not what Wittgenstein says, but what he does not say. For it would be very easy to read this passage in a casual and careless sort of way as asserting a sceptical thesis about language, one that subscribes to the nihilistic point of view that 'there can be no such thing as meaning anything by any word' (Kripke 1982, 55). But in truth Wittgenstein does not employ the example of the arrow-sign to prove that there is no such thing as meaning or clarity in language, or even no such thing as an 'easy case'. Rather, his example simply shows that that whatever else linguistic clarity may be, it is not a property of linguistic signs as such.

To believe otherwise is to subscribe to the magical view of signs. This view insists that the meaning of a linguistic sign is somehow magically conveyed or conjured up all at once, so to speak, by the sign itself (Phillips and von der Ruhr 2005, 174). The source of the magical view of signs is the mistaken belief that if people generally react in the same way to a sign such as →, this implies that the sign must have something *else* called a 'meaning' that explains why they react to it as they do. Wittgenstein aptly summarises the nature of this kind of superstition as follows: 'Some words refer to things, so we create ghosts for other words to refer to' (2003, 384). In other words, we notice that some words refer to material things that have the power to move people (for example, 'my automobile'); so therefore we think that *every* word must refer to something thing-like (its 'meaning') that has the power to instigate human action.

A good example of this way of thinking is H.L.A. Hart's theory that legal rules do (and must!) have a 'core of settled meanings' without which the rule of law would be impossible. Because this view on legal language is so common amongst lawyers and judges (not to mention mainstream law professors) it is important to take the trouble of demonstrating the nature and sources of the metaphysical confusion from which it stems. By way of analogy, Hart's belief that legal norms have a 'core meaning' is like a Platonic mathematician's belief that a norm for generating natural numbers, say 'x + 1', contains or refers to all the natural numbers *right now*, prior to its application. But what would be the sense (*before* the truth or falsity!) of this reference or containment? Any real image or representation that our mathematician might associate with his belief obviously does not itself contain 'all' the natural numbers, for the Platonic mathematical language game stipulates that they are infinite. At best our mathematician might imagine the natural numbers standing in an ordered row that seems to be infinite because it stretches to the horizon and disappears beyond it, like this:

0123456789012345678901234567890123456789012...

Figure 3.3 Natural numbers in an ordered row

Despite what the mathematician may fervently believe in his heart of hearts, however, the norm 'x + 1' does not presently 'mean' that, say, the irrational number *pi* is not in the set of numbers that the norm can be used to construct. Only the *application* of the norm proves (and thus *shows*) that *pi* is not in the set. Likewise, a legal norm such as 'No vehicles in the park' (the hypothetical example that Hart uses) does not presently 'mean' all of the particular vehicles-in-context to which it will and can be applied in the future; rather, its application, now and in the future, will *show* the cases to which it applies. To paraphrase Wittgenstein, the symbol for the class of cases to which a legal norm applies is a list. And seen from the point of view that we are trying to achieve in this paper, what lawyers and judges call 'following the law' is simply an extension of the list of cases to which the law is applied.[10]

And why, pray tell, does Hart think otherwise? Why does he think that legal words *must* have core meanings? Hart's answer to these questions, though correct as far as it goes, yields a *non sequitur*: 'If we are to communicate with each other at all', he says, 'and if, as in the most elementary form of law, we are to express our intentions that a certain type of behaviour be regulated by rules, then the general words we use – like "vehicle" [in the statute "No vehicles in the park"] – *must have some standard instance in which no doubts are felt about its application*' (D'Amato 1996, 57; emphasis added). Hart's answer is a *non sequitur* in this context because the *absence* of doubt about how to apply a legal norm has absolutely no necessary connection to the *presence* of something called the norm's 'meaning'. In other words, although Hart is right that people regularly do not doubt how to use legal signs such as →, this fact no more *has* to be explained by an object called the signs' 'meaning' than the passage of light waves from the sun to the earth must be explained by the hypothesis that space is filled with invisible ether.

Among other things, both of the hypotheses just mentioned violate Ockham's razor, which wisely stipulates that philosophers should not multiply entities beyond necessity. The fact that people have been trained, or have otherwise just picked up, how to use certain words in this or that particular language game is sufficient to explain why they experience no doubt about the usage of the words. Moreover, when a judge simply understands how to use a legal norm such as → without reflecting on

---

10 'The mistake in the set-theoretical approach consists time and again in treating laws [like x + 1] and enumerations [like 0,1,2,3,4,5] as essentially the same kind of thing and arranging them in parallel series so that the one fills in gaps left by the other. The symbol for a class is a list' (Wittgenstein 1978, 461).

it, it is a distortion of language to say, as Hart does, that the judge is using the rule as his 'guide' (1961, 10). Hart's motive for saying this is to distinguish the internal from the external points of view on law: in the former case judges rely on legal norms as the *ground* of their decision, whereas in the latter case an observer of the judge counts the norm as but one of the *causes and conditions* of a judicial outcome that he would like to predict or explain. But while the distinction between grounds and causes is good as far as it goes, it is totally irrelevant to the simple phenomenon of automatic reception that we have been discussing here. People seek guidance when they are in doubt; but since all doubt *eventually* ceases at what Wittgenstein calls the 'bottom level' of signs (1960, 34), so too does the guiding function of legal norms. To be sure, language and the interpretive process can 'guide' us through an unclear norm to a new expression of that norm that we now understand without any more ado; but that final understanding itself does not 'guide' anything – *it is simply how we apply the rule*. Hart's invention of 'core meanings' to explain linguistic clarity and regularities of language use is therefore ultimately unnecessary and circular. It is unnecessary because, as Wittgenstein remarks, 'symbols that are dispensable have no meaning – superfluous symbols signify nothing' (Waismann 1979, 90). And it is circular in the same way that the explanation that was given by Molière's doctor for how opium induces sleep is circular: as Nietzsche remarks, the doctor unhelpfully opined that opium induces sleep because it contains a *virtus dormitiva* – the 'power of making-sleepy' (1927, 392).

Lon Fuller's famous example of a fully operational army truck that veterans want to put on a pedestal in the park as a war memorial cleverly shows how Hart's dogma of core meanings can lead to absurdities in the interpretation and enforcement of legal norms such as 'No vehicles in the park' (D'Amato 1996, 62). But Fuller's example merely shows how the belief that words must always have clear 'core meanings' can produce baleful practical and political effects. In contrast, my concern here is to show that views like Hart's prevent *philosophical* thought from getting clear about the problem of how clarity and obscurity function in various legal language games.

The magical picture of the way language works holds that linguistic signs like → are always attached to what Wittgenstein calls a *Bedeutungskörper* [meaning-body], and as such it is a familiar and remarkably enduring source of confusion in philosophy (1969, 54). In the *Blue Book*, Wittgenstein identifies our inclination to look for some thing corresponding to the noun in sentences like 'What is length?', 'What is meaning?' and 'What is the number one?' (to which list I will add the questions 'What is the meaning of a legal norm?' and 'What is clarity in legal language?') as constituting 'one of the great sources of philosophical bewilderment' (1960, 1). Later, in the first paragraph of his *Philosophical Investigations*, Wittgenstein elaborates on this picture of language by quoting from Augustine's description of how he learned to speak as a young child. In the *Confessions*, Augustine recounts that his elders used words to name objects and that 'by hearing words arranged in various phrases and constantly repeated, I gradually pieced together what they stood for' (Augustine 1961, 29). For Wittgenstein, Augustine's description offers 'a particular picture of the essence of human language', which he characterises this way:

The individual words in language name objects – sentences are combinations of such names. – In this picture of language we find roots of the following idea: Every word has a meaning. This meaning is correlated with the word. It is the object for which the word stands (1958, 2e).

This passage locates in Augustine's primitive idea that a word's meaning is its bearer (the physical object that it may or may not name) the roots of a somewhat more sophisticated idea: namely, that the 'object' for which a word stands is not (or at least not necessarily) its bearer, but rather another ephemeral entity called its 'meaning'. In other words, Wittgenstein is telling us that the more sophisticated idea of the way language works is not different in kind from Augustine's, but is at bottom merely a variation of the primitive picture that Augustine draws.

The magical picture of language that Wittgenstein describes tends to have a curious effect on our philosophizing. If we insist on thinking of linguistic signs as disembodied things that do or do not have meaning in the same way that a sweater does or does not have the colour blue, or a box of marbles has or does not have marbles in it, then certain puzzles can (and do) arise while we are philosophizing, and we can (and do) run around in circles trying to solve them. Thus we ask questions like 'What is clarity in legal language?' and think that the answer *must* be a proposition asserting the existence of a relation between the signs 'clarity in legal language' and something else for which these signs stand: perhaps the one true account of the nature of clarity in legal language. The question presupposes, in other words, something like the following picture of the kind of answer that will satisfy it: 'Answer: the meaning of "clarity in legal language" is [...] such and such'. For convenience, we will shorten the form of the magical picture of language to 'X' R ◻. This expression has the advantage of making visible the essence of the belief that a legal word or statement ('X') must always stand in a relation (R) with something else that is its meaning (◻). The sign ◻ pictures an entity that is not the *same* as 'X', but rather an altogether different thing called 'X''s meaning. In the grip of the magical picture of language we ask questions like 'What is truth, justice and law', and then, thinking that these nouns must stand for their meaning-bodies (◻), we go off on a wild goose chase seeking to find the one and only correct expression of these meaning-bodies.

Now sometimes it comes to pass that we exhaust a very long list of meaning-bodies that we think might correspond to words like 'truth', 'justice' and 'law' without finding any of them to be satisfying. After all, the expression of a meaning is made up of mere linguistic signs, too: its form is simply *'"X" means Y'*. This implies that we must be able to receive the sign 'Y' in a certain way in order to be sure of the meaning of 'X': a process that appears to lead to an infinite regress that is frustrating to those who want to get to the bottom of the way language means what it means. To counteract the puzzlement that continues to nag us after we grow dissatisfied with all of the answers that we give to the questions that our own picture of language ('X' R ◻) leads us to ask, it does not occur to us to change the picture itself on the ground that it is arbitrary and misleading. Rather, we continue to think of language as a disembodied thing, only now we imagine that it is a thing from which all clear meaning has been removed, in much the same way that a naked sheep has been shorn of its wool.[11]

For example, we might think that the legal rule 'No vehicles in the park' has *no* meaning. But rule-scepticism of this sort is nonsensical, in the precise Wittgensteinian sense that it is not bipolar. What could a rule sceptic even *try* to exclude if he said that the legal rule 'No vehicles in the park' has absolutely no meaning? *No meaning as opposed to what?* As we have already seen, the sense of a negation ('not-p') depends on our ability to imagine or depict what is negated (p): 'It is not raining', for example, asserts that water-falling-from-the-sky is not present. What kind of meaning-body could (or do) the signs 'No vehicles in the park' have, such that just *these* imaginable meaning-bodies (□) can be pictured in the manner I earlier pictured the imaginary being called a 'unicorn'? (Be careful! A list of examples is not a norm's meaning – it contains mere instances of the norm's application). Since one cannot look for anything *ad infinitum*, one must, in order to look, have a *method of looking*. But since there is no method of looking infinitely at *all* the possible meaning-bodies of a legal norm, there is no sense in saying *either* that the correct meaning is there *or* that it is not.[12] When it comes to understanding how legal language works, what we need is less magic and more logic.

The logical view of signs

The magical picture 'X' R □ operates as a grammatical rule that is analogous to the syntactical norm 'Never end a sentence with a proposition'. In the latter case those who obey the norm are always checking their prose to see whether there are any sentences that end with prepositions. In just the same way, the picture 'X' R □ compels those who accept it to assert that every word or sentence must have one or more meaning-bodies. Those who find themselves in the grip of the magical view of language let the shadowy object (□) that the picture 'X' R □ tells them the sign 'meaning' must stand for or specify their act of describing meaning, instead

---

11 The best example in American legal theory of this kind of person is Stanley Fish. When Fish asserts that 'formalist or literalist or four corners interpretation is not inadvisable [...] it is impossible', for example, he is not saying that there is a kind of four-corners interpretation that is imaginable and representable, but that is empirically impossible (1991, 56). His sentence does not play the same kind of role as the following sentence does, for example: 'It is impossible for Stanley Fish to lift a thousand pound boulder over his head'. We can imagine, and represent in words or pictures, what it would look like for Stanley Fish to lift a thousand pound boulder over his head, and it is *this* state of affairs that such a sentence would exclude as empirically impossible. But anyone who is reasonably familiar with Fish's work knows that he is not saying that there is some describable practice that 'four-corners interpretation' stands for, and that engaging in this practice is so very difficult for human beings to do that it comes down to being impossible in fact. No, the expression of radical rule-scepticism of this sort is the kind of nonsense that plays the role of a grammatical stipulation: it stipulates in advance (perhaps for political reasons) that the speaker has decided not to call *any* interpretation of a legal text the 'literal' meaning of that text.

12 'Scepticism is *not* irrefutable, but obviously nonsensical, when it tries to raise doubts where no questions can be asked' (Wittgenstein 1974, 73).

of investigating how to describe meaning by unpacking the descriptive techniques that people have laid down for themselves well in advance of any particular act of description. Wittgenstein calls the latter method 'logical' as opposed to 'magical', and he describes its essence in the form of an injunction: 'don't try to specify the act of description by means of the object that is described; but by the technique of description' (1988, 48). Here it is exceedingly important to distinguish *being the meaning of* from *determining the meaning of*. The different ways (techniques) of describing the meaning of an expression are not identical to the expression's meaning. Rather, investigating the techniques helps us clearly understand that there just *are* fundamental differences between different claims of meaning. As D.Z. Phillips recently put it, 'Wittgenstein shows that it is not the sign or rule which determines their application (the magical view), but our practice which shows how in fact the sign or rule are used' (Phillips and von der Ruhr 2005, 173). Please remember: although we are interested in this paper in acquiring perspicuity on the problem of clarity and obscurity in legal language, we have no interest in inventing a grandiose theory of meaning.

That said, what does it mean to say that one can and should pay attention to 'descriptive techniques' rather than chasing after ephemeral meaning-bodies? The magical view of signs asks whether the sign 'X' means what someone says it means ('Y'); the logical view asks what *method of application* (in the case of norms) or *method of comparison* (in the case of propositions) the speaker has followed and whether he has followed it in a standard way within the context of the language game that he is playing. Those in the grip of the magical view are obsessed with the question whether language is determinate or indeterminate (one battleground of the culture war in legal theory between formalism and critical legal studies). Those who use the logical view to get clear about language examine how words like 'determinate' and 'indeterminate' are actually applied – they want to know what speakers *do* when they say that a given text is determinate (or indeterminate). For example, from the logical point of view on language it is possible to notice that the generality of a concept's expression is in tension (if not at war) with its determinacy. What formal logic would call a 'bounded' concept exhausts its meaning in a list of instances. Its extension *is* its meaning. For instance, if the logically bounded function $f(x)$ contains only four instances it is exactly the equivalent of $f(a \lor b \lor c \lor d)$. Nothing could be more determinate than the sign '$f(x)$' in this context. On the other hand, the expression of a general concept is not the equivalent of a list of instances; its generality (and hence its indeterminacy, at least relative to a logically bounded concept) is expressed by the ellipsis in the following expression: $f(x) = f(a \lor b \lor \ldots)$. But observe: the sign '...' does not itself complete the list of cases to which the concept applies. Rather, it acts as a kind of signpost pointing at a method for continuing the series of instances to which the concept can be applied. In short, you need to know the method of application in order to know what the concept 'means', and what it 'means' can only be shown by the application of the method.

Permit me to illustrate this last point by means of one of Wittgenstein's favourite metaphors, which is drawn from a field of mathematics known as projective geometry. Think of the linguistic expression of a legal norm – one that has not yet undergone interpretation in a particular case before a judge or a lawyer – as if it were a two-dimensional shape lying on a plane. Imagine, for example, that the text of the statutory norm 'No vehicles in the park' is figure A in plane I in the following illustration:

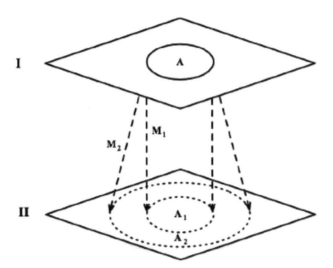

Figure 3.4 Geometrical projection

The point of the metaphor is quite simple: understanding how a judge or lawyer has interpreted (or will interpret) the meaning of a legal norm such as 'No vehicles in the park' is analogous to the task of understanding a geometer's projection of figure A onto plane II. Just as there is, in principle, an infinity of methods of projection in projective geometry (both orthogonal and non-orthogonal), so too there is at least a plenitude of methods for interpreting the meaning of the legal norm 'No vehicles in the park': original intent, the plain meaning of the language, the underlying purpose of the statute, and so forth. In the case of geometry, the projection of figure A onto plane II results in totally different projected shapes depending on which method is used. For example, the use of hypothetical method M_1 (which is orthogonal) produces figure A_1, whereas the use of hypothetical method M_2 (which is non-orthogonal) gives us the different figure A_2. The same kind of thing is true of legal language: a statute like 'No vehicles in the park' will receive one kind of interpretation if the judge adheres to H.L.A. Hart's method of reading its 'core meaning' and a different kind of interpretation if the judge adheres to Lon Fuller's method of looking at the rule's underlying purposes. And even if the ultimate legal result of a particular case happens to be the same whichever theory of interpretation is used, the methods of getting there, including the judges' explanations of the result, will be totally different.

For our purposes, the most important thing to notice about the metaphor of projection is that one cannot infer or judge the nature of figure A just by looking at its projections (A_1 and A_2) alone. Instead, one also needs to know the method of projection, and only with this information in hand can one infer figure A from figures A_1 or A_2. Moreover, it would be pointless to ask which figure on plane II is the 'correct' projection of the figure on plane I if we have already determined that each is a correct application of its respective method of projection. In fact they are both correct! In the *Philosophical Grammar*, Wittgenstein makes use of the projection analogy to say that 'the same thing happens when we depict reality in our language in accordance with the subject-predicate form' (1978, 205). That is, just as you will get nowhere by investigating what figures A_1 and A_2 'mean' without knowing the techniques according to which they were produced, so too you will spin your wheels hopelessly if you ask what a given statement (legal or otherwise) means without paying close attention to the method according to which it was produced and applied. If conservative Justice Scalia and liberal Justice Stevens of the United States Supreme Court were both to say 'Due process of law is an important value in our constitutional scheme', this does not imply that their methods of getting to these words or their methods of applying them are the same. On the contrary, just about every American lawyer knows that their ways of dealing with cases involving the legal concept of 'due process' are radically different. One might say that the two justices always project 'due process' according to different methods of projection despite the fact that there are occasional congruencies in the shape of the resulting figures.

I must emphasise that an investigation of common *methods* of applying words is not the same as an investigation of the common *opinions* of those who apply them. The 'truths' of law and mathematics are not determined by a consensus of opinion, for the opinion that 'X' means Y, however widespread it may be, does not tell us how the sign 'Y' itself is applied. As Wittgenstein puts it, an answer to the question 'How is that meant?' merely 'exhibits the relationship between two linguistic expressions' (1978, 45). No, what is called a 'technique' or 'method' of applying words is not determined by a consensus of opinion, but by a consensus of *action*:

> There is no opinion at all; it is not a question of opinion. They [here, the truths of logic] are determined by a consensus of action: a consensus of doing the same thing, reacting the same way. There is a consensus but it is not a consensus of opinion. We all act the same way, walk the same way, count the same way (Wittgenstein 1976, 183–4).

Thus, if we notice that there are two methods of applying the same statement (a legal norm, for instance), we should not take this to mean that the statement has 'two meanings'; rather, we should take it to mean that in applying the same expression people just proceed according to different methods. Period. To put our motives in this chapter the way Wittgenstein does, we simply draw attention to what people are really doing and refrain from making any grand claims about meaning (Waismann 1979, 186).

Let us consolidate our gains by putting them in the form of a working thesis that is meant to be heuristic rather than explanatory: the degree to which legal language is clear or obscure is not a 'property' of words and sentences as such, but rather a function of whether there is a method (or different methods) of applying it (legal norms) or comparing it with reality (legal propositions) – a consensus of doing-things-with-signs – in this or that *particular* context. As Wittgenstein put it in 1930, 'it is only the method of answering the question that tells you what the question was really about' (Waismann 1979, 79).[13] The clarity of a text has no necessary relationship with the number or the arrangement of the linguistic signs that comprise it. Even a text that is as convoluted as the Internal Revenue Code of the United States can show itself as clear to a tax lawyer. And as Stanley Fish reminds us, a simple statement that seems as vague and unclear on its face as 'throw strikes and keep 'em off the bases' can convey a crystal clear message about what is to be done when spoken by a coach to a pitcher in the context of a major league baseball game (1989, 372).

'How good a description is must be judged by how well it achieves its end', says Wittgenstein, adding that 'if a description makes people do the things you want them to do, it is a successful description' (2003, 394-5). This is a pretty good working hypothesis about what is called 'clarity'. If our investigations of language up to this point have fulfilled their original intention, we should now be in a position to recognise that the clarity or obscurity of a legal statement depends on the form of life in which it is used. As I have said from the beginning, for example, when one considers legal norms from a logical (as opposed to a magical) point of view they are not 'about' anything. Rather, legal norms are signposts pointing at possible uses in a community, or different communities, of law-speakers. Investigating the method or methods of application or comparison that are employed in a particular language game is the key that solves the puzzle of how legal language means or fails to mean *in that context*; other contexts will require other investigations and different keys. If I may be permitted to utter an aphorism, anyone who aspires to fully understand the rule of law must first understand *all* of the implicit laws of rules.

Conclusion: The relationship between Clarity and forms of life

Lawyers and laypersons occupy different planes, so to speak, when they are trying to understand a legal text. Wittgenstein used to say to his classes that 'a blunder is always a blunder in a given speech community' (Munz 2004, 89). I would add to this that the clarity or obscurity of a legal text is always clarity or obscurity within a given speech community. When a lawyer reads a statute or contract, the text is

---

13 Compare the following remarks by Wittgenstein: 'the verification is not *one* token of the truth; it is *the* sense of the proposition. (Einstein: How a magnitude is measured is what it is.)' (1975, 200), and 'Where there are different verifications there are different meanings' (Waismann 1979, 53). Wittgenstein later came to reject this, his most dogmatic form, of verificationism, which seemed to offer a theory of meaning in which 'the meaning of p' = "the methods used to verify that p is the case"'. For example, if we take the case p = 'Ouch!', what method do we use to verify what we are talking about? Wittgenstein's answer: we are not talking *about* anything that could be the case (that's not the role 'Ouch!' plays here), and so it makes no sense to say that the meaning of 'Ouch!' is the method we would use to verify that 'Ouch!' is the case. Nevertheless, paying close attention to the method of application of words in different contexts, including words like 'true' and 'false', continued to be an important element of Wittgenstein's philosophy to the very end.

always received within the context of a form of life that has trained the lawyer to be attentive to certain interpretive possibilities, certain remedial consequences and certain juridical risks and benefits of which the layperson that reads the same text has little if any idea. This means that what is clear to the layperson about a plain-language statute such as 'No vehicles in the park' is clear in a *different way* to a lawyer. Likewise, what is obscure to a lawyer about a given provision of, say, the tax code may also be obscure to the layperson in a totally different way, for the lawyer knows where and how to look for an answer and the layperson does not. Making legal language more accessible to the public by making its expression clearer to laypersons will never efface this fundamental distinction between the legal and non-legal forms of life.

As we have seen, in Wittgenstein's later philosophy the word 'meaning' hangs closely together with the concept 'form of life'. For participants in a linguistic practice to understand one another, Ronald Dworkin writes, 'means not just using the same dictionary, but sharing what Wittgenstein called a form of life' (Dworkin 1986, 63). Accordingly, if we wanted to be charitable to the international movement for more clarity in legal language – a movement that is personified in the members of the organisation called 'Clarity' – then we could read it under the aspect of Wittgenstein's concept of a form of life. We could read it, in short, as a call for laypersons to begin participating with lawyers in the same form of life. But what would such a call really amount to? Surely it would not come down to merely asking laypersons to talk *to* lawyers, or to talk *like* lawyers talk. No, in order to be effective it would have to ask laypersons to *become* lawyers. For lawyers are the only kind of people who could use and understand legal language in the same way that lawyers use and understand it. This tautology is meant to draw attention to the fact that the concept of a 'use of language' is internally related to (entails) the concept of a 'form of life'. The most important sense of this internal relation comes through plainly in the following passage from the *Philosophical Investigations*:

> 'So you are saying that human agreement decides what is true and what is false?' – It is what human beings *say* that is true and false; and they agree in the *language* they use. That is not agreement in opinions but in form of life (Wittgenstein 1958, 88e).

As this passage suggests, to use and understand a statement the same way that a given group of people do has nothing to do with plucking something called the 'clear meaning' of that statement out of one's observation and description of the people's use of it and then talking *about* it (the meaning-body ❑). Although the sign 'meaning' has many different uses, in this context meanings are not things. To use and understand legal language the same way that lawyers do is to use it *as* they do, all the way down. It is to agree in one's behaviour and speech with the legal form of life, and not just to take notice of some*thing* called a 'meaning'. If laypersons really want legal language to be as clear to them as it is to lawyers, then they would use it *as* lawyers use it – they would turn to writing legal briefs and opinion letters instead of letters and poetry. They would, in short, *become* lawyers – and in doing so they would begin to share in the enormous economic and political power that lawyers exercise by virtue of their privileged form of life. The demand for clarity in legal language is thus a demand for admission into the form of life inhabited by lawyers, judges and legislators; it is a demand for a share of their awesome power. But sometimes one cannot acquire power without entering into a kind of Faustian bargain, and this is one of those times. 'Complete clarity in legal language' = 'Every person a lawyer': now *there's* a linguistic equation that gives food for thought.

Chapter 4

Unravelling the Legislator's Tapestry: Judicial Needlework on Encroachment Cases

Anne-Françoise Debruche

The recurring perplexity of non-jurists faced with the distortion between the written words of the law and the outcome of their personal case before the court could very well echo the wry comment of a Lewis Carroll character:

> He thought he saw an Elephant,
> That practised on a fife:
> He looked again and found it was
> A letter from his wife.
> 'At length I realise,' he said,
> 'The bitterness of life!' (1988, 65).

How can the law applied by the judge to a specific case be so different from the written law, especially when such law is embodied in a statute or a code? In order to throw some light on those rather opaque quarters of the law, I will draw inspiration from two different legal areas: comparative law and neighbourhood property conflicts. This comparative approach will include Canada (as an ambassador of the common law), France (as a herald of the Romanist tradition) and Québec (as a mixed heir of those two systems). The material law studied will be neighbourhood conflicts in encroachment cases, an area of private law that all individuals may some day be concerned with.

The encroachment problematic provides a vivid illustration of the gap between the written law and the law as applied. In Canadian provinces of common law, as well as in Québec and France, landowners whose property was trespassed upon may apply to the courts for a demolition order. As they vindicate a real right, whether by means of a real action or of an action in torts, they may feel confident at the outset that the court can do nothing less than to order the suppression of the illegal encroachment.[1] Indeed, French and Québec civil codes uphold the inviolability

---

1 For examples in Canada, see *Gallant v. MacDonald* (1970), 3 Nova Scotia Reports (2d) 137 [Nova Scotia Supreme Court]; *Rossland (City) v. Camozzi* (1994), 47 British Columbia Appeal Cases 161 [British Columbia Court of Appeal]; *Earle v. Martin*, [1998] N.J. n° 353 (Quicklaw) [Newfoundland Supreme Court]. In Québec, see for instance *Gauthier v. Masson* (1897), 27 Supreme Court Reports 575 [Supreme Court of Canada]; *McCarthy v. Smith and*

of this real right.[2] In the other Canadian provinces, this protection flows from the common law rather than from some specific statute:

> Under our system of law, property rights are sacrosanct. [...] The balance of convenience and other matters may have to take second place to the sacrosanctity of property rights in matters of trespass.[3]

However, at some point in the proceedings, they may find out that the road to demolition, notwithstanding their 'sacro-sanct' real right, is in fact the road less travelled. The sidetracks, which range from proprietary estoppel to the discretionary power associated with the injunction remedy, are too numerous to be explored at length here (for further analysis on the topic see Debruche 2007). I will thus focus in this chapter on a single one of them, in order to compare how judges from different legal traditions (France, Québec, Canadian common law) can interpret and apply a written statute or code in an unexpected way; hence eroding its intended predictability. The selected example will be the legislative provisions protecting the improvements made in good faith on another's land, as they have been applied to encroachment cases in the three systems mentioned above.

The mode of acquiring property by incorporation, called in French 'accession', is well know under the French and Québec civil codes.[4] It also exists in English and Canadian common law, as exemplified by sayings such as quicquid plantatur solo, solo cedi [what is planted in the ground belongs to the ground] and aedificatio solo, solo cedit [what is built on the ground belongs to the ground] (among other references for those usages, see Oosterhoff and Rayner 1985, II 1008).[5] The principle of 'accession' means that if someone builds something on the land of another, the

---

Sons (1956) Rapports Judiciaires de Québec, Cour supérieure (C.S.) 48; *Leone v. Deblois*, [1993] Revue de Droit Immobilier 145 [Cour Supérieure du Québec] and in France, Cass. civ. 22 avril 1823, *Sirey* 1823, 381; Cass. civ. 1ère, 21 novembre 1967, *Bulletin civil* I, n° 339, 255; Cass. civ. 3ème, 20 mars 2002, *Bulletin civil* III, n° 71, 61.

2 Article 544 C. civ. (France) defines the right of property as the right to enjoy and dispose of things in the most absolute way while article 545 protects it against expropriation, except in the public interest and with the payment of a compensation. Regarding encroachments, those combined articles have been interpreted as compelling the destruction of the illicit intrusion, see Grenoble, 13 octobre 1965, *Dalloz Sirey* 1966, 168, note C. Givord, and for example Hennion-Moreau (1983, 305) and more generally Lévis (1989) as well as Debruche (2007). In Québec, the courts used to reason in the same way when applying articles 406-407 of the Civil Code of Lower Canada (C.C.L.C.), similar to articles 544-545 C. civ., to encroachment cases. Under the new Civil Code of Québec (C.C.Q.) however, article 953 now expressly authorises any owner to ask for the removal of an illicit intrusion.

3 *Lewvest Ltd v. Scotia Towers Ltd* (1981), 126 Dominion Law Reports (3d) 239, 240 per Goodridge J. [Newfoundland Supreme Court].

4 See in general articles 546-577 C. civ. in France; articles 948 and 954-975 C.C.Q. (former articles 408-441 C.C.L.C.) in Québec.

5 The principle of accession has been stated by Canadian courts more generally and expressly than their English counterparts, for example in *Beaty v. Shaw* (1888), 14 Ontario Appeal Reports 600 [Ontario Court of Appeal] and *Bayer v. Kehran Farms Inc.* (1996), 83 British Columbia Appeal Cases 109 [British Columbia Court of Appeal].

building will be considered the property of the latter rather than the former, unless proven otherwise.[6] But it does not deprive the land owner from claiming the removal of the illicit intrusion, thus entitling him or her to a choice: keeping the building or requesting its demolition.[7] The first branch of the alternative obviously leads, though, to a rather unfair conclusion: someone is entitled to benefit from a construction she never paid for, nor took pains to build. In order to avoid that inequitable shortcoming of the principle of accessio, legislators in France, Québec and Canadian common law provinces adopted statutory provisions designed to protect the improvements made by mistake (in good faith) on another's land. These statutes, or articles in the civil code, either compel the land owner to compensate the builder for the loss of his construction, or allow the builder to retain the land by paying a sum of money (or buy some other real right on the land in order to legalise the intrusion, such as a right of easement).

The provisions protecting the buildings erected by mistake on another's land have been used in encroachment cases to refuse the demolition requested when deemed 'unfair' or 'unjust' by the judge, and to grant damages instead. This application was questionable logically and legally: how could statutes or codes providing for improvements be pertinent in relation to a disparagement (the encroachment)? The objective of this chapter is to show how judges proceeded to bypass or alter the letter of the law relating to improvements on another's land. The image used to enlighten this somewhat arid demonstration will be that of an ingenious needlework (the judicial craft of interpretation) on the tapestry of statutory law. In the first part, I will present the different styles and techniques favoured by the judges as they embroider the black letter of the law. A second part will be devoted to the investigation of the hidden rules governing this judicial craftsmanship.

Judicial embroidery under a comparative lens: different styles and techniques

A comparative study between the French, Québec and Canadian legislation regarding improvements made by mistake on another's land shows three different styles of legislative drafting (thus, three styles of tapestries), and three different relationships between the judge and the statutory rule (so, three distinctive needleworks on those tapestries) when applied to encroachment cases. I will scrutinise them in turn.

---

6 As stated, for instance, in articles 546 and 553 C. civ. (France) and in articles 947 and 955 C.C.Q. (former articles 408 and 415 C.C.L.C.).

7 Thus, the land owner can choose between the inviolability of his real right (as mentioned above) and the privilege conferred by the law of accession. Occasionally though, some common law judges refused demolition on the basis that since the land owner had acquired the property of the intruding building by accession, he could not ask for its removal but only demolish it himself: *National Trust Co. v. Western Trust Co.* (1912), 4 Dominion Law Reports 455 [Saskatchewan Supreme Court]; *Chaiton v. Prudential Nominees Ltd.*, [1985] O.J. N° 392 (Quicklaw) [Ontario High Court]. The English Court of Appeal has affirmed clearly, since then, that demolition was always available despite the accession principle: *London Borough of Harrow v. Donoghue*, [1995] 1 Estates Gazette Law Reports 257.

Undoing geometric predictability: French needlework on article 555 al. 3 Code civil [article 555(3) C. civ]

When dealing with the principle of 'accession' and its diverse applications, the French Civil code [C. civ] preserves in its article 555(3) (albeit rather clumsily in terms of legistic concerns) the interests of the person having built or planted by mistake on the land of another:

> Where the plantings, constructions or works were made by an evinced third party who would not have been liable to restoring the fruits owing to his good faith, the owner may not insist on the suppression of the said works, constructions and plantations, but he has the choice to repay the third party either of the sums referred to in the preceding paragraph.[8]

Although it does not speak of 'improvements', but rather of any type of structure or plantation on another's land, article 555 C. civ. clearly favours the land owner over the mistaken builder. Not only does the former hold the choice of the remedy to grant instead of the demolition he could have hoped for, but the alternative remedy itself consists only of compensating the builder for his expenses according to the mode of evaluation preferred by the land owner. The judge has no share in this arbitration, and the builder is not entitled in any case to retain his construction through buying the land it rests on, or to acquire any real right enabling him to enjoy it where it stands. In short, article 555 C. civ. simply strives to prevent any unjust enrichment on behalf of the land owner who acquires the property of the building by 'accession'; it does not purport to preserve the builder's rights to his unfortunate construction. With regard to the parties, article 555(3) C. civ. does not favour (the builder and the judge in terms of the creativity of the latter); this goal is reached through rather unyielding, unambiguous terms. In that respect and according to our tapestry imaging, it can be likened to a clear-cut geometric design rather than to a complex, multi-layered motive open to several interpretations.

Therefore, it might have come as a surprise to land owners asking for the removal of an encroachment to find such a builder-unfriendly legislative disposition used to avoid the requested demolition when deemed unfair. Arguably, encroachments may seem conceptually linked to constructions built entirely on another's land[9] and thus French courts, including the Court of Cassation, agreed to refer to article 555(3) C. civ. in order to refuse the demolition of encroachments and grant damages instead.[10]

---

8 <http://www.legifrance.gouv.fr/html/codes_traduits/code_civil_textA.htm>, translation G. Rouhette.

9 See the visa of article 555 C. civ. in connection with encroachment cases as soon as 1823 in the jurisprudence of the Cour of Cassation: Cass. civ. 22 avril 1823, *Sirey* 1823, 381; Cass. civ. 16 juin 1903, *Sirey* 1905, I, 329; Cass. civ. 3ème, 14 mars 1973, *Bulletin civil* III, n° 206, 149.

10 Cass. civ. 19 juin 1934, *Sirey* 1935, 151; Cass. civ. 1ère, 4 mai 1959 (2ème espèce), *Sirey* 1960, 171, note A. Plancqueel. But see the opposition of Trib. civ. de Bourg, 9 juin 1911, *D.* 1912, 5, 13.

Since 1977 however, after a decade of indecision,[11] the Court of Cassation has clearly adopted the opposite point of view and upheld it steadily.[12] But what interests us here is that for quite a respectable period of time, French judges admitted the application of article 555(3) C. civ. to protect encroachments made in good faith from demolition and allow compensatory damages *in lieu*. How could such interpretive needlework be devised and engineered?

The discussion on the interpretation and application of article 555(3) C. civ. to encroachment cases flows from the doctrine rather than from the jurisprudence itself; the Court of Cassation being notoriously parsimonious with its motivations (see Touffait and Tunc 1974) and the decisions of the inferior courts, rarely published *in extenso*. From a doctrinal point of view therefore, most authors condemned such an application for the following reasons.[13]

The text of the article itself does not forbid its application to encroachments as it mentions not only 'constructions', but also 'plantations and works'. The latter term may be taken to mean the portion of a building (the encroachment) rather than a complete building (Goubeaux 1969, n° 233; Raynal 1976, n° 16 *in fine*; Terré and Simler 1998, n° 249). Thus, if the author of the encroachment proceeded in good faith, he comes technically under the letter of of article 555(3) C. civ. But numerous authors claimed that the practical effect of the application of that article

---

11 In a first line of cases, article 555 C. civ. was invoked by the defendant, but the Court of Appeal refused to apply it and the Court of Cassation rejected the 'pourvoi' directed against that decision: Cass. civ. 1ère, 13 janvier 1965, *Bulletin civil* I, n° 118, 89; Cass. civ. 1ère, 21 novembre 1967, *Bulletin civil* I, n° 339, 255; Cass. civ.3ème, 15 mars 1968, *Bulletin civil* III, n° 120, 94; Cass. civ. 3ème, 4 juillet 1968, *Bulletin civil* III, n° 322, 248; Cass. civ. 3ème, 11 juillet 1969, *Juris-Classeur Périodique* 1971, II, 16658, note A. Plancqueel; Cass civ. 3ème, 5 mars 1970, *Bulletin civil* III, n° 176, 131. In a second sequence of cases, the Court of Cassation seemed to rectify the criteria used to apply 555 C. civ. to an encroachment rather than to condemn its use absolutely: Cass. civ. 3ème, 8 décembre 1971, *Bulletin civil* III, n° 619, 442 and Cass. civ. 3ème, 8 octobre 1974, *Juris-Classeur Périodique* 1975, II, 17930, note H. Thuillier.

12 Cass. civ. 3ème, 12 juillet 1977, *Bulletin civil* III, n° 313, 238; Cass. civ. 3ème, 26 juin 1979, *Bulletin civil* III, n° 142, 109; Cass. civ. 3ème, 8 juillet 1980, *Juris-Classeur Périodique* 1980, IV, 362; Cass. civ. 3ème, 19 décembre 1983, *Bulletin civil* III, n° 269, 205; Cass. civ. 3ème, 19 février 1984, *Bulletin civil* III, n° 57, 44; Cass. civ. 3ème, 9 juillet 1986, *pourvoi n° 85-10.033*; Cass. civ. 3ème, 5 décembre 2001, *Juris-Classeur Périodique* 2002, II, 10189, note V. Bonnet. Other French jurisdictions followed suit: Paris (2ème Ch.) 29 septembre 1983, *Dalloz* 1984, informations rapides 427, note A. Robert; Versailles (1ère Ch., 1ère sect.) 3 octobre 1983, *Gazette du Palais* 1984, 1, sommaires, 202 and Paris, 21 mai 1993 (2ème Ch.), *Dalloz* 1995, sommaires, 192, note A. Robert. But some did not surrender, such as the Appeal Court of Pau: Cass. civ. 3ème, 5 décembre 2001, *Juris-Classeur Périodique* 2002, II, 10189, note V. Bonnet.

13 Some authors did approve the application of of article 555(3) to encroachments, either because they concurred with the way the Court of Cassation interpreted it in that particular instance (Blin, note under Cass. civ. 1ère, 4 mai 1959, *Juris-Classeur Périodique* 1960, II, 11409 and Solus, obs. under id., *Revue Trimestrielle de Droit civil* 1960, 134), or because they simply agreed with the principle (mostly earlier authors such Baudry-Lacantinerie and Chauveau (1905, n° 377) but also contemporary ones such as Stora (1982)).

to encroachment cases was absurd, and in no case would enable a judge to refuse demolition and grant damages instead. The logic of this assertion appears inescapable. When applied, where does of article 555(3) C. civ. lead to?

> It says only that, when some work has been carried out in good faith on another's ground, the land owner cannot demand its demolition but must, under the conditions it sets out, compensate the builder. One can but wonder through which exegesis it has been understood to mean exactly the opposite and offer to the builder the possibility to acquire the ownership of the portion of land on which he has trespassed.[14]

In other words, of article 555(3) C. civ. is unable to protect the illegal encroachment from demolition. It seems fairly obvious that the legislator could not have contemplated such an eventuality when drafting it (see for example Hennion-Moreau 1983, 312; Cornu 1988, n° 1453; Caron 2002). Not only is it hard to liken the intrusion to the 'increase in value' that disposition refers to,[15] but it also exposes the illicit building portion to demolition if its new owner so wishes (See for instance Bredin 1963; Goubeaux 1975; Raynal 1976, n° 19). Even if it escaped that fate, the legal status of the whole structure would appear very odd indeed. It would become the property of one neighbour for its main part, and of the other for the trespassing part – a 'vertical division' of property (Martin 1971, 1199; Hansenne 1996, n°757).[16] What if the demarcation line went through a bathtub, or a wardrobe? The room divisions might not prove very amenable to the implied partition.

Thus, the application of of article 555(3) C. civ. to encroachment cases is curtailed by the very terms the legislator employs in it. The Court of Cassation has implicitly acknowledged this limitation when excluding such an interpretation, thus restoring the orthodoxy of the geometric perspective associated with the legal tapestry and putting an end to the very creative (although inchoate) judicial needlework that had been undoing it. French land owners requesting the removal of an illicit structure encroaching on their property may now safely trust the protection granted by the civil code to their real right without having to fear the intrusion of the law of *accession* as expanded by judicial fairness.

14　Supra note 10, Note A. Plancqueel (my translation).

15　In that respect, 'the rules of indemnisation prescribed by article 555 become meaningless in this case' (Raynal 1976, n° 21, my translation) and in general the comments made by Hansenne (1996, n° 757).

16　Selling the whole structure and sharing the price would be equally problematic, some authors deeming it 'impossible' (Raynal 1976, n° 17; Hennion-Moreau 1983, 312) despite some ancient authorities hinting to the contrary (Cass. civ. 16 juin 1903, *S.* 1905, 1, 329; Demolombe 1854, n° 691ter; Planiol 1932, n° 2735). Some even suggested installing a dividing panel in the afflicted rooms (Baudry-Lacantinerie and Chauveau 1905, n° 377). All in all, though, it seems the whole building would become inhabitable (Goubeaux 1975, 617-678).

Blurring a classic figure: Québec needlework on articles 417-418 C.C.B.C.

In contrast with the geometric-styled design of article 555(3) C. civ., the dispositions softening the fate of mistaken 'improvements' set in the first Québec civil code, the Civil Code of Lower Canada [C.C.L.C.], seemed to adopt a more classic perspective in terms of legislative drafting and available judicial interpretations. Since article 417 C.C.L.C. reproduced the harsh wording (as seen from the builder's point of view) of article 555 C. civ., including in its third alinea, this temperament was essentially the consequence of article 418 C.C.L.C.[17]

> In the case of the third paragraph of the preceding article, if the improvements made by the possessor be so extensive and costly that the owner of the land cannot pay for them, he may according to the circumstances and to the discretion of the court, compel the possessor to keep the property, and to pay the estimated value of it.

Article 418 C.C.L.C. innovates – one hardly dares say 'improves' – in regard to article 555(3) C. civ. in two respects. First, it provides an alternative remedy to simply compensating the builder for the improvement on the part of the land owner, who is allowed to force acquisition of the disputed land section by the trespassing builder. Second, the judge is expressly invited by the legislator to play an arbitral role: he can veto this compulsory land acquisition if he feels it is unfair for the builder.

Because they offer such an interesting alternative to the benefit of the mistaken builder, even though left to the preference of the injured land owner, articles 417-418 C.C.L.C. were naturally applied to salvage mere encroachments on neighbouring land in addition to buildings erected entirely on it. As early as 1897, the Supreme Court of Canada boldly seized the golden needle of interpretation and openly considered the question in a major Québec case involving such a slight encroachment made in good faith, *Delorme v. Cusson.*[18] In this case, the defendant had reassured the plaintiff as to the location of the dividing line while being unaware he was mistaken as to what he was speaking about. Relying on those reassurances, the defendant had proceeded with the construction of the encroaching building. Although Girouard J., speaking for the Court, denied the demolition requested by means of a real action through another example of legal embroidery,[19] he declared himself favourable to the application of articles 417-418 C.C.L.C. in such cases. According to him, the dissentions relating to the correlative application of of article 555(3) C. civ. in France were due to the

---

17 The past tense favoured here echoes the antique status of that civil code, which was replaced by a new Québec Civil Code starting January 1994. Articles 960-961 of the said Civil Code replaced articles 417-418 C.C.L.C. They will not be studied here because they have not been used in connection to encroachments. This omission is a direct consequence of the insertion in the new code of a new disposition devoted exclusively to encroachments on neighbouring land.

18 (1897), 28 Supreme Court Reports 66.

19 It was held to have been built with the passive acquiescence of the plaintiff, and therefore to be protected by a tacit convention making the encroachment legal.

'defective drafting' of the latter.[20] The Québec legislator had improved it by adjoining article 418 C.C.L.C., which had no equivalent in the French civil code, to article 417 C.C.L.C. mirroring article 555 C. civ. Moreover, as articles 417-418 C.C.L.C. rested on a principle of fairness benefiting the builder in his quality of possessor in good faith, they had to be construed extensively and applied to encroachments as well as to structures wholly located on another's land.[21] Thus, the legislative tapestry encased in articles. 417-418 C.C.L.C. was considerably broadened by the wilful craftsmanship demonstrated by the Supreme Court in *Delorme v. Cusson*. Québec courts subsequently followed the lead and reproduced the pattern in turn, baffling some land owners who had put too great a trust in the inviolability of their real right in the land trespassed upon.[22] But how would a critic's eye appreciate such judicial needlework on articles 417-418 C.C.L.C. in relation to encroachments?

In the first place, the craftsmanship of the Supreme Court has the advantage of being open and explicit where the interpretive needlework of the French Court of Cassation was tacit and lacking in reasoned argument.[23] But laudable as that openness may be, it does not shelter the proposed interpretation from criticism. Undeniably, article 418 C.C.L.C. technically allows the award of damages (or more precisely, of a price paid by the builder to buy the land encroached upon) instead of the demolition initially sought. But beyond this brief harmony between the judicial needlecraft and the original legislative design, the two patterns directly clash in several places.

The first area of conflict lies in the shade of article 417 C.C.L.C.: an encroachment can hardly be considered an 'improvement' in the sense of that disposition.[24] The second and third conflict zones appear within the wording of article 418 C.C.L.C. On the one hand, this article textually endows the injured owner with the ability to compel the acquisition of the land trespassed upon. It is not up to the mistaken builder to claim this alternative remedy for himself, nor to the judge to force it on the unwilling owner.[25] On the other hand, even if the landowner favoured the

---

20 *Supra* note 18, 85.

21 Those dispositions 'rest on undeniable equitable principles, which received the sanction [...] of the greatest interpreters of Roman and natural law', *supra* note 18, 85-86 (my translation).

22 *Boulanger v. Pelletier* (1912) 21 Rapports judiciaires de Québec, Cour du Banc de la Reine 216; *Leclerc v. Cousineau* (1975) Rapports judiciaires de Québec, Cour supérieure 387; *P.G. du Québec v. Doyon*, [1983] Recueils de jurisprudence du Québec, Cour d'appel 592; Frenette (1999, 104-105) approves without any comment this application of the accession principle to encroachment cases.

23 The Supreme Court thus conformed itself to the Québec tradition of judicial argumentation (Brierley and MacDonald 1993, n° 122).

24 As soon as 1896, the famous civilist P.B. Mignault would write that in his view, a wall or a trespassing building portion did not represent 'improvements' under article 417 C.C.L.C. (Mignault 1896, 502). Later authors agreed and defined 'improvements' as works endowed with a certain quality of permanence, susceptible to increase the value of the immoveable (see Lafond 1991, 647; Office de Révision du Code Civil 1978, article 76, al. 2).

25 See nonetheless Martineau (1979, 69), who understood the discretionary power given to the court in an equally unrestricted manner. This interpretation has been disavowed in the later edition of his work by Lafond (1991, 655).

compulsory acquisition remedy, how could he possibly comply with the condition set out in article 418 C.C.L.C. and demonstrate that the encroachment amounts to an improvement 'so costly and expensive' that he or she is unable to compensate the builder for its value?

In light of those considerations, it must be admitted that articles. 417-418 C.C.L.C. do not prove much friendlier to encroachment cases than of article 555(3) C. civ. did. The Québec Court of Appeal realised this in 1937 and tried to restore a more orthodox judicial interpretation over the bold needlecraft proposed by the Supreme Court of Canada in 1897.[26] But Québec judges did not completely forsake the inspiration provided by the latter. In a 1975 decision, Judge Bergeron of the Superior Court insisted upon an economic reading of articles 417-418 C.C.L.C., interpreting them as dispositions promoting a general principle opposing the demolition of costly constructions. On that basis, they had to be applied in a useful manner whenever a judge was seized with a demolition request deemed to be economically flawed – thus, in cases involving encroachments as well and regardless of the good or bad faith of the mistaken builder.[27] Only the adoption of the new Québec Civil Code, which included a provision specifically designed to handle encroachment cases, closed this interpretive sidetrack opened by the expression of judicial fairness (article 992 C.C.Q. and in general Debruche 2007).

Exploring the void: Canadian needlework on statutes concerning improvements on another's land

After perusing the French and Québec civil codes regarding improvements made by mistake on another's land, one is struck by the deep-set, rather overworked style of the related Canadian dispositions. The common law provinces that decided to provide for the protection of improvements made under 'mistake of title' (for example, under the builder's mistaken belief that he is the owner of the land he builds on) are of similar design. They offer the builder a lien (a privilege) on the land built upon until he is compensated for the value of the improvement, unless the judge compels him to acquire this land portion from the injured owner. As an example selected among others (Ontario, Saskatchewan, Alberta and Nova Scotia), the legislation of Manitoba stipulates that:

> Where a person makes lasting improvements on land under the belief that the land is his own, he is or his assigns are entitled to a lien upon the land to the extent of the amount by which the value of the land is enhanced by the improvements, or is or are entitled, or may be required, to retain the land if the Court of Queen's Bench is of opinion or requires that

---

26 *Themens v. Royer* (1937) 62 Rapports judiciaires de Québec, Cour du Banc de la Reine 248. It was followed by *Mc Carthy v. Smith and Sons* (1956) Rapports judiciaires de Québec, Cour supérieure 48.

27 *Leclerc v. Cousineau*, *supra* note 22. Later on, the Court of appeal itself turned around and yielded again to the lure of article 417 C.C.L.C. in *P.G. du Québec v. Doyon*, *supra* note 22.

that should be done, according as may, under all the circumstances of the case, be most just, making compensation for the land if retained, as the court may direct.[28]

At the core, the legislative tapestry portraying the legal fate of improvements on another's land rests on a few simple lines. The judge is empowered to decide which builder benefits from it (what is a 'lasting improvement', was there a 'mistake' as to the ownership of the disputed land, etc.) and which remedy will be granted (mainly, a monetary compensation from the land owner[29] or the acquisition of the property of the land trespassed upon).[30] But this minimalist artwork half-disappears under a flourish of words making it appear deceptively complicated, to satisfy the legislative concern (typical of common law drafting) to be as comprehensive and complete as possible.

Some Canadian judges confronted with encroachment cases were quick to realise how convenient such statutes would prove to solve them once and for all. Unlike French or Québec judges, they usually enjoyed (and still do) the ability to refuse 'unfair' demolitions on the basis of the discretionary power associated with the grant of the remedy of injunction and to substitute damages in lieu. But those substituted damages were allowed as compensation under the law of torts. They did not imply the conveyance of the land encroached upon, whose legal status thus remained unclear (Debruche 2007). In that light, provincial statutes protecting improvements made under mistake of title went further than the discretion associated with the injunction remedy, because they precisely allowed the judge to compel the injured land owner to sell the disputed portion of land to the mistaken builder.

Those equitable concerns prompted some very creative judicial needlework on the statutes regarding improvements under mistake of title in order to apply them to encroachment cases. In so doing, the craftsmanship used by the courts matched in its intricacy and flourish the legislative style of drafting they were working upon. First of all, from a purely textual point of view, they had to construe as widely as possible the expression 'lasting improvement', to allow it to cover mere encroachments in addition to buildings wholly erected on somebody else's land. This they did, considering for example as 'lasting improvements' the encroachments by the portion of a house, by a wall or a roof, by the foundations of a bathroom, by a side-door and even by a concrete sidewalk.[31] Some judges stated to that effect

---

28 *Law of Property Act*, Continuing Consolidation of the Statutes of Manitoba, c. L.90, s. 27. See also the *Conveyancing and Law of Property Act*, Revised Statutes of Ontario 1990, c. C. 34, s. 37; the *Act respecting Improvements under Mistake of Title*, Revised Statutes of Saskatchewan 1978, c. I-1; the *Law of Property Act*, Revised Statutes of Alberta 2000, c. L-7 and the *Land Registration Act*, Statutes of Nova Scotia 2001, c. 6, s. 76(2). In general about those statutes, see Hurlburt (1978, 108-109).

29 Whose payment may be guaranteed by the concession of a lien to the mistaken builder, such as in the Manitoba legislation cited above at *supra* note 28.

30 Or even, in Nova Scotia, an easement benefiting the trespassing building: *Land Registration Act*, *supra* note 28.

31 *Sel-Rite Realty Ltd. v. Miller* (1994), 20 Alberta Law Review (3d) 58 [Alberta Queen's Bench]; *Noel v. Page* (1995), 47 Real Property Reports (2d) 116 [Ontario Court of Justice]; *344408 Alberta inc. v. Fraser*, [1999] A.J. N° 133 (Quicklaw)[Alberta Queen's Bench]; *Gay*

that the expression actually meant a lasting improvement for the land belonging to the mistaken builder, rather than for the land trespassed upon.[32] Others limited the application of the condition linked to the 'lasting improvement' to the grant of the lien, thus freeing the compulsory sale of the disputed land from complying with it.[33] In the second place, the Canadian courts invoked the mischief rule to justify the liberal interpretation they were making of the statutes regarding improvements made under mistake of title in the case of encroachments on neighbouring land. According to the said mischief rule, a statute amending a defect in the common law (the 'mischief') is to be construed liberally rather than restrictively. Therefore, the expression 'lasting improvement' could be construed liberally, as well as the other conditions in the statutory disposition (for instance, the construction on 'another's land' when the predecessor in title of the parties owned both portions of lands at the time of the encroachment).[34]

Having thus expertly embroidered the black letter of the statutory law, Canadian judges accessed the inner void of the legislative canvas, radiating from the adjective 'just'. The judge, say the statutes, decides both if it is fit to grant a remedy to the mistaken builder, and which type of remedy is the most adequate considering all the circumstances of the case: a lien, the compulsory sale of the land encroached upon or even an easement in Nova Scotia. The first branch of this wide judicial discretion recalls the exercise of the discretion associated with the grant of the injunction remedy. It is to be exercised judicially.[35] The courts will thus often check if the balance of convenience favours the plaintiff builder, and if he would suffer a hardship if the remedy was withheld.[36] But judges can also refer generally to what is 'just under all the circumstances of the case',[37] or where 'equity' or 'justice' points to.[38] The second branch of the judicial discretion nesting in the void of the statutory tapestry concerns the type of remedy to grant. When the 'improvement' is an encroachment, there can be no question of bestowing a lien because it is conditional on the payment of compensation by the land owner according to the increase in value of his land

---

v. Wierzbicki (1967), 63 Dominion Law Reports (2d) 88 [Ontario Court of Appeal]; *Ward v. Sanderson,* (1912) 1 Dominion Law Reports 356 [Ontario Divisional Court]; *Vewcharuk v. Boucher,* [1999] S.J. N° 72 (Quicklaw)[Saskatchewan Queen's Bench]; *James v. Brock,* (1926) 2 Dominion Law Reports 880 [Manitoba King's Bench]; *Mildenberger v. Prpic* (1976), 67 Dominion Law Reports (3d) 65 [Alberta Supreme Court].

32 *Gay v. Wierzbicki, supra* note 31; *James v. Brock, supra* note 31, severely criticised in that respect by *Mohl v. Senft* (1956), 63 Manitoba Reports 492 [Manitoba Queen's Bench].

33 *Gay v. Wierzbicki, supra* note 31, followed by *Noel v. Page, supra* note 31 and *Mildenberger v. Prpic, supra* note 31.

34 *Sel-Rite Realty Ltd. v. Miller, supra* note 31 and *Gay v. Wierzbicki, supra* note 31; reversing [1966] 2 Ontario Reports 372 [Ontario High Court].

35 *Gay v. Wierzbicki, supra* note 31.

36 *Noel v. Page, supra* note 31. The fact that the defendant builder acted in good faith is given weight also: *Ward v. Sanderson, supra* note 31; *Aumann v. McKenzie,* (1928) 3 Western Weekly Reports 233 [Manitoba King's Bench]; *Gay v. Wierzbicki, supra* note 31; *Noel v. Page, supra* note 31; *Vewcharuk v. Boucher, supra* note 31.

37 *Mildenberger v. Prpic, supra* note 31.

38 *Sel-Rite Realty Ltd. v. Miller, supra* note 31.

(which the encroachment is obviously not). Thus, except in Nova Scotia, judges can only grant the builder the opportunity to buy the land he encroached upon.[39] But at this point, some courts even went a step further in their needlecraft and put the void to a creative use of their own. They estimated that if they could do more (ordering the compulsory sale of the portion of land), they could do less by granting an easement even if the statute did not expressly allow them to do so.[40]

The hidden rules of craftsmanship

The interpretive ability and creative resourcefulness of judges confronted with encroachments on neighbouring land thus appears rather remarkable, whether it blooms under Romanist (civil law) or common law skies. But this judicial craftsmanship has to abide by a certain set of rules and limitations, flowing both from the legislative tapestry they work upon and from the overall structure of the legal system they belong to. In this second part, I will attempt to describe and contrast the principles governing – often in an implicit manner – the judicial artwork on statutes and codes relating to improvements on another's land. Those hidden rules of craftsmanship derive from three different sources: the legislative style and content of the disposition subjected to interpretation (the 'canvas' judges work upon); the rules governing statutory interpretation in general (amounting to a 'catalogue' of canons and techniques); and finally, the amount of respect due to a supreme judicial body acting as a sort of 'chief designer' in interpretive matters.

Being true to the canvas: Interpretation or re-creation?

As I observed in the first part, legislative styles in connection with mistaken improvements vary considerably from one system to another. Evidently, the words and content of the interpreted statute or code affect the margin of appreciation that judges will enjoy when applying it to a borderline case, such as an encroachment on neighbouring land.

Under the French Civil code, judges found apparently no room to manoeuvre. In order to express the unequivocal way in which of article 555(3) C. civ. presented itself as alien to the encroachment *problématique*, I compared it to a geometric-styled tapestry whose hard lines forbade its application to buildings not erected totally on another's land. Despite its relative legistic clumsiness, the message delivered by article 555(3) was audibly clear and logically inescapable. Since applying it to encroachments leads to an absurd legal situation (a 'vertical' co-ownership undesirable from a mere practical point of view), it should have been readily admitted that such an application was to be avoided as being totally useless in order to protect the illicit building from demolition.

---

39 *Vewcharuk v. Boucher, supra* note 31 and already *Gay v. Wierzbicki*, [1966] 2 Ontario Reports 372 [Ontario High Court].

40 *Hindelka and Makowecky v. Rosten* (1982), 5 Western Weekly Reports 395 [Saskatchewan Queen's Bench]; *Vewcharuk v. Boucher, supra* note 31 and for a similar measure, *344408 Alberta inc. v. Fraser, supra* note 31.

Therefore, the French example shows that even clear-cut legislative drafting is powerless in keeping judicial creativeness at bay, especially when the call of fairness pervades judges' ears in hard cases like some sort of luring siren song. Encroachment cases, normally leading to demolition according to the strict letter of the law, often cast such equitable spells. Under that influence and at least for a while, French courts did not hesitate to interpret of article 555(3) C. civ. in a way completely opposite to its very terms.

The case of Québec and articles 417-418 C.C.L.C. is a minor variation on the French theme. The legislative canvas was less exclusive and slightly more amenable to encroachment cases. It provided an adequate remedy (compulsory acquisition of the land trespassed upon), even if it reserved it to the land owner rather than to the judge or the mistaken builder. So judges had to bend article 418 C.C.L.C. to their equitable purposes too, but they were able to do so more discreetly than French judges because the content of the interpreted legislative disposition proved more encroachment-friendly.

Contrasting with those Romanist illustrations, the common law example drawn from the construction of statutes concerning improvements made by mistake on another's land shows a unique synergy between judge and legislator. The aforesaid statutes were clearly not designed to cover encroachment cases,[41] a point some lawmakers made obvious by subsequently amending their legislation to protect encroachments in a separate section. Thus in Manitoba, the legislator added in 1931 a section specifically devoted to encroachments after the section regarding improvements following an over creative interpretation of the latter to save an encroachment from demolition.[42] But in the provinces where no specific disposition pertaining to encroachments exists (Ontario, Saskatchewan, Alberta), the courts have displayed a multi-faceted, shining creativity in construing the statutes on improvements so as to apply them to encroachment cases.

This interpretive craftsmanship bore on the hard lines of the legislative canvas, that I likened to a Japanese motive to emphasise its basic simplicity. And 'hard' did those main lines prove when it came to applying them to encroachments: construing the expression 'lasting improvement' to comprehend a mere trespass, notably, asked for some very inventive judicial needlecraft. But after complying, however forcefully and questionably, with the few hard lines of the legislative tapestry, judges were rewarded by accessing the void reserved for them in the center of the design. Called

---

41 The earlier jurisprudence in connection with mistaken improvements dealt mainly with buildings erected totally on another's land: see for instance *McGregor v. McGregor* (1880), 27 Grant's Chancery Reports 470 [Ontario Chancery]; *O'Grady v. McCaffray* (1882), 2 Ontario Reports 309 [Ontario High Court], *McGibbon v. Williams* (1897), 24 Ontario Appeal Reports 122 [Ontario Court of Appeal]; *Chandler v. Gibson*, [1901] 2 Ontario Law Reports 442 [Ontario Court of Appeal].

42 *Law of Property Act* 1931, Revised Statutes of Manitoba 1987, c. L.90, s. 28, reproduced in s. 28 of the current *Law of Property Act*, Continuing Consolidation of the Statutes of Manitoba, c. L.90. The decision which probably prompted this modification in 1931 was *James v. Brock*, *supra* note 31. In Nova Scotia, both dispositions (regarding improvements and encroachments) were adopted simultaneously a few years ago: *Land Registration Act*, Statutes of Nova Scotia 2001, c. 6, s. 76(2) and (3).

by the statute itself to apply it when it seems 'just' to them and to grant the likewise 'just' remedy considering the equity of the case, Canadian judges are treated as lawmaking partners by the legislator. Indeed, the legislator assumes the general part of the lawmaking task and leaves the particular expression of the law to the courts, to be defined according to the piecemeal fashion characteristic of case-law.

As a consequence, the content of the law regarding improvements made by mistake on another's land cannot be ascertained just by reading the statute and trying to figure out how judges interpreted its terms ('lasting improvement', 'mistake', etc.). Part of this law flows from the case-law filling the void deliberately created in the statute by referring to the 'just' discretion of judges when applying it. More than an interpretation, what I see here is a judicial creation in a legislative space willingly left open: judicial needlework is expressly invited to fill the blanks in the canvas. Therefore, Canadian litigants are openly advised to take case-law into account when trying to determine how such a statute will be applied to their case. As opposed to the false certainties flowing from the strict design of article 555 al. 3 C. civ. and 417-418 C.C.L.C., the Canadian statutes regarding improvements make no mystery of the potential uncertainties associated with the way judges will choose to apply them in a particular case. At least, litigants in common law are alerted to the creative power vested in the judges by the legislator himself – their civil law counterparts are not so fortunate.

Abiding by the catalogue of canons and techniques: A very plastic guide

Judicial craftsmanship, as expressed in interpretive needlework on legislative canvases, has to take into account a certain array of general rules associated with the art of statutory interpretation. In common law as in Romanist systems, the examples drawn from the application of statutes or codes regulating improvements to encroachment cases allow us to observe very vividly how judges pay heed to those general rules.

In France, the interpretive power connected with the application of legislation to specific cases represents the cornerstone of the relative freedom of appreciation judges traditionally enjoy. Following the French revolution, they were not allowed to create general legal rules anymore (by means of *arrêts de règlement*, see article 5 C. civ.), but had the duty to interpret the legislation when necessary to avoid any *déni de justice* [denial or want of justice] (see article 6 C. civ.). Ever since, the hierarchy of legal sources underlying, among others, the civil code, has confined judges to applying the legal rule rather than enunciating it. In the early nineteenth century imagery, this subservient position has been crystallised in images such as the judge 'mouth' or even 'slave' of the legislative law.[43] It is thus only through developing statutory interpretation as an art and craft that French judges have been able to reclaim some of the normative power they had been stripped of by the new

---

43 Montesquieu (1964, 589) bequeathed the image of the judge 'mouth' of the law to later jurists; the more demeaning representation of the judge 'slave' of the law flowed for example from a revolutionary circulary of the 27th of November, 1791, cited by Nivet (1998, 161).

order.[44] The technique of literal interpretation, favoured by most of the *exégètes*, did not meet the needs of the industrial revolution in the last quarter of the nineteenth century and gave way to the more liberal approach which still prevails today. Many authors have proposed comprehensive theories meant to clarify the steps of judicial interpretation (see for example Geny 1919; Ost and Van de Kerchove 1989). But the courts themselves do not feel particularly compelled to refer to those scholarly works, nor to explain how they interpret this or that legal rule in the light of interpretive techniques as a whole (a general constatation acknowledged for example by Moreau-Margrève and Delnoy 1978, 31-33).

This judicial preference for liberal interpretation of the legal written rule is evident in the treatment of article 555(3) C. civ. by French courts when they decided to apply it to encroachments on neighbouring land. When the judicial sense of fairness is called upon by hard cases such as those frequently provided for by the encroachment problematic, the ability to interpret the legislative norm as widely as possible represents a precious tool – a golden needle to enlarge and even redesign the legal rule seen as useful for equitable purposes. In so doing, French judges do not have to do much of the embroidering themselves, especially when the liberal interpretation comes from the Court of Cassation. The latter, as I have seen with the application of article 555(3) civ. to encroachment cases, often prefers a cautious silence to an argument bound to elicit criticism. It is thus left to authors, as noted also, to fill the interpretive gaps and when necessary, to criticise the tentative fillings. Furthermore, freedom of interpretation also means the freedom for a court to change its mind, or propose a new pattern. Again, the Court of Cassation is unafraid to do so, as it demonstrated in relation to article 555(3) C. civ. in the matter of encroachments. Those twists and turns in the interpretive craftsmanship are no more overburdened by explanations than the initial needlework was.

The implicit guidebook to interpreting the Québec Civil code appears, on the surface at least, very similar to the French one. Québec judges, mirroring their French counterparts, do not voice a law of their own as common law judges do. In civil matters, they are only entrusted with the application of the civil code to individual cases. Therefore, to avoid being accused of denial of justice,[45] they also tend to interpret their code in a liberal fashion (Mignault 1935-1936, 109; Walton 1980, 95; Côté 1999, 37-39). Below the surface however, things have proved more complicated. Outer common law influences, first from the Judicial Committee of the

---

44 For an in-depth, comprehensive analysis of the official (statutory-bound) and unofficial (relative freedom through interpretation) portrait of the French judge, see the 'outside-in' study by Lasser (1994-1995).

45 Prohibited in Québec as in France at first by article 11 C.C.L.C., then by section 41.2 of the *Interpretation Act*, L.R.Q., c. I-16.

Privy Council,[46] then from the Supreme Court of Canada,[47] often confused the Civil code with a mere statute and thus interpreted it in a rather strict manner (as a sample of the critics from Québec (see Azard 1965; Baudouin 1975).[48] This confusion has been greatly reduced nowadays, and the Supreme Court currently vows to treat the Civil code as a code according to the Romanist tradition.[49]

At the time of *Delorme v. Cusson*, the Supreme Court was definitely not accustomed to handle the Québec civil code as a Romanist judge would. It thus seems out of character to observe the Court interpreting those articles with such liberality in order to protect encroachments from demolition. At root, this liberal attitude simply anticipates the broad interpretation that would be given to similar common law statutes regarding improvements a few decades later. But on the face of it, the interpretive needlecraft exhibited by the Supreme Court of Canada follows the implicit guidebook provided to any Romanist judge. It even refers to the French code and displays more argumentative flourish than the French Court of Cassation. The Court acts here both as a judge and a scholarly author, attempting to convince the parties as well as the legal community at large that the proposed interpretation of articles 417-418 C.C.L.C. is the most appropriate one. But in so doing, the Supreme Court of 1897 also reveals the magnitude of its interpretive power: strict in general, its interpretation of the Québec civil code can also become liberal when deemed necessary according to equitable considerations. It is not confined to technical interpretive rules that would have to be followed by the book. Thus, interpretive needlework as practiced by the Supreme Court proves as free as the craftsmanship displayed by the Cour of Cassation – in a more loquacious form.

Canadian judges holding office in common law provinces enjoy a similar freedom, but it takes root in a different type of theoretical soil. Voicing a law of their own – the common law – it is only natural to find them interpreting strictly or restrictively the concurrent legal source – statutory law – when it alters the existing case law. The literal rule, or ordinary meaning rule, expresses this spontaneous tendency to construct statutory law in a strict manner. This basic interpretive rule implies to understand the words used by the legislator according to their usual, everyday meaning (for example Sullivan 1994, 1-34; Poirier and Debruche 2005, 398-399;

---

46 See for instance *Robinson v. Canadian Pacific Railway*, [1892] Law Reports – Appeal Cases 481, 487; *Québec Railway Light, Heat and Power Co. v. Vandry*, [1920] Law Reports – Appeal Cases 662, 672-673 and the critics formulated Walton 1980, 90-96; Mignault (1922-1923, 1936-1937); Normand (1986-1987) and Brierley and MacDonald (1993, n° 51-52). For the improvement in the interpretive method of the Privy Council regarding Québec civil law, see for instance *Laverdure v. Du Tremblay*, [1937] Law Reports – Appeal Cases 666, 677.

47 The Supreme Court of Canada has become the final appeal court for Canada in 1949. Before 1949, its decisions could be appealed before the Privy Council, see Poirier and Debruche (2005, 296).

48 As for the Supreme Court, see for example *Lamontagne v. Québec Railway, Light, Heat and Power Co.*(1915), 50 Supreme Court Reports 423, 427; *Town of Montreal West v. Hough*, [1931] Supreme Court Reports 113, 120-121.

49 As in *Cie Immobilière Viger Ltée v. Giguère*, [1977] 2 Supreme Court Reports 67, 76 and *Banque Nationale du Canada v. Houle*, [1990] 3 Supreme Court Reports 122, 145. Québec authors have taken due notice and approve (Baudouin 1986; Glenn 2001).

and in general Zimmerman 1997). It rests on the larger presumption in favour of the 'stability of the law', which implies that statutes must always be interpreted, when possible, as not altering the common law (Coombe 1989; Bell and Engle 1995, 167-183; Poirier and Debruche 2005, 398-399). This presumption also underlies the distinction between limitative (restricting the basic rights and liberties of individuals) and favourable (expanding those rights and liberties) statutes. The former, which tend to restrict any existing right, are to be construed restrictively and the latter, which have the opposite effect, in a liberal fashion (Côté 1999, 587-628; Poirier and Debruche 2005, 431-433; and in general Côté 1997).[50] But the relationship between statute law and common law is not necessarily a competitive one. A statute can also complete the common law, for instance by reaching a goal unattainable by common law rules, or provide a remedy for a gap or defect in the existing common law. To sustain the legislative action in the first case, judges have devised the golden rule: it purports that the statute will be interpreted so as to enable it to produce the desired effect (Hopkins 1937, 689-696; Bennion 2002, 745-750).[51] In the second case, the mischief rule implies that a statute mending some imperfection in the common law is to be construed largely rather than strictly or restrictively, so as to broaden its remedial action.[52]

As a result, it appears that the judicial guidebook for statutory interpretation hosts varied rules susceptible to point in opposite directions in a given case, depending among other things on how the judge perceives the relationship uniting the interpreted statute to the existing common law. In addition, the nature of those interpretive guidelines is purely persuasive; they do not bind the courts as an imperative legal rule would. They are, to quote Lord Reid in *Maunsell v. Olins*, 'their servants, not their masters'.[53] Judges can use them to sustain their discretion when interpreting a statute and frame it in a reasoned, coherent discourse, but they are not bound to use one over the other.[54]

This discretionary power is evident in the specific hypothesis I study here: the application of statutes on improvements to encroachment cases. The guidelines supposed to encompass the interpretive needlework of Canadian judges were clearly contradictory. On the one hand, the presumption for the stability of the common law pleaded for a restrictive interpretation of the statutes concerning improvements

---

50 Remedial statutes are generally deemed favourable as well (Sullivan 1994, 176-177).

51 See also *Maunsell v. Olins*, [1975] Law Reports – Appeal Cases 373, 391 [House of Lords]; *A-G. v. Prince Ernest Augustus of Hanover*, [1957] Law Reports – Appeal Cases 436 [Court of Appeal]; *Boma Manufacturing Ltd. v. Banque Canadienne Impériale de Commerce*, [1996] 3 Supreme Court Reports 727, 781.

52 The mischief rule conventional point of origin is the *Heydon's Case* (1584) 76 English Reports 637 and is also named teleologic or purposive (Sullivan 1994, 36-44; Langan 1969, 40-43, 96-99; *Laidlaw v. Toronto metropolitain*, [1978] 2 Supreme Court Reports 736).

53 [1975] AC 373, 382.

54 A superior court can thus impose the product of a particular statutory interpretation, but not the means (for example, the guidelines themselves). About the judicial freedom to apply those interpretive rules, see for example Robertson (1998, 72-107), Poirier and Debruche (2005, 403-405). The event of their statutory 'codification' does not alter this discretionary nature (see Tucker 1985; d'Amato 1989).

on another's land. Those statutes undeniably altered the existing common law, which upheld the unamended principle of *accession*. The principle calling for strict or restrictive interpretation in the case of limitative statutes also leads to the same effect, since the statutes on improvements curtailed the real rights of owners whose land was trespassed upon. Moreover, the literal rule certainly did not encourage one to understand the term 'lasting improvements' as including mere encroachments on neighbouring land. On the other hand however, the mischief rule obviously favoured the extensive construction of statutes governing improvements made by mistake. Those statutes remedied a defect in the existing common law in relation to the law of *accession*. They strove to prevent an uneconomic and often unfair demolition, as well as an unjust enrichment on the part of the land owner. Therefore, in light of that *ratio legis* enhanced by the concurring application of the golden rule, they should be given the greatest extension possible. In a way, the Canadian courts had to choose each time between the equity of the land owner (protected by the first set of interpretive guidelines) and the equity of the mistaken builder (shielded by the mischief and golden rules). As I have seen, when they decided to favour the second one they relied on the mischief and golden rules rather than on the literal rule and others. Through this preference, Canadian judges demonstrated the extent of the discretion they enjoy in relation to statutory interpretation, as well as the unpredictability associated with the contradictory nature of the principles supposed to guide this craftsmanship.

Submitting to the chief designer – Where there is one

In the two systems partaking of the Romanist tradition, thus in France and Québec, judicial activity on the civil code (as well as on statutes in general) proceeds under supervision by a court specifically endowed with such a mission. Interpretive needlework on legislative norms is thus screened in some way by a sort of chief designer entitled to veto any pattern of which it does not approve. In France, this role belongs to the Court of Cassation; in Québec, it is shared *de facto* by a bicephalous authority: the Supreme Court of Canada on the one 'head' and the Québec Court of Appeal, on the other.

In France, I have observed that the Court of Cassation regally assumes its function as chief designer in interpretive articles. I saw how the Court approved of the application of article 555(3) C. civ. to encroachments for a while, and then ousted it categorically. In the meantime, its position was unclear because the Court of Cassation does not express itself freely. It is bound by the formal language imposed by the types of actions brought before it (the types of *pourvois* [appeals]), as well as by the argumentation used by the parties and by the criticised court of appeal. Therefore, the Court of Cassation appears in terms of legal interpretation as a tight-lipped chief designer, albeit an authoritative one: when it has selected a certain pattern, the courts below must follow. Except when this chief designer suddenly changes its mind, the advantage of such a function is that judicial needlecraft on the civil code is more predictable. Therefore, in the line of cases selected here, a French plaintiff should not fear to see article 555(3) C. civ. applied to his detriment. Judges should heed the interpretation retained steadily by the Court of Cassation since 1977 and refuse to use it to withhold the demolition requested. However, should they choose not to do so, the plaintiff knows he can appeal to the Court of Cassation to strike the forbidden interpretive needlework off the canvas – even if such recourse is long and costly.

In Québec, matters are less certain because the supervision power is shared by two distinct entities: the Court of Appeal and the Supreme Court of Canada. Within provincial boundaries, the Court of Appeal is the supreme authority regarding the interpretation of the Québec civil code. Composed of judges trained in the civil law tradition, it usually behaves more or less as the French court of Cassation does. But above the Québec Court of Appeal sits the Supreme Court of Canada, composed of three Québec-trained judges and a majority of six common law professionals.[55] In *Delorme v. Cusson* in 1897, it was the Supreme Court that acted as chief designer regarding the interpretation of articles 417-418 C.C.L.C. It declared them applicable to encroachment cases and Québec courts followed this lead by way of citations not unlike the technique of precedent. In 1937, the Court of Appeal issued an opposite point of view. But it encountered some difficulty in finding an audience among Québec judges. Some courts simply continued to refer to the opinion of the Supreme Court over the contrary position adopted by the Court of Appeal. Therefore, the bicephalous nature of the judicial authority empowered to supervise the interpretation of the Québec Civil Code leads to an occasionally divided jurisprudence. Unpredictability naturally stems from this division. But the upper hand often belongs to the Supreme Court owing to its superior position in the hierarchy.

Thus, in conclusion, a comparative approach bearing on civil and common law systems shows that one possible explanation of the gap between what the written law says and what is decided judicially lies in the duality of legal actors called upon to design and apply a certain rule to a specific case. This duality also stands as one of the reasons the legal language appears complex. As a consequence, the parties to a case are often unable to predict how it will be decided even if they have access to the set of relevant rules beforehand. When statutory law is concerned, common law and civil law systems share the same fate: the fact that at least part of the rules are enacted by one legal source (the legislator) and then applied by another (the judge) leads to a certain opacity as to their nature and content. This opacity is undeclared in Romanist systems such as France or Québec, because the civil code makes no formal reference to judicial interpretation and seems to stand alone, clear and bright. But in common law systems, the opacity is paradoxically lessened by the frank avowal of the partnership uniting the legislator and the judge in the very words of the statute to be applied.

---

55 *Supreme Court Act*, Revised Statutes of Canada (1985), c. S-26, articles 4 and 6. About the formation of the Court chambers in relation to the legal system involved by the appeal, see Wheat (1980). But those accommodations remain far from sufficient (Brierley and MacDonald 1993, n° 53).

Chapter 5

Customising The Model Law on International Commercial Arbitration

Maurizio Gotti

The ongoing internationalisation of English provides a useful and interesting insight into the ways in which linguistic and legal elements interact in the construction of discourse. Such a construction is characterised by complex interaction that combines, opposes and often merges elements of globalisation and localisations. It contains evidence of hybrid forms of discourse which are highly representative of socio-cultural identities (see Robertson 1992; Wright 2000). Legal discourse is rooted in local communities from which it emerges but is at the same time increasingly subject to international pressures and conventions. As a result, it has become a fertile ground for exploring and analysing intercultural variations at both the textual level and at the level of the interpretative schemata that shape the semantic-pragmatic traits of the professional community they belong to (Bhatia, Candlin and Gotti 2003). Contemporary legal systems are subject to regional and global forces which impact on legal norms and legal texts (Potter 2001; de Sousa Santos 2002). This process is most evident in domains involving globalisation processes as they have relevant consequences on the discourse produced by both native and non-native practitioners working in intercultural and cross-cultural settings (Levi and Walker 1990; Frederickson 1996; Salmi-Tolonen 2004, 1187-1188).

A case in point is represented by the discourse of international commercial arbitration. Indeed in the last few decades, arbitration has become a common tool worldwide for settling international commercial disputes. The wide acceptance of this adjudication procedure has itself been promoted by the growing internationalisation of commercial exchanges and by the many advantages that arbitration offers compared to litigation (Bernstein and Wood 1993, 3-4; Sanders 1999, 2-6). The high level of recourse to international arbitration has given rise to a widely felt need for greater harmonisation of the procedures to be followed. This has in turn led to the elaboration of a Model Law to be used as a guide by law-makers in national governments to produce their own individual statutory provisions for commercial arbitration.

The intention of this chapter is to analyse the text of the *UNCITRAL Model Law on International Commercial Arbitration* (ML) adopted by the United Nations in 1985[1] including its explanatory note; and the related *Arbitration Rules* (AR)

---

1 The Model Law was subsequently incorporated into the laws of several countries with varying constitutional, socio-cultural and economic conditions. Legislation based on the UNCITRAL text has been enacted in many countries, such as Australia, Bahrain, Belarus,

(1986).[2] The purpose of this analysis is to highlight cases of indeterminacy and then to identify the drafters' motivations for these less precise choices. The chapter goes on to consider the ways in which many of the cases of indeterminacy identified have been improved and thus clarified by the process of adapting these texts to the various national environments. My aim here is to draw out the factors that have determined such diverging outcomes.[3]

Indeterminacy in the Model Law

Generally speaking, the UNCITRAL texts show great concern for conceptual or terminological 'unambiguity' and explicit textual schematisation – a feature which is indicative of the emphasis normally placed by common law legislation on precision and detail for action in specific circumstances (Campbell 1996). However, a closer examination of these texts reveals several instances of vagueness, as the following analysis will demonstrate.

Indeterminate lexis

Despite the recurring claim that precision is a prominent feature of legal discourse and one of its distinctive qualities (Mellinkoff 1963; Solan 1993; Tiersma 1999),

---

Bermuda, Bulgaria, Canada, Croatia, Cyprus, Egypt, Germany, Greece, Guatemala, Hong Kong Special Administrative Region of China, Hungary, India, Iran, Ireland, Kenya, Lithuania, Macau Special Administrative Region of China, Madagascar, Malta, Mexico, New Zealand, Nigeria, Oman, Peru, Republic of Korea, Russian Federation, Scotland, Singapore, Sri Lanka, Tunisia, Ukraine, Zimbabwe and some states in the USA (California, Connecticut, Florida, Oregon and Texas).

2 The Model Law is available at <http://www.uncitral.org/pdf/english/texts/arbitration/ml-arb/06-54671_Ebook.pdf> while the Arbitration Rules are available at http://www.uncitral.org/pdf/english/texts/arbitration/arb-rules/arb-rules.pdf>. Note that only the Model Law is considered as a legislative text per se.

3 The analysis presented in this chapter is based on the results of two recent research projects. The former is an international research project entitled *Generic Integrity in Legislative Discourse in Multilingual and Multicultural Contexts* (<http://gild.mmc.cityu.edu.hk/>). The project investigated 'the generic integrity of legislative discourse by analysing the linguistic and discoursal properties of a multilingual corpus of international arbitration laws drawn from a number of different countries, cultures, and socio-political backgrounds, written in different languages, and used within and across a variety of legal systems' (Candlin and Gotti 2004b, 7-8). Some of the results of the project are presented in Bhatia, Candlin, Engberg and Trosborg (2003) Bhatia, Candlin and Gotti (2003); and Bhatia, Candlin and Engberg (forthcoming). The latter is a research project on *Intercultural Discourse in Domain-specific English* funded by the Italian Ministry of Research and coordinated by the University of Bergamo in collaboration with the Universities of Milan, Naples, Turin, Verona and IUSM Rome (<http://dinamico.unibg.it/cerlis/>). The focus of the project is on intercultural communication as it appears in the language of law, business communication, politics, diplomacy, research institutions and EU institutions. Some of the results of the project are presented in Candlin and Gotti (2004a; 2004b).

there are several exceptions to this rule. One of the least consistently precise areas is lexis, which may be to a certain extent referentially fuzzy. In particular, the 'studied interplay of precise with flexible terminology' (Crystal and Davy 1969, 213) sometimes allows subjective, if not arbitrary, interpretation. Indeed, legal English appears to tolerate insignificant differences (see 'tolerance principle', Endicott 2000, 1) and deliberately uses 'weasel words' (Mellinkoff 1963, 21) that is words and expressions which have flexible meanings. Often, these words are indefinite adjectives, which are particularly gradable and vague because of their 'borderline indefiniteness' (Fjeld 2001, 644; see also Warren 1988). Examples commonly pointed to are: 'reasonable, 'substantial', 'satisfactory', 'negligent', 'unconscionable' (for more examples see Mellinkoff 1963, 21-22). Such terms allow judges to use their own discretion in deciding on their applicability based on the circumstances. For example, the expression 'unjust in the circumstances' as used in 'to have been unjust in the circumstances relating to the contract at the time it was made' (Maley 1994, 27) leaves ample room for judicial discretion. Tiersma (1999, 83) also provides the example of the deliberately vague expression 'prudent investor rule' in use in many US states to refer to the requirement that a trustee in charge of investing money on behalf of another should behave like a 'prudent investor'.

In keeping with this approach the drafters of the Model Law have purposely adopted vague terms in several sections to allow the arbitrator a greater freedom of interpretation.[4] Below is an example of how the broad discretionary powers of the judging authority are facilitated by expressions such as 'the necessary measure', where the evaluation of what is to be considered a 'necessary measure' is left to the arbitrator(s):

> [...] any party may request *the court or other authority* specified in article 6 to take *the necessary measure*, unless the agreement in the appointment procedure provides *other means for securing the appointment* (ML 11(4); emphasis added in italics, as in all quotations in the chapter).

As can be seen above, the limit on the intervention of the judging authority is vaguely qualified by the expression 'other means for securing the appointment', where the adjective 'other' cannot be decoded in a specific way as it is linked to a referent of uncertain meaning. Moreover, the reference to the legal body that is to solve any possible dispute is not stated explicitly but indicated with the vague expression 'the court or other authority'. This is due to the fact that the text is meant to be a Model Law to be applied in various contexts, and therefore it is the national laws that will determine who the judging body is to be. This 'openness' of the text is clearly visible in the formulation of article 6 of the Model Law, in which the sentence is left purposely incomplete:

---

4 This drafting technique is usually adopted in international treaties, covenants and conventions. It is known as 'constructive ambiguity' (where the meaning of the settled text is not clear) by lawyers and diplomats. For general discussion on the topic, see Blomquist (2006, 308-309). For a specific discussion on international commercial law see Lindsay (2003, 1296-1300) and WTO Dispute Settlement Body Special Session (2005, 2).

The functions referred to in articles 11(3), 11(4), 13(3), 14, 16(3) and 34(2) shall be performed by ... [Each State enacting this model law specifies the court, courts or, where referred to therein, other authority competent to perform these functions] (ML 6).

Many of the indeterminate adjectives used in the UNCITRAL texts concern quantification, which is often left open to the judgement of the arbitrator. Indeed, the decodification of the semantic value of adjectives such as 'substantial' or 'sufficient' is very subjective:

> An arbitration is international if: [...]
>> (b) one of the following places is situated outside the State in which the parties have their places of business: [...]
>>> (ii) any place where a *substantial* part of the obligations of the commercial relationship is to be performed or the place with which the subject-matter of the dispute is most closely connected (ML 1(3)(b)(ii)
>
> The parties shall be given *sufficient* advance notice of any hearing and of any meeting of the arbitral tribunal for the purposes of inspection of goods, other property or documents. (ML 24(2)).

Other indeterminate adjectives (or their adverbial forms) are used to refer to time. An example of these is 'prompt(ly)':

> Subject to an agreement by the parties, the arbitral tribunal shall, *promptly* after its appointment, determine the language or languages to be used in the proceedings (AR 17(1)).

At times, this flexible word occurs in clusters with other 'weasel words' such as in the expression 'as promptly as possible':

> The appointing authority shall, at the request of one of the parties, appoint the sole arbitrator *as promptly as possible* (AR 6(3)).

Here, the adverbial phrase gives the appointing authority the freedom to fix the period of time in which the appointment is to be made. The rationale behind the use of such a flexible phrase is that – since the parties have not been able to reach an agreement on the appointment of the arbitrator within the time limit specified by the Rules (article 6(2)) – the choice is handed over to an 'appointing authority', whose decisional powers are seen as indisputable since no binding time limit is set for this task. This is considered the most reasonable solution to a problem which the parties have not been able to solve.

'Weasel words' are also used to refer to the behaviour of the parties, which is to be governed by common sense. Indeed, the use of adjectives such as 'appropriate', 'reasonable and justifiable' is quite frequent, as can be seen in the following excerpt:

> [...] unless the parties have agreed that no hearings shall be held, the arbitral tribunal shall hold such hearings at an *appropriate* stage of the proceedings, if so requested by a party (ML 24(1)).

The reference to common sense and shared views is not at all surprising, as it is in keeping with the idea itself of arbitration, which is a less formal procedure of dispute resolution based on the presupposition that the parties accept the arbitrator's personal opinion and final judgement. In line with this presupposition, it is therefore legitimate for the arbitrator to decide what is appropriate or inappropriate according to his own discretion:

> Unless otherwise agreed by the parties, either party may amend or supplement his claim or defence during the course of the arbitral proceedings, unless the arbitral tribunal considers it *inappropriate* to allow such amendment having regard to the delay in making it (ML 23(2)).

The same consideration holds for such phrases as 'undue delay':

> A party who knows that any provision of this Law from which the parties may derogate or any requirement under the arbitration agreement has not been complied with and yet proceeds with the arbitration without stating his objection to such non-compliance without *undue delay* or, if a time-limit is provided therefor, within such period of time, shall be deemed to have waived his right to object (ML 4).

The concept of 'public policy' is also quite vague and, in the end, it is left to the arbitral court to provide an appropriate interpretation having due regard to the circumstances of the case:

> Recognition or enforcement of an arbitral award, irrespective of the country in which it was made, may be refused only [...]
> (b) if the court finds that: [...]
> (ii) the recognition or enforcement of the award would be contrary to the *public policy* of this State (ML 36(1)(b)(ii)).

Moreover, definitions in the UNCITRAL texts are frequently accompanied by expressions such as, 'include(s), but is/are not limited to', which usually introduces a number of interpretations to be given to a specific term. However, such a list does not cover the semantic field in an exhaustive way:

> The term "commercial" should be given a wide interpretation so as to cover matters arising from all relationships of a commercial nature, whether contractual or not. Relationships of a commercial nature *include, but are not limited to*, the following transactions: any trade transaction for the supply or exchange of goods or services; distribution agreement; commercial representation or agency; factoring; leasing; construction of works; consulting; engineering; licensing; investment; financing; banking; insurance; exploitation agreement or concession; joint venture and other forms of industrial or business co-operation; carriage of goods or passengers by air, sea, rail or road (ML 1(1) note).

This open-ended definition of 'commercial' has led to different interpretations in different countries, with the result that this term has sometimes been submitted to strict delimitations of meaning in a number of cases. In several countries, for instance, this definition has been interpreted according to the *expressio unius est exclusio alterius* principle, which stipulates that if something is not included in a list, it is thereby excluded (Gibbons 2003, 49). Thus, the attribution of a limited semantic value to the term 'commercial' led an Indian party to contend that its agreement with Boeing (an American company) to provide consultancy services for the promotion of the sale of Boeing aircraft in India could not be regarded as a 'commercial' transaction.[5] The dispute resolution judgement instead opted for the broader meaning of the expression 'commercial' that is, it should

> be construed broadly having regard to the manifold activities which are an integral part of international trade today (Pathak 1998, 182).

Modal auxiliaries and hedging expressions

Indeterminacy of interpretation may also be caused by the use of certain modality markers, and in particular by some modal auxiliaries which create vagueness due to their polysemy. Many of them have epistemic or dynamic as well as deontic values.[6] Thus, to arrive at an adequate interpretation of modality in normative texts, it is necessary to explain the link between linguistic semantic values and the social pragmatic setting of the provisions under consideration (Klinge 1995). The vaguest modal auxiliaries are those expressing probability ('may', 'might'), tentative possibility ('could'), tentative assumption ('should') or hypothetical prediction ('would'). Some of them are not very frequent in normative texts (Gotti and Dossena 2001). This is particularly the case of distal forms such as 'should' and 'would', which are extremely rare in the arbitration texts considered in this chapter. Indeed, 'should' does not appear at all in the text of the Model Law, although it is found in one of the footnotes, where it expresses obligation (Model Law 1985, 1). However, in this example, the use of 'should' rather than the mandatory 'shall' creates uncertainty of meaning in so far as it could be perceived to convey a weaker degree of the obligation expressed, as if some sort of advice were implied by the text, while in other contexts the pragmatic meaning to be attributed to this auxiliary is strongly deontic and allows no discretionality of interpretation on the part of the reader, as can be seen in the following examples drawn mostly from the explanatory note:

> The term "commercial" *should* be given a wide interpretation so as to cover matters arising from all relationships of a commercial nature, whether contractual or not (ML 1(1).note)

> Although the grounds for setting aside are almost identical to those for refusing recognition or enforcement, two practical differences *should* be noted (ML explanatory note, para 44).[7]

The expression 'it should be noted', in particular, is often used to signal the way which the reader is expected to understand a term or an article:

---

5 *R.M. Investment and Trading Co. Pvt. Ltd. v. Boeing Co.* A.I.R. 1994 SC 1136.

6 The distinction of modality into deontic, dynamic and epistemic is drawn from Palmer (1986; 2001).

7 Please note that the *Explanatory Note by the UNCITRAL Secretariat on the Model Law on International Commercial Arbitration* is for informational purposes only and not an official comment.

[...] *It should be noted* that 'recourse' means actively 'attacking' the award; [...] (ML explanatory note, para 41).

The semantic value of the advice to be attributed to the use of 'should' is more appropriate in the following case, in which a motivation for the use of certain procedures instead of others is pointed out as a justification for the suggestion made:

> [...] These instances are listed in article 6 as functions which *should* be entrusted, for the sake of centralization, specialization and acceleration, to a specially designated court or, as regards articles 11, 13 and 14, possibly to another authority (e.g. arbitral institution, chamber of commerce) [...] (ML explanatory note, para 15).

The other distal form 'would' also occur in the Model Law: twice in the text itself and ten times in the explanatory note. Its use is mainly linked to hypothetical discourse:

> The conditions set forth in this paragraph are intended to set maximum standards. It *would*, thus, not be contrary to the harmonization to be achieved by the model law if a State retained even less onerous conditions (ML 35(1) note).
> Recognition or enforcement of an arbitral award, irrespective of the country in which it was made, may be refused only: [...]
> (b) if the court finds that: [...]
> (ii) the recognition or enforcement of the award *would* be contrary to the public policy of this State (ML 36(1)(b)(ii)).

As can be seen in the above excerpt, the use of the conditional 'would' rather than the present tense (quite possible in this case) makes the formulation of the hypothesis much less certain. The same tentative tone can be seen in the explanatory note, where the use of this modal auxiliary is preferred to the present tense, which would be less vague and would convey a more definite pragmatic value:[8]

> [...] According to article 1(2), the Model Law as enacted in a given State *would* apply only if the place of arbitration is in the territory of that State [...] (ML explanatory note, para 12).

The use of an indeterminate expression containing 'would' is somewhat surprising here, particularly when the sentence does not convey a hypothesis but rather a plain fact. It is clear in this case that the use of the present tense would be more appropriate. Here are some more examples:

> [...] While this approach is understandable in view of the fact that even today the bulk of cases governed by a general arbitration law *would* be of a purely domestic nature, the unfortunate consequence is that traditional local concepts are imposed on international cases and the needs of modern practice are often not met (ML explanatory note, para 5).

---

8 For further discussions on the definite pragmatic value of the indicative present, see Gerbe (2006, 289-296), Cornu (2000, 272), Bergeal (2001, 193).

[...] It may be noted that the article does not deal with enforcement of such measures; any State adopting the Model Law *would* be free to provide court assistance in this regard (ML explanatory note, para 26).

'May' is also an auxiliary likely to cause indeterminacy. In fact, since it can express both deontic permission and epistemic possibility, its meaning and pragmatic functions are quite flexible. The deontic meaning is the one most frequently found in normative texts, and this is also the case with the UNCITRAL texts. The value of permission is often made more evident by the placing of the parties or the arbitratror(s) in the grammatical subject position and by the use of 'harmonic' expressions (Hoye 1997) such as 'provisions':

A party who knows that any *provision* of this Law from which *the parties may* derogate or [...] (ML 4).

In other instances of the texts analysed, the semantic value of 'may' denotes epistemic possibility:

[...] Also any expert report or evidentiary document on which the arbitral tribunal *may* rely in making its decision shall be communicated to the parties (ML 24(3)).

The two semantic values sometimes appear in the same article; in the following case, for example, there is an alternation between deontic and epistemic uses of 'may':

Unless otherwise agreed by the parties, the arbitral tribunal *may*, at the request of a party, order any party to take such interim measure of protection as the arbitral tribunal *may* consider necessary in respect of the subject-matter of the dispute. The arbitral tribunal *may* require any party to provide appropriate security in connection with such measure (ML 17).

In some instances, the indeterminacy implicit in this modal auxiliary gives rise to the possibility of both interpretations. It is only after a more complete analysis of the context that the more appropriate semantic value becomes clear. This is the case in the following excerpt, where the use of the word 'fact' implies that the possibility of the parties making an agreement is to be ascribed to eventuality rather than permission:

Where a provision of this Law refers to the *fact* that the parties have agreed or that they may agree or in any other way refers to an agreement of the parties, such agreement includes any arbitration rules referred to in that agreement (ML 2(e)).

There are no cases of 'might' either in the Model Law itself or in the explanatory note. There are, instead two instances of 'could' in the explanatory note to the Model Law. These are used to convey the semantic value of tentative possibility:

[...] While the need for uniformity exists only in respect of international cases, the desire of updating and improving the arbitration law may be felt by a State also in respect of non-international cases and *could* be met by enacting modern legislation based on the Model Law for both categories of cases (ML explanatory note, para 9).

The use of 'can' is equally consistent: in all four instances where it is used in the Model Law, it indicates dynamic possibility. Three of these four uses contain passive forms, as in the following excerpt:

> The award deals with a dispute not contemplated by or not falling within the terms of the submission to arbitration, or contains decisions on matters beyond the scope of the submission to arbitration, provided that, if the decisions on matters submitted to arbitration *can* be separated from those not so submitted, only that part of the award which contains decisions on matters not submitted to arbitration may be set aside; [...] (ML 34(2)(a)(iii)).

As pointed out by Trosborg (1997, 106-107), the use of passive sentences, having a non-human grammatical subject and in which no agent is clearly mentioned, introduces a high degree of vagueness as in this case it may be difficult to establish who is to be considered responsible for the actions, permissions, obligations mentioned in the text. Another example of this non-human 'thematic topicalisation' (Bowers 1989, 284) can be seen in the following article, which avoids any specification of the performer(s) of the action mentioned:

> After the award is made, *a copy* signed by the arbitrators in accordance with paragraph (1) of this article shall be delivered to each party (ML 31(4)).

Uncertainty of interpretation is also caused by the use of hedging expressions such as lexical verbs like 'appear', 'seem', 'suggest', or common nouns, adjectives and adverbs expressing vagueness like 'about', 'almost', 'apparent(ly)', 'approximate(ly)', 'around', 'most', 'essentially', '(un)likely', 'maybe', 'perhaps', 'possibility', 'possible/y', 'potentially', 'presumable/y', 'probable/y', 'quite', 'slight(ly)', 'some', 'somewhat'. Although these are commonly used in everyday communication to express tentativeness and possibility (Holmes 1984), they have also been found in the normative texts examined here, both in the Model Law and in the explanatory note. For instance, there are two instances within the text of the Model Law where the hedging adjective 'likely' appears in articles dealing with the impartiality and independence of arbitrators. Below is the first one:

> When a person is approached in connection with his possible appointment as an arbitrator, he shall disclose any circumstances *likely* to give rise to justifiable doubts as to his impartiality or independence [...] (ML 12(1)).

The use of this particular adjective reinforces the tone of vagueness which characterises the section of the Model Law dealing with the composition of the arbitrary tribunal (Chapter III). Indeed, the requirement of independence and impartiality is not stressed explicitly as mandatory but expressed in an extremely vague way, simply requiring that attention should be drawn to these issues:

The court or other authority, in appointing an arbitrator, *shall have due regard* to any qualifications required of the arbitrator by the agreement of the parties and to such *considerations* as are *likely* to secure the appointment of an independent and impartial arbitrator and, in the case of a sole or third arbitrator, shall *take into account* as well *the advisability* of appointing an arbitrator of a nationality other than those of the parties (ML 11(5)).

Hedging verbs are also used in the explanatory note. For example, verbs such as 'appear' and 'seem' signal non-commitment:

[...] Even most of those laws which *appear* to be up-to-date and comprehensive were drafted with domestic arbitration primarily, if not exclusively, in mind. [...] (ML explanatory note, para 5).

As evidenced by recent amendments to arbitration laws, there exists a trend in favour of limiting court involvement in international commercial arbitration. This *seems* justified in view of the fact that the parties to an arbitration agreement make a conscious decision to exclude court jurisdiction and, in particular in commercial cases, prefer expediency and finality to protracted battles in court (ML explanatory note, para 14).

Tentativeness is often provided by indeterminate expressions occurring in clusters as can be seen in the following examples, where the use of 'it is advisable' in the first excerpt is accompanied by 'as closely as possible', and 'may' by 'proper' in the second excerpt:

[...] *It is advisable* to follow the model *as closely as possible* since that would be the best contribution to the desired harmonization and in the best interest of the users of international arbitration, who are primarily foreign parties and their lawyers (ML explanatory note, para 3).

If an application for setting aside or suspension of an award has been made to a court referred to in paragraph (1)(a)(v) of this article, the court where recognition or enforcement is sought may, if it considers it *proper*, adjourn its decision and *may* also, on the application of the party claiming recognition or enforcement of the award, order the other party to provide appropriate security (ML 36(2)).

The use of these clusters, besides other hedging expressions such as 'caution' and 'might', is determined by the significant obstacles that settlement negotiation may encounter in certain countries because of the local tradition of arbitration procedures, which Cremades aptly pointed out:

Traditionally, it was an agreed doctrine within the world of arbitration that an arbitrator's duty shall not be mixed with any mediating activity or intent to reconcile. This was one of the greatest dangers widely highlighted in arbitration seminars as it was stated outright that an arbitrator who initiated conciliation or mediation was exposed to the risk of an eventual challenge (Cremades 1998, 162).

However, even in these countries such inflexible positions have been questioned and – mainly due to the influence of the UNCITRAL Model Law – the new local provisions on arbitration often include an obligation for the judge to facilitate conciliation between the parties throughout the proceedings.

Discussion

As the above analysis has shown, the UNCITRAL texts contain several instances of indeterminacy. This is partly due to the very nature of these normative texts. As discussed in previous studies (Mellinkoff 1963; Bhatia 1993; Solan 1993; Tiersma 1999; Gotti 2005), normative texts have to conform to a double constraint: 'the law must simultaneously be both general and specific enough' (Hiltunen 1990, 66). Indeed, on the one hand, they have to be very precise in defining the obligations they are meant to impose or the rights they confer. On the other hand, they have to refer to a very wide and sometimes unpredictable range of possible applications that such rules may involve. To comply with this need, they have to be as all-inclusive as possible (Bhatia 1993, 102). However, this need for all-inclusiveness may determine some vagueness and indeterminacy in the wording of the texts themselves (Olmsted 1991; Endicott 2000; Hjort-Pedersen and Faber 2001; Bhatia, Engberg, Gotti and Heller 2005), mainly due to the adoption of general terms conveying wide semantic values, with the result that their meaning in the context of those provisions is not as clear as expected.

The presence of vague textual formulations in the UNCITRAL texts is due to several reasons: like all normative texts (see 'indeterminacy claim', Endicott 2000, 1), the Model Law, its explanatory note and the Arbitration Rules aim to be as all-inclusive as possible in order to be valid in the widest range of applications. Thus, they make use of general terms conveying wide semantic values, with the result that their meaning in these articles is not as clear as expected. This need for all-inclusiveness is particularly strong in these articles, as the main objective of the drafters of the UNCITRAL texts is to keep the scope of their application as broad as possible. Indeed, these texts are not related to any specific, geographically-based arbitral organisations, but they are meant to be truly international in their perspective so as to achieve 'the desired harmonisation and improvement of national laws' (ML explanatory note, para 2).

Moreover, in many articles the Model Law is worded in a vague way so as to allow more freedom to the parties involved. This high degree of flexibility can be clearly noticed, for example, in the following excerpt drawn from the UNCITRAL Arbitration Rules, in which the possibility of avoiding the application of the official regulations is presented as deriving from any modifications that 'the parties may agree in writing':

> Where the parties to a contract have agreed in writing that disputes in relation to that contract shall be referred to arbitration under the UNCITRAL Arbitration Rules, then such disputes shall be settled in accordance with these Rules subject to such modification as the parties may agree in writing (AR 1(1)).

Another reason for the vagueness of the UNCITRAL texts is that the drafters have been careful to adopt 'weasel words' in order to allow the arbitrator greater freedom and to guarantee the maximal use of the discretionary powers of the judging authority to decide what is appropriate or inappropriate. This arbitrariness is in line with the idea itself of arbitration, which is a less formal procedure of dispute resolution based on the presupposition that the parties are willing to accept the arbitrator's personal opinion and final judgement, and also with the informal, diplomatic resolution process that such international agreements rely on.

A further rationale for the 'openness' and flexibility of the UNCITRAL texts is that they are meant to be a model to be used by State parties to produce their own individual statutory provisions for commercial arbitration and thus fulfil the widely felt need for greater harmonisation of the procedures to be followed to solve international disputes. The indeterminacy of the text is therefore meant to facilitate the process of adoption of the model, a procedure which implies not only the adaptation of the original discourse to the typical features and resources of the national tongues, but also its adjustment to the cultural needs and legal constraints of each specific country.

This requirement explains why the text of the UNCITRAL arbitration rules has mainly an informative function, as it implies some sort of adaptation on the part of the user of the clauses presented. This is in line with the results of Salmi-Tolonen's (2003) analysis of the Finnish Arbitration Act compared with the UNCITRAL Model Law, which confirm her hypothesis that the functions of national law and international law are slightly different: expository and descriptive in the case of international law, and directive in the case of national law.

Customising the Model Law

Many of the cases of indeterminacy seen above have been improved in the process of adaptation of these texts to the various local environments. The formulation of national regulations has been greatly conditioned by specific factors, depending strictly on the different cultural, linguistic, legal and socio-economic environments in which this adaptation has taken place. To evidence the nature of such modifications, I will carry out a comparison in this section between specific parts of the UNCITRAL texts and those of the regulations enacted by two Italian arbitrations chambers – the Milan Arbitration Chamber (MAC)[9] and the Bergamo Arbitration Chamber (BAC)[10] – and the Venice Court of National and International Arbitration (VENCA).[11]

Drafting traditions

Important elements of a legal system are its drafting traditions and stylistic conventions (Bhatia, Candlin and Evangelisti Allori forthcoming). These may influence arbitration discourse significantly, as can be seen in the differentiation between civil law and common law texts: the former are mainly characterised by generality, while the latter prefer particularity. It is commonly asserted that civil law

---

9 Available at <http://www.mi.camcom.it/show.jsp?page=327160>.
10 Available at <http://www.bg.camcom.it/>.
11 Available at <http://www.venca.it/index.html>.

statutes are written in terms of principle whereas common law statutes are written in detail as

> The civil code draftsman is eager to be widely understood by the ordinary readership, whereas the common law draftsman seems to be more worried about not being misunderstood by the specialist community (Bhatia 1993, 137).

This conceptual differentiation is reflected in the drafters' stylistic choices. In common law legislation, sentences are very long, consisting of three or more main clauses, each modified by many subordinate clauses. This remarkable sentence length depends on the great number of details to be inserted and the need that specifications should be precise and clear (Mellinkoff 1963; Gustafsson 1975; Tiersma 1999; Gotti 2005). Civil law sentences are shorter, with a less strict use of paragraphing. This makes the understanding of the sentences easier, but renders the reconstruction of the relationship between the various sentences more complex.

The adherence of the UNCITRAL texts to a more traditional legal style is demonstrated by the lengthy and complex structure of most of its sentences. As can be seen in Table 5.1, the average sentence length is greater in AR than in the other three texts which – although written in English – are part of the civil law system.

Table 5.1 Average sentence length in the corpus analysed (from Belotti 2003, 33)

	Average sentence length
AR	43.1
MAC	37.0
BAC	34.4
VENCA	29.8

The reason for this discrepancy lies in the fact that the UNCITRAL texts tends to include all possible information in a single sentence, thus increasing the density of information. The more complex structure of legal discourse in these texts is confirmed by the data concerning sentence types. As Table 5.2 shows, AR has more complex sentences than the Italian texts. MAC, BAC and VENCA, on the contrary, contain more simple and compound sentences.

Table 5.2 Distribution of sentence types (from Belotti 2003, 34)

	AR		MAC		BAC		VENCA	
Simple	5	17%	9	19%	15	28%	4	33%
Compound	1	3%			2	4%	5	42%
Complex	24	80%	36	77%	37	68%	3	25%
Complex-compound			2	4%				

An example of this complexity can be seen in article 11(5) of the Model Law which uses four subordinate clauses and three coordinated clauses (see p.98).

The longer sentence length of the UNCITRAL texts is also favoured by their stricter adherence to the tradition of English legal language, as can be seen in the frequent use of binomial expressions, such as the crystallised forms *ex aequo et bono* and 'null and void'; and the free collocations 'independent and impartial arbitrator' and 'documents and other materials'. Moreover, sentences in the UNCITRAL texts are lengthened by the frequent use of multinomials joined by alternative/ complementary coordination:

> The parties may be *represented or assisted* by persons of their choice. The names and addresses of such persons must be communicated in writing to the other party; such communication must specify whether the appointment is being made for purposes of *representation or assistance* (AR 4).

Linguistic conventions

The analysis of arbitration texts has also shown examples of discrepancy due to variations in linguistic conventions. This can be seen, for example, in the way juridical obligation is signalled. This concept is traditionally expressed by the modal 'shall' in the UNCITRAL texts, as is customary in English legal discourse. Italian legal discourse, instead, often adopts a present indicative to state legal provisions, thus emphasising the actuality and applicability of the legal provision and also implying that the law draws its force from the natural order of things rather than an order imposed by human agents. This tense is frequently used also in the regulations of Italian arbitration chambers and arbitral courts written in English:

> The appointing authority *shall*, at the request of one of the parties, appoint the sole arbitrator as promptly as possible. In making the appointment the appointing authority *shall* use the following list-procedure [...] (AR 6(3)).

> In the event the Parties have not appointed the Arbitrator/s and not designated a different appointing authority within the applicable terms, the arbitrator/s *is/are appointed* by the Court [...] (VENCA 10).

This preference for the present tense is also part of the drafting tradition of another country belonging to the civil law system, that is, France (Gerbe 2006, 267-302). As Garzone's (2003, 206) analysis has shown, the simple present indicative – rather than the deontic modal *devoir* – is the form customarily used to convey both the prescriptive and the performative functions of normative and legislative texts.

The faithful observation by the UNCITRAL texts of the linguistic conventions of English legal discourse can also be seen in the choice of lexis. For instance, the Model Law contains archaic or very formal expressions such as 'agreed upon' (for 'agreed on'), 'commencement' (for 'beginning'), 'furnish' (for 'produce'), 'notwithstanding' (for 'regardless of') and compound forms like 'thereof', 'thereon' and 'thereto' which are typically related to the register of legal writing (see Bowers 1989; Gotti 2005). These texts also include Latin lexical items, such as *interim* and *ipso jure*, and complementary binomials (Gustafsson 1984) like *de jure* or *de facto* and *ex aequo et bono*. Also a French expression, *amiable compositeur*, is present,[12] borrowed from the language of international arbitration. In these texts, Latin expressions are not usually translated or paraphrased, as the target readers' knowledge of their meaning is taken for granted (indeed, the texts are exclusively aimed at legal experts). Latinate and French forms, instead, do not occur at all in some of the Italian arbitration rules (such as BAC) or are very few in others (in MAC and VENCA). The same can be said for archaic words, as can be seen in Table 5.3.

Table 5.3 Type and number of occurences of archaic words (From Belotti 2002, 132)

	AR	MAC	BAC	VENCA
Forthwith		1		
Hereinafter	1			
Such (used as adjective)				
Therefore	2	2		
Therefor	2	2		
Therein		1		
Thereof	2	3		3
Thereon	2			
Thereto	2			
Total	11	9	0	3

Cultural constraints

Anecdotal evidence of arbitration practices suggest that the cultural environment greatly influences the outcome of the arbitration procedure. It is clearly visible in those cases in which the national legislation imposes specific obligations in compliance with local customs and traditions: for example, countries such as Korea and Saudi Arabia uphold requirements of nationality and/or residence for a person to serve as arbitrator (Jarvin 1999, 60). Saudi Arabia also requires arbitrators to be male and of the Islamic faith (Saleh 1992, 549). These criteria impose serious restrictions on the choice of arbitration in an international dispute and are usually taken into consideration by non national parties when they have to fix the site of an arbitration case with a party residing in one of those countries. But even when cultural differences are not so evident, it is impossible to guarantee a perfectly homogeneous process, as the various legal patterns of the countries involved will re-emerge in some of the

---

12 There is as such no direct translation of this expression into English. The concept allows an arbitrators to decide the dispute according to the legal principles s/he believe to be just (equity).

procedures described or in a few of the principles set out. Such professional traits will not only characterise the written texts, but will be present in the minds of the arbitrators themselves, who – no matter how neutral and culturally open they wish to be – will be conditioned by their own specific legal philosophy. This emergence of the arbitrator's educational and professional background may create problems in the assessment of the parties' behaviour and generate negative consequences on the outcome of the proceedings themselves, a risk international arbitrators are fully aware of:

> [A]n arbitrator, without relinquishing the most impartial frame of mind, may nonetheless remain very distant, in educational and cultural terms, from the particular party or its counsel. In such a case, difficulties are likely to arise which have nothing to do with the probity of the arbitrator in question. They are due solely to the fact that said arbitrator reveals a greater intellectual propensity to grasp every detail of the arguments put forward by one party, while encountering objective and honest difficulties in understanding the submissions of the other(s) in the same way. Albeit unwillingly, the conduct of the arbitrator may thus adversely affect the equal treatment of the parties (Bernini 1998, 42).

A similar opinion is expressed by Lalive, who remarks that:

> [Participants in international arbitration] have different origins or places of business, different educations, methods, reactions or Weltanschauungen. In short, what has perhaps struck me more than anything after many years of arbitral practice, either as advocate or as arbitrator, is the capital role played by what may best be called '*conflicts of cultures*' between the parties (as well as their respective counsel) and, as a result, by difficulties of 'communication' between them and arbitrators (Lalive 1992, 80, italics in the original).

In spite of the growing international arbitration culture, the national influences traced in the arbitrators' behaviour may prove particularly harmful and often rely on the arbitrators' unfamiliarity with one of the parties' site rules and practices. This is the reason why in recent legislation on arbitration there is a growing tendency to offer the parties a more comprehensive set of procedural rules rather than leaving the conduct of the proceedings completely to the discretion of the arbitral tribunal, an approach in line with the UNCITRAL Model Law. This process of harmonisation, however, is very hard to carry out, and even if all the procedures were to be unified, some differences would still remain in their perception at a local level. The reason for this is to be found in the underlying professional background:

> Our own legal cultures remain, for the time being, in certain areas, an important limiting factor to harmonisation because [...] the application of the same rule may lead, despite all good intentions, to strikingly different results (Lazareff 1999, 36).

As seen above, the UNCITRAL provisions dealing with the impartiality and independence of arbitrators are characterised by a high degree of indeterminacy. As discussed earlier, the requirement of independence and impartiality is not stressed explicitly as mandatory but expressed in an extremely vague way, simply requiring that attention should be given to the problem. This requirement, instead, is clearly stated as a strict obligation in some national texts, with the use of a strong deontic modal auxiliary such as 'must' and the explicit mention of situations that may impair such impartiality:

> Every arbitrator must be and remain independent of the parties involved in the arbitration (article 7(1) *Rules of Arbitration of the International Chamber of Commerce*).
>
> An arbitrator must be impartial and independent (article 17(1) *Rules of the Arbitration Institute of The Stockholm Chamber of Commerce*).
>
> All arbitrators conducting an arbitration under these Rules shall be and remain at all times impartial and independent of the parties; and none shall act in the arbitration as advocates for any party. No arbitrator, whether before or after appointment, shall advise any party on the merits or outcome of the dispute (article 5(2) *Rules of the London Court of International Arbitration*).

This greater precision can be explained by the high degree of autonomy enjoyed by the arbitrator(s) during the entire procedure (Borris 1994), as no jury is involved in the proceedings and since the majority of the disputes in international commercial arbitration are of a technical and complicated nature. It is important, therefore, that the decision-making process should be totally transparent and that the arbitrator(s) should be impartial and independent. This need is particularly felt in certain contexts, where the custom of non-standard arbitration has often been regarded as too sensitive to the parties' interests and pressures. This provides an explanation for the specific rules that several local sets of provisions have laid down to regulate the conduct of appointed arbitrators. In particular, the regulations laid down by a few Italian arbitration chambers contain specific codes of conduct concerning such important issues as the arbitrator's competence, impartiality and independence, which are largely modelled on the Criteria of Arbitral Ethics (*Criteri di Deontologia Arbitrale*) enacted by the Italian Arbitration Association in 1999 (Bartolini and Delconte 2001). The codes of conduct included in MAC and BAC consist of fifteen articles, covering various aspects connected to the problem of arbitrators' impartiality and independence and regulating the conduct of arbitrators in a very detailed way, as from the time they accept the appointment and throughout the entire arbitration procedure. Also VENCA has a specific article (article 13) stating explicitly that the appointed arbitrator is expected to send a written statement expressing his independence and impartiality and declaring he has no connections with the parties involved in the arbitration process. BAC also includes the need for a Roster of Arbitrators (section 6) and outlines in detail the characteristics of a potential arbitrator and of the application procedures. The specification of a roster of arbitrators stresses the wish of this arbitration chamber to exercise strict control over the competence and reliability of prospective arbitrators. In addition as regards the procedure for challenging an arbitrator, AR indicates the grounds for challenge in general terms, only mentioning 'justifiable doubts as to his impartiality or independence' (article 10). BAC (section 8.1), instead, makes a clear reference to the reasons for challenging an arbitrator and refers to a precise external source of jurisdiction for their specification:

> The party may reject the arbitrator in the cases specified in Section 51 of the Italian Code of Civil Practice (BAC 8(1)(2)).

In the Arbitration Law of the People's Republic of China the grounds for challenging the appointment of arbitrators are also mentioned in very specific terms, and are exemplified in a close relationship with any 'one litigant' or 'the attorney', 'private meetings with the litigants or with their attorneys' or acceptance of 'invitation of the litigants or their attorneys to dine' or acceptance of 'gifts' (Bhatia, Candlin and Wei 2001, 10). This implication of possibilities of bribery or influence may be prompted by particular socio-cultural factors specific to that country, a hypothesis which finds confirmation in the words of an expert on Chinese law, Professor Jerome Cohen from New York University, quoted by Jane Moir in an article in the South China Morning Post (5 October 2001):

> The longer my experience as either an advocate or an arbitrator in disputes presented to Cietac [China International Economic and Trade Arbitration Commission], the graver my doubts have become about its independence and impartiality. [...] At a minimum, I would surely no longer advise clients to accept Cietac jurisdiction unless the contract's arbitration clause required the appointment of a third country national as presiding arbitrator (quoted in Bhatia, Candlin and Wei 2001, 8).

Target readers

The socio-economic environment in which legal provisions are issued has also influenced the style adopted in customising the UNCITRAL normative texts. An example can be seen in the regulations enacted by the Milan and Bergamo Arbitration Chambers and the Venice Court of National and International Arbitration. These institutions are situated in one of the most industrialised areas in Northern Italy, where a large number of small enterprises operate successfully on foreign markets. Their sets of rules are intended for a number of business people running small and medium-sized companies and wanting clear indications on how to resolve commercial disputes without recourse to ordinary justice. This explains the higher degree of user-friendliness encountered in their texts, which can be noted in several cases. One instance is the fact that they include standard arbitration clauses – such as the clauses for a sole arbitrator, for an arbitral tribunal and for a multi-party arbitration – which can be adopted verbatim and completed easily by the reader, as may be seen from the following examples:

> *Arbitration agreement* (a)
> The undersigned (b) ....and .... considering that a dispute has arisen on the subject (c) .... agree to defer this dispute to the decision of (d) .... to be appointed in accordance with the Rules of the National and International Arbitration Chamber of Bergamo, which the parties expressly declare they know and which they accept in full.
> The arbitrators / the sole arbitrator shall decide according to the rules and regulations .... / fairness (specify what is relevant).
> The language of the arbitration shall be ....

Notes

a) The arbitration agreement is a document that is stipulated when the dispute has already arisen between the parties and in the absence of a precautionary arbitration clause.
b) Specification of the name and residence, or in the case of companies, the head offices of the parties.
c) Reference, also expressed in general terms, of the subject under dispute, with possible reference to the contract out of which the dispute originated.
d) Specification of the number of arbitrators (one or three) (BAC, Arbitration agreement).

Clause for Sole Arbitrator
All disputes arising out of the present contract[1], including those concerning its validity, interpretation, performance and termination, shall be referred to a sole arbitrator according to the International Arbitration Rules of the Chamber of National and International Arbitration of Milan, which the parties declare that they know and accept in their entirety.
The sole arbitrator shall decide according to the norms [...][2].
The language of the arbitration shall be [...].

Notes

a) Where the arbitration clause is contained in a document other than the contract to which it pertains, the contract referred to shall be indicated.
b) The parties may indicate the norms applicable to the merits of the dispute; alternatively, they may provide that the arbitrator decide ex aequo et bono (MAC, Clause for Sole Arbitrator).

The texts above have the form of ready-to-use specimens and are thus very easy to copy and complete. Instead, the UNICITRAL arbitration rules, on which the Italian texts are modelled, are mainly informative and imply some sort of adaptation on the part of the user of the clauses presented:

Model arbitration clause
Any dispute, controversy or claim arising out of or relating to this contract, or the breach, termination or invalidity thereof, shall be settled by arbitration in accordance with the UNCITRAL Arbitration Rules as at present in force.
Note
Parties may wish to consider adding:
(a) The appointing authority shall be .... (name of institution or person);
(b) The number of arbitrators shall be ...... (one or three);
(c) The place of arbitration shall be ..... (town or country);
(d) The language(s) to be used in the arbitral proceedings shall be ... (AR 1).

Moreover, the shorter sentence length and the higher average number of simple and compound sentences of the Italian texts (see above section on '*Drafting traditions*') determine a positive impact on their level of readability and make them easier to process, which strengthens their greater degree of user-friendliness.

Conclusion

The process of customisation of the UNCITRAL Model Law and Arbitration Rules has provided interesting insights into how normative discourse may change when adopted by countries relying on different cultural, linguistic and legal conventions. In being taken as a model, these sets of rules have been made simpler to decode, thanks to criteria which are typical of the Plain Language Movement (Asprey 1991; Wagner and Cutts 2002; Kimble 2003) and typically marked by the use of smaller number of words per sentence, extensive use of simple and compound sentences and adoption of common lexis. In addition, these texts have been made much more user-friendly by means of the provision of model clauses to be copied verbatim and simply completed with one's specific details. These changes are to be attributed to the different target readers. The UNCITRAL texts are exclusively aimed at legal experts, while the arbitration rules are also intended for business people wanting clear indications on how to resolve commercial disputes without recourse to ordinary justice.

Furthermore, in the re-writing process implied in the customisation of the original texts, the vagueness and indeterminacy of the original texts – mainly due to the aim of the Model Law and the Arbitration Rules to be as all-inclusive as possible in order to be valid in the widest range of applications – have been eliminated, and specific references to the local situation have been inserted so as to make the resulting texts correspond more closely to the legal and socio-cultural traits of the national target users. This can be seen, in particular, in the analysis of the specificity of information included in the various texts, which differs significantly, due to discrepancy in socio-cultural expectations and practices. A relevant case in point was found in the comparison of the various clauses concerning the grounds for challenging the appointment of arbitrators: in the UNCITRAL texts they are expressed in more general terms, while in the other texts the constraints are specified in greater detail.

The textual discrepancies observed in this analysis are a clear proof of the problems that arise in the process of establishing closer harmonisation in legal normative discourse at a global level. These problems become particularly evident when 'model' texts have to be adopted in various contexts, thus giving rise to interesting differentiations in the resulting texts. These variations are to be attributed not only to the languages in which the final texts are expressed but also to the different cultural traits and legal traditions of the communities for which they are meant. In spite of the desire to make international arbitration texts 'unbound' (Paulsson 1981) typical of the processes of harmonisation and globalisation, the differentiations observed in the arbitration rules formulated at a local level are the result of conscious and deliberate decisions by national drafters, and demonstrate that the source texts have merely offered the input on the basis of which new autonomous texts have been created taking into consideration the local socio-legal environment and the needs of the final users.

Chapter 6

Is the Chinese Legal Language more Ambiguous and Vaguer?

Deborah Cao

Language is inherently indeterminate. Linguistic uncertainties sometimes lead to legal disputes[1] and become matters of contention in court (for example see Schane 2002; Stratman 2004). The Chinese language, like any other language, is inherently indeterminate, but one may ask: are all languages equally indeterminate or are some languages more indeterminate than others? In our case, one may wonder: is the Chinese language, and for the purpose of this analysis, the Chinese legal language, more ambiguous and vaguer than English and the English legal language? In this chapter, I will address some of these issues using examples from Chinese statutes. My first aim will be to identify certain inherent linguistic features of the Chinese language that may render the Chinese legal language prone to uncertainty. I then discuss drafting issues in Chinese law that may have contributed to ambiguity and vagueness. Lastly, I will consider the pragmatic legal implications of the contention that the Chinese legal language is more ambiguous and vaguer than English. In this chapter, 'uncertainty' is used interchangeably with 'indeterminacy' (for discussions on indeterminacy and the law see Bix 1993; Stratman 2004; Bathia 2005). 'Chinese linguistic uncertainty' is used as a general term to cover the uncertain and indeterminate property of the Chinese language including linguistic vagueness, generality and ambiguity. Vagueness, generality and ambiguity are distinguishable (see Williamson 2001), but they are also relative, and sometimes may overlap (see Schane 2002).

Uncertainty in Chinese law

It is commonly acknowledged that contemporary Chinese law suffers from excessive generality and vagueness. Correspondingly, a highly flexible and contextualist approach to law seems to prevail among Chinese lawmakers and lawyers. Peerenboom (2002, 247, 251) argues that Chinese legislation is characterised by excessive generality and vagueness, omissions, undefined terms and inconsistencies. He cites examples of Chinese equity joint venture law, criminal law, and civil law. Keller (1994), in his study of Chinese law, concludes that generality and flexibility are the guiding principles in Chinese legislative drafting; colloquially referred to by legislative officials as

---

1 See for example, *Raffles v. Wichelhaus* 2 Hurl. and C. 906, 159 Eng. Rep. 375 (Ex. 1864); and *Frigaliment Importing Co. v. B.N.S. International Sales Corp.*, 190 F.Supp. 116 (S.D.N.Y. 1960).

the policy of 'preferring the coarse to the fine' (ibid. 749). He further argues that generality and flexibility captures the essential guide in Chinese lawmaking that legislation must reflect the unitary nature of the state while satisfying the needs of regional diversity. This also accords with the principle of legislative stability as it permits the effective amendment of the law through changes in interpretation rather than through alterations to the actual statutes (Keller 1994, 750). The justification offered for this central doctrine is that national legislation must be general and flexible so that it can be implemented throughout the country and adapted to local conditions (Keller 1994, 749). As Keller (1994, 752) notes, Chinese lawmakers have not, in general, attempted to use legislative language supported by rules of construction to strengthen the internal structure and order of positive law. They prefer instead, particularly in relation to primary legislation, that the specific meanings attached to legislative language shift with their contexts. Similarly, Chinese administrative bodies also have a preference for broadly drafted laws that leave them free to act as they see fit in specific circumstances (Keller 1994, 752).[2]

In this regard, Potter (2001, 11) agrees that Chinese laws are intentionally ambiguous and are replete with vague passages that do not lend predicability or transparency to the regulatory process; but he believes that this is a consequence of legal instrumentalism prevailing in China that gives policy makers and officials significant flexibility in legislative interpretation and implementation. In contrast, Peerenboom (2002, 251) submits that there may be many reasons for generality and vagueness in Chinese law, pointing specifically to the following reasons: many of China's laws are modelled after the laws of civil law countries, which are typically more general and broadly drafted than statutes in common law countries; China is a vast country undergoing profound changes, so broadly drafted laws and regulations allow sufficient flexibility in implementation to meet local conditions. He also suggests that the traditional emphasis on particularised justice characteristic of the Confucian tradition and the socialist emphasis on uniting practice and theory combined with the pragmatic orientation of current leaders all favour laws that are statements of general principles that must then be interpreted and applied to particular situations by local officials and administrators (Keller 2002, 251). Regardless of the reasons, such excessive generality and vagueness often undermine the predicability and certainty of Chinese law.

Chinese linguistic features of uncertainty

In this section, I explore the linguistic issues that may have contributed to the uncertainty in Chinese law as has been identified by the aforementioned legal scholars, examining specifically the linguistic nature of the Chinese language, legal language

---

2 Keller (1994, 749), citing Ma Xiaohong, points out that the principles of generality and flexibility in contemporary Chinese lawmaking have a close parallel with the Chinese imperial legislative tradition. Ma Xiaohong, cited in Keller, believes that the late imperial Ming and Qing legislation was characterised by generality of language, and contemporary Chinese legislative theorists often praise and invoke the views of imperial lawmakers in support of their contemporary practices.

and legislative drafting practice. Chinese is different from English in its linguistic form in that the Chinese language uses characters as its linguistic representation (as opposed to an alphabet), and in how the Chinese characters are structured to express meaning, for example, grammar. Two linguistic features stand out in Chinese when compared with European languages: firstly, the absence of inflection that is words[3] can assume a variety of grammatical functions without morphological change; and secondly, omission that is grammatically significant indicators can be omitted. These are the inherent linguistic features of the Chinese language.

Chinese characters are not words in the strict English sense and as such they can vary in meaning as their context changes. Even in the same general context, a character may have several different meanings. Chinese characters are more like word roots than words. There are no changes in the character in relation to tense, number, gender, person, or case; and there are no articles such as the English 'the' and 'a'/'an'. Since the Chinese language does not have definite and indefinite articles as in English or other European languages, this aspect becomes more obvious when translating between Chinese and European languages, for example English. When translating into Chinese, the articles in English are often omitted. This can sometimes give rise to problems, as considerable meaning variation may result with or without the use of articles.

When Chinese texts are translated into English, there is the additional problem of the rare use of linguistic markers for plural nouns with no markers for plural verbs. As a result ambiguity often arises as linguistically it is uncertain whether singular or plural meanings are intended. In many instances, the translator has to make the arbitrary decision of using or not using articles or choosing between the singular and plural in English, thus arbitrarily eliminating the uncertainties contained in the original Chinese text. This also arises when English is translated into Chinese: the definite article or plural form in English are omitted and their meanings lost in the translation; often introducing uncertainty when it was not there in the original text (for inter-lingual uncertainty in law, see Cao 2007b).[4]

One source of uncertainty is that Chinese does not have grammatical categories of tense or aspect (see for example Yang and Huang 2004). There are particles that function as tense markers, but they are rarely used. As a result, the Chinese language is not a tense-prominent language like English and while the equivalence of tenses can be indicated by temporal adverbs or particles, more often than not, they are implied from context. There are two kinds of uncertainty related to the lack of tense: (1) the rare use of particles or tense markers; and (2) certain tenses in English cannot be expressed in Chinese.

---

3 In this chapter, 'word' is used to describe Chinese characters for convenience.

4 I had first hand personal experience of the uncertainty caused by the lack of pluralisation when I was asked for an opinion in a dispute involving two Chinese parties in Australia where the contract was written in Chinese. A Chinese phrase used in the contract was written in the singular form, but one party argued that it should be understood in the plural form. The uncertainty appeared because no distinction is normally made between singular and plural nouns in Chinese.

Another source of uncertainty in Chinese comes from omission. The language offers the option to omit grammatically significant and other parts in language use. The resulting elliptical sentence is a major source of structural ambiguity. Ambiguities of this kind may disappear and the meaning may become clearer if the omitted parts are supplied.

Apart from these inherent linguistic features that contribute to uncertainty, Chinese language users also have a linguistic habit of using words with uncertain meanings. Such vague and general expressions are commonly used in ordinary speech and ordinary written texts. They are also used in law (to be discussed later). For instance, a common word in Chinese is the use of *deng* (meaning 'etc.', 'such as', 'including') in Chinese legal texts. The habitual and sometimes over-frequent use of *deng* which allows for open-ended interpretations can cause a great deal of uncertainty and ambiguity. A further problem is that *deng* can indicate both open-endedness when listing things and can also be used to end a listing, a closure, to be all inclusive, depending on actual use and context.

Uncertainty in Chinese legal language

The following section will examine a major Chinese statute, the Criminal Code, to demonstrate how the various linguistic features discussed above and other factors render the Chinese legal language vague, general and imprecise.

The Chinese Criminal Code (*Xingfa*) is one of the most important basic laws in the Chinese legal system. It was originally promulgated in 1979 and has been amended a number of times in 1997, 1999, 2001, 2002, 2005 and more recently in 2006. The 1997 amendment was virtually a rewrite of the original code, substantively and substantially changing many of the provisions; increasing the total number of articles from 192 in eight chapters to 452 articles in ten chapters. A close reading of the Criminal Code reveals that there are many instances of linguistic uncertainty at the lexical and syntactical levels. These uncertainties caused by the inherent and other features of the Chinese language include lexical, grammatical and syntactical ambiguity, vagueness and generality.

Two provisions are worthy of closer examination; namely articles 338 and 339 relating to environmental crimes:

第三百三十八条　违反国家规定，向土地、水体、大气排放、倾倒或者处置有放射性的废物、含传染病病原体的废物、有毒物质或者其他危险废物，造成重大环境污染事故，致使公私财产遭受重大损失或者人身伤亡的严重后果的，处三年以下有期徒刑或者拘役，并处或者单处罚金；后果特别严重的，处三年以上七年以下有期徒刑，并处罚金。

[Article 338 Anyone who, in violation of the state regulation, release[s], dump[s] or dispose[s] radioactive waste[s], waste[s] containing pathogen of contagious disease[s], toxic material[s] or other hazardous waste[s] to land, water [and/or] atmosphere, [and/or] cause[s] [a] serious environmental pollution accident, [and/or] result[s] in serious consequence[s] causing serious loss to public [and/or] private property or personal injury [and/or] death is punished by no more than three years' imprisonment or detention, and is also punished with a fine, or is only punished with [a] fine; for [those accidents resulting in] particularly serious consequence[s], no less than three years' and no more than seven years' imprisonment is imposed together with [a] fine (my translation)].[5]

Similarly,

第三百三十九条 违反国家规定，将境外的固体废物进境倾倒、堆放、处置的，处五年以下有期徒刑或者拘役，并处罚金；造成重大环境污染事故，致使公私财产遭受重大损失或者严重危害人体健康的，处五年以上十年以下有期徒刑，并处罚金；后果特别严重的，处十年以上有期徒刑，并处罚金。

未经国务院有关主管部门许可，擅自进口固体废物用作原料，造成重大环境污染事故，致使公私财产遭受重大损失或者严重危害人体健康的，处五年以下有期徒刑或者拘役，并处罚金；后果特别严重的，处五年以上十年以下有期徒刑，并处罚金。

以原料利用为名，进口不能用作原料的固体废物、液态废物和气态废物的，依照本法第一百五十二条第二款、第三款的规定定罪处罚。

[Article 339 Anyone who, in violation of the state regulation, dump[s], stockpile[s] or dispose[s] solid waste[s] from outside the border to inside the border is punished by no more than five years' imprisonment or detention and a fine. Anyone causing serious environmental pollution incident[s], resulting in serious loss to public [and/or] private property or serious harm to human health, is punished by no more than five years' and no less than ten years' imprisonment and by imposing [a] fine. For [those resulting in] particularly serious consequences, [they are punished] by more than ten years' imprisonment and [a] fine].

Anyone [who does] not have the approval of the relevant department[s] in charge under the State Council [who] import[s] without authorisation solid waste[s] as raw material[s], [and/or] cause[s] serious environmental pollution accident[s], result[s] in serious loss to public [and/or] private property or serious harm to human health, is punished by no more than five years' imprisonment or detention, and is also punished with [a] fine. For [those accidents resulting in] particularly serious consequences, no more than five years and no less than ten years' imprisonment is imposed together with [a] fine.

Anyone who import[s] solid waste[s], liquid waste[s] and waste gas in the name of raw material[s] which cannot be used as such is punished under sections 2 and 3 of article 152 of this Act.]

There are a number of linguistic uncertainties in the above two provisions. Firstly, all the articles 'the' and 'a' are added in the English translation.[6] Secondly, since Chinese does not distinguish in most cases between singular and plural forms as stated earlier, when translating Chinese into English, we may have to decide whether certain nouns should be translated and understood as singular or plural forms. In this

---

5 All translations in this chapter are provided by the author.

6 Note that in a Chinese court, only the law enacted in the Chinese language is valid, not English or any other translation. Thus, some of these uncertainties will not become an issue while others will.

particular case, there are ambiguities due to the lack of number markers in Chinese, but common sense tells us that words such as 'waste' and 'disease' in this context would not result in any substantive deviation or change in the meaning of the Act. Also, in Chinese, words such as 'waste' are collective nouns, and do not present the problem of singular versus plural forms. Besides, even in common law, it is often stated and it has become an established rule of statutory interpretation that the singular form may represent the plural and vice versa (see for example the *UK Interpretation Act 1978* s. 6(c)).[7]

However, this is not always the case. Another phrase which is the equivalent of 'cause serious environmental pollution accident' in Chinese can be understood as 'an accident' or 'accidents'. Would it mean that a person has to cause more than one such accident to be criminally liable or just one accident is sufficient? Such an issue would arise in both Chinese and English. Common sense may also tell us that it is likely that it means one accident if such an accident satisfies the qualification stated in the provision. Similarly, 'fine' is imposed, and it could be one fine or many fines, although common sense and a reasonable understanding may dictate that one fine was intended. For another noun in article 339, the equivalent of 'anyone who does not have the approval of the relevant departments in charge under the State Council', 'departments' here can be either 'a department' or 'departments'. This ambiguity is more serious in practical terms than the examples discussed above. Since the Chinese version does not specify whether it is singular or plural, and the word 'department' is qualified by 'the relevant' without specifying which department, and given the Chinese bureaucracy and lack of transparency in general, this could potentially mean numerous and countless numbers of departments that are either closely related or remotely related from which one has to obtain approval. This could potentially be a source of uncertainty.

In summary, the use or non-use of singular and plural markers and lack of definite and indefinite articles are very much present in this Criminal Code, giving rise to some ambiguities, although in many cases, not all cases, such ambiguities can be clarified or made clear from context or by a common sense approach. This situation is similar in most Chinese statutes in general.

Thirdly, apart from grammatical ambiguity, there is also a syntactical or structural ambiguity in article 338 as in:

> [...] Anyone who, in violation of the state regulation, releases, dumps or disposes radioactive wastes, wastes containing pathogen of contagious diseases, toxic materials or other hazardous wastes to land, water [and/or] atmosphere, [and/or] causes a serious environmental pollution accident, [and/or] results in serious consequences causing serious loss to public [and/or] private property or personal injury [and/or] death is punished [...].

Here the main verbal phrases 'releases, dumps or disposes...' and 'causes a serious environmental pollution accident' have parallel structures in Chinese. It could well and reasonably be understood as to mean that anyone who releases, dumps or disposes the prohibited materials commits an offence under the Act. Equally, it could

---

7 See for example *Re Toal Application for Judicial Review* [2006] NIQB 44, para 10.

also mean that anyone who causes a serious environmental pollution accident is also liable under the Act. Linguistically speaking, such interpretations would be correct. However, according to Wang (2004), a legal scholar from China, in terms of the law, under article 338, the criminal liability arises only when one causes a serious environmental pollution accident which leads to the serious consequences of heavy losses of public or private property or human casualties. This means that a person can release, dump or dispose any of the prohibited materials without committing any offence. Furthermore, a person can also release, dump or dispose the prohibited materials causing an environmental pollution accident and still not commit any offence under the Act, so long as the serious environmental pollution accident does not result in the serious consequences of heavy losses of public or private property or human casualties. The act is only an offence when serious consequences as described in the Act result thereof. One may say that this interpretation is possible or acceptable in the Chinese provision. One may also say that this is a stretched and very restricted interpretation. In any event, the Chinese sentence is very loosely structured linguistically so that we can say that either interpretation is possible. Thus, the provision is ambiguous and uncertain linguistically.

We can also detect a structural ambiguity in article 338 in some of the noun phrases used. These words are stringed together without the equivalent of the English 'and' or 'or' as in the case of *gongsi caichan* in article 338, 'resulting in serious loss to public [and/or] private property'. Here in Chinese, the commonly used phrase *gongsi caichan* is literally 'public private property' which can mean either 'public and private' property or 'public or private' property. The Chinese can say without the omissions *gonggong caichan he siyou caichan* [public property and private property] or *gonggong caichan huo siyou caichan* [public property or private property], but in most cases, a short hand form is used *gongsi caichan*. One possible interpretation is that 'or' is intended in the Criminal Code.

Another example in article 338 is *renshen shangwang* [literally 'personal injury death'], so it could mean 'personal injury and death' or 'personal injury or death'. It is ambiguous as to whether death must be involved for the offence to be committed. This is important as the offence under Chinese law, as mentioned earlier, very much depends on the seriousness of the conduct. However, in this case, we have no definitive way of knowing it. A reasonable understanding is that it could mean either injury or death but it must have produced serious consequences.

Hence a clearer (or as clear as one can or should be) translation of articles 338 and 339 could be (in any event English is not the language of the court in China):

> Article 338 Anyone who, in violation of the state regulation, releases, dumps or disposes radioactive wastes, wastes containing pathogen of contagious diseases, toxic materials or other hazardous wastes to land, water *or* atmosphere, *causing a* serious environmental pollution accident *that results in* serious consequences causing serious loss to public *or* private property or personal injury *or* death is punishable by no more than three years' imprisonment or detention, and is also punished with a fine, or is only punished with a fine; for those accidents resulting in particularly serious consequences, no less than three years' and no more than seven years' imprisonment is imposed together with a fine (emphasis added in italics as in all quotation in the chapter).

Article 339 Anyone who, in violation of the state regulation, dumps, stockpiles or disposes solid wastes from overseas to China is punished by no more than five years' imprisonment or detention and a fine. Anyone causing serious environmental pollution incidents, resulting in serious loss to public or private property or serious harm to human health, is punished by no more than five years' and no less than ten years' imprisonment and by imposing a fine. For those resulting in particularly serious consequences, more than ten years' imprisonment and a fine are imposed.

Anyone who does not have the approval of the relevant departments in charge under the State Council imports without authorisation solid wastes as raw materials, causing a serious environmental pollution accident that results in serious loss to public or private property or serious harm to human health, is punished by no more than five years' imprisonment or detention, and is also punished with a fine. For those accidents resulting in particularly serious consequences, no more than five years and no less than ten years' imprisonment is imposed together with a fine.

Anyone who imports solid wastes, liquid wastes and waste gas in the name of raw materials which cannot be used as such is punished under sections 2 and 3 of article 152 of this Act.

Fourthly, we can also see that in both articles 338 and 339, the words yanzhong [serious], *zhongda* [serious, major or heavy] and *tebie yanzhong* [particularly serious] are used a number of times. These words are general or vague in Chinese and English. In fact, such words are typical expressions of vagueness or imprecision as they indicate borderline cases and there can be no clear determination as to whether or not such words apply to a particular situation. So, one may wonder how 'serious' would be considered 'serious' or 'particularly serious'. We have no way of knowing as nowhere in the Code are these words further qualified or described. However, they touch on an extremely important aspect in Chinese criminal law.

As pointed out, in Chinese criminal legislation, determining what constitutes a criminal and capital offence can turn on interpretations of phrases such as 'serious', 'large amount' or 'special circumstances' (Belkin 2000). These are the most obvious and most frequently used words of vagueness in the Code. These words are frequently employed to describe the degree of the seriousness of crimes, extent of harms or damage done by criminal acts and the amount of money involved in crimes for the purpose of prescribing penalties and punishment. In this regard, the legal definition of crime in the Chinese criminal law is relevant. Article 13 of the Criminal Code stipulates that:

A crime refers to an act that endangers the sovereignty, territorial integrity and security of the States, splits the State, subverts the State power of the people's democratic dictatorship and overthrows the socialist system, undermines public and economic order, violates State-owned property, property collectively owned by the working people, or property privately owned by citizens, infringes on the citizens' rights of the person, their democratic or other rights, and any other act that endangers society and is subject to punishment according to law. However, if the circumstances are obviously minor and the harm done is not serious, the act shall not be deemed a crime.

According to Wang (2004, 153), in this legal definition of crime, what we should notice is not only the material characteristic of a crime in China, but also the requirement as to what constitutes a crime. According to Chinese criminal law and, principally, for the general definition of a crime, any harmful conduct will not be treated as a crime 'if the circumstances are obviously minor and the harm done is not serious' (Wang 2004, 153). In the theory of Chinese criminal law, 'the circumstances' are closely linked with the degree of the social harmfulness caused by the conduct. In the Specific Part of the Criminal Code, the circumstances or the degree of the social harmfulness shall be clearly defined (Wang 2004). This is reflected in the form of actual harmful consequences and the sum of the illegal money involved. In some cases, it might be also reflected in the criminal method or criminal mind, but in these cases, the final decisive factor in what constitutes a crime is still the actual harmful consequences (Wang 2004, 153). As Wang points out, because of this requirement of 'the circumstances', the Chinese criminal law builds up its unique 'guilty line' for differentiating guilty and innocent. Accordingly, most conducts which are treated as innocent in Chinese criminal law because they are below 'the guilty line' would constitute crimes in other legal systems (Wang 2004).

Thus, the seriousness of an act and the seriousness of its social consequence determines whether the act constitutes a crime or not and the punishment accordingly, but the vague words 'serious' and 'particularly serious' in the Criminal Code would pose considerable problems in the application of the law and in people's understanding of the law.

Therefore, it is not surprising that the Supreme People's Court issued an explanation for these words in these sections of the Criminal Code, The *Interpretation of the Supreme People's Court Concerning Certain Issues Related to the Specific Application of Law in Hearing of Criminal Cases regarding Environmental Pollution* (2006). The *Interpretation* by the Court is specifically issued with regard to the explanation as to what constitutes 'serious loss', 'particularly serious consequences', and 'serious harm' in articles 338 and 339, quantifying what they mean. The *Interpretation* states:

Article 1: Any of the following situations falls under '*serious damage to public [and/or] private property*' referred to in articles 338, 339 and 408 of the Criminal Code:
1. causing damage to public [and/or] private property in the amount of more than ¥300,000 *yuan*;
2. causing the loss of the basic functions or permanent damage to basic agricultural land, protected forest land [or] forest land for special purposes of more than five *mu*, other agricultural land of more than ten mu, [or] other land of more than twenty *mu* [a Chinese measurement];
3. causing the death to forest or other forest trees of more than fifth cubic metres, or causing the death to more than 2500 young trees;
Article 2: Any of the following situations falls under '*serious consequences of personal death [or] injury*', or '*serious harm to human health*' referred to in articles 338 and 339 of the Criminal Code:

1. causing the death of more than one person, serious injury of more than three persons, [or] light injury of more than ten persons, or serious injury to more than one person and light injury to more than five persons;

2. causing the occurrence [or] spread of [a] contagious disease, or causing people to be poisoned constituting a situation as classified in Sub-Category III of emergency public health incident as set out in the Plan of the State Emergency Response to Sudden Public Health Incidents;

3. other situations 'causing serious consequences of personal death [or] injury' or 'causing serious harm to human health'.

Article 3 Any of the following situations falls under '*particularly serious consequences*' referred to in articles 338 and 339 of the Criminal Code:

1. causing loss to public [or] private property of more than one million *yuan*;

2. causing the occurrence of situations involving water source pollution [or] people evacuation that are specified in the emergency environmental incidents in above subcategory II as stated in the Plan of State Emergency Response to Sudden Environmental Incidents;

3. causing the loss of the basic functions or permanent damage to basic farm land, protected forest, special purpose forest land of more than 15 *mu*, and more than 30 *mu* of other land for agricultural use, [or] other land of more than 60 *mu*;

4. causing the death of forest or other trees of more than 150 cubic meters, or the death of more than 7500 young trees;

5. causing the death of more than three persons, serious injury to more than ten persons, light injury to more than 30 persons, or serious injury to more than three persons and light injury to more than ten persons;

6. causing the occurrence [or] spread of [a] contagious disease constituting a situation above those as classified in Sub-Category II of emergency public health incident as set out in The Plan of the State Emergency Response to Sudden Public Health Incidents;

7. other situations with particularly serious consequences.

In the above English translation, the [or] and other words inserted are made at my discretion and they in fact constitute further uncertainty. The *Interpretation* thus clarifies the meaning of some of the imprecise words in the original Act. However, the *Interpretation* was issued in 2006, almost ten years after the original Act took effect. It makes one wonder how the cases were decided in the intervening years. Obviously, the Chinese courts did decide cases during those years. One can speculate that the courts must have used a common sense approach in understanding what these words entailed and how serious a particular criminal act would be commonly perceived by ordinary people and by the courts themselves in the circumstances.

Fifthly, in articles 338 and 339, we can see there are other words of imprecision, for instance, 'relevant departments', 'loss of public or private property'. This is not to say that statutory provisions drafted in English in common law countries do not contain similar expressions, but normally, as is the case in English law, they are defined in the law itself. For instance, the UK *Animal Welfare Act 2006 (c45)*, uses the vague adjective 'appropriate' to qualify the substantive 'national authority' (as in 'appropriate national authority'), but the general interpretation section of the Act clearly defines what 'appropriate national authority' means; that is, it refers to (a) in relation to England, [to] the Secretary of State; and (b) in relation to Wales, [to] the

National Assembly for Wales (2006, 34, para 62). Another example drawn from the same Act is the use of 'local authority' which is defined to refer specifically to

> (a) in relation to England, [to] a county council, a district council, a London borough council, the Common Council of the City of London or the Council of the Isles of Scilly, among others (ibid., 35).

Generally in English statutes, when a particular word or a phrase used is general or vague but carries legal significance, their definition is expressly contained in the same statute. The same rule generally applies when an ordinary word which may carry an uncommon meaning is used in a statutory provision. For example, the interpretation provision of the *UK Animal Welfare Act* defines the ordinary word 'premises' so as to include 'any place and, in particular, –[…] (a) any vehicle, vessel, aircraft or hovercraft; (b) any tent or movable structure' (2006, para 62, 35).[8]

In contrast, if we look at the Chinese Criminal Code, general and vague words are not normally defined or described.[9] For the example cited above, the Criminal Code does not provide any definition or description as to what may constitute 'loss to public or private property' in article 338. The Supreme People's Court also recognised this and issued an explanation in the *Interpretation of the Supreme People's Court*

---

8 Similarly, as Economy reports (2004, 102, citing Nagle 1996), China's Water Pollution Prevention and Control Law states that 'enterprises and other undertakings which cause serious water pollution must eliminate pollution within a stipulated time'. What constitutes 'serious' water pollution is not self-evident, nor is the meaning of 'enterprises and other undertakings […]'. The *US Clean Water Act 1977*, in contrast, specifies in great detail the type and amount of pollution that particular sources may emit through the procedures for establishing effluent limitations and water quality standards and through the permit process. Economy (2004, 102) writes that it is difficult for the Chinese to know what is prohibited and what can be called to account through legal redress. In one case, when a local environmental protection bureau attempted to sue a local chemical company for failing to pay its discharge fees over a two-year period, the bureau at first could not decide whether the basis for the suit rested on the enterprise's failure to pay for small amounts of its discharge fees or its failure to pay over-standard fees. Moreover, the local court, scheduled to hear the case, pointed out that inconsistencies between national regulations and local rules might make a suit difficult. Economy (2004, 102) says that ambiguity in laws also permit conscious exploration by enterprises or other actors, and the Chinese even have a saying: 'national policies, local countermeasures', to describe the practice of exploiting the ambiguity of national laws and regulations to figure out ways around them.

9 This is not to say that Chinese statutes do not have definitions. In fact, Chinese statutes normally give some definitions to the key terms at the beginning of statutes. For instance, in the Environmental Protection Law of the People's Republic of China (1989), article 2 states: '"Environment" in this law refers to the total body of all natural elements and artificially transformed natural elements affecting human existence and development, which includes the atmosphere, water, seas, land, minerals, forests, grasslands, wildlife, natural and human historical relics, nature reserves, historical sites and scenic spots and urban and rural areas, among others.' But such definitions are usually restricted to a very few key terms in a statute, in the Environmental Protection Law, 'environment' is the only definition. Furthermore, one can also argue many of the terms that are used to define the key terms need definition themselves, for instance, what is considered 'wildlife' as used in the above definition.

Concerning Certain Issues Related to the Specific Application of Law in Hearing Criminal Cases Involving Environmental Pollution (2006):

> [...] The "loss to public or private property" referred to in this Interpretation includes the damage and destruction to property directly caused by the environmental polluting act, the reduction of the actual value of the property, and the costs incurred for the necessary and reasonable measures adopted to prevent the expansion of the pollution and the elimination of the pollution.

Another relevant factor in relation to imprecise words used in law is that in the common law, words that are not defined or even words that are defined in a particular statute, are always subject to judicial interpretation and application. Thus, for many words that are not defined in the statute proper, judicial interpretation in legal precedent is referred to and applied in subsequent cases. However, in the Chinese legal system, case law in terms of judicial interpretation does not constitute a source of law and Chinese judges do not elaborate or give reasons.

On the whole, in the Chinese Criminal Code, there are many words of generality and vagueness, such as 'public interest', 'justified self-defence', 'wilful criminal act', 'work units concerned', 'other laws', 'other regulations'. These words are not defined or elaborated. We may further note that even in the judicial interpretation by the Supreme People's Court cited above, there are further linguistic uncertainties in the use of punctuation, the use of 'and/or', 'other particularly serious situations', among others.

Possible Reasons for the Legislative Uncertainty in China

As we have seen, the Chinese statutory language as represented in the Criminal Code has vague, ambiguous, general and otherwise imprecise words and contains other linguistic features of this kind. We have also seen that such imprecision can be attributed to both the inherent linguistic features in the Chinese language in terms of grammatical and structural uncertainty and the deliberate use of the language through the choice of imprecise lexical words. In this regard, consideration of the Chinese legal system as a whole may be relevant.

China is largely a civil law country. Statutory laws constitute the main source of law. Unlike common law jurisdictions such as the United States or the United Kingdom, there is no strict precedential concept for case law. In theory, each case stands as its own decision and will not bind another court. Judges' decisions are usually not accompanied by lengthy written legal opinions and reasoning. Judicial decisions do not have any legally binding precedential effect on other cases. However, in practice lower people's court judges often attempt to follow the interpretations of the laws decided by the Supreme People's Courts. Case law does not constitute precedent and has no binding force, thus judicial or statutory interpretation in the common law sense of statutory provisions does not play a significant part in the legal system. The court applies the law as proclaimed by the legislature. However, an important source of law is the judicial interpretation (or judicial explanation) issued from time to time by the Supreme People's Court and the Supreme People's

Procuratorate of China. Their interpretations are important guides for procurators, lawyers and judges. These are not always interpretations arising from actual court cases. They are in the form of *jieshi* [interpretation or explanation], *yijian* [opinion], official answers, letters in reply, notices and other similar forms, a measure that amounts to the re-creation of detailed rules and new rules (Ji 2004).

Judicial interpretation in China dates back to 1954, shortly after the founding of the People's Republic of China. The national authorities found it necessary to issue such explanations to cope with the problems that arose in handling cases. The Standing Committee of the National People's Congress (NPC), the Chinese national parliament, passed the *Decision on Interpretation of Law* in 1995 which provided that those questions connected with specific application of laws and decrees should be interpreted by the Supreme People's Court. Thus the highest judicial body in China was formally conferred with the power of enacting judicial interpretation. This power was also confirmed by further legislation afterwards in the *Organic Law of People's Court of the People's Republic of China* in 1979. Furthermore, the Standing Committee of the NPC later adopted a resolution on the improvement of interpretation work of Chinese laws, providing that

> an interpretation of questions involving the specific application of laws and decrees in court trials shall be provided by the Supreme People's Court, and an interpretation of problems concerning the concrete application of laws and decrees in procuratorial practices shall be prescribed by the Supreme People's Procuratorate.

Furthermore, if there is any difference in principle between them, the Standing Committee of NPC will make final determination for interpretation or decision. Thus, the judicial interpretation has been considered as a formal source of law.[10]

The fundamental purpose of judicial interpretation by the Supreme People's Court and the Supreme People's Procuratorate is to clarify the issues raised in legal practice and to unify the understanding of law (Wang 1995, 572). The Procuratorate's interpretations of law are not binding and are of a guiding nature while the Court's interpretations are binding. Specific to the legal practice of criminal law, the Chinese judicial interpretation has the following functions (Wang 1995):

1) Indicating how to correctly understand the meaning of the law;
2) Explaining the issues of the law;
3) Indicating the concrete standard of sentencing within the statutory punishments;
4) Clarifying the guilty line and line for giving a heavier punishment when the law requires 'serious circumstances' or 'particularly serious circumstances';
5) Clarifying the limitation of time for a particular law;
6) Explaining how to implement laws.

---

10 According to judicial statistical data, about 4,000 judicial interpretations have been made by the Supreme People's Court alone or jointly with the Supreme People's Procuratorate from 1949 to 2000 (Zhai 2002).

Wang (1995, 575) points out that with function (4), it is typical for the Chinese legislature to use 'serious circumstances' in law as the threshold for convicting for an offence and to have 'particularly serious circumstances' as the indicator for the heavier punishment in Chinese criminal law, and the 'circumstances' need common knowledge to be understood, but it does not usually work well and therefore judicial explanation is needed for further description (Wang 1995, 575).

Wang (1995) further highlights that when compared with judges' opinions in case report of the courts in the United States and the Federal Republic of Germany, Chinese judicial interpretation typically covers a broader scope. The Chinese Supreme Court and Supreme Procuratorate have to do so mainly because of the general or incomplete character of the law (Wang 1995). As in other countries, Chinese judicial explanations help to make the issues clear (Wang 1995, 577). Furthermore, in accordance with the tradition of continental law which Chinese law follows, a basic law should remain stable, but the changing social situations requires the law to make a timely response to them (Wang 1995, 577).[11]

Another consideration in the discussion of imprecise Chinese legal language is that the matter is also related to the problem of poor drafting. Peerenboom (2002, 252) points out that, while PRC laws treat many issues in a general way, they often fail or omit to address some substantive legal issues. Presumably, such omissions are intended to afford greater flexibility in implementation or indicate a lack of consensus at the time of implementation. At other times the omission seems to be a mere oversight. Peerenboom (2002) argues that often the only possible explanation for the many omissions, inconsistencies, contradictions, and related maladies that plague much of China's legislation is poor drafting, the lack of practical experience and appreciation for law-making hierarchies on the part of the drafters (for discussions of Chinese legal drafting, see Wu Daying, Ren Yunzheng and Li Lin 1992, 700-725. For discussion of vagueness and ambiguity in Chinese law, see Ross and Ross 2000).

Several judicial interpretations to the Criminal Code, judicial interpretations have been issued in recent years.[12] Most of these interpretations and opinions from the Supreme People's Court and the Procuratorate were issued to clarify vague wording in the Criminal Code, or to quantify or specify what certain general, ambiguous or vague words mean, for instance, *qingjie yanzhong* (circumstances [of the offence] are serious), *qingjie jiaoqing* (circumstances [of the offence] are light or not serious), *shu'e juda* (the amount [of money involved] is huge), *shu'e jiaoda* (the amount is rather large) in relation to property damage, bribery and others to determine appropriate punishment.

---

11 Wang (1995, 577) points out that, theoretically, the Chinese legislature can make use of the method of legislative explanation to clarify or further expand the laws, which is already provided in Chinese law and is demanded by the legal circle in China, but due to the current strenuous tasks of legislative works and the legislative tradition, the Chinese legislature has not yet attended to these relatively small and routine matters.

12 For example see *The Interpretation of the Supreme People's Court and the Supreme People's Procuratorate Concerning Certain Issues Related to the Specific Application of Law in Handling Criminal Cases Involving Gambling* (2005); *The Interpretation of the Supreme People's Court Concerning Certain Issues Related to the Specific Application of Law in Handling Criminal Cases Involving Undermining Production Safety in Mines* (2007).

Another aspect, although not directly related to the issues under consideration here, is the poor and improper use of language in Chinese law in general, and in the writing of court decisions by judges in China. Chinese courts are required to publish their decisions, but many have failed to do so. One reason, as reported, for not publishing judgements by some of the courts is believed to be the numerous linguistic errors found in court decisions and the poor writing skills of judges. Some courts feel too embarrassed to publish such poorly written works. Linguistic errors found in Chinese decisions include ungrammatical or wrong usage, use of slang, inappropriate use of words, accidental omission or addition of words, typographical errors, punctuation errors, impropriate use of classical Chinese mixed with colloquialism, mistakes in writing litigants' names, among others. It was reported that some judges in Sichuan Province were accorded with disciplinary and financial sanctions in 2004 for the numerous linguistic errors in their judgements after the court in Sichuan held that a linguistic error in a court decision rendered the judgement a wrong decision (see Cao 2004).

Possible Legal Consequences of Chinese Linguistic Uncertainty

A number of implications can be drawn from the foregoing discussion. Language used in law as in other areas is characterised by indeterminacy, or 'open textureness' as Hart (1961/1992) calls it, with a core of 'settled meaning' and a 'penumbra of uncertainty'. The English legal language is not immune from imprecise and ambiguous expressions (see Solan 2004; Charnock 2006). English legal jargon such as 'fair and reasonable', or 'due process of law' is vague and elusive. So are abstract legal expressions such as 'justice', 'due diligence' and 'reasonable endeavours'. However, I see the Chinese language and legal language as more indeterminate than its English counterpart. If we describe this indeterminacy in terms of Hart's 'core' and 'penumbra', the Chinese settled core would seem smaller and the penumbra and open textureness larger. If this is the case, then, would Chinese law be more uncertain than common law in English?

I believe that Chinese law should not be more uncertain than English law, but in reality, it is, at present and for the foreseeable future. Major reasons, I believe, are the lack of coherent and consistent legal narrative in China; the lack of precedent which may settle indeterminate cases in reference to a settled past legal history as it exists in English common law; and furthermore, the lack of an independent judiciary in China. Legal rules and judicial interpretation I refer to here differ from legislative interpretation practised in China when the Supreme People's Court issues binding legislative interpretation to define statutory provisions. This is very different from case law determined on the basis of legal dispute and precedent.

Endicott (2000), in his study of indeterminate language and law in English, points to a paradox in law. On the one hand, he notes that, for law and the rule of law, there is a consensus about the requirements: law must be open, clear, coherent, prospective and stable (for instance, see Raz 1979). Law that fails to meet these requirements would not be law, and a legal system that lacks them to some degree is defective in a legal sense (Endicott 2000, 185). So, either such linguistic 'unclarity', be it vagueness, ambiguity or generality, must be eliminated in the language used in law, or law and rule of law cannot be attained and arbitrary government will result. On the other hand, linguistic uncertainty is inherent in language, and cannot be eliminated, thus is 'ineliminable' from a legal system (Endicott 2000, 190). Furthermore, law commonly appeals to moral considerations, and such general moral evaluative considerations are necessarily vague. This is the most important source of vagueness in law (Endicott 2003, 114). Not every law needs to be vague, but all legal systems necessarily have vague, general and uncertain laws. In fact, it is inconceivable for a community to be completely regulated with precise and exact laws (Endicott 2000, 190). Given the above dilemma, Endicott argues that a vague law does not necessarily represent a deficit in the rule of law. By the same token, replacing a vague law with a precise law does not necessarily bring a community closer to the ideal of the rule of law (Endicott 2000, 191). But what is important here is that the judiciary plays a critical role in making law certain and stable.

In China's case, due to historical reasons and the influence of the civil law system and other legal and political reasons, its judiciary has not been able to fulfil the necessary role in stablising the law. The judiciary has been perennially weak and ineffectual. Furthermore, due to the lack of established legal rules and principles as they exist in common law, uncertain laws enable authorities to make arbitrary decisions or exempt their actions from the law as happens not infrequently throughout China's modern history. For instance, in common law, one long established rule in contract law is the parole evidence rule that a written instrument is deemed the complete and final expression of the contract parties and cannot be varied or contradicted by oral evidence. There are also numerous legal rules governing legislative interpretation in common law (see for example Côté 1999; Holland and Webb 2003; Bennion 2007) In China, courts in recent years have started to formulate legal rules, but they are not systematic and not binding. There is not yet a coherent body of legal principles or rules.

As we know, all languages are inherently uncertain, but an argument could be advanced that some languages may be more uncertain and indeterminate than others. As shown by the examples cited in this chapter, certain linguistic features in Chinese may be prone to produce more uncertainties when compared with other languages, such as English. I argue that the Chinese legal language is more uncertain than the English legal language. In this regard, a German jurist, Grossfeld (cited in Weisflog 1987, 206) believes that the English legal language, compared with the German legal language, is less concentrated or more 'open-textured'; and English legal concepts are vaguer. There are different views as to whether one language may be more ambiguous than others. For instance, Bally (1944) was sceptical of the idea, but Jespersen (1964) did not rule out *a priori* the possibility that some languages could be less inadequate than other languages, or that ambiguities may increase with the development of a language, both cited in Kooij (1971, 3-4).

In addition, it seems that Chinese language users, in this case, Chinese lawmakers and legal drafters, often take advantage of linguistic uncertainty. Inappropriate and defective use of language in Chinese legislation produces more uncertainty. Another observation is that Chinese legal language tends to be ordinary, that is, very close to ordinary, non-technical, non-specialist Chinese. The Chinese legal language has a growing legal vocabulary. However, in terms of syntax and other grammatical features, legal Chinese is very much like ordinary formal Chinese, which is in sharp contrast to legal English with an obsession with precision, sometimes bordering on excessiveness and incomprehensibility. Legal Chinese is often just as loose as ordinary Chinese. Improvement has been noted in recent years but adequate expression in Chinese legal drafting within the linguistic constraints is critical. Further improvement in this area will undoubtedly reduce some of the uncertainties in Chinese law, even though indeterminacy in language and law can never be eliminated, in Chinese and other tongues.

PART 2
An International Perspective

Chapter 7

Conceptual and Textual Structure in Legislative Texts

Andreas Lötscher

Legislative texts are often difficult to understand, for various reasons. Most important is the fact that the very function of such texts imposes specific limitations on their organisation and formulation. They have to be structured in small units, articles and paragraphs, which can be connected by overt linguistic means only to a limited degree. Moreover, legal texts may consist only of normative statements, for example, they are not allowed or allowed only to a very limited degree to contain purely informative additions, such as commentaries, explanations, metalinguistic remarks, or instruments commonly used in ordinary language to make texts more understandable. And finally, legal statements must be abstract and general, whereas easy understanding is helped by citing specific examples.

How can we then make legal texts transparent under such difficult conditions? Several strategies and principles have proven to be useful in daily practice. One such useful strategy originates from the general principle of showing the content structure in the formal structure of the lexicon and the text.

Comprehensibility of laws: a difficult issue

In this chapter, it is argued that legal texts can only partially fulfil the requirements of the necessary linguistic qualities such as clearness, simplicity and precision. First, these qualities often are contradictory in themselves, second legal texts are subject to specific textual restrictions, limiting the usual possibilities of making texts more comprehensible. As a way out of these problems, it is proposed to concentrate on the quality of transparency, exploiting the iconic qualities of texts: texts can show the structure of their content in their form.

Textual qualities of laws

'There are three rules for writing a novel. Unfortunately, no one knows what they are' (Somerset Maugham, cited in Brodie 1997, 15). When drafting laws, the situation seems different. Everybody knows the three rules: laws must be clear, simple and precise. *The Joint Practical Guide* (2003, 1) is just one representative authority among many that demands laws to be:[1]

(1) clear, easy to understand and unambiguous
(2) simple, concise, containing no unnecessary elements
(3) precise, leaving no uncertainty in the mind of the reader.

Some of these qualities do not appear specific to laws, but rather self-evident requirements for any text that has a practical purpose: laws as factual texts should present their information in a straightforward way; there is no reason for them to be redundant, verbose, poetic, or rhetorical. Comprehensibility is a basic quality of any texts intended to communicate content rather than to provide intellectual or aesthetic pleasure. *Prodesse* is the key word, the rhetorical *delectare* is to be neglected.

In a deeper sense, however, the need for these qualities can also be derived from the very function of laws as institutions of a democratic state. Quality must follow function. Clearness and precision guarantee legal certainty; they are an essential condition for the consistent interpretation of a text by all those involved – legislator, enforcement authority, citizens addressed by the law, judges. Otherwise no one could be sure whether they are following a regulation as it has been conceived by the legislator and will be applied by the authorities or by the courts. Simplicity is just another requirement for clarity. Unnecessary words make formulations less transparent, opaque, without making them more precise.[2] To illustrate my point, let us examine the following rule and see how its clarity may be improved by simple restyling as suggested by Kimble (2004):

Before restyling – Current rule 8(e)(2)
When two or more statements are made in the alternative and one of them if made independently would be sufficient, the pleading is not insufficient by the insufficiency of one or more of the alternative statements.

After restyling
If a party makes alternative statements, the pleading is sufficient if any of them is sufficient (Kimble 2004, 40).

If laws are clear, simple and precise, then hopefully they are easy to understand. When drafting laws, comprehensibility is more than simply a quality of a good text. It has political implications (see for example Champeil-Desplat 2006; Bergeal 2006). Sometimes, it is argued that laws are 'special' purpose texts, which by their nature can and must be understood only by lawyers (Murphy 2006). If this argument is used to justify the use by lawyers of special linguistic rules or deviant styles and word usage, then it is misguided. Language can only function if all people in a linguistic community use the same rules, whether the product is simple or complex. Laws in most

---

1 For other examples, see Tercier (1999, 261).

2 In the Swiss tradition and lore of law drafting it goes without saying that one has to avoid irrelevant verbiage in statements and formulations; as such the example above before restyling never would have been accepted.

cases are equally applicable to non-lawyers as they are to lawyers. In a democratic society laws should be understood by the persons to whom they apply so that they can judge for themselves what the implications of a provision are and are not dependent on lawyers to do this for them. Incomprehensibility implies inequality (see for example Cacciaguidi-Fahy and Wagner 2006, 22, 24, 28). Comprehensibility also can contribute to the acceptance of laws: only a law that can be understood by the average citizen is perceived to be a fair law (Kindermann 1986).[3] Laws are not normally the sort of texts that are loved by their addressees.[4] They contain prohibitions, duties such as paying taxes, and punitive sanctions. If one has to communicate a message that is not very welcome to the addressee, one should be particularly careful in formulating it. In this sense, laws have to comply with what is normally expected of well drafted texts, which includes their being comprehensible.

Last but not least, laws should be visually, structurally and terminologically well-ordered texts in a general way: they should be formulated in a coherent and consistent way, and this is so just for politeness. If you want to treat your addressee in a decent way, you should give your message a decent form, irrespective of its content. This is especially true of texts of some importance, issued by institutions claiming legitimate authority. This is the way a legislator and in a broader sense the State can treat its addressees in a polite manner and show respect to them. Laws must be of a high linguistic quality, regardless of whether a specific text has to be understood by the average reader or just by specialists. Orderliness is not necessarily the same as clarity, precision, or even simplicity. Nevertheless, it can contribute to a better understanding and to more transparency.

The arguments put forward here have been repeated so often that they have almost become trite (Lang 1994; Rorvig 1999). It is no secret that laws are not normally good texts in the sense described. In fact, it is a common criticism that laws are incomprehensible and lack transparency (see Scott and Zuleeg 2005). Yet, repeating the arguments seems to have little effect on the quality of laws. To vary Somerset Maugham's quote: 'everybody seems to know the three rules for writing a law, unfortunately no one seems to know how to apply them'.

On a closer look, there are some good reasons why this situation persists. Laws by their nature are rather 'special' and 'problematic' texts. One major problem is that, ultimately, the three rules are contradictory. Usually, they cannot be achieved simultaneously: you can not be simple and precise at the same time. Precision implies more detailed and thus less simple formulations; it means elaborate and complicated formulations that mention additional details. More details are less easy to process and render the flow of the text less clear. Sometimes precision is more necessary

---

3 See also the even more radical position cited in the foreword by Sir Thomas Bingham to Cutts (1994, 5): 'Absence of clarity is destructive of the rule of law.' A similar thought, concerning simplicity, can be found with Seneca (Epistolae, 94, 38) *'Legem enim brevem esse oportet, quo facilius ab inperitis teneatur'* [The law must be short, in order to be understood more easily by the uneducated].

4 'Addressee' is understood here as a subset of the 'audience of a text' (Smith 2003). For further discussion on the concept of addressee and audience theory, see Dan-Cohen (1984) and Stevenson (2003).

than simplicity. Precision may require formulations which are complicated enough to become clumsy and hard to understand. As an example, article 21(2) of the Swiss *Loi fédérale sur l'assurance-vieillesse et survivants (RS 831.10)* [Federal Act on Old-Age and Survivors' Insurance][5] defines the point in time at which the right to receive an old-age pension begins:

Art. 21 Rente de vieillesse
[1] Ont droit à une rente de vieillesse:
a. les hommes qui ont atteint 65 ans révolus;
b. les femmes qui ont atteint 64 ans révolus.
[2] Le droit à une rente de vieillesse prend naissance le premier jour du mois suivant celui où à été atteint l'âge prescrit à l'al. 1. Il s'éteint par le décès de l'ayant droit.

[Art. 21 Old-age pension
[1] The right to an old-age pension is held by:
a. men who have reached the age of 65;
b. women who have reached the age of 64.
[2] The right to an old-age pension arises on the first day of the month following that in which the age specified in paragraph 1 is attained. It expires on death].[6]

Given the different rights of men and women and the need to define the relevant point in time precisely, it is not possible to simplify this rather difficult formulation and to say, for example: 'Le droit à une rente de vieillesse prend naissance à l'âge de 65 ans' [The right to an old age pension starts at the age of 65 years old].

The following formulation for fixing tariffs for health treatment in health insurance further illustrates the point:

Art. 55 Etablissement des tarifs par les autorités d'approbation
[1] Lorsque, pour les traitements ambulatoires ou hospitaliers, les frais moyens par assuré et par année dans l'assurance de soins obligatoire augmentent au moins deux fois plus que la moyenne de l'évolution générale des prix et des salaires, l'autorité compétente peut ordonner que les tarifs ou les prix de l'ensemble ou d'une partie des prestations ne doivent plus être augmentés, aussi longtemps que la différence relative du taux annuel de croissance est de plus de 50 % comparée à l'évolution générale des prix et des salaires (*Loi fédérale sur l'assurance-maladie (RS 832.10)*).

[If the average costs per insured person and year for compulsory health insurance for in-patient and out-patient treatment increase by at least twice the general increase in prices and salaries, the authority responsible may order that the tariffs or prices for all or for specific services may not be increased, so long as the relative difference in the annual growth rate amounts to more than 50 per cent measured against the general increase in prices and salaries (Federal Act on Health Insurance)].

In this provision, no condition mentioned can be omitted; otherwise a relevant condition will be omitted. In addition, the last part is rather difficult to understand

---

5 Unless otherwise stated all examples used in this chapter are drawn from Swiss legislation.
6 All translations provided in this chapter are my translations.

for simple mathematical reasons: it is hard for the average reader to work out what the relative difference between the annual increase in health costs and the increase in general prices and salaries are. But the provision provides a precise rule of when it is possible to stop the increase in prices for health services.

Simplicity does not necessarily result in comprehensibility either. Regulations can theoretically be made simpler by giving them a more general, abstract formulation. The implications and consequences of a statement are more difficult to draw from an abstract formulation than from more specific formulations. A good example of the comprehension difficulties that arise from an abstract formulation is the definition of 'livraison des biens' [supply of goods] in the *Loi fédérale régissant la taxe sur la valeur ajoutée (RS 641.20)* [Federal Act on Value Added Tax].[7]

> Art. 6 Livraison de biens
> [1] Il y a livraison lorsque le pouvoir de disposer économiquement d'un bien est accordé à une personne en son propre nom
> [There is a supply if a person acquires the power of economic disposal over the goods in his own name].

'Livraison' [supply] comprises every form of change of possession, such as selling, giving away, exchanging, etc. The definition is general enough to include any forms of change of possession that are not foreseeable in reality. To the lay reader, it is so general and abstract that s/he has to think for a while before realising that selling also is a form of change of possession. In any case, it may be simpler than listing every form of change of possession one can think of – and safer than a list – but nevertheless hard for anyone who reads it for the first time.[8]

Thus, the possibilities of simplification are often limited; and after simplifying formulations wherever possible, you are still left with many provisions that are not easy to understand. Ultimately, if the drafter has to chose between simplicity and precision, precision must usually be evaluated more highly.

Comprehensibility strategies in ordinary language

The conflicts between precision and simplicity are of a fundamental nature; and they arise in ordinary language as well as in specialised texts. To remedy such conflicts, everyday language has developed various strategies. Some of these are:

Contextuality Everyday communication makes use of contextual information and Grice's (1975) conversational rules in the interpretation of utterances. You do not have to be too specific in formulating a thought, since you can rely on the contextual

---

7 The consolidated texts of Swiss laws published in the *Recueil systématique du droit fédéral* are accessible at <www.admin.ch>. Texts from Swiss legislation are cited in French, German and Italian.

8 Whether a formulation should be more abstract or more specific (and enumerative) is also a question of principle and the judicial system: abstract formulations give more freedom of interpretation to the enforcement authorities and the courts. On the other hand, Tiersma (1999, 83) shows that in practice a list is not equivalent to an abstract general term.

information and the principles of efficient communication. No utterance can ever be as precise as intended, but you can rely on the fact that the addressee will complete the information necessary for understanding from other information accessible in the communication situation and the rest of the text. As a result, your contribution will be sufficiently precise even if you omit important information and you can keep your formulations relatively simple.

Variation In ordinary language communication, one often tries to make a statement understandable by formulating the same thought in several different ways. One can look at a concept from different points of view, whereby none of the different wordings for the same thought may be entirely appropriate, but all the wordings when taken together can transmit the meaning intended by complementing each other.

Summaries and elaborations In everyday texts, one hardly ever communicates a thought in one single passage. Rather one starts and/or ends a report or an argument with a summary of the content and adds details to it at the appropriate moments. A summary enables the reader to build up an overall concept of the framework, to focus their expectations in the appropriate directions and to fill in the details as efficiently as possible in the given whole.

Concreteness and exemplification Concrete information is more understandable than abstract information, because one can draw implicational information directly from factual knowledge rather than by applying general rules of logic. An abstract assertion can be made more easily comprehensible by amplifying it with specific examples. A specific example illustrating a general abstract statement, however, usually has less relevance and reliability than the general statement.

Explanatory elaboration When it is difficult for a reader to find the relevant implications or presuppositions of an assertion, the writer can help him by supplying this information himself. Thus the author may explain the causal background of the events described and their further consequences. He thereby creates a network of primary and secondary information.

Metalinguistic commentaries The author can support the understanding of a text by giving metalinguistic comments on the thread of thoughts, on the structure of the argument, on the particular function of a specific proposition in the whole of the text. Ordinary language texts usually move simultaneously on different communicative and functional levels, not only with regard to the implicit message, but also on the level of the explicit linguistic structure.

Limitations of comprehensibility strategies in laws

Unfortunately, in many cases the above strategies used in ordinary language to enhance comprehensibility do not apply to laws: laws cannot be contextualised as freely as ordinary language. They provide universally applicable rules and are formulated without regard to a specific context or situation. Not only do they have to be written more precisely than everyday texts in order to be understood outside a specific context; they are also read without a connection to a context, which makes processing more difficult than in the usual case. Of necessity, laws are written in an impersonal, formalised style. The technical, specialised language and impersonal style causes legislative texts to be of an exclusive character that is not easily accessible to persons who lack the required specialist knowledge.

More importantly, the fundamental principle *lex iubeat, ne doceat*, laws must formulate provisions, not argue or give explanations, applies.[9] Thus laws in a way are extremely 'monofunctional' texts allowing only normative statements as elements. There are good reasons for this restriction. The sole purpose of a law is to lay down rules. If statements other than regulations were allowed, one could never be sure of the sense in which a statement should be interpreted. An explanation or example could be interpreted as a normative statement, and vice versa. The principle also implies 'expressive parsimony': giving two or more parallel or similar formulations for one and the same regulation is out of the question. Were this to be done, no one could decide which formulation was relevant. This is a fundamental difference from the strategies of ordinary language, where redundancy is one of the most effective means of ensuring comprehension. From this restriction, it follows that almost all of the comprehensibility strategies mentioned above, such as giving explanations, commentaries, specific examples for abstract statements, metalinguistic remarks explaining the thread of thought, are not applicable to legal texts.

Evidently, when one has to do without such strategies of helping the reader through a complex and abstract text, it is rather difficult to create easily comprehensible texts.

Iconicity and transparency

What then can we do to improve the clarity and comprehensibility of legal texts? Do we have to accept these difficulties and assume that laws by their nature lack transparency? I do not think so. If we cannot achieve simplicity, we can at least strive for maximum transparency. Situations and rules may be very complicated, and it may be difficult to formulate laws in a simple way, but this does not mean that there are no ways of improving transparency. Complex texts with complex content may require more efforts to process, but they need not be opaque. Complexity does not inevitably mean lack of clarity.

Well-ordered texts tend to be transparent. There are basic cognitive reasons for this. What is a well-ordered text? A basic principle is to present a thought in the order and with the structure that an ordinary reader would employ in his own thought processes. This way of developing a thought appears 'natural' and 'logical'. The reader finds the thoughts in the order in which he expects them without much reflection. A text appears 'natural' when it is organised sequentially according to the most effective cognitive reception and text processing strategies at hand, in the same way that people instinctively organise und present a complex thought. It appears

---

9 The idea must be quite old, as it is mentioned in Seneca (Epistolae 94, 38): '*lex iubeat, non disputet*' [The law must command, not discuss].

'logical', if it is organised structurally so as to resemble the cognitive structuring of the correlated complex thought. Semiotically, this amounts to exploiting the iconic possibilities of any textual representation of a conceptual structure. It consists in modelling the superficial material structure of a text according to the conceptual structure of the content and the temporal order of the processing of a thought.

Another principle of good ordering consists in being systematic, in that one uses the same organising principles throughout the whole text. If one follows this principle, readers tend to form expectations and appropriate reception strategies, and they need not analyse the whole structure of a text every time a new subject is dealt with in order to find out how it is organised.

To sum up, if you are not allowed to explain and clarify the complex content and the structure of regulations by examples, explanations and metalinguistic commentaries, it is at least possible to achieve more transparency and comprehensibility by applying, wherever possible, the iconic principle in the textual organisation.

This strategy, an elementary principle of the semiotics of communication, is of course not new; it has long featured in all kinds of legal texts (see Ames 1980; Leeds-Hurwitz 1993; Ost and Van de Kerchove 1992; Jackson 1992). The principles of logical, natural and systematic ordering of texts have been applied by writers for centuries (see Jackson 1987; Faralli and Pattaro 1988; Jackson 1993; Freeman 1998). Accordingly, in what follows I will often mention well-known principles, which are also applied explicitly or implicitly in works such as *The Joint Practical Guide* (2003) or in Cutts (1994; 2000). In most cases, these rules are formulated by chance/haphazardly, in response to specific cases, without any systematic discussion of the problems and potential for making laws more comprehensible. My aim is to develop a more general view on these strategies and to demonstrate how the many specific rules can be seen as applications of very general strategies. I will base my argument on the drafting rules used within the Swiss Federal Administration, in which the principles of 'plain legal language' are more readily accepted than in many other administrations.[10] Nevertheless, some of the examples demonstrate that optimal solutions are difficult to find in any tradition.

Moreover, it is not always evident what specific rules and strategies derive from a general principle. Even when we know the general principle, applying it in a specific case is not always straightforward. From the presentation below of examples for solutions one might get the impression that it is evident why a formulation is a bad one and how one could find a better one; or one could conclude that the solution is obvious and that everybody could have found it. But all the examples of unsatisfactory formulations I present below are taken from authentic texts, (in many cases from drafts that have been subsequently restyled before final adoption and publication), written by experts in law drafting. This may provide adequate evidence that it is a

---

10 All drafts for federal acts are checked for their linguistic correctness and quality by a Committee for legal drafting, (Commission interne de rédaction (CIR), see its website <http://www.bk.admin.ch> -> La Chancellerie fédérale > Organisation de la Chancellerie fédérale > Secteur Conseil fédéral > Services linguistiques) made of jurists and linguists. This ensures professionalism and application of interdisciplinary know-how in drafting and a coherent practice.

far from trivial task for law drafters to find good solutions and to apply the general principles in individual cases. A well-ordered structure is sometimes evident only after it has been achieved with a measure of creative effort. What it would be is not immediately obvious in a badly written text.[11]

Levels of iconicity and transparency

This chapter explores the possibilities of iconic transparency at the different linguistic levels of a text: layout, terminology, sentence structure and paragraph structure. Each level shows its specific structural problems, and for each level, specific maxims can be formulated, not all new to law drafting. But they can be seen as the result of the same basic principles of creating transparency by structural clarity, and a unified view and a systematic application of these principles can provide a more coherent framework for law drafting.

Layout and transparency

The iconic principle works most obviously on the typographic level. When you can see a structure on paper, you can detect the content structure of the text much more quickly. This is the concept on which the lay out organization of legal texts in most countries is based, for example. the structuring of the units of a text into subparts such as sections, subsections, articles, paragraphs, letters etc.; and the typographical rules that make such subdivisions visible. The text presented as in the lay out structure after restyling below, which follows the requirement mentioned in the final sentence of the text before restyling, is easier to process due to its structure:

Before restyling
15. As far as possible, the enacting terms shall have a standard structure (subject matter and scope – definitions – rights and obligations – provisions conferring implementing powers – procedural provisions – implementing measures – transitional and final provisions)
The enacting terms shall be subdivided into articles and, depending on their length and complexity, titles, chapters and sections. When an article contains a list, each item on the list should be identified by a number or a letter rather than an indent (*Interinstitutional Agreement of 22 December 1998 on common guidelines for the quality of drafting of Community legislation* (1999/C 73/01)).

After restyling[12]
15 (1) As far as possible, the enacting terms shall have the following standard structure:

---

11 There is one more fundamental point to writing clearly: Unless you have well ordered ideas you cannot write a well ordered text. But then, thoughts are only made clear by writing a clear text, and texts usually become clear only after much rewriting, as all of us know.
12 All restyling is my own restyling.

  a. subject matter and scope,
  b. definitions,
  c. rights and obligations,
  d. provisions conferring implementing powers,
  e. procedural provisions,
  f. implementing measures,
  g. transitional and final provisions.

(2) The enacting terms shall be subdivided into articles and, depending on their length and complexity, titles, chapters and sections.

(3) When an article contains a list, each item on the list should be identified by a number or a letter rather than an indent.

Although the strategy of showing the logical structure of a provision in its typographical presentation seems to be universally accepted and used in western law drafting, there are substantial differences among the different countries and their drafting traditions. They have developed differing guidelines which, generally speaking, make texts more transparent by using a variety of type faces, narrower or wider spaces between lines, and clearly identifiable indentations (Cutts 1994, 9f). In some systems, the numbering is not fully systematic in that indents without numbering or letters are used at the lowest level or the optical structure of a statement is blurred by mixing phrases and numbering:[13]

(1) Where a person—

> (a) has entered, or proposes to enter, into a timeshare agreement on which this Act applies as offeree, and
>
> (b) has received the notice required under section 2 of this Act before entering into the agreement,

the agreement may not be enforced against him on or before the date specified in the notice in pursuance of subsection (2)(a) of that section and he may give notice of cancellation of the agreement to the offeror at any time on or before that date (*Timeshare Act* 1992, as cited in Cutts 1994, 56f.).

The different listing systems show that any efforts to make the structure of a text more transparent by typographical means usually lead to the introduction of more text structuring instruments, such as numbering or adding headings to sections. This goes beyond a purely typographical means of the presentation of a text. On the other hand, these elements would not make sense without typographical structuring. Generally, a system of making texts more transparent on the typographical level usually involves a combination of layout rules and structure marking devices.

One caveat has to be added to the merits of typography: typographic transparency is no cure-all for making laws comprehensible and transparent. The clear typographical structure of a text must correspond to a real logical structure; it has iconic quality only if there is a similarity between the material appearance and the logical form. It is easy to construct texts that are perfectly structured typographically, but which in reality are a confusion of *membra disjecta* [scattered fragments]. Such texts do not

---

13 Within the Swiss law drafting system, this way of organisation of a paragraph is not allowed.

become less opaque as a result of their elaborate typography (see below section on '*Use layout according to logical structure*').

Transparency in vocabulary and terminology

Another instance of iconicity which may contribute to greater clarity can be found in the well-ordered use of vocabulary. Identity or differences among concepts should be visible in the structure and use of vocabulary. This is the rationale of the rule 'same meaning, same form', to which the rule 'different meanings, different forms' can be added. This implies consistent use of vocabulary.

Same meaning, same form In ordinary language, the rhetorical maxim of *variatio delectat* [variety is the spice of life] is often followed. Repetition is regarded as boring and bad style. In legal texts, precision and clarity are more important than stylistic elaboration. Variety in vocabulary results in a lack of transparency, because it is no longer clear whether the different expressions used relate to one or more concepts.[14] Once a specific expression for a concept has been introduced, the same expression should be used throughout the text. Moreover, a specific fact should be described from the same point of view. In the next example, in the first draft, the expressions 'action' [action] and 'intenter' [to file, to bring, to institute] are used in first paragraph, in the second paragraph 'prétention' [claim] and 'élever' [to raise], although in both cases the same actions are meant. In the second case, obviously a different, more specific description of the same situation is given. This blurs the fact that the same condition is indicated in both cases:

Art. 17 Cumul d'actions
(1) Lorsque *l'action* est *intentée* contre plusieurs consorts, le tribunal compétent à l'égard d'un défendeur l'est à l'égard de tous les autres.
(2) Lorsque plusieurs ~~prétentions~~ *actions* qui présentent un lien de connexité entre elles sont ~~élevées~~ *intentées* contre un même défendeur, chaque tribunal compétent pour connaître de l'une d'elle est compétent (Projet de Loi fédérale de procédure civile – [Draft Federal Act on Civil Procedure]).

[Art. 17 Joinder of actions
(1) If an *action is filed* against two or more defendants, the court that is competent for one defendant is competent for all defendants.
(2) If two or more ~~claims~~ actions with connected subject matter are ~~raised~~ filed against the same defendant, any court is competent that is competent for any one of the ~~claims~~ actions].

---

14 The point is considered here from the perspective of iconicity. There is another related perspective, that of the maxims used by judges in the interpretation of laws: when different words are used, one has to presume that different meanings are intended. Judges have a different approach to the relevance of variation than people in ordinary conversation do. But still, this maxim of interpretation derives from the general maxim of relevance of Grice (1975). The underlying assumption is that if the legislator had intended to communicate the same meaning, he would have used the same words, an assumption not made so strictly in ordinary language.

Correlated meaning, correlated form Less obvious on the level of the vocabulary structure is the use of corresponding expressions for corresponding concepts, for instance in the same terminological field. In the example below, the expressions 'consonorité nécessaire' [Mandatory joinder of parties] and 'consorité simple' [simple joinder of parties] are combined as contrasting expressions in the headings of the two articles. The two situations designated are contraries, being related by a negation: 'necessary – not necessary = optional' The corresponding terms used traditionally – 'nécessaire' [necessary], 'simple' [simple] – do not reflect this relation; lexically they have no semantic connection at the level of the original lexical meaning. It would be more transparent to use antonyms that form a lexical pair and thereby to show at the level of the vocabulary that the two expressions reflect opposing situations. (The original formulation also breaks the rule of 'same expression for the same concept' in the formulation of the regulation itself).

> Art. 63 Consorité nécessaire
>> Les parties à un rapport de droit qui n'est susceptible que d'une décision unique doivent agir ou être actionnées conjointement.
> Art. 64 Consorité simple *facultative*
>> Les personnes dont les droits et les devoirs résultent de faits et de fondements juridiques semblables peuvent agir ou être actionnées comme consorts simples *conjointement* (Projet de Loi fédérale de procédure civile).

> [Art. 63 Mandatory joinder of parties
>> The parties to a legal relationship in respect of which only one decision may be made must file actions or have actions filed against them jointly.
> Art. 64 Simple *Voluntary* joinder of parties
>> Persons whose rights and obligations arise from circumstances or legal grounds that are similar may file actions or have actions filed against them as simple joint parties *jointly* (Draft Federal Act on Civil Procedure)].

Transparency in formulations

Same formulation for same kind of provision The principle of using vocabulary that reflects identity or differences in content also applies to entire statements. When you have to describe the same situation in two statements, you should use the same wording for it. The example below illustrates how confusion can arise when two different formulations are used for the same action; you do not know whether the action to be taken by the state in subparagraph (a) is the same as that in subparagraph (b). In fact, there are no differences between the two on this point. Confusion is also created by the differences in the word order between the two subparagraphs. It is helpful for comprehension to use the same clause structure in all parallel cases:

> Before restyling
> Le montant des contributions globales accordées au promoteur est fixé en fonction de l'effet. Il:

a. se *monte à 80% au plus des coûts* occasionnés par les innovations pouvant être pris en compte;
b. *comprend une contribution* de la Confédération représentant *50% au plus des frais* de gestion et d'administration pouvant être pris en compte.

[The amount of the global contributions to the organising body is determined according to the effect. It:
a. *amounts to a maximum of 80% of the costs attributable to the innovations in question*;
b. *includes a contribution from the Confederation* to the management and administrative costs amounting to *a maximum of 50% of the attributable costs*].

After restyling
Le taux des contributions est fixé en fonction de l'effet écologique et agronomique des projets et des mesures ainsi que de leur efficacité. Il s'élève à:
a. *80% au plus des coûts* pouvant être pris en compte s'il s'agit de contributions allouées pour la réalisation de projets ou de mesures;
b. *50% au plus des frais* pouvant être pris en compte s'il s'agit de contributions allouées pour la couverture des frais de gestion et d'administration (Projet de Loi fédérale sur l'agriculture).
[The amount of the global contributions is determined according to the ecological and agronomic effect of the projects and the measures as well as their efficiency. It amounts:
a. *to a maximum of 80% of the attributable costs* in the case of contributions for the implementation of the projects and measures that result in innovations;
b. to *a maximum of 50% of the attributable costs* in the case of contributions to the costs of management and administration (Draft of the revised Federal Act on Agriculture)].

Type and grammatical structure of provisions Transparency necessitates that one should be able to recognise the type and the relevant normative content of a provision from its formulation. A certain situation or action can be considered from different points of view, and consequently a description of this situation can be formulated in different ways. A formulation for such a situation or action can be organised in grammatically different ways, depending for example on the specific verb chosen. From a normative perspective, it is important to formulate a provision in a way that shows the logically and normatively relevant parts and relations within the situation described as directly as possible. Accordingly, the following principle can be stated: formulate a provision in such a way as to make its type and logical structure evident by its grammatical form. Thus by its iconic quality, the structure of a sentence can make the relevant structure of the provision more conspicuous.

In the next example, the draft provision is formulated as a possible action of the court. This action involves a party, who is given a more detailed description ('la partie manifestement hors d'état de conduire elle-même son procès' [a party who is clearly unable to conduct his own case]). On closer inspection, a condition for taking a specific action is found to be concealed in this description of the person involved. It would be more transparent to formulate this condition in a conditional clause. This would show the logical structure of the provision more directly, which consists in a connection of a condition with a consequence:

Before restyling

Art. 62 Partie hors d'état de procéder

> Le tribunal peut engager la partie manifestement hors d'état de conduire elle-même son procès à constituer un mandataire.

[Art. 62 Party unable to conduct own case

The court may request a party who is clearly unable to conduct his own case to instruct an agent].

After restyling

Art. 62 Incapacité de procéder

> Si une partie est manifestement incapable de procéder elle-même, le tribunal peut l'inviter à commettre un mandataire (Projet de Loi fédérale de procédure civile).

[Art. 62 Inability to conduct own case

If a party is clearly unable to conduct his own case, the court may request him to instruct an agent (Draft for a new Federal Act on Civil Procedure)].

Remember the addressee (who has a duty or a right?) Another way to conceal the relevant points of a provision is to omit to mention who the person involved in an action is, whether as the one who has a duty or who has a right. One can also blur the relevant point by changing the perspective. Often the drafter of a provision who works for the authorities concerned looks at a situation from the point of view of the authorities and formulates the provision accordingly. But in many cases, what should be regulated in the first place is not the reaction of an authority to the action of an individual, but the right of this individual. Thus the provision should be formulated from the point of view of the individual. The next example indicates which claims can be accepted from the standpoint of the court; however, the provision in fact states a rule for the person who wishes to file a claim: he is the one who will initiate this action. The provision thus restricts the specific right of a party rather than giving the court a specific competence to decide.

Before restyling

Art. 46 Intérêt juridique

> Les demandes et requêtes sont irrecevables faute d'intérêt digne de protection.

[Claims and applications are inadmissible unless there is an interest that is worthy of protection.]

After restyling

Art. 46 Intérêt juridique

> La qualité pour intenter une action ou présenter une requête est subordonnée à l'existence d'un intérêt juridique ou d'un intérêt digne de protection (Projet de Loi fédérale de procédure civile).

[The right to file an action or application is dependent on their being a related legal interest or interest worthy of protection (Draft for a Federal Act on Civil Procedure)].

Do not combine different types of information in one single provision Transparency requires that a formulation should not combine contents of different normative type. One way to violate this principle involves merging definitional and normative elements in one statement, usually a definition. This practice is not uncommon in EU directives. Often, definitions include elements which conceal a prohibition or a command. In the following example, the definition of 'installateur d'un ascenseur' [installer of a lift] includes properties which are not necessarily fulfilled by the average 'installer of a lift', namely that of complying with a provision contained in the same directive – what about the installers that do not comply with these requirements? Are they not regarded as installers under the directive?

4. Aux fins de la présente directive:
– l'installateur d'un ascenseur est la personne physique ou morale qui assume la responsabilité de la conception, de la fabrication, de l'installation et de la mise sur le marché de l'ascenseur, *et qui appose le marquage "CE" et établit la déclaration "CE" de conformité* (my emphasis),
[...]
– le fabricant des composants de sécurité est la personne physique ou morale qui assume la responsabilité de la conception et de la fabrication des composants de sécurité, *et qui appose le marquage "CE" et établit la déclaration "CE" de conformité* (my emphasis) (article 1(4) *Directive 95/16/EC*).

[– The 'installer of a lift' shall mean the natural or legal person who takes responsibility for the design, manufacture, installation *and placing on the market of the lift and who affixes the CE marking and draws up the EC declaration of conformity*
[...]
– The 'manufacturer of the safety components' shall mean the natural or legal person who takes responsibility for the design and manufacture of the safety *components and who affixes the CE marking and draws up the EC declaration of conformity*].[15]

In the next example, a definition of 'air' is combined with a delimitation of the scope of a directive. It is rather puzzling to see 'ambient air' defined in a roundabout way as outdoor air only. In reality, what the formulation is intended to accomplish is to restrict the provisions of the directive to outdoor areas. Transparency would require that this restriction of the scope of the directive is stated explicitly and not packed in a definition of ambient air:

Aux fins de la présente directive, on entend par:
– 'air ambiant': l'air extérieur de la troposphère, *à l'exclusion des lieux de travail* ['ambient air' means outdoor air in the troposphere, *excluding work places*] (my emphasis) (article 2(2) *Directive 2002/3/EC*).[16]

Do not introduce norms tacitly A provision should mention the point that is regulated and not regulate any aspect of some other matter that is only of minor overall importance. It sometimes happens that in a specific, restricted view, procedural problems are explicitly dealt with while the matters that constitute the main point of some action are tacitly presumed as given. For example, article 67(1) below presupposes that the intervening person has successfully filed a request; this important requirement is not expressly mentioned in the provision itself, although, it is one of the main points of the whole provision, and should be introduced explicitly as one of the basic requirements of the procedure.

Before restyling
Section 4: Intervention
Art. 66 Conditions
Le tiers qui rend vraisemblable un intérêt juridique personnel à ce qu›un procès pendant soit jugé en faveur de l›une des parties peut intervenir à titre accessoire en tout temps.
Art. 67 Requête
[1] *La requête en intervention* indique:
    a. le motif de l'intervention;
    b. la partie en faveur de laquelle elle a lieu.
[2] Le tribunal statue après audition des parties.

[Section 4: Intervention
Art. 66 Requirements
[1] Anyone who credibly asserts a personal legal interest in an ongoing dispute being decided in favour of one or other of the parties *may intervene in the proceedings at any time as a joint party.*
Art. 67 Application
[1] *The application to intervene* contains:
    a. the grounds for intervention;
    b. the details of the party in favour of whom intervention is being made.
[2] The court decides *on the application* after hearing the parties].

After restyling
Art. 66 Intervention
[1] Quiconque rend plausible un intérêt juridique à ce qu'un litige pendant soit jugé en faveur de l'une des parties *peut en tout temps présenter une requête en intervention.*
[2] *La requête en intervention* indique:
    a. le motif de l'intervention;
    b. la partie en faveur de laquelle elle a lieu.
[3] Le tribunal statue après avoir entendu les parties (Projet de Loi fédérale de procédure civile).

[Art. 66 Intervention
[1] Anyone who credibly asserts a personal legal interest in having an ongoing dispute decided in favour of one or other of the parties *may apply to intervene in the proceedings at any time.*
[2] *The application to intervene* contains:
    a. the grounds for intervention;
    b. the details of party in favour of whom intervention is being made.

[3] The court decides *on the application* after hearing the parties (draft for a Federal Act on Civil Procedure)].

Transparency in text structure

Insofar as text structure can reflect the logical and conceptual structure of a regulation it can have iconic qualities and thereby create transparency. There are several different aspects to this.

One thought – one provision One of the simplest rules of iconicity on the level of text structure is not to combine two or more provisions into the one sentence; or: 'one thought – one provision'; 'one provision – one thought'. Paragraph 1 of the following example combines a provision on the calculation of export contributions for fruit juice and the point in time at which they are paid – in fact, this is not very visible in the original wording, but this is what it should mean. These two aspects of the regulation concern two different subject matters and should be formulated separately:

> Before restyling
> Art. 7 Calcul des contributions à l'exportation
> > [1] Les contributions à l'exportation de concentré de jus de pommes et de poires sont calculées *d'avance par période d'exportation selon des taux uniformes* sur la base (my emphasis):
> > > a. d'un calcul du prix de revient [...]
>
> [Art. 7 Calculation of export contributions
> [1] The export contributions for apple and pear juice concentrates are calculated *in advance of each export period according to standard rates* on the basis of: a. a calculation of the cost price [...]].

> After restyling
> Art. 7 Calcul des contributions à l'exportation
> > [1] Les contributions à l'exportation de concentré de jus de pommes et de poires *sont allouées selon des taux uniformes. Ceux-ci sont calculés d'avance par période d'exportation, sur la base* (my emphasis):
> > > a. d'un calcul du prix de revient [...] (Projet de révision de *Ordonnance sur les fruits et les légumes,* RS 916.131.11).
>
> [Art. 7 Calculation of export contributions
> [1] The export contributions for apple and pear juice concentrates *are granted according to standard rates: They are calculated in advance of each export period on the basis of:* a. a calculation of the cost price [...] (Draft for the revision of Ordinance RS 916.131.11 relating to Fruits and Vegetables)].

Do not mix up provisions of different types in one text unit The elaborate systems of multi-layered subdivisions in most laws only make sense if their respective parts have a thematic unity, differentiating them from other parts. It is especially important that smaller parts such as lists should meet this requirement and be thematically homogeneous. When two provisions are thematically distinct, they have to be organised in different textual unities. An article such as the one cited below does not comply with this principle in that it mixes up several different subject-matters and types of provisions in a uniform list. This way of presentation lacks transparency, and in any case there is no correspondence between the homogeneous structure of the list and the differences in the regulation types:

Article premier
Champ d'application   Purpose of the regulation
1. Le présent règlement établit les règles générales
en matière d'hygiène des denrées alimentaires à
l'intention des exploitants du secteur alimentaire
en tenant particulièrement compte des principes
suivants:

a) la responsabilité première en matière de   Principles of the regulation
sécurité alimentaire incombe à l'exploitant du
secteur alimentaire;
b) il est nécessaire de garantir la sécurité
alimentaire à toutes les étapes de la chaîne
alimentaire depuis la production primaire.
[...]
f) il est nécessaire de fixer des critères
microbiologiques et des exigences en matière
de contrôle de la température fondés sur une
évaluation scientifique des risques;
g) il est nécessaire de garantir que les denrées
alimentaires importées répondent au moins
aux mêmes normes sanitaires que celles
produites dans la Communauté, ou à des normes
équivalentes.

Le présent règlement s'applique à toutes les   Scope
étapes de la production, de la transformation et
de la distribution des denrées alimentaires ainsi
qu'aux exportations. Il s'applique sans préjudice
d'exigences plus spécifiques en matière d'hygiène
alimentaire
(*Règlement No 852/2004 (CE)*).[17]

Use layout according to logical structure   As mentioned, a clearly structured layout only makes sense if it corresponds to the logical structure of the text. In the following example, taken from the *Joint Practical Guide* (2003, 17) the version before restyling is cited as an example of drafting that should be avoided because of its over-complexity, and the revised version is proposed as the text to be preferred.

---

17 Official translation available at <http://eur-lex.europa.eu/LexUriServ/LexUriServ. do?uri=OJ:L:2004:139:0001:0054:EN:PDF>, 3.

Before restyling
The market prices of [product X] shall be the prices ex-factory, exclusive of national taxes
and charges:
    (a) of the fresh product packaged in blocks;
    (b) raised by an amount of [EUR X] to take account of the transport costs necessary.

After restyling
(1) The market prices of [product X] shall be the prices ex-factory of the fresh product
packaged in blocks, exclusive of national taxes and charges.
(2) Those prices shall be raised by an amount of [EUR X] to take account of the transport
costs necessary (cited in the *Joint Practical Guide* (2003, 17)).

The main logical problem of the original version, however, is not over-complexity,
but the different logical status of the letters (a) and (b) within the provision. (a)
indicates the type of product to which the provision is applied, (b) indicates the way
the market price is to be calculated; elements of this calculation, however, appear
in the introductory part of the provision as well. The revised version still is not
systematic in this point, in that the various aspects to be considered in fixing a price
for a product, namely the relevant shape of the product and the elements of the price
that are to be included or excluded, are intermingled in the textual organisation. A
more transparent presentation, separating these two aspects in a more clear-cut way,
would be:

After second restyling
The market prices of [product X] shall be the prices ex-factory of the fresh product
packaged in blocks:
    (a) exclusive of national taxes and charges;
    (b) raised by an amount of [EUR X] to take account of the transport costs necessary.

Organise complex provisions according to natural ordering principles As set out
earlier, a complex text appears to be well-ordered and comprehensible when it is
organised sequentially following the usual cognitive strategies of dealing with a
complex mental structure. There are a few evident general principles for this, the
most important being:

- give a general description before going into details
- describe the normal case before describing the special case
- describe the normal case before describing deviant cases
- follow the chronological order of events.

Following the chronological order in a description is clearly an instance of iconic
presentation of a situation. The other principles are based on the fact that processing a
text means constructing a model of a reality (for cognitive models of text processing
see, for example, Rickheit and Strohner 1999). It is much easier to construct a model
by starting with an overall structure and filling in details than having to assemble
individual pieces to make a whole. The principle of text organisation in this case

amounts to leading the reader through a model in the chronological sequence he would choose himself for orientation:

- applied to the usual text units in a law, this gives the following general rules for organizing complex provisions
- general provision before exceptions
- general provision before special cases
- general provision before details
- chronological order.

These rules appear to be simple and self evident; nevertheless, one can easily find laws where they are neglected. The following example excerpted from a draft provides a good illustration of how not to organise a provision. In the first paragraph, a general rule and an exception are stated in the one paragraph. The second paragraph is apparently a definition of a term contained in the first paragraph, but on closer inspection it introduces certain duties. In the third paragraph, more duties are mentioned, but the relationship between these duties and the ones alluded to earlier is not clear:

Before restyling

Art. 64 Contrôles

[1] La production, l'encavage et le commerce de vin sont soumis au contrôle de la comptabilité de cave afin que les appellations et désignations soient protégées. Le Conseil fédéral peut prévoir des exceptions si la protection n'en souffre pas, notamment pour les entreprises qui se limitent au commerce de vin en bouteilles et ne pratiquent ni importation ni exportation.

- General rule; but who is controlling whom (addressee)?
- Exception (in same paragraph)

[2] La comptabilité de cave comprend:·
a. la déclaration d'encavage et
b. la tenue d'un livre de cave comprenant toutes les opérations de cave ainsi que l'ensemble des transactions.

Definition of 'comptabilité de cave' (referring to para 1, first sentence)

[3] Le Conseil fédéral fixe les obligations auxquelles sont soumis la production, l'encavage et le commerce de vin et édicte les dispositions détaillées relatives aux contrôles, notamment en ce qui concerne l'enregistrement, les annonces, la tenue d'une comptabilité de cave et l'inventaire annuel

- Apparently details, but what are these additional obligations (are they in addition to para 1; or is this repetition)?
- Essential details on 'contrôle' (para 1)

(RS 916.146 Projet d'Ordonnance sur le contrôle du commerce des vins [RS 916.146 draft Ordinance on the Control of Wine Trade]).[18]

The restyled version below shows an organisation of the text according to natural principles of ordering general and special information:

After restyling[19]

Art. 64 Contrôles

[1] Afin que les appellations et désignations soient protégées, quiconque produit et encave du vin ou en fait le commerce doit :
a. établir une déclaration d'encavage;
b. tenir un livre de cave dans lequel doivent figurer toutes les transactions et opérations de cave.

General rule: general duties of wine producers and traders

[2] Le Conseil fédéral peut prévoir des exceptions notamment pour les entreprises qui se limitent au commerce de vin en bouteilles et n'effectuent ni importations ni exportations, pour autant que ces exceptions ne nuisent pas à la protection des appellations et des désignations.

Exceptions to the first paragraph

[3] Il fixe les charges auxquelles sont soumis la production, l'encavage et le commerce de vin

Details on the first paragraph

---

18 [[1] The production, cellar storage and trading of wine are subject to the control of the cellar accounting system in order to protect the appellations and designations. The Federal Council may provide for exceptions provided this does not prejudice protection, particularly for businesses that confine their activities to trading in bottled wine and which do not import or export wine.
[2] The cellar accounting system comprises: a. the cellar storage declaration and b. the keeping of a cellar book recording all the cellar activities as well as all the transactions.
[3] The Federal Council stipulates the obligations that apply to production, cellar storage and trading of wine and issues detailed provisions on controls, particularly with regard to the registration, notification and retention of cellar accounts and the annual inventory].
19 [[1] In order to protect the appellations and designations, anyone who produces and cellars wine or who trades in wine must: a. issue a cellar storage declaration; b. keep a cellar book that must record all the transactions and cellar activities].
[2] The Federal Council may provide for exceptions, particularly for businesses that confine their activities to trading in bottled wine and which do not import or export wine, provided such exceptions do not prejudice the protection of the appellations or the designations.
[3] It stipulates the charges that apply to the production, cellar storage and trading of wine].

Conclusion

The social or economic problems laws have to deal with are often intricate, and so are the concepts the legislators choose for their regulations. Thus, simplicity taken in an absolute sense cannot be achieved in a forward way, nor can it be the foremost quality of a law. But if laws cannot be simple they can have a transparent structure at least. By transparency we can achieve relative comprehensibility even in complex situations. Transparency means showing the structure of thoughts in the structure of the text as directly as possible. Of course, a thought that is not clear cannot be presented in a transparent way. Transparency therefore also means giving a clear structure to clear thoughts. When we make efforts to create a transparent text we are forced to clarify our thoughts and concepts. Efforts for transparency on the linguistic level can have an educational effect on the conceptual level. But clarity and plain language in laws means also that once we have developed a clear concept it should be allowed to be formulated in a visual transparent way.

Chapter 8

Finland Makes its Statutes Intelligible: Good Intentions and Practicalities[1]

Aino Piehl

Since the 1970s, Finland has been seeking to clarify the language of statutes with a view to making them more intelligible to the public. This has been a common objective for statutes written in both of the national languages: Finnish and Swedish. Previous to that, clarity was understood in terms of internal and mutual consistency of statutes. The primary aim at that time was to establish the expressions and lexicon of Finnish statute language, and also to ensure that statutes were drafted in grammatically correct and idiomatic Finnish language.

Today, modern legislation is expected to evolve in many directions, and clarity of language is an objective that must vie with other demands for the drafter's attention: the financial and administrative impacts of a statute have to be assessed; alternative forms of guidance must be considered; and the consistency of a proposed statute with the Finnish Constitution, Community Law and international treaties must all be evaluated. These considerations must also be stated explicitly, while the extent to which a statute is intelligible continues to depend largely on the interest and abilities of the drafter.

From 'translatorese' to the language of Finnish statutes

As part of the Kingdom of Sweden from the Middle Ages until 1809, Finland was subject to Swedish laws. As a result, translators were responsible for formulating the language of statutes written in Finnish for much of its history, and this has had a significant impact on the evolution of the language. While some of the older laws were translated into Finnish, none of these translations were ever printed. Royal Ordinances, on the other hand, were translated and printed in the 16th and 17th centuries. These translations adhered closely to the structure of the Swedish source text, and their meaning could be quite obscure in Finnish, as equivalents had to be found for many concepts and this often meant simply using the Swedish, Latin or French expressions in the Finnish text; or resorting to word-for-word loan translations of Swedish expressions. It was not until 1735 that the first official position for a

---

1 The author wishes to thank Daryl Taylor for the translation of this chapter which was originally written in Finnish.

Finnish language translator was established in the Swedish civil service (see Pajula 1960, 71, 82, 87).

The first printed law in the Finnish language was a translation of the Swedish law of 1734 published in 1759. This law was a major reform and its wording in Swedish had been drafted carefully with a view to concise expression. The high standard of the source text was also apparent in the translation, even though this largely continued to adhere closely to the structure of the original. This law also remained in force for a long time, as Swedish laws continued to be applied even after Russia had conquered Finland in 1809. Finland then became an autonomous grand duchy directly subordinate to the Tsar, while its internal administration and judiciary continued to work in the Swedish language. The comprehensive process of legislative reform continued slowly, and so new translations of the 1734 law were prepared again in the 1860s and 1890s.

A major social shift occurred in Finland after the middle of the 19th century. As elsewhere in Europe, the idea of a nation state was beginning to gain ground in Finland, and nationalist officials in the universities and administration took the view that society should function in the Finnish language spoken by the majority of the population. Many of these leading figures in the Finnish national consciousness movement were originally Swedish speaking, but had changed their language in pursuit of their ideals. These efforts began to hone and sharpen the Finnish language to meet the needs of a modernising society in a wide range of fields. The leading figures in this process also sought to improve the language of statutes. For example Elias Lönnrot and August Ahlqvist, both early professors of the Finnish language, were involved in work to translate laws into Finnish and to expand the legal lexicon (Pajula 1960, 184-185).

In 1863, on the recommendation of nationalist Finns, Tsar Alexander II issued a decree seeking to grant the Finnish language the status of a language of public administration within 20 years; meaning that Finnish-speaking Finns would have to be able to transact business with public authorities in their native language by no later than 1884. This meant that the language of statutes gradually gained support from other uses of the Finnish language in public administration. It was not until 1902, however, that a Decree of the Tsar confirmed the status of the Finnish language as fully equal to Swedish in public administration (Pajula 1960, 222).

Throughout the 19th century, statutes were usually drafted in Swedish, even though Finnish-speaking civil servants were already engaged in such work in the closing years of this century. The statutes were also translated into Finnish and published. Finnish became the language of drafting when Finland elected its first unicameral Parliament in 1907 and more than 90 per cent of the new Members of Parliament were Finnish speaking. It was at this point that statutes began to be translated from Finnish into Swedish.

In 1917 Finland became an independent State with two statutory national languages: Finnish and Swedish. With 89 per cent of the population the Finnish speakers were in a large majority (*Finlandssvenskarna 2005 – en statistisk rapport* 2007, 7). Although Finnish had already become established as a language of legislative drafting, many civil servants were still either native speakers of Swedish or had mainly studied and worked in the Swedish language. This meant that the impact of Swedish on the language of statutes and administration in particular was substantial and many structures and expressions were alien to the Finnish language. The language of statutes was specifically criticised for these failings in sources such as *Lakimies* – the Finnish language journal founded in 1903 by the Association of Finnish Lawyers, one aim of which was to develop Finnish as a language of law. In 1929, for example, suspicions were expressed in this journal that 'the people who write and amend laws nowadays are no more familiar with the laws of language than with those of society' (Ahava 1929, 219–228).

As the statutes suffered from shortcomings of both language and legislative drafting, the idea of establishing a body to inspect them was entertained, and a special law inspection division was set up at the Ministry of Justice in 1936. This division was responsible for inspecting legislative drafting and for taking care of the linguistic quality of statutes, which meant ensuring that completed statutory proposals conformed to established legal linguistic usage and were precise and consistent (Tyynilä 1984, 258-259). The aim of law inspection was thus to consolidate the forms and expressions of legal language. Finland's new standard language was still seeking a uniform, established style in many other specialised fields where it likewise continued to suffer from lexical deficiencies. Philologists also studied the evolution of language from this point of view. No consideration was given, on the other hand, to the question of whether the statutes and the language of public administration were intelligible from the point of view of safeguarding the rights of ordinary people.

General intelligibility was nevertheless a fundamental principle of lexical development. This was also the justification for seeking to avoid the use of Greek and Latin loan words or of loans from contemporary languages in the statutes. Instead of these, Finnish language elements were recombined to coin new words or new meanings were given to existing expressions. The range of special legal and administrative concepts was still quite narrow and the lexicon did not differ substantially from ordinary language, as too little time had elapsed to allow any domain of special terminology to evolve. The rule of law also generally applied to familiar and concrete matters and no specialist expertise was usually necessary for understanding the statutes.

Seeking general intelligibility instead of conformity of expression

It was only in the 1970s that any real call was heard for the language of statutes to be intelligible to the public at large, although the idea had surfaced sporadically at earlier stages in the history of Finnish legal language. When a special legal drafting body was first proposed in 1877, it was considered important for such a body to be able to ensure that the law would be clear and intelligible to the people. The proposal was not supported by the national consciousness movement at that time, however, as it did not allow for the fact that readily intelligible laws drafted in Swedish would in any case remain incomprehensible to the majority of Finns on the other side of the language barrier (Tyynilä 1984, 72-79).

The call for intelligibility was heard again in the 1950s when a committee was appointed in 1953 to consider reorganising the process of drafting legislation. The report of this committee stressed that laws had to be readily intelligible to the general public (Tyynilä 1984, 309-310). The same aspiration was repeated in the justifications for the proposal given in the government bill when the reforms were enacted in 1959. The final reorganisation saw the establishment of the Law Drafting Department and associated Bureau of Legislative Inspection at the Ministry of Justice. However, the terms of reference formulated for these units in 1960 no longer referred in any way to the intelligibility of laws; and instead the goal of legislative inspection was to produce statutory proposals drafted in legal language that was free from error, precise and consistent (Tyynilä 1984, 319-336).

Only over a decade later was the time ripe for the notion of intelligibility as such. A universal interest in achieving democracy and social equality also focused attention on the intelligibility of language used by public authorities, which was understood to derive from the language of statutes. And this language had to be intelligible so that members of the public could find out about their rights and ensure that those rights were respected. Beginning in the late 1960s these ideas also encouraged the Finns to take an interest in ensuring that ordinary people could understand the language of statutes and public administration.

In the 1970s, the Law Drafting Department of the Ministry of Justice issued instructions for writing intelligible statutes and official communications. Courses on this subject involving language specialists were also arranged for officials. It was also at this time that the first guidebooks were published specifically for civil servants, focusing on linguistic features that hamper understanding, such as abstract expressions, cumbersome sentence structures and a lexicon that is alien to the public at large. The earliest efforts were made by the Law Drafting Department of the Ministry of Justice, when it published instructions for officials drafting statutory proposals and other civil servants called *Ymmärrettävää virkakieltä* [*Intelligible Administrative Language*] in 1974 (see Rontu 1974). A second impression of these instructions was soon prepared, and in 1977 they were published again in an enlarged edition (Rontu 1977).

The idea of clarifying official language was thus greeted with enthusiasm, and in 1979 the government appointed a Committee on Administrative Language to consider what should be done to achieve this objective. This committee included representatives of public authorities, including those charged with the task of drafting legislation, together with linguists, plain language experts and specialists in communications and public relations. The committee completed its report, *Kieli ja virkakoneisto* [the *Language and the Machinery of Administration*] in 1981. This report analysed the various types of official language and the reasons for their obscurity. The committee proposed several measures to improve the situation, many of which were subsequently implemented. Indeed these proposals may be considered the basis of procedures employed even nowadays with a view to clarifying the language used by public authorities.

The decision on administrative language and its consequences

One of the most important proposals made by the committee was that the Council of State should issue a decision on measures to improve the use of language by public authorities. The *Valtioneuvoston päätös toimenpiteistä valtion viranomaisten kielenkäytön parantamiseks* [*Decision on Administrative Language*] took effect in the following year (1982), and required central government agencies to ensure the intelligibility of documents issued to private individuals. The decision only applied to central government agencies; courts of law were to attend to their own language practices, while the use of language by local government was the responsibility of local councils. The decision was repealed in 2000, but a corresponding duty was prescribed in the 2003 *Hallintolaki* [the *Administration Act*],[2] imposing a general requirement of good language usage on all public authorities:[3] 'Public authorities shall use appropriate, clear and intelligible language' (Ibid., paragraph 1 section 9).

The *Decision on Administrative Language* also included some concrete directions on language use. It discouraged the use of expressions that were not widely known or were not clear in context. Authors were urged to explain the concepts that they employed. Public authorities were also required to report to the Ministry of Finance, and with respect to drafting of statutes also to the Ministry of Justice, on the steps that they had taken to implement the decision. Training of officials responsible for drafting statutory proposals had to pay greater attention to skills in language use. The decision appointed the Research Institute for the Languages of Finland to serve as a specialist in clear language use, assisting public authorities in resolving problems in this field.

After the decision, government agencies set about organising staff training courses in clear and intelligible language use. Courses were also arranged for the officials responsible for drafting proposed statutes, providing an appreciation of the factors that influence intelligibility. The lecturers retained for these courses were researchers at the Research Institute for the Languages of Finland, which received an increased budget allocation enabling it to establish positions in the 1980s and 1990s for four researchers specialised in clarifying official language. A special training unit was set up at the Institute, the clients of which were mainly central and local government agencies. The Research Institute also prepared a guidebook promoting clear official language in 1980 and a new guidebook in 1992. Articles on intelligible official language began to be published in a 'good official language' column of the *Virallinen lehti / Officiella tidningen* [Finnish *Official Gazette*]. The column has continued to this day.

Following the report of the Committee on Administrative Language the Ministry of Justice prepared a new *Lainlaatijan opas* [the *Legal Drafter's Manual*], published in 1996. This publication discusses some of the features that influence

---

2 Available at <http://www.finlex.fi/en/laki/kaannokset/1982/en19820598.pdf>.

3 The *Administration Act* does not apply to courts of law, police investigations or central authorities responsible for supervising the legality of official actions, even in their dealings with the public. This hardly means, however, that these authorities would not be expected to follow the principles of good governance.

the intelligibility of a text, such as aspect, information content, sentence structure and choice of terminology. It also points out that deliberate use of unclear wording does not constitute appropriate drafting. The *Legal Drafter's Manual* provides many instructions on how to formulate a text more intelligibly, and these instructions are illustrated with examples. It also states the aim of gradually removing from the statutes expressions that are archaic and alien to ordinary language, and replacing them with more familiar terms. At several points it refers to the progress that can be made simply by observing the *rule of three*: a section of a statute should include no more than three paragraphs; a paragraph should comprise no more than three sentences; and a sentence should have no more than three clauses (Ibid., 121-138). The Manual is currently being revised.

The committee report stressed the importance of training university students in writing, particularly in the fields of law, social sciences and economics. Law students currently take compulsory courses in Finnish and communications, and a course in the language of statutes enabling the student to learn about such matters as the features that promote or impair the intelligibility of a text. The report also focused on the importance of in-service training for civil servants. For many years civil servants gained their introduction to legislative drafting on courses at the government training centre. These courses also included a module on clarity and intelligibility of the language of statutes, which was taught by language specialists. The officials who draft statutory proposals are still trained in this way, and government departments have also continually retained language specialists to teach writing courses for officials engaged in preparing statutory proposals in order to maintain the high profile of intelligibility.

The Decision on Administrative Language also sought to improve the quality of statutes and official communications in the Swedish language, and to this end a 1988 government resolution established the Swedish Language Board at the Council of State to promote the clarity and intelligibility of legal and administrative Swedish used in Finland. This Board also publishes manuals and guidelines. The first manual, *Svenskt lagspråk i Finland* [Swedish legal language in Finland], was published in 1986 even before the Board had been appointed, and several revised impressions of this work have subsequently appeared. The Board also issues recommendations on questions of language and arranges training in association with the Research Institute for the Languages of Finland. By contrast no official body has been established to promote the intelligibility of statutory proposals and official communications in Finnish.

The Decision on Administrative Language and the evolution of the language of statutes

The *Decision on Administrative Language* also attracted considerable interest among philologists. This led to several students' theses investigating the impacts of the *Decision on Administrative Language* on statutes which were prepared at universities in the 1980s and 1990s. These studies focused on the sentence structures used in statutes, which the Committee on Administrative Language had identified as the main reason for obscurity in texts. For example, Päivi Naskali (1992) and Asta Virtaniemi (1992) compared statutes from the late 1980s to older statutes and to studies of them. The investigations specifically reviewed features of sentence structure that were considered to reveal something about the clarity and intelligibility of a text. These features were the length of a sentence and clause in words, the number of clauses in a sentence, the number of sub-clauses and their status in the sentence, and the number of nominalisations in a sentence such as clause equivalents, participle modifiers and other expressions that are used to eliminate sub-clauses (see Table 8.1 for examples of nominalisations).

Table 8.1 A sentence of statute language containing several nominalisations (Directive 20/2002/EC, article 5)

Radiotaajuuksien käyttöä **koskevien** oikeuksien jakamismenettelyn on oltava avointa, selkeää ja syrjimätöntä	
sanotun kuitenkaan *rajoittamatta* niitä erityisperusteita tai -menettelyjä,	Without prejudice to specific criteria and procedures adopted by Member States
joita jäsenvaltiot ovat omaksuneet	
	to grant rights of use of radio frequencies
radiotaajuuksien käyttöä **koskevien** oikeuksien *myöntämiseksi*	
	to providers of radio or television broadcast content services
radio- tai televisio-ohjelmien sisältöpalvelujen tarjoajille	
yleistä etua **koskevien** tavoitteiden *saavuttamiseksi* yhteisön oikeuden mukaisesti.	with a view to pursuing general interest objectives in conformity with Community law,
	such rights of use shall be granted through open, transparent and non-discriminatory procedures.

Table 8.1 compares the same sentence in the English and Finnish versions of *Directive 20/2002/EC of the European Parliament and of the Council on the authorisation of electronic communications networks and services*,[4] juxtaposing equivalent clauses and expressions aside from the main clauses. The main clause comes at the start of the Finnish version and at the end of the English version, and is

---

4 English version available at <http://eurlex.europa.eu/LexUriServ/LexUriServ. do?uri=CELEX:32002L0020:EN:HTML; Finnish version available at <http://eur-lex.europa. eu/LexUriServ/LexUriServ.do?uri=CELEX:32002L0020:FI:HTML>.

shown with a shaded background. The participle modifiers are marked in boldface and other nominalisations are italicised in the Finnish text. (NB! The English version also employs many structures other than clauses.) The Finnish sentence has 40 words and two clauses with three participle modifiers and three other nominalisations. The English sentence has 54 words in a single clause.

The studies showed that changes had occurred with respect to the features identified by the Committee on Administrative Language. In particular, it was noted that sentences had shortened and included fewer clauses than in older statutes. This progress seems to have continued into the new millennium, as the length of sentences in terms of words and clauses is now also clearly shorter than in statutes dating from the late 1980s (see Table 8.2). This is evident from my study of statutes from 2002 and 2003 (Piehl 2006, 187). Sentences in Finnish can seem surprisingly short in terms of the number of words, but this is simply because the language has no articles and few prepositions, with the corresponding linguistic functions expressed instead using case endings on the words. As the example in Table 8.2 shows, the actual words are fairly long.

Table 8.2 Sentence length and number of clauses in Finnish legislation

	Words/ sentence	Clauses/ sentence	Words/ clause
Finnish legislation			
1960s			
Mäkitalo (1968)	23.1	2.3	-
Niemikorpi (1991)	22.4	2.4	9.6
1970s			
Language and the Machinery of Administration (1981)	21.0	2.3	9.2
1980s			
Naskali (1992)	18.9	2.1	9.1
Virtaniemi (1992)	19.6	2.0	10.0
2000s			
Piehl (2006)	14.9	1.5	10.1

These findings should nevertheless not be understood to mean that the statutes have evolved in an exclusively favourable direction, even when understood in purely structural terms. The studies indicate that the average number of words in a clause has increased, even as the number of words in a sentence has fallen. This is probably because various nominalisations such as clause equivalents and participle modifiers have been employed to eliminate the sub-clauses that were previously used and express the same content in the main clause. These devices tend to make clauses and sentences more complex and hamper intelligibility. For example, anything expressed using a participle modifier can nearly always also be said with a relative clause. The findings of Naskali (1992), Virtaniemi (1992) and Piehl (2006) indicate that while the use of relative sub-clauses has been decreasing, the use of participle modifiers in statutes has risen considerably. This development continued unchecked even after the *Decision on Administrative Language*, and despite the efforts made through guidelines and training to reduce the use of participle modifiers (see Table 8.3). Even so, statutes in the new millennium have also increasingly employed relative sub-clauses.

Table 8.3 Percentage of clauses with participle modifiers and relative pronouns in Finnish legislation

	Percentage of clauses with participle modifiers	Percentage of clauses with relative pronouns
1920s Naskali (1992)	32.6	42.9
1980s Virtaniemi (1992)	64.8	16.7
2000s Piehl (2006)	99.3	18.5

European Union membership revives translatorese in legislation

Finland joined the European Union in 1995, thereby returning to a state of affairs in which translated texts are an important factor in Finnish legislation. European Union Directives have to be implemented through Finnish legislation, and the implementing statutes are influenced by the Finnish language versions of the Directives. Opinions of the extent of this influence on legislation vary between a high estimate, according to which 80 per cent of legislative projects are linked in some way to the European Union, and a low estimate suggesting that the European dimension affects only 20 per cent of projects. Two-thirds of the government bills submitted to the Finnish Parliament in 2003 and 2004 had some connection with Community Law (*Paremman sääntelyn toimintaohjelma* [the *Better Regulation Programme*] 2006, 112–113). Finnish statutes are also affected by European Union Regulations, which have direct effect in all member states.

Community Law has a heritage that is alien to Finland. The regulation of European Union statutes is more detailed, and perhaps for this reason also more verbose, with a greater number of clauses and more complex sentence structures (for an analysis of the flaws of European legislative drafting, see Tanner 2006). There is also often a tendency to seek impressive and declarative formulations of a kind not found in Finnish legislation. There may likewise be a greater inclination in European Union statutes towards unclear formulations resulting from compromise. The translation strategy of the European Union for statutes has been for none of the language versions to deviate far from the mode of expression of the source text. Finnish translation policies have also been highly conservative, especially in the early stages, and translators were instructed to stay close to the source text (Stenqvist 2000, 22).

Finnish politicians, public authorities and other users of Community Law statutes thus encountered a rather alien statute style in European Union legislation. They found the Finnish language Community Law statutes particularly strange. This is evident from the responses to a questionnaire that I sent to civil servants in Finnish central government departments in 1998. More than 80 per cent of the respondents felt that European Union texts in Finnish were hard to understand. The reasons given for this were, in particular, convoluted sentence structures (70 per cent of respondents) and alien terminology (64 per cent of respondents). About half considered the European Union texts that they had read in other languages to be more difficult than corresponding national statutes in the same language (Piehl 2000). I repeated this questionnaire again in 2007, and it provisionally appears that impressions of the difficulty of texts and of the reasons for this remain similar to those indicated in 1998 (Piehl, forthcoming). A public debate was held at the time of accession on whether the language of Community Law statutes would impair the language of Finnish statutes. Finland's Parliamentary Ombudsman later claimed that such a development had indeed occurred (reported in Finland's leading national daily newspaper *Helsingin Sanomat* on 30 May 2000). Officials responsible for drafting statutory proposals also feel that Community Law statutes have impaired the standard of legislation in Finland (*Better Regulation Programme* 2006, 140).

The effects of Community Law statutes do not seem to be especially prominent in the sentence structure of Finnish statutes, however. The findings of a comparison that I made between the features of laws enacted in 2002 and 2003 and those of their corresponding Directives indicate that sentences in the Directives are clearly longer in terms of both the number of words and the number of clauses used. They also contain at least as many nominalisations per clause as there are in Finnish statutes, despite using more sub-clauses. For example, there are still more participle modifiers in the Directives than in Finnish statutes (see Table 8.4) (Piehl 2006, 4).

Table 8.4 Length of sentences and clauses and percentage of clauses with participle modifiers and relative pronouns in Finnish/EU legislation

	Words/ sentence	Clauses/ sentence	Words/ clause	Percentage of clauses with participle modifiers	Percentage of clauses with relative pronouns
Finnish legislation 2002-2003	14.9	1.5	10.1	99.3	18.5
EU legislation in Finnish	19.8	2.2	9.1	101.6	22.5

A special guidebook, *Lainlaatijan EU-opas* [the *Legal Drafter's Guide to the European Union*],[5] has been prepared for implementing European Union Directives and was first published by the Ministry of Justice in 1997. This guidebook imposes the same requirements on Finnish statutes based on Community Law Directives as apply to statutes arising from purely domestic processes. The guidebook also notes that although the language of Community Law statutes differs from the language that is familiar in Finland, this is no justification for changing the language of Finnish statutes, which should evolve on its own terms. Problems arise, for example, due to the use of terms in the Directives that differ from those used in Finnish statutes, and due to unclear wording. According to the guidebook, the main rule is to use the terms of the Directives, but to deliberate carefully before changing the established terminology of the Finnish language. Even though the aim is to avoid modifying the interpretation of Directives in the course of national implementation, the *Legal Drafter's Guide to the European Union* nevertheless encourages the writer to aim for intelligibility:

> If the lack of clarity has not arisen at the translation stage, but is chiefly the outcome of a political compromise, then careful consideration should be given to how the Directive will be implemented. The writer must then take care to ensure that the national implementing provisions are formulated in clear language (*Legal Drafter's Guide to the European Union* 2004, 58).

Finnish civil servants were also given guidance on how to influence the formulation of Community Law statutes at the preparatory stage. The second government development programme for legal drafting published by the Ministry of Justice in 2000 gave civil servants involved in preparing Community Law statutes the objective of ensuring that those statutes would be intelligible to the general public. This is not a new idea for the European Union, but was also proposed in the 1998 *Inter-institutional Agreement on common guidelines for the quality of drafting of Community legislation.*[6] The latest Finnish development proposals for legal drafting make no separate reference to language, even though they stress the importance of participating in work to improve the quality of Community legislation.

Intelligibility: The aim but not always the outcome

There is unanimous agreement nowadays on the point that the language of statutes and public administration must be intelligible to the average member of the public. This has also been imposed as an aim in drafting statutory proposals in the latest guidelines and development programmes, such as the *Better Regulation Programme*[7] of autumn 2006 and the *Bill Drafting Instructions*[8] that were originally issued in

---

5 Available at <http://www.om.fi/25714.htm>.

6 Available at <http://eur-lex.europa.eu/LexUriServ/LexUriServ.do?uri=CELEX:31999 Y0317(01):EN:NOT>.

7 Available at <http://www.vnk.fi/julkaisukansio/2006/j08-paremman-saantelyn-toiminta ohjelma-osa-1/pdf/fi.pdf>.

8 Available at <http://www.om.fi/uploads/7b3b69oecmj2dy2.pdf>.

Finnish in 2004. The syllabus of law school programmes and of training for legal drafters working in government departments now includes modules on the factors that affect intelligibility. The Bureau of Legislative Inspection at the Ministry of Justice also reviews most statutes, and especially Acts of Parliament. However, there has been an ongoing debate in Finland since the 1980s on inadequacies in the quality of legislation and on the obscurity of statutes. The Finnish Parliament, for example, has complained about inadequacies in government bills on several occasions. Why is it that these good intentions do not seem to be realised, even though their importance has been stressed by imposing a legal duty on public authorities to pay attention to these aspects?

There are many reasons for the persistence of textual obscurity. Partly the problem lies in the function and character of the texts in question. Matters subject to regulation have become increasingly specialised and technical, making them ever more difficult to understand without expertise in the sector concerned. 21st century decrees, in particular, include quite detailed regulations. Community Law statutes also introduce further elements of this kind into Finnish legislation (*Better Regulation Programme* 2006, 140, 153). On the other hand, Acts of Parliament and Community Law statutes tend to function at a high level of generality, and it can be difficult to link phenomena described at this level to the concrete world that is familiar to the ordinary reader, nor are general abstract concepts of much use in so doing. The details of the legal system and practice that are necessary for interpreting statutes are likewise not fully explained in the statutes. Indeed statutes are also intended for a very broad range of users, and this can make it very difficult to formulate a text that is equally suitable for all of them.

A reason for obscurity can also be found in the procedures for preparing legislation. The Committee on Administrative Language originally observed that the drafter is always responsible for the intelligibility of a statute. Nowadays, however, it seems that the drafter has been left to bear this burden alone. No organised help or guidance in tackling problems of language use or feedback on intelligibility is available when the drafter is actually composing the statutory proposal. The content of courses on how to draft statutes remains divorced from the actual work of doing so, and legal inspection occurs at such a late stage that major reformulations of statutory proposals are no longer possible. One worthy opportunity to secure feedback on the intelligibility of statutes would be through discussions with the people who translate them, as all Finnish statutes are translated into Swedish. Unfortunately this has not been considered as a viable means of systematically improving the quality of texts drafted in the Finnish language, and translations are also generally made only at a very late stage. The instructions for preparing statutory proposals also fail to advise the drafter to pay attention to planning the linguistic style of a statute at the beginning of the project, and aspects of language only come to the fore at the finishing and polishing stage.

The Committee on Administrative Language did propose several measures, however, whereby government departments and other public authorities could be assigned responsibility for the linguistic quality of statutory proposals. They were required to arrange staff training and to conduct regular quality reviews of the texts that they produced. A responsible person from the authority was to be appointed to perform the latter duty, which would also involve disseminating new instructions and recommendations to colleagues (see *Language and the Machinery of Administration* 1981). The *Decision on Administrative Language* also obliged public authorities to consider the standing arrangements that they would install to ensure the quality of statutes and other official written communications. They were required to report on these measures to the Ministry of Justice in respect of statutes and to the Ministry of Finance in other areas (Iisa and Piehl 1992, 112). With the exception of training, however, these instructions and recommendations were largely ineffectual. Training was also generally voluntary and often tended to appeal, in particular, to officials who were already interested in clarity of written expression and who were otherwise adept in this respect.

Minimal resources and a dearth of appreciation are also reasons why the goals of intelligibility and clarity have not been more energetically pursued, and legal drafters have been assumed to be able to tackle these aspects unassisted. These shortcomings in appreciation have not solely been a problem for the language and intelligibility of statutes, but it is evident from development proposals in recent years that preparing statutes has in general not been a matter of high priority for government departments in Finland. The programmes have criticised the leadership of government departments for failing to take an interest in improving the preparation of statutes or allocating the necessary resources to this activity. If legal drafters are constantly required to work in haste, then they will not have enough time to consider how their texts are composed or to attend to many other factors that affect the quality of statutes.

Following the parliamentary elections of spring 2007 the incoming government included implementation of the Better Regulation Programme in its programme. This programme once again stresses the point that legal drafters need training and support if they are to be able to formulate better statutes. At the time of writing the new government has not been in office long enough to allow any conclusion as to which programme proposals will be implemented and in what form. Ideally the goal of intelligible statutes will be given a realistic opportunity to become more than a mere aspiration.

Chapter 9

The Swedish Approach to Clear Legislation and Clear Official Texts

Barbro Ehrenberg-Sundin

Introduction

Sweden has always been ahead of the rest of the world in the quest for clarity in the law (Asprey 2003, 23). Indeed, there is a long history of support for greater clarity in Swedish legislation. The 1783 Ordinance for the Royal Chancery under King Charles XII required that

> the Royal Chancellery in all written documents endeavour to write in clear and plain Swedish and not to use, as far as possible, foreign words.

Today, the main source of initiative for making legislation and other legal documents as clear as possible is the Swedish Cabinet Office and its Director-General for Legal Affairs.[1] As early as 1982, an *Ordinance on the Duties of the Government Offices* stipulated that the Director-General for Legal Affairs of the Cabinet Office is responsible for 'high quality in the legislation and the administration' and for ensuring that 'the language in Acts and other Decisions is as clear and simple as possible' (*Förordning (1996:1515) med instruktion för Regeringskansliet* [the *Ordinance on the Duties of the Government Offices*]).

This latter task is the responsibility of language experts in the *Granskningsenheten* [the Division for Legal and Linguistic Draft Revision] at the Ministry of Justice. One of the many roles of these language experts is to encourage government officials to use a plain language approach in their drafting. There is also a special EU Language Service which is responsible for promoting clear and simple EU legislation. In addition, a special committee appointed by the Government – the *Klarspråksgruppen* [the Plain Swedish Group] – has the mission to encourage Swedish authorities to embrace plain language in their work.

The purpose of this chapter is to provide a review of the three functions outlined above, in the hope that the Swedish Government's support for plain language might serve as an inspiration to others. In a Parliamentary Bill (2005), adopted by the *Riksdag* [Parliament] in December 2005, the Swedish government proposed four new objectives for its national language policy (see *Bästa språket – en samlad svensk språkpolitik* (prop. 2005/06:2) [Best language – a concerted language policy for

---

[1] For further explanations on initiating legislation and other legal documents in Sweden, see Ehrenberg-Sundin (2002, 3-4).

Sweden]). One objective was to emphasise the importance of plain language activities by stating that 'public Swedish must be cultivated, simple and comprehensible'.[2] The benefits of such activities are well defined, debated and approved of in the legal literature: plain language writing helps maintain faith in public institutions; it enhances democracy and the rule of law; it makes administration more efficient and thus saves both time and money (see Kimble 1996-97; Asprey 2003; Cacciaguidi-Fahy and Wagner 2006, 21). But in order to achieve these goals, these plain language initiatives must be carried out in a systematic way and be an integrated part of every central, regional and local authority's normal activities. They must have sufficient resources, both in terms of professional expertise and financial resources. In this respect, Sweden still has a long way to go.

The 'Swedish way' is to start at the very top – firstly, to make the language and structure used in national legislation as clear as possible; secondly, to influence government authorities at all levels, central, regional and local, to start their own plain language activities; and thirdly, to help make EU texts as clear as possible. These three approaches have been carried out in the Division for Legal and Linguistic Draft Revision, by plain language experts and by a special Committee set up by the Government for promoting plain language activities: the Plain Swedish Group. Since July 1, 2006, however, the activities of the Plain Swedish Group have been taken over by a new state body: the *Språkrådet* [the Language Council].[3]

The Swedish approach to clear legislation: Statutes for clear drafting

The law in Sweden provides a legal basis for plain language use. Article 26 of the *Ordinance on the Duties of the Government Offices* (1982) stipulates the legal basis for the Division's work within the various ministries. Article 7 of *förvaltningslagen (1986:223)* [*Administration Procedure* Act] provides the legal basis for greater clarity in the work of government authorities and requires that the said authorities 'must endeavour to express themselves in a comprehensible manner'. In addition, article 7 of the *Verksförordning (1995, 1322)* [*Government Authorities and Agencies Ordinance*] requires the director-general to ensure that the authority uses a plain Swedish approach when drafting official documents.

Since 1976, the work on encouraging clarity in the language used in statutes and other legal instruments has been supported by language experts and lawyers working at the Ministry of Justice. There are now five language experts and five legal revisers whose responsibility is to check the quality of drafts from all the ministries. The main task of the division's legal advisers (who are all associate judges) is to review statutes and other proposals to be submitted to the Swedish Parliament. The purpose of the legal advisers' review is to make sure that the laws and decisions are well reasoned, lucid and uniform in legal technique and that they are not anticonstitutional.

---

2 The other three objectives are: Swedish is to be the main language in Sweden; Swedish is to be a complete language, serving and uniting society; and everyone is to have a right to language; to develop and learn Swedish, to develop and use their own mother tongue and national minority language and to have the opportunity to learn foreign languages.

3 See <http://www.sprakradet.se/plain_language>.

The work of the language experts is to improve the quality of the texts so that they can be easily read and understood by the general public. This revision takes place one or two weeks before the Government decides on the text and it is, of course, an important checkpoint. As such the division has a key role in legislative drafting in the ministries as no Government Bill (including proposed Acts), no Government Ordinance or Committee Terms of Reference can be sent to the printers without the division's approval.

This ongoing process, which has been in place for more than 30 years, emanates from the idea that laws must be clear and user-friendly, because these texts have an impact on decision-making at all levels of society. The work of the division to a large extent also influences the wording of more detailed provisions issued by public authorities, as well as other texts such as brochures or web site information.

Revision alone does not guarantee lucid laws

While the final revision is an important mechanism for checking the linguistic quality of the texts, this revision alone does not guarantee lucid laws. Typically, at the final revision stage there is little time, and as a result the language experts deal mainly with linguistic concerns such as sentence structure, archaic or misleading words, phrases and forms, syntax problems, unclear passive voice and nominalisation. The visual structure and presentation of the contents are difficult to change at such a late stage.[4] In addition to reviewing draft documents, the legal language experts have also developed other approaches in a bid to achieve greater clarity. These include:

- Changing ineffective text models and creating prototypes
- Offering special seminars and training sessions for drafters
- Writing handbooks, guidelines and articles on clear drafting
- Giving advice by telephone or e-mail and on the website Klarspråk [clear language]
- Taking part in the work of law Commissions that are appointed by the Government to redraft legislation.

An example of such a Commission was the Income Tax Law Commission, which was responsible for redrafting and consolidating more than 30 acts and thousands of supporting amendments with a new and more comprehensible *Inkomstskattelagen* (1999:1229) [the *Income Tax Act*]. One of the language experts was appointed as an expert to the Commission to rewrite the very lengthy and complicated Swedish social insurance legislation. The objective of this Commission was to develop legislation with a more logical and user-friendly structure and make it easier to read and understand (see *Socialförsäkringsbalk* (2005:114) [the *Social Insurance Code*]).[5]

---

4 For further discussion on the importance of the visual presentation and structure of normative texts and their impact on Clarity, see Flückiger (Chapter 1).

5 Available at <www.regeringen.se/sb/d/108>. English summary (2005, 31).

In its attempt to arrive at greater clarity, Sweden has, over the years, adopted a number of techniques which are used to make legislation easier to read and understand. They include the following characteristics:

- The act normally has a very short title (*Vallagen*) [The Elections Act][6]
- There is a table of contents, often in the very first article
- The act is normally divided into chapters with chapter headings, and the chapter often start with a summary of the chapter's contents
- The structure of the act depends on how it will be used and by whom, it must be logical and user friendly; the principle "from the general to the specific" is preferably used in the different parts of the act
- Informative subheadings, sometimes in the form of a question, give a clear picture of the structure and contents of the act. – *How much rent must the tenant pay?*
- Each article has no more than three paragraphs in it
- Vertical lists are often used for procedures, conditions and so forth
- References to provisions in another act are formulated in such a way that the reader gets a fair picture of what the provision referred to is about
- Clear and simple language is used, if possible gender neutral language, according to existing guidelines.

The Division is also keen to explore the use of contents lists and summaries as a mechanism to make legislation more accessible to a wider audience, particularly those who are accessing information on the Internet where publication of the full text is unlikely to be of use to the majority of readers. It is the division's belief that such summaries should be prepared by the drafters to reduce the possibility of misleading or incorrect information.

Changing ineffective text models

In addition to legislation, other government documents (such as Commission reports, administrative decisions, explanatory parts of bills, administrative decisions and committees' terms of references)[7] have been the subject of improvements efforts. One of the key features of the efforts to improve clarity has been a move away from the chronological narrative approach which has characterised traditional government texts. Under the new approach, drafters now begin by focusing on the proposals or decisions made by the Government and then go on to set out the supporting

---

6 See Vallagen (2005: 837) [Elections Act], especially chapter 1 (table of contents) and chapter 7 (informative subheadings), available at Swedish statutes in translation <www.sweden.gov.se/sb/d/3288>.

7 A good example of the non-chronological/narrative structure is Chapter 5 of the *Best Language* (2005:06/2) Bill, available in Swedish at <www.regeringen.se/sb/d/108/a/50761>, and which shows the proposals followed by the motivation (arguments). The new model is not a narrative one, but is more focused on the result (*what* does the government propose and *why*, and *which* consequences will the proposal have and so forth).

arguments. The adoption of this outcome driven approach by the Government and the Swedish Parliament (which is also now using this clearer 'the-result-first' model or 'emphatic approach'[8] in its reports on legislation from the standing Committees) has given rise to a trickle down effect to agencies at all levels of the Government.

The experience of the Division suggests that altering inefficient writing habits is not an easy task since such drafting in particular is influenced and governed by tradition. If members of Parliament are to be convinced of the merits of the new model, they must see tangible benefits. As such, reforms of the drafting approach takes time and there needs to be a strategy which is persuasive, diplomatic, yet persistent. The experience in Sweden suggests that as members of Parliament become accustomed and familiar with the new 'emphatic approach', resistance gradually disappears. A key element in overcoming resistance is to target important standards documents as evidence of the commitment and support for greater clarity.

Promoting greater clarity: The plain Swedish group

In a bid to encourage all government authorities to use greater clarity in their writing, the Government appointed a Plain Swedish Group as early as 1993. The aim of the group was to build a network of contacts at almost every level of government authority. On July 1, 2006, the group was incorporated into a new state body: The Swedish Language Council.[9]

The Plain Swedish group carried out a variety of projects and activities including:

- Bringing together knowledge, ideas and experiences from various plain language projects in Sweden and abroad
- Arranging plain language conferences in support of greater clarity
- Delivering lectures and seminars on plain language to the government's agencies
- Publishing a plain language bulletin
- Awarding the Plain Swedish Crystal.

The group was made of judges, linguists, information managers and political scientists, appointed as members of the group on a voluntary basis. The participation of judges from the Supreme Courts was seen as greatly enhancing the standing of the movement and in convincing lawyers and senior officials of the merits of plain language. The group was supported by a secretariat consisting of two language consultants.

Despite limited resources, the impact of the Plain Swedish Group has been impressive. More than half of all Swedish government agencies are currently involved in plain language work. This stands in sharp contrast to the position in 1994 when the group started its campaigning and 65 percent of the authorities felt

---

8 In Swedish 'the result-first' structure or model is called the '*emfatisk disposition*'. It can also be translated in English as the 'emphatic approach'.

9 See <http://www.sprakradet.se/klarspråk>.

no need to participate in plain language work at all (see *Klarspråksbulletinen* [the *Plain Swedish Bulletin*] 2002; surveys were also sent out in 1994, 1996, 1999 and 2006).[10]

In 2001, the Plain Swedish Group also initiated an evaluation of the comprehensibility of public agencies texts. While this evaluation found that archaic and obscure language as well as long and convoluted sentences had almost disappeared from bureaucratic language, there remained a lot to be done in other respects to make the documents more user-friendly. The evaluation (see footnote 11) indicated that the root of the comprehensibility problems lay mostly in the failure to take account of the reader's needs, in both the content structure and presentation of the text. Specifically, many of the documents lacked the meta-comments such as summaries and informative sub-headings needed to guide the reader through the text.[11]

Based on the results of the evaluation, a checklist to be used by government officials was developed. It contained a total of 35 questions, all crucial to the comprehensibility of the text, the readers' needs, the message, text structure and textual cohesion, syntax and words and phrases. The checklist was then developed into an interactive web test in 2002, the so-called *Klarspråkstestet* [plain language test].[12] A new version of the test was developed in 2006, specifically aimed at drafting administrative decisions and letters. The test can be used free of charge by anyone who wants to revise an existing text or simply learn how to write in a reader-friendly way.[13]

In addition to the work of the Plain Swedish group, the efforts of achieving greater clarity have been supported by the large corpus of language consultants who are graduates of a special two and half years language and communication programme at the University of Stockholm. One of the aims of this programme is to put in place a training and development support initiative to teach how to write clear, precise and straightforward Swedish, tailored to the readers' needs.

Guidelines and handbooks for clear legal language

A number of guidelines have been developed over the years, and issued by the Prime Minister's Office. The first set of guidelines for clear language in laws entitled *Language in Acts and Other Statutes* appeared as early as 1967. From a current

---

10 A summary in Swedish of the result of all the inquiries can be found on the *Sprakradet's* website, see *Klarspråksgruppens enkätresultat* [result of surveys] at <www.sprakradet. se/2067>. A summary in English of the results from the 1994-1999 surveys is also published in the *Plain Swedish Bulletin* (2002).

11 Published in *På väg mot ett bättre myndighetsspråk* (2001) [Towards better Swedish in public authorities] by the *Statskontoret* [Swedish Agency for Public Management], see <www.sprakradet.se/2067>.

12 For further details on the web test see Baedecke and Sundin (2002) available at <http:// www.plainlanguagenetwork.org/conferences/2002/sweden/>.

13 The new version of the plain language test is available at <www.sprakradet. se/2065>.

perspective they look very unsophisticated but their recommendations attracted considerable attention from lawyers when they were issued. The government's motivation for issuing these first guidelines lay in its belief that if openness and efficiency in public administration was to be encouraged, then official texts and, first of all, legislation needed to be clear and user-friendly. As such, the democratic guarantee of access to the law and the rule of law required a commitment to clarity. The guidelines asked drafters to

- Use modern and comprehensible vocabulary and modern forms
- Avoid 'the noun disease' and unusual prepositional phrases
- Avoid long and complex sentences with embedded subordinate clauses
- Avoid vagueness and unnecessary variation.

In 1979, *More Guidelines for The Language of Legislation* were published This supplement set out principles for making the language gender-neutral and provided guidance on the use of headings and sub-headings and the merits of lists for multiple conditions, requirements or rules. More importantly, the Government at the time declared that the drafters had to follow the guidelines, not only when drafting new Acts and Ordinances but also when drafting amendments. It prescribes that as soon as a substantial amendment is made, the language of the amended article must be modernised when and if necessary to ensure its clarity. As a result the Government was able to put in place an ongoing process of modernisation of the legislation; hence, the consolidated version of a law usually contains both old-fashioned style and contemporary, ordinary language. In the 1980's, more guidelines were published including the so-called *Svarta listan* [black list], which focused on showing how inflated, formal and difficult legal phrases could be replaced with more comprehensible alternatives.[14] At the time of publication, these suggested alternatives were already in widespread use in new and amended legislation which had been approved by the director-general for legal affairs in each ministry. As a result, the traditional arguments against such a move on the basis of impoverishing the legal language were not heard.

In addition to the mentioned guidelines, the Prime Minister's Office issued handbooks addressed to the ministries and the State Commissions on how to draft government bills, State Commission reports, administrative decisions and State committee terms of reference. Moreover, the prime Minister's Office has issued style guides addressed to all public authorities in Sweden to ensure uniform writing so far as punctuation, abbreviation etc. are concerned.[15] The central authorities were also issued with a handbook on how to draft regulations. Other guidelines on how to draft, Government Bills, Administrative Decisions, State Commission Reports and State Committee Terms of Reference have also been issued. The Division also publishes a style guide on a regular basis, *Myndigheternas skrivregler* [*A Styleguide*

---

14 The black list is available for consultation at <http://www.regeringen.se/content/1/c6/01/97/75/e28ebb27.pdf>.

15 Most of these can be found at the Government's web site, see <www.regeringen.se/sb/d/3251>.

for Public Authorities], addressed to the ministries, the Parliament and all public authorities in Sweden.

How we influence the European Union documents

When existing European Union legislation was being translated into Swedish in the early 1990's, many Swedes worried about the complicated language it contained. The Swedish translators adopted the continental style with longwinded articles and long and complicated sentences, as the requirement is not to split sentences up. One sentence in French or English must also be one sentence in all other EU official language versions. In this respect, the quality of the translation is very heavily dependent on the quality of the source text.

There were also complaints about the long titles of the directives and regulations, not to mention the preamble (commonly know as recitals) often written in the form of a single long convoluted sentence made up of one hundreds words or so. Verbosity, contracted sentences, long attributes, EU jargon: all this made EU legislation difficult or impossible to translate into modern Swedish. Therefore, Sweden felt that the language of those translations reverted back several decades in respect of the developments to simplify and clarify legal language. Research carried to that effect proves that this was indeed the case (Sheiki 1998; Ehrenberg-Sundin 2000, 2004; Ekerot 2000; Parés 2002; Hofman 2003; Nilsson 2004; Wallin 2004).

So, the question became clear: what can Sweden do to help in making EU texts clearer and simpler? This question, and an answer to it, was in fact raised several years ago by a Commission Report *Swedish in the EU* (1998, 14). Some of the proposals in that report are now beginning to bear fruit. Over the last few years, efforts to promote plain language in the European Union context have increased. For instance, an EU Language Service as part of the Division for Legal and Linguistic Draft Revision at the Ministry of Justice has been set up. Its principal channel is a website[16] which has been set up to

- Support the Swedish translators and legal revisers, mostly in terminology matters
- Encourage the Swedish EU-delegates, who take part in various EU working groups, to pay attention to the guidelines for clear drafting that recently appeared in the EU and to use what influence they have to improve the wording and structure of the legal documents handled by those groups – both the source text and the Swedish translation
- Influence Sweden's positions on the regulatory reform work in the EU, by suggesting that the reform work also should include rewrites in plain language, and not only include methods like deregulation, consolidation or the use of impact analysis, which are the main issues of the Better Lawmaking Program.

To achieve the above, several methods are used.

---

16 See <www.regeringen.se/sb/d/2750>.

Consistent guidelines and recommendations

The website lists several guidelines and recommendations for EU texts written in Swedish on:

- How to comment on draft EU legislation, while still under consideration by the European Commission, the Council of the European Union or the European Parliament
- How to request linguistic corrections in legislation that has been adopted
- How to draft a text in a clear way so that it will become easier to translate; those guidelines are also translated and adopted into English and French and issued by the Translation Centre for the European Union Bodies in Luxemburg[17]
- How to find the right expression when drafting or translating texts about EU matters; this style guide,[18] issued in September 2005 is produced in cooperation with the Swedish translation departments in the EU institutions.

The Swedish translators and legal revisers also use the guidelines for plain legal drafting and other style guides, issued by the Swedish Prime Minister's Office, which I mentioned earlier. The web site also provides access to the EU institutions' own agreement on the editorial quality of Community legislation since December 1998 and *the Joint Practical Guide for the drafting of Community legislation* [the *Joint Practical Guide*],[19] which appeared in Swedish in 2003.[20] It is important that people taking part in EU working groups where legislative acts are drafted and debated know that the institutions have actually agreed that

- Legislative acts must be clearly, simply and precisely drafted
- Consideration must be given to the individuals who will be affected by the legislative acts and the people responsible for implementing them
- Overly long articles and sentences, unnecessarily convoluted wording and excessive use of abbreviations should be avoided.

In other words, these EU guidelines stipulate that EU legislation must be appropriate for its target group and clearly and simply worded.

---

17 See <www.cdt.europa.eu>.

18 *Redaktionella och språkliga frågor i EU-arbetet* (2005) [*Editorial and Linguistic Issues on Implementing EU Legislation*] available at < http://www.regeringen.se/content/1/c4/34/95/f58bd44d.pdf>.

19 Arising out of the *Interinstitutional Agreement of 22 December 1998 on Common Guidelines for the Quality of Drafting of Community Legislation,* Available at <http://eur-lex.europa.eu/LexUriServ/LexUriServ.do?uri=CELEX:31999Y0317(01):EN:NOT>.

20 See <http://eur-lex.europa.eu/sv/techleg/index.htm>.

Helpful networking

Some forty government agencies and all ministries have appointed one or more contact persons for EU language issues. These contact persons are the gateway to the experts at the agency or ministry. They channel up-to-date information from the EU Language Service to the experts and help the translators at the institutions to quickly get hold of the right expert when they have questions about terminology, for example. This is very important, as decisions often have to be very quick as to which term to use in certain context. If a suitable term is not used, the consequences may echo through the various types of ensuing legislation for years to come.

The EU Language Service, in turn, works closely with the different translation departments and lawyer-linguists in Brussels and Luxemburg and with language organisations in Sweden. Smooth cooperation enables all the parties involved to produce consistent recommendations on matters of style and terminology. As a result, there is a close cooperation between the Swedish translators working in the different EU institutions and I believe that this cooperation is rather unique. This also applies to the link they have to Swedish ministries and authorities through the EU Language Service.

Political influence

Clear and simple regulations are an issue to which Sweden gives priority. One of the objectives of the EU Language Service is to monitor and influence this issue. A great deal of work is now being done in the EU on better regulation. The Commission's action plan for better and simpler legislation (June 2002) contains a series of suggestions on how to improve quality, for example by impact analyses and broader consultation procedures. The proposals are embodied in the *Interinstitutional Agreement on Better Law-Making* (2003) (for further discussion on the *Interinstitutional Agreement*, see Flückiger, Chapter 1).

In connection with the negotiations on this agreement, Sweden emphasised the requirement for linguistic and editorial clarity in legislation. During the Convention on the Future of Europe, Sweden also suggested an addition to the new constitutional treaty on this very point, though unfortunately to no avail in the final negotiations (see Ehrenberg-Sundin 2004). But plain language thinking is finally taking root in the EU, and the pressure must be kept up.

Broaden the network and share best practice!

It would be a very fruitful exercise to set up networks with counterparts from all the Member States to share best practices in the field of clear legislation. Many States have accepted principles of drafting that are surprisingly similar (for a comparative analysis see Ehrenberg-Sundin 2000). Clarity, simplicity, precision, accuracy and plain language are common standards of good quality legislation both in the common law and civil law drafting styles (see for example the various *Chartes de la qualité de la réglementation* [Charters of quality drafting] of the different ministries of France;[21] *Report on Statutory Drafting and Interpretation: Plain Language and the Law in Ireland 2000).*

The problem of good standards and recommendations not being known and therefore not applied by drafters is universal. It is important that such standards and recommendations do not become an empty gesture. It is also very important that new models be developed and tested. The criticism of existing drafting techniques (see for example Butt and Castle 2001; Cutts 2001; Cutts and Wagner 2002) should be considered in such pivotal work and best practice should be shared between countries.

Efforts to improve the source texts in the Commission

During the last few years some steps have been taken to improve the quality of EU legislation drafts in English or French (see for example Robinson 2005). The Commission's Legal Revisers Group assists the different Directorates General to revise legislative drafts at an early stage, and also offer seminars in legislative drafting. At this early stage when the draft exists in only one language, far-reaching changes can be suggested if the legal revisers believe them necessary.

Unfortunately, the strict, short deadlines and the volume of work often prevent the revisers from achieving the standard they would like. But, obviously, this kind of support is really needed. As legislation is drafted by the technical department for the sector concerned, the draftsman is seldom a lawyer but a veterinarian or an economist with no training at all in legal drafting. And mostly s/he writes in a foreign language. Due to this fact there is a tendency for the drafters to follow precedent and continue using phrases and expressions that have been used in earlier provisions or legislation.

A systematic approach to improve drafting is needed

Sweden welcomes the steps taken by the Commission's Legal Service, but more has to be done to improve the quality of EU drafting. What concrete measures and what resources and competence will be needed internally is, of course for the EU institutions to think about and decide upon. There must be, though, strategic approaches, effective structures and adequate resources.

As I have mentioned, the Swedish experience is that there is a lot to be gained if language experts and lawyers, as well as experts of the subject matter, cooperate in drafting legislation; and that political support and support from central administration is crucial. This is also needed in the European Union. Otherwise there might be a risk that better regulation work will not include enough action to ensure that the structure, presentation and language of the rules will be as clear as the citizens of the Union are hoping for. Impact assessment, consultation, consolidation, deregulation,

---

21 For example the Charte de la qualité de la réglementation du Ministère de la défense available at <http://www.thematiques.modernisation.gouv.fr/UserFiles/File/C42-2%20doc%202 b%20Processus%20labellisation%20VF%2016%2005%2007.pdf>.

good formal and legal quality and easy public access on the Internet are all important components in better regulation work; but, they are not enough if legislation is to be understood and applied in the way it was intended.

For instance, the *Joint Practical Guide* produced by the institutions' own legal services, clearly states that sentences should be short; but yet recommends the following model provision, which contains a very long sentence once the gaps in between the brackets are filled in.

> Since the objectives of the action to be taken (*specify the objectives*) cannot be sufficiently achieved by Member States (*give reasons*) and can therefore, by reason of (*specify the scale or effects of the action*), be better achieved at Community level, the Community may adopt measures, in accordance with the principle of subsidiarity as set out in Article 5 of the Treaty. In accordance with the principle of proportionality, as set out in that Article, this (*name of the act*) does not go beyond what is necessary in order to achieve those objectives.

In practice, it turns out like this:

> Since the objectives of the proposed action, namely to coordinate activities in the Member States to regulate and supervise safety and to investigate accidents and to establish at Community level common safety targets, common safety methods, common safety indicators and common requirements of safety certificates, cannot be sufficiently achieved by the Member States and can therefore, by reason of the scale of the action, be better achieved at Community level, the Community may adopt measures in accordance with the principle of subsidiarity as set out in Article 5 of the Treaty. (91 words) In accordance with the principle of proportionality, as set out in that Article, this Directive does not go beyond what is necessary in order to achieve those objectives.

And this is a provision which appears in most EU laws!

Why plain language is worthwhile

The benefits of clear and effective communication between government and the public and business are well defined and approved of in Sweden. Plain language writing helps maintain faith in public institutions. It enhances democracy and rule of law and makes administration more efficient and thus saves both time and money. And last but not least, it inspires the civil servants to do a good job.

It is, of course, a natural aim in a democracy to want to ensure openness and clarity within the public administration. In Sweden, the principle of public access to documents was expressed for the first time in 1766 in the *Freedom of the Press Act*, now a constitutional law (*Constitutional Act 1949*). This principle facilitates the free democratic exchange of views, thereby contributing to the democratic legitimacy of decisions. It also strengthens the control of the administration by the public and the media, and contributes to making the administration more efficient. But the principle of accessibility to documents does not function well if documents are not easy to read and understand. Hence, one can argue on that basis that plain language is a prerequisite of openness. The actual cost of poor writing in government and law are certainly beyond calculation. In Sweden, there are no large-scale evaluations or inquiries made to measure the actual costs of poorly written documents or the actual gains of rewriting documents in plain language. Some authorities measure the time and cost wasted as a result of complaints, confusion and claims occasioned by, for instance, a certain letter or form sent out by the authority in question.[22]

The current efforts to make the majority of citizens use the Internet services that the Swedish authorities provide, are, of course, in the long run both time and cost saving for the government. In this context, the use of plain language is of utmost importance: the information provided on the websites must be comprehensible to anyone using it; otherwise nothing will be gained by using the new technology. It is evident, that the self-service function made possible by the new e-society will not be worth the effort if instructions and information on websites are too difficult to understand.

The central tax authority, for instance, offers many different types of information and service on its Internet Portal, including the possibility to approve income tax return forms, already filled in by the authority based on the figures for the year in question.[23] Last year, six and a half million Swedes had the opportunity to complete their tax return on the Internet or by sms (using their cell-phones). More than one million people made use of this possibility. The ongoing simplification of tax return forms, which started in the late 1970s, is only one example of a reform in Sweden, which includes rewrites and simplified routines as well as making use of new technology. The guiding star of this reform has been and still is to make life easier for the general public and to reduce costs at the same time.

A Government Bill proposes a concerted language policy for Sweden

In September 2005, the Swedish Government submitted the *Best language – a concerted language policy for Sweden (2005)* bill to the Parliament. In it, the Government proposed four new objectives for national language policy, namely:

- Swedish is to be the main language in Sweden
- Swedish is to be a complete language, serving and uniting society
- Public Swedish is to be cultivated, simple and comprehensible

---

22 As an example in 2005, the National Social Insurance Board sent out a letter to 900 000 senior citizens concerning changes in their pension benefits. As the letter was written in legalese, it caused thousands of inquiries as people did not understand the content of the correspondence. The cost to the Insurance Board in terms of phone calls and e-mails, not to mention the loss of public confidence was incalculable. The letter was re-written in plain language and tested on focus groups including the original intended readers (senior citizens). Three tests were carried out, because the rewrites were simply not good enough and had to be improved step by step. The cost for these focus groups tests and rewrites was marginal, compared to the cost the first letter has involved.

23 See <www.skatteverket.se>.

- Everyone is to have a right to language: to develop and learn Swedish, to develop and use their own mother tongue and national minority language and to have the opportunity to learn foreign languages.

The main reason for this proposal is that the language situation in Sweden has evolved in a number of ways. Firstly, five languages have been granted the official status of minority languages (standard Finnish, Tornedal [Meänkieli], Sami, Romani, Yiddish); secondly, one ninth of the population are from a non-Swedish background; for many of them (including immigrants) Swedish is their second language. In addition, there is an increasing use of English in many areas of society, such as in higher education and research, which in the long run could lead to domain losses.

The language policy must take account of the overall language situation in the country. One aspect of this situation is that everyone whose first language is not Swedish must be able to retain and develop their mother tongue. At the same time, in order to respond to internalisation and the development of society, good opportunities must be available to acquire knowledge of English and other foreign languages. Moreover, clear and comprehensible official texts are a pre-condition for a living democracy (see *Mål i mun* SOU 2002:2, Chapter 9 [Speech – Draft Action Programme for the Swedish Language]).

Therefore, the Government considered that a reinforced and coordinated language planning organisation was needed. A new language planning body, The Swedish Language Council, was organised from 1 July 2006 and it was coordinated with the existing *Institutet för språk och folkminnen* [Institute for Dialectology, Onomastics and Folklore Research in Uppsala].[24] The new body is based on the activities conducted by the former Swedish Language Council and the Finnish Language Council in Sweden and, last but not least, the activities of the Plain Swedish Group in the Government Offices. Other new areas of work for the Language Council deal with sign language and the promoting of the national minority languages. The Swedish Terminology Center, though, remained an independent body but works closely with the new language planning body. The language experts and the EU Language Service continue to work as before within the Government Offices. With this new coordinated language body, the activities of the Plain Swedish Group will be widened to cover the current language situation in Sweden. More importantly, the plain language issues will now be considered in a more concerted way and in a broader context through this new organisation.

Conclusion

The Swedish experience with efforts to encourage clear legislation and official texts has highlighted a number of important lessons for other jurisdictions seeking to advance the cause of legal clarity. The support and sponsorship of ministers, politicians, and senior public servants is paramount to mobilising a broad and lasting commitment across all sectors of government. In addition placing the effort on a legal

---

24 See <www.sofi.se>.

footing sends a clear signal of the government's commitment and the importance it attaches to clear language and effective communication. A genuine cooperation between plain language experts, lawyers and other experts when reforming texts helps create the conditions for success while authorities must have adequate resources to plan and carry out systematic plain language activities. Finally the intended readers and users of texts have an important contribution to make to the clarity and plain legal language efforts and they should be engaged with as stakeholders in the entire process.

Chapter 10

What, How, When and Why – Making Laws Easier to Understand by Using Examples and Notes

Ben Piper[1]

> The legislative drafter also labours under another difficulty. Writers of other documents are at liberty to set their work out in the form that best suits the task of conveying their intention. However, the legislative drafter is obliged to follow a form that enables the bill as drafted to be debated in accordance with the standing orders of the parliament that is to consider it. This means that the bill must be divided into separate clauses and that for the most part material that is merely illustrative of the intended effect of the legislation must not be included.
>
> These handicaps go to make the conveyance of meaning in legislation particularly difficult (Pearce and Geddes 2001, 3).

The intention of this chapter is to show that it is no longer necessary for drafters to labour under this difficulty. Through the expeditious use of notes[2] and examples, legislative drafters can now illustrate more clearly the intended effect of what they write, resulting in legislation that is more accessible to a wider range of readers, and that is easier to interpret and apply (for further discussion on the impact of statements, explanatory notes, examples, summaries and overviews in legislative drafting, see Sullivan 2001; Carter and Green 2007).

While this chapter is primarily concerned with legislative drafting, my observations should also have validity with respect to contract drafting, as it is an activity that is similar to legislative drafting (see Kimble 1992; for a comparative analysis on contractual and statutory interpretation see Kirby 2003) and was the first area to explore the adoption of notes and examples (Battistoni 2005, 4).

While the conceptual foundations of using notes and examples to improve clarity are well established in the plain language literature (Sullivan 2001), the purpose of this chapter is to use working examples to provide insights into the opportunities that the use of notes and examples provide for legislative drafters in practice,

---

1 At the time this paper was written I was a legislative drafter in the Office of the Chief Parliamentary Counsel, Victoria, Australia. The views expressed in this paper are my personal views and do not necessarily represent the views of that Office.

2 Note that I am not referring here to notes as 'marginal notes' (sections headings) as understood for example in the UK. For an analysis of the use of marginal notes in the interpretation of legislation, see Simanba (2005).

particularly the opportunity to improve their ability to communicate. While the evidence presented is largely anecdotal and primarily based on my own personal experience as a legislative drafter, it serves to illustrate the potential promise which notes and examples hold out for improving the clarity of legislation. It is hoped that by illustrating this potential promise, more legal writers/drafters will be encouraged to use this valuable tool.

Potted personal and Victorian history of the use of notes and examples

I first started using notes in about 1990 at a time when Victorian legislative drafters were permitted to insert notes as footnotes on the relevant page of a law. Unfortunately soon after 1990 this permission was retracted, and notes were then only permitted to appear as an endnote. These endnotes appeared among other material at the end of laws and were very difficult to find.[3] I thus attempted to use notes only on a handful of occasions in the 1990s, and during that period, I only used the occasional textual example.[4]

In 2000, the *Interpretation of Legislation Act 1984 (Vic)* [the *Interpretation Act*] was amended to recognise notes and examples as part of Victoria's laws (section 36(3A)). From the start of 2001, Victorian legislative drafters have been able to insert notes and examples immediately after the provisions to which they relate, confident that those notes and examples form part of the law in which they appear.

Examples – old style

For many years, most English-speaking jurisdictions (including Victoria) have used what I call 'textual examples'; that is an example that appears as part of the text of a law. The 'classic' textual example is something like the following from section 6 of the *Jobseekers Act 1995* (C.18)(U.K.):

> (2) those regulations may [...] provide that a person–
>> (b) may restrict his availability for employment in any week in such circumstances as may be prescribed (for example, on grounds of conscience, religious conviction or physical or mental condition or because he is caring for another person).

In jurisdictions that do not expressly provide for examples, this is basically the only way that an example can be put forward with the confidence that it forms part of the law. By its nature it is clearly part of the text of the law.

---

3 This material includes such things as extended publishing histories and notes, notes containing information about the Parliamentary history of the Bill that became the Act, indexes and reproductions of items of the relevant law that had been passed, but that had not yet come into operation.

4 These are examples that form part of the text of a law. They are discussed in more detail in the next section.

There is another sort of textual example that is handled differently by different jurisdictions. Again, the very next sub-section of the *Jobseekers Act* provides an example of this alternative form:

> (3) The following are examples of restrictions for which provision may be made by the regulations–
>
> (a) restrictions on the nature of the employment for which a person is available;
>
> (b) restrictions on the periods for which he is available; [...].

Had this provision been drafted in Victoria in 1995, the opening words would have been written along the following lines:

> (3) Without limiting sub-section (2), the regulations may provide for– [   ].

In other words, legislative drafters in Victoria would not have stated that the specific instances were examples, even though that is clearly what they regarded them as. Given that we have always had a concern that our specific lists of instances create the danger of causing the general empowering words to be read down despite our express words that that is not to happen (this is particularly so in the case of long specific lists), the U.K. approach has considerable attraction, as something that is explicitly called an example is far less likely to be used to read down the general words of which it is an example.

There is also a hybrid form of the Victorian and U.K. approaches. I have come across examples in Ontario that adopt wording similar to the Victorian wording, but that also insert a sub-section heading above that wording stating 'Examples' (see section 347 *Education Act, R.S.O. 1990, c.E.2*; section 13 *Municipal Act 2001, S.O. 2001, c.25*).

Although textual examples have some attractions, they have the disadvantage that they are not a suitable vehicle for telling a story (see below pp. 187-189). This is because narrative examples often need a few sentences for their telling and usually refer to people in one form or another. Generally, if they were put into the middle of a provision it would be almost impossible to properly read the provision, as the example would be more of an obstacle than an aid to understanding.

I therefore argue that only narrative examples have the potential to communicate with readers in new ways. As Rudolph Flesch (1949, 38) stated years ago:

> Whenever you write about a general principle, show its application in a specific case; [...] tell a pointed anecdote. These dashes of colour are what the reader will take away with him. Not that he will necessarily remember the illustration or anecdote itself; but it will help him remember the main idea.

While at present it is perhaps too radical to suggest that we illustrate every general principle in our laws with a dash of colour, I do suggest that we do it in cases where readers might have more difficulty than usual in understanding a general principle. And in those cases the only thing suitable for the job is a narrative example or a decent note.

Potted history of elsewhere

Various jurisdictions in Australia (the Commonwealth, New South Wales, Queensland) have used notes and narrative examples in their legislation since at least the early 1990's. For instance, extensive worked notes and examples appeared in the Commonwealth's social security legislation in 1991 (see section 8(11) *Social Security Act 1991*). Of those jurisdictions that use notes and examples, in some it is clear that they form part of the law (see *Interpretation Act 1984 (Vic)*) while in others it is not so clear (see *Interpretation Act 1987 (NSW)*), and in some jurisdictions it is a factor that varies from Act to Act. There are also some differences in these jurisdictions as to whether or not examples can extend the law (for a more detailed discussion see Barnes 2004).

With respect to other common law jurisdictions, some including India, the United Kingdom and a number of U.S. jurisdictions have used textual examples for quite some time (see for example section 6 *Indian Evidence Act 1872*; *Occupier's Liability Act 1957* (UK)). Others such as New Zealand and a number of Canadian jurisdictions occasionally use narrative examples in the way that I will be advocating in this chapter (see for example section 36 *Personal Property Securities Act 1999* (New Zealand)).

A threshold issue

From a strict legal point of view there is not much point in having notes and examples in laws unless it is clear that they are actually part of the law, and have the same status as the operative provisions of the law, or, at the very least, that they are matters that can be taken into account in interpreting the laws to which they relate. More particularly, it is highly undesirable to have a situation where there is an express statement that if there is a conflict between a provision of a law and an example of that provision, the provision of the law prevails. This is the case in at least several jurisdictions in Australasia (see for example section 15AD *Acts Interpretation Act 1901(Cth)*; section 14D *Acts Interpretation Act 1954 (Qld)*). It is undesirable because a situation then arises where on the face of the law it appears that the law does not achieve the intention of the writer of the law. For instance, take the following hypothetical definition and example in relation to an injury compensation scheme:

'medical service' includes–
   (a) the provision of any article needed to operate, run or repair any medical equipment;
Examples[5]
Examples of things referred to in paragraph (d) include electricity, water, lubricating oil and replacement filters and batteries.

Paragraph (d) only refers to articles, but the very first example is 'electricity', which is hardly an 'article' in the strict sense of that word. It appears the drafter

---

5 Bold in the original. All bold typeset provided in the examples given are in the original text of the Acts cited.

really intended to refer to the 'thing' in paragraph (d) rather than 'article'. If this provision appeared in a Queensland law, a court would be bound to find that the provision prevailed and that electricity therefore could not be considered to be a medical service, even though it appears to have been within the contemplation of Parliament/the drafter that electricity should be a medical service. However, in Victoria it would be open to a court to find that electricity was a medical service.

This is because Victoria inserted in 2000, with effect from 1 January 2001, the following provisions in its *Interpretation Act*:

> An example (being an example at the foot of a provision under the heading **'Example'** or **'Examples'**), diagram or note (being a note at the foot of a provision and not a marginal note, footnote or endnote) in an Act or subordinate instrument forms part of the Act or subordinate instrument [...] (emphasis in the original) (s. 36(3A)).
>
> If an Act or subordinate instrument includes at the foot of a provision under the heading **'Example'** or **'Examples'** an example of the operation of the provision, the example –
> (a) is not exhaustive; and
> (b) may extend, but does not limit, the meaning of the provision (emphasis in the original) (s. 36A(1)).[6]

In the case of our hypothetical provision, I suggest that the Victorian result is the more desirable outcome.

At the same time as the Victorian provisions were introduced, a decision was made allowing Victorian legislative drafters to insert notes immediately after the provision to which the note applied. Should other jurisdictions be tempted to introduce similar provisions, I recommend on the basis of my experience with the *Interpretation Act* provisions, that paragraph (b) immediately above be split into the following two paragraphs:

> (b) may extend the meaning of the provision; and
> (c) does not limit the meaning of the provision unless the contrary intention appears.

This rewording gives examples more scope. It also overcomes the possibility that it can be argued that negative examples (that is, examples of what is not covered by a provision) are not part of the law (see section on '*Setting limits*' for more details).

I should also mention that in some jurisdictions, individual Acts have set out their own interpretation provisions with respect to the examples that appear in them (see Barnes 2004, 10). This is, of course, the only option contract drafters have, but it is also something individual legislative drafters may wish to consider doing in jurisdictions that have no Interpretation Act provisions dealing with notes and examples.

---

6 The Act is available at:
   <http://www.dms.dpc.vic.gov.au/Domino/Web_Notes/LDMS/PubLawToday.nsf/
   2184e627479f8392ca256da50082bf3e/0BAFA192804A8E0CCA257296001EFC87/
   $FILE/84-10096a090.doc>.

Introduction to the notes and examples

The examples of notes and examples that follow are a representative sampling of the notes and examples I have inserted, or attempted to insert, into Victoria's laws. To keep faith with anyone who might have been attracted by the title to this chapter, my first four groups of examples reflect that title. Those groups are not mutually exclusive, nor were they ever intended to be comprehensive. After the four groups I have taken the liberty of including some other types of notes and examples. There are undoubtedly many other types.[7]

What?

It is the lot of the legislative drafter from time to time to write something that, at first glance, and perhaps even at second and third glance, appears, to put it kindly, to be strange. In the past all we could do was write these provisions and hope that users would realise from the context, or from their deeper knowledge of the relevant environment, what the 'strange' provision was attempting to do. Notes, in particular, now provide us with a means to provide all readers of our laws with an explanation of what is going on.

Example no. 1

Recently, Victoria attempted to standardise the enforcement provisions in three related Acts: the *Dangerous Goods Act 1985* [the *Dangerous Goods Act*]; the *Equipment (Public Safety) Act 1994*; and the *Occupational Health and Safety Act 2005*. The latter Act had already been enacted with the model provisions, and it was my role to insert replicas of those model provisions into the other two Acts. One of the provisions which had to be replicated provided for the administrative review of certain enforcement decisions – these were defined as 'reviewable decisions'. The *Dangerous Goods Act* had a section 10A that also provided for the administrative review of decisions made under that Act. For purposes of uniformity, it was thus necessary to include the following provision in section 10A:

(2A) Sub-section (1) does not apply to any reviewable decision.

This had the result that on the face of section 10A, any decision under the Act could be reviewed except 'reviewable' decisions. As I was sure that this would cause confusion, I therefore included the following note immediately after sub-section (2A):

Note: A 'reviewable decision' has the meaning given by section 20 – see section 3(1). Reviewable decisions are excluded from sub-section (1) because they are dealt with by Part IIA. Essentially, a wider range of people may apply for the review of a reviewable decision and there is a process of internal review available in respect of those decisions.

---

7 There is not much purpose to be served by creating these classifications other than for the sake of convenience.

Example no. 2

A provision was inserted into the *Liquor Control Reform Act 1998* [the *Liquor Control Act*] that required people who were required by another provision of the Act to complete a responsible service of alcohol course to produce evidence that they had completed the course, if they were asked to do so by an inspector (section 108A). This provision had the following exception:

> (3) Sub-section (2) does not apply if the licensee, permittee or person acting on behalf of the licensee or permittee has not completed the required program or course, or did not complete the program or course within a required period.

At first glance this seems to be creating a loophole by saying that a person can avoid the provision by not doing the course. On further reading, it becomes clear that while it is a means of avoiding the provision, it would in fact be unreasonable not to have this provision. But to avoid readers spending a large amount of time trying to fully understand the relevant provision, I decided it would be helpful to provide the following explanation:

> Note: Sub-section (3) ensures that a person does not commit an offence by failing to produce evidence that does not exist. If the evidence does not exist the person would have committed a more serious offence under section 108 in not complying with the licence or permit conditions [these conditions required that the person do the course] (*Liquor Control Reform (Underage Drinking and Enhanced Enforcement) Act 2004*).

Example no. 3

Another provision I had to insert into the *Liquor Control Act* was the following:

> **3B. Where supply occurs if off-premises request made**
> For the purposes of this Act, if liquor is provided to a person who was not on licensed premises at the time the person ordered the liquor, the supply of the liquor to the person occurs at the place where the liquor provided was appropriated to the person's order [...].

The phrase 'appropriated to the person's order' is not the sort of phrase I use in legislation (or anywhere else, for that matter). In fact I objected to its use for a long time. Unfortunately it related to an issue that was of great importance to a relatively common type of prosecution under the Act, and it was a phrase on which several courts had offered their opinions in the past. For this reason, the instructing Department insisted that the phrase continue to be used. However, it also was sufficiently moved by my concerns to expressly request the inclusion of examples illustrating what the phrase meant. Hence:

> **Examples**:
> 1. A customer sits down at a kerb-side table of premises operated by the holder of a general licence. She orders a glass of wine. The waiter takes the order to the bar, where a glass is filled. The waiter then takes the glass to the customer. In this scenario the wine in

the glass is supplied to the customer at the bar because that is where it was appropriated to the customer's order.

2. A customer orders the home delivery of a carton of beer by phone from the manager of premises licensed to supply liquor for consumption off the premises. The customer pays for the beer by providing his credit card details over the phone. The manager selects the beer from the fridge, and a staff member delivers the beer to the customer's house. In this scenario the beer is supplied to the customer at the fridge because that is where it was appropriated to the customer's order.

Example no 5

In the recent standardisation exercise I described in example no. 1, it became necessary when amending the *Dangerous Goods Act*, to move two offence provisions that were very inconveniently located for the purposes of the changes we were making. These sections had a subject matter that had nothing to do with the amendments we were inserting. The only way to move the provisions was to re-enact them in a different place in the Act. However, I was concerned that in doing this it would appear that we were creating new offences. I therefore inserted a note after the section stipulating:

> Note: This section re-enacts section 15 of the Act as it was before the commencement of section 9 of the *Dangerous Goods and Equipment (Public Safety) Acts (Amendment) Act 2005.*

How

Example no. 1

Several years ago the Victorian Government decided to regulate public auctions of land. Concern had been expressed, in particular, about the widespread practice of the making of bids on behalf of the sellers at auctions of land, without it being disclosed on whose behalf the bids were being made. Obviously those bids could not be genuine bids, and they were seen as unfairly pushing up the prices obtained at auctions, as genuine bidders at those auctions had no way of knowing that they were bidding against dummy bidders. One of the provisions of the proposed bill, the *Estate Agents and Sale of Land Acts (Amendment) Bill 2003*, stated:

> **42. Offence to falsely acknowledge bid**
> A person at a public auction of land must not falsely claim to have made a bid, or falsely acknowledge that he or she made a bid […].

The instructing Department was concerned that readers of the new law would wonder how someone could falsely claim or acknowledge that they had made a bid. Thus for the exposure draft that was released for public comment before the law was presented to Parliament I prepared the following example at the Department's request:

Ron is trying to sell his house by public auction. His brother Jim agrees to help him. Just before the auction starts Ron introduces Jim to Maria, the auctioneer, and all 3 of them have a chat.

The auction starts. At one point the bidding seems to stop. The reserve price is still a mere hope on the horizon. To get things going again Maria takes a bid from a convenient tree. (In doing this, she commits an offence against section 36C(2).) One of the previous bidders is suspicious and asks Maria to identify the last bidder. Maria points to Jim and asks him to acknowledge making the last bid. In accordance with his pre-auction discussion with Maria, Jim raises his hand. In doing so he commits an offence against this section. He is not guilty of an offence against section 36B because he did not make a bid at the auction.

If Jim had made a bid and Maria had accepted the bid, Maria would have committed an offence against section 36C(1).

The Department was satisfied that this enabled readers to readily understand how the provision worked, and, to the best of my knowledge, no concerns were ever expressed about the provision.[8]

Example no. 2

I was again asked to make an amendment to the *Liquor Control Act*. There was existing provision for the controllers of a liquor licence to nominate a person ('a nominee') to operate the licence (section 54(1)). Once a nomination took effect the nominee assumed a number of the responsibilities of the licence controllers (section 54(9)). I was asked to insert a provision explicitly specifying certain circumstances in which a person ceased to be a nominee (this was in addition to some existing provisions that enabled a person to stop being a nominee), and to then provide that on such a cessation, the licence holders re-assumed their responsibilities. There was no problem with the first part of this instruction, and I produced the following sub-section in the provision:

(10)   A person ceases to be a nominee on ceasing to manage or control the licensed premises in circumstances in which that cessation is, or is likely to be, permanent.

However, there was a problem with the second part of the instruction, as the existing provisions were structured in a way that made it unnecessary to do anything – those provisions already achieved the desired result. The instructing Department was not satisfied with this advice in that they had had considerable problems in practice in getting people to understand what occurred when a person ceased to be a nominee under the existing provisions. I therefore offered to include the following note under sub-section (10):

---

8 This example was the first narrative example I ever drafted. Like many others it remained in the Bill when it was first introduced into Parliament but did not survive the re-introduction of the Bill following an election. I also note that its style shows glimpses of what may be possible for drafters in the future.

Note: On a person ceasing to be a nominee, section 53(4) ceases to apply. This has the effect under section 53 of re-imposing liability as a licensee or permittee on the directors or members of the committee of management (as the case may be) of the body holding the licence or permit.

When

In Victoria work injuries are covered by a statutory compensation scheme. The *Accident Compensation Act 1985* regulating this scheme is frequently amended. Often when amendments are made, the provisions as amended only apply to injuries that occur after the amendments come into operation. Frequently in the past our practice in these situations was to include a new sub-section at the end of the section where a relevant amendment had been made stating that the section as amended by the amending Act only applied to injuries that occurred after the amendments came into operation. Often these new sub-sections appeared physically many sub-sections after the sub-sections to which they applied.

Several years ago I attempted an alternative way of dealing with these provisions. I created a Part at the back of the Act that contained details of all of the amendments that had particular starting times. In the body of the Act, after each amendment that had a particular starting time I inserted a note. Examples of such notes are:

Note: Paragraph (c) does not apply with respect to injuries that occur before the date of commencement of section 8 of the **Accident Compensation and Transport Accident Acts (Amendment) Act 2003**—see section 265.

Note: Subsections (15) to (18) only apply to claims for compensation under this section made after the date of commencement of section 4 of the **Accident Compensation and Transport Accident Acts (Amendment) Act 2003**—see section 266(1). Also, those subsections do not apply to workers who had been injured before that date until the expiry of 18 months after that date—see section 266(2).

Why

An amendment to the *Accident Compensation Act 1985* inserted a formula to be used in the calculation of certain lump sum payments to injured workers. One element of the formula, item 'A' of section 115B, could have one of two alternative meanings (either a gross amount or a net amount), depending on whether or not the relevant Minister had published a certain document. This was a very unusual provision that appeared to provide the Minister with an arbitrary power, so the following note was provided:

Note: The purpose of this provision is to enable the Minister to respond to possible policy changes in relation to the taxation of settlement payments by the Commonwealth Government.[9]

Providing connections

So far I have not discussed the most common circumstance in which notes are used by drafters generally. This is the situation where a provision of a law relies on, or is significantly affected by, another provision of the law that is not in its immediate vicinity. To assist readers in this circumstance it is common to provide a cross-reference. For example, in an amendment of the *Road Safety Act 1986*, the following provision was inserted:

174. Liability of operator
    (1) A person is guilty of an offence if—
        (a) the person is the operator of a vehicle; and
        (b) the vehicle is in breach of a mass [...] limit [...] .
Note: The penalties that apply in respect of the offence created by this section are set out in section 178 (*Transport Legislation (Amendment) Act 2004*).

It is now unusual in Victoria for penalties to be separated from the offences to which they relate. But this was an exceptional case because the penalty depended on whether the offender was a body corporate or not, and on which of three separate categories of offence the transgression fitted into. Section 178 covered almost two pages, and the penalties it contained applied to section 174 and to four other sections. As a result a reader of the Act would only encounter section 178 if s/he read the Act sequentially, something which is unlikely to occur when the law in question relates to heavy transport vehicles. Notes in this circumstance are thus very helpful to readers, and I think most drafters now recognise that.

Making sure it is covered

Another very common circumstance in which examples are used relates to a concern that a provision covers a specific factual situation. In the past these situations were the cause of much disputation with instructors, as they needed the certainty that a common circumstance would be covered. Drafters were worried that the inclusion of specific circumstances would risk causing the generality of the relevant provision to be read down. By inserting examples after provisions both of these problems are addressed, and this approach may even enable examples of what is not intended to be covered to be given – although, as previously mentioned, the legal effectiveness of these negative examples is open to question in Victoria.

---

9 If certain policy changes that were in the offing had been made, recipients of the pay-outs would have suffered significant tax disadvantages unless the appropriate gross or net amount was used for item 'A'.

This provision appeared in a rewrite of section 5 of the *Transport Accident Act 1986* dealing with how a person's pre-accident earnings were to be calculated after a compensable accident:

> (3) This sub-section applies, if during the 12 months immediately before the relevant day, there was, as a result of any action taken by the earner, a significant change in his or her earnings circumstances that resulted in the earner regularly earning, or becoming entitled to earn, more on a weekly basis than he or she was earning before the change occurred (*Transport Accident (Amendment) Act 2004*).[10]

The original provision contained a number of textual examples that were augmented by the inclusion of the following examples directly underneath this provision:

Examples
Examples of a change of circumstances to which this sub-section would apply include a change of job, a promotion, a move from part-time to full-time employment, or a pay increase arising from the achievement of performance standards. This sub-section does not apply to a pay rise applying across an industry.

Maths 'stuff'

Another common circumstance in which examples, in particular, are used, is if a provision contains mathematical calculations. For instance an amendment to the *Accident Compensation Act 1985* included the following:

> (10) A number determined under the A.M.A. Guides must be rounded to the nearest whole percent.

The Department asked to include an example of how this provision would work. In providing the following examples I also took the opportunity to make it clear that the ordinary rules of mathematics applied to this situation:

Examples:
A final degree of impairment of 9.5% must be rounded to 10%. A final degree of impairment of 8.4% must be rounded to 8% (*Accident Compensation and Transport Accident Acts (Amendment) Act 2003*).

Incidentally, the first example was deliberately chosen, as 10% was a very significant threshold in the provision as significant benefits were only available to those who had a 10% or more degree of impairment.

---

10 I had best insert a 'what' note here, as this sub-section reads strangely by itself. Another sub-section in the section took effect if sub-section (3) applied. It was a device I used to break-up the material.

Reminder

In re-enacting section 10B of the *Dangerous Goods Act*, a provision that conferred a power of delegation on various people and authorities, it was envisaged that the delegates would include people and bodies who were not under the administrative control of the Department administering the section. It thus wanted to be able to impose conditions on how the delegations it conferred were exercised, and requested the insertion of a provision in the section to achieve that effect. I advised that this power was already conferred by the *Interpretation Act*. The Department was concerned that future administrators of the section would be unaware of that fact, so the following note was added to the bottom of the section:

> Note: Section 42A(1)(b) of the **Interpretation of Legislation Act 1984** provides that a person delegating a power or function may specify conditions or limitations on the exercise of the power or function by the delegate.

Setting limits

In the amendments prepared in relation to the *Sale of Land Act 1962*, the following offence was created:

> (5) The person must not do any thing with the intention of preventing, causing a major disruption to, or causing the cancellation of, the auction.

In contemplating what might or might not be a 'major' disruption, I thought it might be helpful to attempt to provide some guidance, particularly as a major disruption had to be something that was not so major that it led to the cancellation of the auction. I was also concerned to ensure that it could not be argued that any disruption to an auction was a major disruption. Thus:

> **Example**:
> Fred attends a public auction of a house he intends bidding for. His son accompanies him to the auction with a radio. At one point during the auction, Fred's son whispers into Fred's ear. Fred immediately interrupts the auctioneer to announce that Essendon has just beaten Carlton at the match at the MCG. While this announcement causes the auctioneer to lose concentration and to stop taking bids, she is quickly able to resume the auction. Fred has not caused a major disruption to the auction.
> Harry attends a public auction of a house he intends bidding for. Shortly after the auction starts he sets off a stink bomb. It is not possible to resume the auction until the fumes from the bomb have dissipated, which takes 30 minutes. Harry has caused a major disruption to the auction and has thus committed an offence against sub-section (5) (*Estate Agents and Sale of Land Acts (Amendment) Bill 2002*).[11]

---

11 This example has been critically discussed by O'Brien (2005, 50) one of my colleagues and fellow advocates of the use of examples and notes.

Sadly this example did not make it into the law that was passed by the Victorian Parliament. However, if it had been, it would have caused the courts a headache, as my first example, which arguably is attempting to limit the scope of the provision, is not, according to the *Interpretation Act*, allowed to do so.

On the other hand, courts follow the general principle that they must attempt to give some meaning to a legislative provision. This is the primary reason why I have recommended that other jurisdictions modify the Victorian *Interpretation Act* if they intend to follow the example of Victoria (see above p. 185).

The possibilities are intriguing, if examples were able to both expand and limit provisions at the same time. For instance, drafters would be able to attempt to put boundaries on concepts such as what is 'reasonable' in particular circumstances by providing examples of what is, and what is not, reasonable (in much the same way as I tried to do in the last example with respect to what was, and what was not, a major disruption).

Explanatory notes in amending legislation

It has been the practice for some time now in the Australian Capital Territory to include an explanatory note immediately after every one of its amending provisions in its statute law revision Acts. These are Acts that make a variety of minor technical amendments to other Acts. In Australia generally explanatory notes normally appear all together as a separate document that is either physically attached to, or that accompanies, the relevant Bill. Often these notes simply paraphrase the provisions of the Bill which they explain, but they can be used to provide material as to why an amendment is being made, how it relates to other provisions and how it is intended to take effect. They can also include examples (see Barnes 2004, 10 ff). In some Australian jurisdictions these notes are written by the drafter of the Bill, in others (the Commonwealth, Victoria) by the instructing Department.

The A.C.T. practice is something that I commend to attention. There is obviously a concern that if a provision is to be inserted as an amendment, and that provision has a note or example, in the amending provision you will have either that note or example and the explanatory note that accompanies the amending provision.[12] There is some danger that readers may feel overwhelmed by this subsidiary material. It has been observed that the text of the law can become lost in these A.C.T. Acts, despite the fact that a lot of effort has gone into making these laws both visually effective and attractive.

However, taken as a whole I believe it is an initiative that is worthy of consideration for use on a wider basis. It is also a welcome reversal of a trend in Australia towards the increasing incomprehensibility of amending laws. Unfortunately, it has significant resource implications as this approach is dependant on notes that contain helpful explanatory material. In practice, however, the majority of explanatory notes

___
12 I note that the explanatory note falls by the wayside when the amendment actually occurs. I should also mention that the Victorian Law Reform Commission in the late 1980's strongly advocated the adoption of the practice of placing explanatory notes with the provisions that they were explaining.

in Australia are anything but explanatory and this means that much more work than occurs now would need to be done if the A.C.T. model was adopted.

The dark side

But is it not dangerous to use notes and examples, and can they be misused?

At the outset, I should stress that notes and examples should be drafted with the same rigour and attention as if they were part of the law even in those jurisdictions where they are not formally part of the law. I would argue that notes and examples are no more dangerous than anything else in the law, and that if they are used intelligently and with care they will considerably enhance the prospect that a law will be understood as it was intended to be understood. Notes and examples have the potential to ensure that a law is understood by far more people than might be the case if they are not used. At the very least they have the potential to save readers of laws much time by explaining how a provision fits in with other provisions of the law.

Given the potential benefits of notes and examples I think the risk of having a mistake in a note or example causing a law to be misinterpreted is well worth taking. And in a jurisdiction such as Victoria, for instance, it is possible that a note or example may help overcome mistakes in provisions themselves. I refer, for example, to the hypothetical example I posited earlier (see, p. 183) which might enable electricity to be considered to be an 'article' in an infelicitously worded provision.

With respect to misuse, my colleague Paul O'Brien (2005) cites examples of examples that contain material that really should have been in the provision to which the example is attached. This is a very legitimate concern, and I have seen a number of other examples of it myself. In fact there is sometimes a very fine line as to where material should be placed. However, certainly in jurisdictions that have Interpretation Act provisions like Victoria's, this particular misuse probably does not matter in terms of the legal effect it has, as the material in the example has to be read as part of, and as extending, the provision.

Conclusion

This chapter has attempted to illustrate the contribution which examples and notes can make to improve the clarity and overall effectiveness of laws. The examples provided were selected from real life experiences with a view to highlighting the diverse range of circumstances in which notes and examples can be used. While the widespread adoption of notes and examples is unlikely to occur in the short term I hope that this chapter will stimulate a wider and more informed debate on what I consider to be the frontier of a new dimension in communication by drafters.

Chapter 11

The Illusion of Clarity: A Critique of 'Pure' Clarity Using Examples Drawn from Judicial Interpretations of The Constitution of The United States

M. Douglass Bellis

Introduction

In this chapter, my aim is to establish that the goal of perfect clarity in legal writing is illusory, but that a relative clarity can be obtained through sufficient sensitivity to the assumptions of the cultural context in which the writing takes places and is intended to be used.

Googling the concept 'clarity in legal texts' produced over 310,000 separate web pages dealing with this issue. If nothing else is clear, it is clear that there is great interest in clarity in legal texts. Unless there were a widespread feeling that legal texts, especially laws, were hard to read, such a result would be unlikely. The existence of organisations for improving legal writing like Clarity is itself proof there is such a widespread feeling.

Yet no one seems in principle to oppose using clear language to write laws. While there is argument over what constitutes clarity (Cutts 2000; Sullivan 2001; Asprey 2003; Kimble 2006; Wagner and Cacciaguidi 2006), about whether or not what passes for clear language may at times actually be ambiguous and imprecise (Dickerson 1964; Endicott 2000; Graham 2001; Solan 2004), I could find no real defence of opaqueness and unreadability per se, even by scholars whose papers struck this untutored lawyer as, well, rather opaque and unreadable (Welle and Farber 1981).

Why then do reasonable observers complain that the law is sometimes unclear? The law is conventionally seen as a command of the sovereign (Hobbes 1651; Derrida 1990; Hunt and Wickham 1994), so why would the sovereign want to make, or 'negligently' allow, the law's demands to be unclear? And so risk the frustration of the sovereign's purpose in enacting them?

Obfuscating influences in the best of times

There are probably a number of factors influencing the answer to this question.

Haste

The haste of lawmaking results in less than carefully thought out prose. Politicians make laws in response to the political imperatives of the moment, often driven by unforeseen or uncontrollable events. Drafters therefore rarely write laws in calm academic retreats without time pressure. Drafters cannot always be primarily interested in the clarity and efficiency of the language used. They simply want to get the job done as quickly as possible. In many countries drafters, working in or with government ministries or parliamentary committees, try to balance the demands of politics, the egos of politicians, and the exigencies of deadlines with the effort to achieve a simple expression of legislative intent in commonly used phrases. It is not surprising they do not always succeed. Perhaps it may be more surprising that they often do not even try to succeed. While it is said that to have respect for laws or sausage you should never see either being made, perhaps seeing the real life circumstances of the law making process might make us empathise more with its poor practitioners.

Politics

Politics may unintentionally constrict the linguistic options of the drafter. How we talk about a problem often defines the problem for us emotionally. Is 'the right to abortion' a 'right to choose' and a 'protection of the right to individual privacy in the most intimate personal matters, free from governmental interference'? Or is a prohibition on abortion a 'pro-life' measure, guarding the 'right to life', the most fundamental of the rights for which governments are formed, as recognised at the beginning of the Declaration of Independence of the United States?

There may be neutral ways to talk about this, but most people who have strong feelings are likely to talk about it in non-neutral terms. Politicians either have an emotional connection with the laws they make, or else they are gearing those laws in part to audiences who have such a connection. Either way, they will want words that reflect the emotional spin they are trying to achieve. Sometimes these words carry potentially ambiguity-creating connotations. While many anti-abortion activists recognise and intend exceptions to the prohibitions they seek, as for example, to save the life of the pregnant woman, and sometimes in cases of rape or incest, the concept of a prohibition on abortion as protecting the life of the 'foetus' or 'unborn child' rather cuts against any exceptions. On the other hand, many proponents of abortion feel there are certain instances, when the pregnancy is at full term, for example, when abortion is inappropriate unless very compelling reasons indicate its necessity. Yet the logic of abortion as a human right of the pregnant woman rather cuts against this. Either set of political terminology, used in draft legislation, may obscure these intentions and subtleties, and perhaps defeat them. Yet the political instinct to use them may be compelling.

Sometimes, too, the political process leads to phrasing that is intentionally unclear. Various factions can agree on the words to use, but disagree as to their purport. Each of these factions may resort to trying to plant in the record such seeds of legislative history as will ultimately yield the fruit of the desired interpretation in the courts. One of the reasons courts may be wise in their reluctance to recur to legislative history may be because it can be quite contrived and even self contradictory. If the situation that gave rise to the statute made the language of the statute unclear, that same situation is likely to affect the legislative history. The court finds itself studying two unclear documents instead of only one.

The policy maker who asks the drafter to use an intentional lack of clarity realises there is uncertainty in the text, but considers the chances the policy maker's views will prevail in the interpretation are sufficiently great as to warrant the risk that they won't. Usually a more straight forward expression of intent would arouse otherwise sleeping opposition. With the ambiguity, the opposition, too, is willing to risk an adverse ruling from the courts, but hopes to get its interpretation instead. This sort of lack of clarity most often arises in very closely contested bills, where neither side is very sure of getting its way in a straight up or down vote.

The 'draft it yourself' approach

The members of some parliamentary bodies were in the past their own principal drafters. Some contemporary members, especially those with legal training, still think they are equipped to do the drafting themselves. Rarely would they attempt an entire bill, but they may have a particular section of the bill that they wrote themselves. This may set some parts of a draft bill in concrete, leaving in ambiguities and oddities of phrasing, and perhaps inconsistencies with the rest of the bill text.

The 'let interested others do it for me' approach

However, most laws are no longer directly drafted by the legislators themselves. Outside drafters, whether from the government or lobbyists, may have their own agendas. These agendas may not include clarity. Such drafters and even some legislators sometimes obscure their true intent in verbosity or misleading terminology or convoluted cross references. They hope to avoid argument and ease the passage of less attractive portions of the bill by hiding them. Often the debate focuses on the overall purpose of the bill, so many details may safely ride under cover of unclear language. You must dig to find them. They may only be discovered by the courts and litigants years later. When they are discovered, they may be difficult to understand. They may not even have the intended effect. Their own obscurity finally may defeat their purpose, but if it does not, the lack of clarity has served those who chose it well.

Fitting it in what's already there

Many countries have an extensive body of existing laws, often derived from various sources and found in various forms such as decrees of the executive power, rules, and court decisions as well as in constitutions and statutes. New laws are often amendatory in nature, and so must 'fit in' to the pre-existing structure. In the case of laws whose sources are in court decisions or other non legislative matter, the option of combining the two in a new document does not exist. Disparities of wording can arise from this fact. In other situations, the new written text may be somewhat difficult to follow because key elements depend on the extrinsic source of law. Even where all the legal materials are in a single statute or code, a lack of clarity may arise. Many drafters are disinclined to reword and rearrange existing law as extensively as they otherwise would when amending it, because that existing law is already authoritatively interpreted and familiar to its users in its current form.

At some point what was perhaps a small and minor part of the original law through amendment can take on (relatively, at least) gargantuan proportions. See the Appendix at the end of this article, containing section 552 of title 5 of the United States Code, as an example of this. This section was a separate Act grafted upon an existing chapter of the Code, which itself was originally an entire and separate Act, later incorporated into an enacted title of the United States Code. Through these successive condensations, the 'real estate' of section numbers and other subdivisions available for expansion dwindled to nothing. As a result, the prose is very dense, and there is a risk that definitions originally intended for the first Act will apply awkwardly given the special purposes and terminology of the later Acts.

If we were drafting title 5 of the United States Code as a fresh matter, we would reorganise this and other laws enacted into it, in order to make the subdivisions of title 5 more in proportion to each other. The impulse to enact the United States Code, title by title, a process still not complete, grew out of a desire to have a symmetrical and harmonious body of law arranged in an organised fashion. Here is an unintended consequence of that desire, which turns out to be largely self-defeating. Had the various laws remained independent, there would be less need to fit any of them onto Procrustean beds. The subdivisions would permit greater expansion without bursting at the seams.

Why not simply revise the old and new laws together in order to make them read better? Periodically this makes sense, but to do it frequently leaves the law in confusion and gives its authoritative interpreters not enough time to settle its usage. Confronted with new wordings and textual organisational schemes, courts will be tempted to change interpretations in ways not intended. Politically the process of revision invites substantive changes along the way that would not be proposed but for the convenient vehicle law revision presents. This may not in itself damage clarity, but its possibility makes such law revisions less likely. To the extent they might have contributed to clarity, that contribution is therefore lost.

For this reason, the drafter usually feels compelled to leave the settled part of the law unmolested and simply add some new ideas, even though doing so may harm the overall readability of the text. Unsettling the entire text for the cognoscenti is not always worth improving its access for the uninitiated.

Job security

One is tempted to suggest another motive for making simple ideas complex. Lawyers who have created a complex statutory scheme are often in demand to interpret it after its enactment. If there is no ambiguity there is no demand for their services. Likewise those portions of the bar who habitually work with a particular law do at times rather see themselves as a mystical priesthood. They would rather not have the holy of holies exposed to the profane gaze of the uninitiated multitude. For both economic and emotional reasons, they cling to the comfortable obscurity of their expertise.

Amateurism

Even non-experts and non-lawyers have certain expectations of legal language. They want a certain grandeur of tone that seems 'fitting'. In many cases such people do have a hand in writing the law. They are not professional legislative drafters and they want to make the most of their moment in the sun. They want to leave such marks as will indelibly show their participation in the process and its importance. Sometimes they succeed in doing so, to the detriment of clarity.

Too many warriors, no chief

Too many cooks spoil the stew, and too many drafters confuse the draft. In most modern settings, there are a number of people involved in writing a statute, and in many cases they never talk to each other or agree upon a common basis for proceeding with their work. The draft passes through many hands and many layers of review on its way to enactment. No one person normally has complete control of its contents throughout its journey. Indeed, given the complexity of many areas the law is asked to regulate, it is unlikely that one person will at the same time have both the substantive expertise and the drafting expertise needed. But a side effect of this is greater confusion in the drafts. No one person is sure just what the draft contains. The draft may well be a compromise in language reflecting more the relative power of the various participants than an overall understanding of the purpose or effect of the draft.

Letting those who administer the law write themselves blank cheques

Another source of lack of clarity comes when those who administer the laws have a great part in drafting them. People who execute laws naturally want as much flexibility and discretion reposed in themselves as possible. In benign situations this is to allow them to make equitable adjustments in detail so as to achieve the purposes of the legislation and substantial fairness for all the persons affected by it. In less benign situations, it is the tool of despotic governments to create an illusion of the rule of law while allowing in reality an untrammelled authority to the despot.

Clarity for whom?

So for a variety of mostly bad reasons, the law becomes clouded and obscure, even though no one, if asked, would say they intend that to happen.

Once we have enough time, and professional drafters who are allowed to draft in peace, though, the battle may not be won. In deciding how to search for the holy grail of clarity, there is another question we must now ask. Clarity for whom? Who is the audience of the legal text?

We often start by assuming the general public will be the interested parties and that every legal text should be equally accessible to the reader on the street (Mellinkoff 1963; Tiersma 1999; Asprey 2003; Adler 2006). Should the laws that govern us not be accessible to us without professional help? Well, yes, when we are talking about laws that might affect us in our daily lives, such as criminal laws, and perhaps personal earned income tax laws. But what about laws dealing with taxes on butterfly straddles? Maybe it is the tax accountant to whom they are addressed, and we may safely assume that tax accountant has a certain professional vocabulary that mystifies both lay people and lawyers. Yet if they are our audience we might well want to speak to them in their own language, a technical language which for that very reason is precise and clear to them. No laymen in their right minds would try to determine the tax consequences of such a transaction without consulting a tax lawyer or accountant well versed in these matters. There is little point in writing the law as if it were a novel to be read by the general public.

A law text dealing with judicial procedure might use terms, say for the compulsory and optional joinder of parties to a law suit, that grow out of the ancient forms of action. Though these terms have evolved and in any case are somewhat quaint and old fashioned sounding, they still are easier for the courts to understand than would be entirely new terms. It is unlikely that persons not trained in the law would really be interested in these matters. For the few who are, the loss of simplicity through the substitution of clear, but lengthy explanation may not be worth it. They can google the technical terms to the extent they need them, even if those terms are strange to them. In many cases the accretion of precedent has filled in gaps caused either by ambiguity in technical terms that were originally non-technical terms. Such gaps may also grow out of the changing circumstances in which the law is being implemented, circumstances impossible to see in the original instance but not difficult to interpolate by sound judgment. For in many cases, today's technical term is yesterday's common speech, frozen in time and made technical by formal interpretation to deal with the felt necessities of the times. Just because it is not current slang does not mean we should avoid it. Continuity with past usage and continuing settled meanings of the old terms without change argue we should not. We sometimes define our terms in a legal text to shorthand a complex idea into a general and shorter term. This improves readability and clarity. For the same reason, if the case law gives us a ready-made defined term, we should not refuse to use it. We should also allow its evolution through future usage and juridical interpretation. The practical utility of this approach outweighs any theoretical objections to it.

So perhaps some of the wailing about the lack of clarity in legal writing comes from our lack of appreciation for the audience intended to be addressed and our lack of appreciation for the practical circumstances in which legislation is drafted.

Even if we add all these causes together, though, it still surprises us that there should be such an uproar about legal writing, especially legislative drafting, and its lack of clarity. Could there be some other, more fundamental reason this concern is so strong and so persistent over time? I think there is, and one that few observers have mentioned, so far as I am able to make out.

A deeper problem than we may have thought

Before we can write about anything clearly, we must understand it clearly. Rarely do we ask ourselves probing questions about whether that is possible. We should. The answer may induce a little needed humility.

In the cave

Even in ancient times, Socrates, as portrayed by Plato, seemed doubtful that our sense perceptions completely corresponded to ultimate reality. Consider the metaphor of the observer of shadows reflected on the cave walls in the Republic, book vii (Plato, Lee (trans.) 1955). People are imagined as living in a cave, facing the back wall without the ability to turn back, with a fire burning behind them, and between them and the fire, various objects are carried by unseen passers by. They cannot see the objects, or that they are being carried by passers by, but only the shadows the objects cast on the cave walls. They will have no reason not to believe these flickering images are actual things. They will not know they are shadows. In this analogy, even the objects which are held up behind them are only images of real things, so the observers are seeing merely the shadows of imitations of the real thing.

Similarly, what we see has some relationship to reality, but it is not the whole picture and at times can deceive rather than enlighten us. Yet in many cases, that is all we have to go on, so we try our best to understand something which we do not really see clearly. In such a case it is not surprising that our written descriptions of it might in some fundamental sense lack clarity. Even if they seem clear, they may be in error when judged against ultimate objective reality. Of course, Plato is more concerned with an understanding of what is ultimately good than epistemology in general, but as he would merge the good and the true, later commentators are not wrong to use his analogy in a broader sense than he may have originally intended it.

An interlude, but not a happy one

For a while, the age of faith in Europe simply avoided the question of what is reality. Authority, ultimately religious authority, was the intellectual lodestone and the source of truth. To question the basis of that authority was in many cases unimaginable and in all cases dangerous to one's health and fortune. So the question of whether clarity was possible was not much asked.

The confused and confusing writings of the European dark and early middle ages may serve as an example of the results of this lack of questioning. Consider Isadore's *Etymologies* (2004), in its time considered the compendium of all knowledge. Today it is rarely read and requires a good deal of research to understand. Things of great general interest are mixed with details of dubious truth and with forgettable trivia. There is little evidence of an overall coherent theory of relationships between things. Though organised, its structure ultimately confuses. Perhaps it served the practical needs of its time as well as our encyclopaedias do ours today. Yet no one would now read it as we do Plato, and its influence on the modern mind is almost nil. Could this mean that clarity is least achieved when we least think about whether it is possible?

Back in the cave

But the Renaissance of classical learning, and in particular, Descartes (2006), brought the question into the open again. How do we know what we think we know? How do we know that what we perceive through our senses really is there, or if there, has the characteristics we imagine it to have? Cartesian doubt was originally intended as a kind of thought experiment to help separate the fundamental from the accretions of unexamined assumption, not least those of the dark and middle ages. But it took on a life of its own and raised in a very direct way the question of whether we can really know anything. That question has never really returned to the shadows. Worse, each attempt to resolve it by establishing some base certainty that is irrefutable, has failed.

This has had serious consequences for both science and religion, but even in our more humble backwater of legal writing, it is fraught with implications. How can we write clearly about something which we are unable to understand clearly?

Locke (1632-1704) and perhaps Hume (1882) made an effort to solve the riddle raised by Cartesian doubt by basing our knowledge on sense perceptions, and the associations we make between them (Smith 1902). We can rely on things we directly sense, and the conclusions we draw from applying logic to them. But the infinite regress continues to haunt us and make their solutions not entirely persuasive. How do we know we can rely on our sense perceptions? What are optical illusions in that case? What about phenomena that occur where no one is there to sense them? Does the tree not fall in the forest even when there is no one to see and hear it fall?

Ultimately, we have no real proof that our perceptions of reality correspond with its facts. Kant (2003), in impenetrable prose, expounds the theory that we cannot, even in principle, derive truth from the use of pure reason alone (though he leaves open the possibility of direct inspiration—a not very satisfying alternative, since there is no way of distinguishing such an inspiration from delusion). I suppose this proves that even those who address this fundamental question are capable of a lack of clarity.

But is there not a difference between reality and law?

Modern experimental physics has shown in fact what Kant argued in theory. The light slit experiments confound our notions of time and space no less than does the math of special relativity and the spatial paradoxes of general relativity. Yet in some ways, the two seem to contradict each other as well. We do not seem to be able to grasp reality entirely, at least not by using our every day common sense assumptions, or even the current conventions of theoretical physics. Our partial perceptions of the world are incomplete and self-contradictory. The seemingly solid material things of everyday life must in some sense be rather like the shadows on Plato's cave walls. And if Socrates was right in identifying the good with the true, this must spill over into the moral world, as well.

Might not our moral perceptions, correct as they are within the limits of our own experience and for our immediate purposes, sometimes fail to correspond with even more general norms that apply across a range of experiences and purposes?

Another answer?

Given the fact that our fundamental grasp of reality is unclear, we must wonder whether, in a legal or any other context, clarity of expression is possible. Probably in some fundamental sense it is not. This is important to us as seekers after verbal clarity. If our concepts cannot entirely correspond with physical reality, how much less so are they likely to correspond to the social reality which is in some sense the basis of law? Can that social reality be built upon an epistemology that has no certain centre? Can it exist independently of our other uncertainties?

If not, we may now have a basis for a more satisfying answer to the question of why there are so many complaints about the lack of clarity in legal documents. If clarity is impossible everywhere, it is surely impossible in legal writing. But why does this bother us so much in that context?

Why we care

Unlike many other types of documents, legal writings are widely read. Usually they govern over an extent of territory. With growing international trade and relations, that extent is getting larger and more diverse. That means more and more people with differing backgrounds have occasion to ponder legal documents that apply in that territory. A wider variety of experiences forming those doing the pondering creates more opportunities for misconstruction.

Then, too, people are concerned about legal documents in a way they are not about other writings. Legal documents have practical consequences and limit or enhance people's freedom of operations. Literature may inspire or amuse us. A law controls us and often either imposes sanctions or benefits. We do not take the possibility of sanctions or benefits lightly. We strain to understand legal writings because we expect or fear important consequences in our lives from them.

Clarity of expression may be impossible because we cannot clearly express a reality we cannot, even in principle, understand. Yet it is in legal writing especially that we seek clarity, because of the gravity of its consequences. But in seeking certainty in legal writings we are bound to be frustrated in our search for understanding, just as we are in general with any sort of writing, and, indeed, in any sort of such search. If we do not know that clarity is impossible, even in theory, we may complain about its lack most vociferously where it is most likely to hurt, or help, us. Legal writing would certainly be a candidate for that place.

Should we give up?

Should we throw up our hands and conclude the search for clarity is a waste of time? Does this mean that all legal writings must be obscure and fundamentally unsound? Not really.

First of all, there are surely degrees of lack of clarity. To say that ultimately no human writing, legal or otherwise, can capture entirely a reality we cannot completely understand does not mean it cannot capture any part of it. Even the shadows on the cave walls have some relationship to the reality they reflect. How might we seek this relative, if not absolute, clarity?

Clarity of expression might be possible for all practical purposes, if we accept certain premises in common about the nature of reality and in particular about the nature of human relationships, whether we can prove them or not. Most legal systems do indeed start with such premises, some perhaps stated in a written Constitution, some by tradition, and others through a consensus (whether real or fictional) of that society or influential members of it, at some point in time. So for the purposes of legal writing in any particular legal setting, we often do not have to worry whether the subjects and objects about which we write really exist. We just agree to assume that they do. While they may differ from legal system to legal system, culture to culture, country to country, and even region to region, in any given place and time where there is a stable system of laws in effect, there is a sort of consensus about these issues we may implicitly rely upon.

Still not home free

This would neatly solve our search for clarity and end this article, were it not for one additional, unpleasant fact. Precisely because the ultimate premises of legal systems vary from time to time and place to place, isolating those that we may rely upon in any particular time and place is a very dubious endeavour. The premises are rarely if ever contained in the text to be interpreted. It would probably be almost humanly impossible to do so, as it is impossible to create a mathematical system without some unproven and unprovable premises. Outsiders to a given set of social conventions can easily be misled by applying their own social conventions to the words that seem to have a common meaning. More often than not, much of what we see as a lack of clarity is really a lack of understanding, our lack of understanding, of the cultural assumptions of those who wrote the text we are trying to decipher.

Law, as we use it in day to day life, is not a brooding omnipresence in the sky, awaiting our discovery through the application of right reason to obvious premises. Rather it is the result of enactment through social convention normally through some formal command of an authority generally recognised in a particular society. Societies are not static and hermetically sealed from one another, so the conventions are always changing, even when the text remains identical. *Littera scripta manent* [written words remain], but the context that gives them their meaning changes. Later understandings of the 'original intent' of the text become blurred by changes in the consensus and modes of expression current among, not to mention the felt needs of, the people governed by it.

An example from the United States Constitution

In the American context, we can see this in the history of interpretation of its written Constitution, most of which was established by a mostly British colonial people whose protestant and Whig assumptions were so axiomatic that Jefferson said many of the ideas of the declaration of independence (and so arguably the Constitution of 1787) were simply in the air as agreed commonplaces and did not represent any deep philosophical constructs or novel perceptions. They were, at least to the colonists, self-evident. The English and the Europeans did not happen to share those assumptions, however. Only some luck, and the difficulties of crossing a large ocean, spared us Americans the inconveniences of what might otherwise have been a rather nasty and potentially violent debate with much better armed and more numerous foes. We escaped that fate until the 20th century, when we were better prepared materially, if less prepared philosophically, to handle it. Arguably we are still engaged in it in the 21st.

The lack of common assumptions, though, is not exclusively to be found in our external relations. Today, learned judges and professors give interpretations of the 'plain meaning' of the American Constitutional text that would surprise, and perhaps terrify, anyone brought up with the conventions of 18th century American thought and discourse.

An interesting if trivial example of this is the question, now rather seriously debated, about the meaning of that clause in Article I of the Constitution that states that

> every order, resolution, or vote to which the concurrence of the Senate and House of Representatives may be necessary (except on a question of adjournment) shall be presented to the President of the United States.

for his approval before taking effect and, if not approved, be returned for a vote on whether to override his disapproval. Commentators since the early 20th century have been troubled by this rule and whether it might apply to the power given to Congress in another part of the Constitution to propose amendments to the Constitution.

That part (Article V) of the Constitution says that

> The Congress, whenever two thirds of both Houses shall deem it necessary, shall propose amendments to this Constitution [...] which [...] shall be valid to all intents and purposes

as part of this Constitution, when ratified by the Legislatures of three-fourths of the several States […]

Since the Article I clause does not say, 'Except as provided in article V […]', some modern commentators wonder why the proposal of amendments under Article V, because two thirds of both (always interpreted as 'each') House must agree, does not require the assent of the President. Yet from the very first proposal of amendments (drafted by the main drafter of the Constitution itself, James Madison) neither the Congress nor the President regarded that assent as required. When an effort to overturn an early amendment reached the courts, they dispatched a similar argument without any real discussion, as self-evidently wrong.

The modern commentators are imposing a 19th (or even 20th) century convention of drafting on an 18th century document. In the 19th century, the style of American drafting took a turn for the worse, as the still provincial Americans looked to England and the European code system of laws for models, forsaking the elegant and simple style of Jefferson. Ironically, formalism, and something that would strike the 18th century mind as pettifogging narrowness of interpretation, replaced the goal of 'plain English' and the conversational style that is so evident, and so pleasing, in 18th century American prose, not least the Constitution.

The courts and early commentators had no doubts that the assent of the President was not required for proposed amendments, because of the wording 'Whenever two-thirds of both Houses shall deem it necessary'. This is not a legislative act requiring the consent of each House separately, but a kind of joint political decision requiring only their collective judgment that the necessity had arisen. It was felt to be a specific that controlled the general without the addition of a niggling 'Notwithstanding Article I' or 'Except as provided in Article V'. Requiring the consent of the President would manifestly allow situations to arise in which both Houses thought amendment necessary, but none could be proposed because the President demurred. That would violate the plain sense of the sentence, as understood by 18th and early 19th century readers. So it was easily interpreted in the way all commentators feel it should be by those who wrote and spoke its language. Only later, when foreign influences had corrupted America's original enlightened purity of speech did doubts arise. Some of the methods suggested for resolving those doubts would do considerable violence both to the language of the Constitution and the separation of powers it endeavoured to create. Luckily, these fevered imaginings of professors are relatively unlikely to take hold in our courts. But it is a good illustration of a lack of clarity that arises from a lack of understanding of the linguistic and cultural assumptions of the authors of a text.

Oddly, in a modern civil law country, the so-called rule of proportionality might have led courts to a similar result as has been obtained in the United States, without worrying about the apparently sweeping nature of the general rule. In general, though, such a rule of construction is not recognised in the United States, or for that matter in most common law countries, and would be viewed in the United States as a shocking arrogation of power by the judiciary. In civil law countries where the courts profess an abject subservience to the text of statutes, the rule is considered as a logical interpretation of the imprecision inherent in the legislative mind. The result is the same, but the reasoning and cultural assumptions used to get to it are quite different.

Another one

Just as such misunderstandings of a text can arise with the passage of time, with its concomitant changes in culture and linguistic convention, they can arise when two different cultures seize upon the same words to construct a legal text. An example of this may be found in a passage from the English bill of rights, a product of the Glorious Revolution of 1689, relating to the privileges of members of Parliament. After a stirring prologue that still quickens the Whiggish heart of Americans, the Parliament advises and the sovereign enacts the following rule: 'That the freedom of speech and debates or proceedings in Parliament ought not to be impeached or questioned in any court or place out of Parliament'. The Americans, in adopting their Constitution almost a century later, mimicked this provision by saying, in Article I, 'and for any Speech or Debate in either House, they [the members of the respective houses] shall not be questioned in any other place.' This text in Britain has become the foundation of a rather surprising (to Americans at least) prohibition on the use of what we call legislative history to determine the meaning of a statute. The idea seems to be that any recourse to parliamentary debate or similar materials is an impeachment or questioning of the freedom of debates and speeches and proceedings. Perhaps the passive voice lends itself to this interpretation better than the American version. However, it is rather unlikely that the Whigs in 1689 thought they were laying down a rule for the consideration of legislative history, nor have the Americans ever interpreted their similar language as providing one. Instead, the Americans, perhaps consistent with their tendency to see everything in individual rather than collective terms, have interpreted these words as conferring an individual immunity on legislators from any suit, civil or criminal, or any other penalty, other than that which might be imposed by their own House for disorderly behaviour, for anything said or done in connection with their legislative duties. Indeed, it protects their committee reports and other legislative history from being the basis of any suit against them for libel, slander, or any other wrong they might do in their legislative capacity. Thus, the legislative history may be an even more forthright source of legislative intent than otherwise. Ironically, some concern has arisen in our courts that there is too much recourse to legislative history, and a kind of parole evidence rule has asserted itself as a check on that tendency. But no one has suggested an interpretation of the speech and debate clause at all similar to that which until recently was current in Britain. Here we see a mutation not only as between different cultures, the British and American, but over time as well, as the meaning of the phrase has evolved, though somewhat differently, in each country.

These two examples show us how the same words can mean something different over time and as between different nations, even nations with such similar cultural roots as Britain and the United States. These differences in interpretation, I have argued, arise from the different felt needs of the differing (in time or place) cultures that have been called upon to make the interpretations. Clarity is a creature of its time and place, and so relative and not absolute.

An implication

Perhaps this is one reason projects like the ongoing rewrite of the Federal Rules of Civil Procedure in the United States have a special salience. While the rules may have been clear enough in the context of the times and circumstances that first gave them their birth, changing conditions and perhaps even changing cultural assumptions call for changes in language that, in our context today, we might even venture to call clarifications. We are not necessarily wiser, nor is our language purer, than the original drafters and their language, but changing times require changing texts, just to stay in the same place.

Another, even bigger one

Now, as the growing interaction between peoples and nations slowly merges us into a diverse world culture, we have many more occasions to be exposed to the legal texts founded on cultures not our own. Even where we share a language with the cultures, and much more so when we do not, we must be humble in our approach. To impose our notions of clarity on others is not simply morally indefensible, it is impractical.

As we need to forge common understandings of rules to guide our lives in common, we must first concentrate on understanding the differing cultural assumptions that form the base of the various subcultures within and among the nations and regions of the world. Once we understand these, we may move toward a greater uniformity, and thus toward the underpinnings of a common sense of clarity. More likely, for the foreseeable future, we will need to have varying texts, or at least varying approaches to interpretation, to make a given text or texts do the work of cross cultural communication.

Because we may have a long time to wait before a more general consensus on what constitutes clarity can form, we might better spend our time on the often humbling task of understanding cultural variation and less time pretending to paper it over with words.

Appendix

Below is set forth section 552 of title 5 of the United States Code ((2005) Administrative Procedure Public information; agency rules, opinions, orders, records, and proceedings) in its splendid entirety, to demonstrate the constraints of working with a pre-existing structure. In reality, this section was an entirely separate (and none too clearly drafted) Act; the very important Freedom of Information Act. That Act provides for general public access to the workings and documents of the Government; an early effort to assure 'transparency'. The Act, though, was embedded in an enacted part of the United States Code (not all of which is technically the official law of the United States). The drafter felt constrained by the pre-existing structure to make this a single section, necessitating quite a lot of subdivision. The purpose of the United States Code, to organise and make uniform in style the general and permanent laws of the United States may be somewhat self-defeating if that purpose is understood to include making those laws more readable and accessible to the public.

(US Code Collection (2005)

TITLE 5 > PART I > CHAPTER 5 > SUBCHAPTER II > § 552
§ 552. Public information; agency rules, opinions, orders, records, and proceedings
Release date: 2005-05-18
(a) Each agency shall make available to the public information as follows:
(1) Each agency shall separately state and currently publish in the Federal Register for the guidance of the public—
(A) descriptions of its central and field organization and the established places at which, the employees (and in the case of a uniformed service, the members) from whom, and the methods whereby, the public may obtain information, make submittals or requests, or obtain decisions;
(B) statements of the general course and method by which its functions are channeled [sic] and determined, including the nature and requirements of all formal and informal procedures available;
(C) rules of procedure, descriptions of forms available or the places at which forms may be obtained, and instructions as to the scope and contents of all papers, reports, or examinations;
(D) substantive rules of general applicability adopted as authorized by law, and statements of general policy or interpretations of general applicability formulated and adopted by the agency; and
(E) each amendment, revision, or repeal of the foregoing.
Except to the extent that a person has actual and timely notice of the terms thereof, a person may not in any manner be required to resort to, or be adversely affected by, a matter required to be published in the Federal Register and not so published. For the purpose of this paragraph, matter reasonably available to the class of persons affected thereby is deemed published in the Federal Register when incorporated by reference therein with the approval of the Director of the Federal Register.
(2) Each agency, in accordance with published rules, shall make available for public inspection and copying—
(A) final opinions, including concurring and dissenting opinions, as well as orders, made in the adjudication of cases;
(B) those statements of policy and interpretations which have been adopted by the agency and are not published in the Federal Register;
(C) administrative staff manuals and instructions to staff that affect a member of the public;
(D) copies of all records, regardless of form or format, which have been released to any person under paragraph (3) and which, because of the nature of their subject matter, the agency determines have become or are likely to become the subject of subsequent requests for substantially the same records; and
(E) a general index of the records referred to under subparagraph (D);
unless the materials are promptly published and copies offered for sale. For records created on or after November 1, 1996, within one year after such date, each agency shall make such records available, including by computer telecommunications or, if computer telecommunications means have not been established by the agency, by other electronic

means. To the extent required to prevent a clearly unwarranted invasion of personal privacy, an agency may delete identifying details when it makes available or publishes an opinion, statement of policy, interpretation, staff manual, instruction, or copies of records referred to in subparagraph (D). However, in each case the justification for the deletion shall be explained fully in writing, and the extent of such deletion shall be indicated on the portion of the record which is made available or published, unless including that indication would harm an interest protected by the exemption in subsection (b) under which the deletion is made. If technically feasible, the extent of the deletion shall be indicated at the place in the record where the deletion was made. Each agency shall also maintain and make available for public inspection and copying current indexes providing identifying information for the public as to any matter issued, adopted, or promulgated after July 4, 1967, and required by this paragraph to be made available or published. Each agency shall promptly publish, quarterly or more frequently, and distribute (by sale or otherwise) copies of each index or supplements thereto unless it determines by order published in the Federal Register that the publication would be unnecessary and impracticable, in which case the agency shall nonetheless provide copies of such index on request at a cost not to exceed the direct cost of duplication. Each agency shall make the index referred to in subparagraph (E) available by computer telecommunications by December 31, 1999. A final order, opinion, statement of policy, interpretation, or staff manual or instruction that affects a member of the public may be relied on, used, or cited as precedent by an agency against a party other than an agency only if—

(i) it has been indexed and either made available or published as provided by this paragraph; or

(ii) the party has actual and timely notice of the terms thereof.

(3)

(A) Except with respect to the records made available under paragraphs (1) and (2) of this subsection, and except as provided in subparagraph (E), each agency, upon any request for records which

(i) reasonably describes such records and

(ii) is made in accordance with published rules stating the time, place, fees (if any), and procedures to be followed, shall make the records promptly available to any person.

(B) In making any record available to a person under this paragraph, an agency shall provide the record in any form or format requested by the person if the record is readily reproducible by the agency in that form or format. Each agency shall make reasonable efforts to maintain its records in forms or formats that are reproducible for purposes of this section.

(C) In responding under this paragraph to a request for records, an agency shall make reasonable efforts to search for the records in electronic form or format, except when such efforts would significantly interfere with the operation of the agency's automated information system.

(D) For purposes of this paragraph, the term 'search' means to review, manually or by automated means, agency records for the purpose of locating those records which are responsive to a request.

(E) An agency, or part of an agency, that is an element of the intelligence community (as that term is defined in section 3(4) of the National Security Act of 1947 (50 U.S.C. 401a (4))) shall not make any record available under this paragraph to—

(i) any government entity, other than a State, territory, commonwealth, or district of the United States, or any subdivision thereof; or

(ii) a representative of a government entity described in clause (i).

(4)

(A)

(i) In order to carry out the provisions of this section, each agency shall promulgate regulations, pursuant to notice and receipt of public comment, specifying the schedule of fees applicable to the processing of requests under this section and establishing procedures and guidelines for determining when such fees should be waived or reduced. Such schedule shall conform to the guidelines which shall be promulgated, pursuant to notice and receipt of public comment, by the Director of the Office of Management and Budget and which shall provide for a uniform schedule of fees for all agencies.

(ii) Such agency regulations shall provide that—

(I) fees shall be limited to reasonable standard charges for document search, duplication, and review, when records are requested for commercial use;

(II) fees shall be limited to reasonable standard charges for document duplication when records are not sought for commercial use and the request is made by an educational or noncommercial scientific institution, whose purpose is scholarly or scientific research; or a representative of the news media; and

(III) for any request not described in (I) or (II), fees shall be limited to reasonable standard charges for document search and duplication.

(iii) Documents shall be furnished without any charge or at a charge reduced below the fees established under clause (ii) if disclosure of the information is in the public interest because it is likely to contribute significantly to public understanding of the operations or activities of the government and is not primarily in the commercial interest of the requester.

(iv) Fee schedules shall provide for the recovery of only the direct costs of search, duplication, or review. Review costs shall include only the direct costs incurred during the initial examination of a document for the purposes of determining whether the documents must be disclosed under this section and for the purposes of withholding any portions exempt from disclosure under this section. Review costs may not include any costs incurred in resolving issues of law or policy that may be raised in the course of processing a request under this section. No fee may be charged by any agency under this section—

(I) if the costs of routine collection and processing of the fee are likely to equal or exceed the amount of the fee; or

(II) for any request described in clause (ii) (II) or (III) of this subparagraph for the first two hours of search time or for the first one hundred pages of duplication.

(v) No agency may require advance payment of any fee unless the requester has previously failed to pay fees in a timely fashion, or the agency has determined that the fee will exceed $250.

(vi) Nothing in this subparagraph shall supersede fees chargeable under a statute specifically providing for setting the level of fees for particular types of records.

(vii) In any action by a requester regarding the waiver of fees under this section, the court shall determine the matter de novo: Provided, that the court's review of the matter shall be limited to the record before the agency.

(B) On complaint, the district court of the United States in the district in which the complainant resides, or has his principal place of business, or in which the agency records are situated, or in the District of Columbia, has jurisdiction to enjoin the agency from withholding agency records and to order the production of any agency records improperly withheld from the complainant. In such a case the court shall determine the matter de novo, and may examine the contents of such agency records in camera to determine whether such records or any part thereof shall be withheld under any of the exemptions set forth in subsection (b) of this section, and the burden is on the agency to sustain its action. In addition to any other matters to which a court accords substantial weight, a court shall accord substantial weight to an affidavit of an agency concerning the agency's determination as to technical feasibility under paragraph (2)(C) and subsection (b) and reproducibility under paragraph (3)(B).

(C) Notwithstanding any other provision of law, the defendant shall serve an answer or otherwise plead to any complaint made under this subsection within thirty days after service upon the defendant of the pleading in which such complaint is made, unless the court otherwise directs for good cause shown.

[(D) Repealed. Pub. L. 98–620, title IV, § 402(2), Nov. 8, 1984, 98 Stat. 3357.]

(E) The court may assess against the United States reasonable attorney fees and other litigation costs reasonably incurred in any case under this section in which the complainant has substantially prevailed.

(F) Whenever the court orders the production of any agency records improperly withheld from the complainant and assesses against the United States reasonable attorney fees and other litigation costs, and the court additionally issues a written finding that the circumstances surrounding the withholding raise questions whether agency personnel acted arbitrarily or capriciously with respect to the withholding, the Special Counsel shall promptly initiate a proceeding to determine whether disciplinary action is warranted against the officer or employee who was primarily responsible for the withholding. The Special Counsel, after investigation and consideration of the evidence submitted, shall submit his findings and recommendations to the administrative authority of the agency concerned and shall send copies of the findings and recommendations to the officer or employee or his representative. The administrative authority shall take the corrective action that the Special Counsel recommends.

(G) In the event of noncompliance with the order of the court, the district court may punish for contempt the responsible employee, and in the case of a uniformed service, the responsible member.

(5) Each agency having more than one member shall maintain and make available for public inspection a record of the final votes of each member in every agency proceeding.

(6)

(A) Each agency, upon any request for records made under paragraph (1), (2), or (3) of this subsection, shall—

(i) determine within 20 days (excepting Saturdays, Sundays, and legal public holidays) after the receipt of any such request whether to comply with such request and shall immediately notify the person making such request of such determination and the reasons therefor, and of the right of such person to appeal to the head of the agency any adverse determination; and

(ii) make a determination with respect to any appeal within twenty days (excepting Saturdays, Sundays, and legal public holidays) after the receipt of such appeal. If on appeal the denial of the request for records is in whole or in part upheld, the agency shall notify the person making such request of the provisions for judicial review of that determination under paragraph (4) of this subsection.

(B)

(i) In unusual circumstances as specified in this subparagraph, the time limits prescribed in either clause (i) or clause (ii) of subparagraph (A) may be extended by written notice to the person making such request setting forth the unusual circumstances for such extension and the date on which a determination is expected to be dispatched. No such notice shall specify a date that would result in an extension for more than ten working days, except as provided in clause (ii) of this subparagraph.

(ii) With respect to a request for which a written notice under clause (i) extends the time limits prescribed under clause (i) of subparagraph (A), the agency shall notify the person making the request if the request cannot be processed within the time limit specified in that clause and shall provide the person an opportunity to limit the scope of the request so that it may be processed within that time limit or an opportunity to arrange with the agency an alternative time frame for processing the request or a modified request. Refusal by the person to reasonably modify the request or arrange such an alternative time frame shall be considered as a factor in determining whether exceptional circumstances exist for purposes of subparagraph (C).

(iii) As used in this subparagraph, 'unusual circumstances' means, but only to the extent reasonably necessary to the proper processing of the particular requests—

(I) the need to search for and collect the requested records from field facilities or other establishments that are separate from the office processing the request;

(II) the need to search for, collect, and appropriately examine a voluminous amount of separate and distinct records which are demanded in a single request; or

(III) the need for consultation, which shall be conducted with all practicable speed, with another agency having a substantial interest in the determination of the request or among two or more components of the agency having substantial subject-matter interest therein.

(iv) Each agency may promulgate regulations, pursuant to notice and receipt of public comment, providing for the aggregation of certain requests by the same requestor, or by a group of requestors acting in concert, if the agency reasonably believes that such requests actually constitute a single request, which would otherwise satisfy the unusual circumstances specified in this subparagraph, and the requests involve clearly related matters. Multiple requests involving unrelated matters shall not be aggregated.

(C)

(i) Any person making a request to any agency for records under paragraph (1), (2), or (3) of this subsection shall be deemed to have exhausted his administrative remedies with respect to such request if the agency fails to comply with the applicable time limit provisions of this paragraph. If the Government can show exceptional circumstances exist and that the agency is exercising due diligence in responding to the request, the court may retain jurisdiction and allow the agency additional time to complete its review of the records. Upon any determination by an agency to comply with a request for records, the records shall be made promptly available to such person making such request. Any notification of denial of any request for records under this subsection shall set forth the names and titles or positions of each person responsible for the denial of such request.

(ii) For purposes of this subparagraph, the term 'exceptional circumstances' does not include a delay that results from a predictable agency workload of requests under this section, unless the agency demonstrates reasonable progress in reducing its backlog of pending requests.

(iii) Refusal by a person to reasonably modify the scope of a request or arrange an alternative time frame for processing a request (or a modified request) under clause (ii) after being given an opportunity to do so by the agency to whom the person made the request shall be considered as a factor in determining whether exceptional circumstances exist for purposes of this subparagraph.

(D)

(i) Each agency may promulgate regulations, pursuant to notice and receipt of public comment, providing for multitrack processing of requests for records based on the amount of work or time (or both) involved in processing requests.

(ii) Regulations under this subparagraph may provide a person making a request that does not qualify for the fastest multitrack processing an opportunity to limit the scope of the request in order to qualify for faster processing.

(iii) This subparagraph shall not be considered to affect the requirement under subparagraph (C) to exercise due diligence.

(E)

(i) Each agency shall promulgate regulations, pursuant to notice and receipt of public comment, providing for expedited processing of requests for records—

(I) in cases in which the person requesting the records demonstrates a compelling need; and

(II) in other cases determined by the agency.

(ii) Notwithstanding clause (i), regulations under this subparagraph must ensure—

(I) that a determination of whether to provide expedited processing shall be made, and notice of the determination shall be provided to the person making the request, within 10 days after the date of the request; and

(II) expeditious consideration of administrative appeals of such determinations of whether to provide expedited processing.

(iii) An agency shall process as soon as practicable any request for records to which the agency has granted expedited processing under this subparagraph. Agency action to deny or affirm denial of a request for expedited processing pursuant to this subparagraph, and failure by an agency to respond in a timely manner to such a request shall be subject to judicial review under paragraph (4), except that the judicial review shall be based on the record before the agency at the time of the determination.

(iv) A district court of the United States shall not have jurisdiction to review an agency denial of expedited processing of a request for records after the agency has provided a complete response to the request.

(v) For purposes of this subparagraph, the term 'compelling need' means—

(I) that a failure to obtain requested records on an expedited basis under this paragraph could reasonably be expected to pose an imminent threat to the life or physical safety of an individual; or

(II) with respect to a request made by a person primarily engaged in disseminating information, urgency to inform the public concerning actual or alleged Federal Government activity.

(vi) A demonstration of a compelling need by a person making a request for expedited processing shall be made by a statement certified by such person to be true and correct to the best of such person's knowledge and belief.

(F) In denying a request for records, in whole or in part, an agency shall make a reasonable effort to estimate the volume of any requested matter the provision of which is denied, and shall provide any such estimate to the person making the request, unless providing such estimate would harm an interest protected by the exemption in subsection (b) pursuant to which the denial is made.

(b) This section does not apply to matters that are—

(1)

(A) specifically authorized under criteria established by an Executive order to be kept secret in the interest of national defense or foreign policy and

(B) are in fact properly classified pursuant to such Executive order;

(2) related solely to the internal personnel rules and practices of an agency;

(3) specifically exempted from disclosure by statute (other than section 552b of this title), provided that such statute

(A) requires that the matters be withheld from the public in such a manner as to leave no discretion on the issue, or

(B) establishes particular criteria for withholding or refers to particular types of matters to be withheld;

(4) trade secrets and commercial or financial information obtained from a person and privileged or confidential;

(5) inter-agency or intra-agency memorandums or letters which would not be available by law to a party other than an agency in litigation with the agency;

(6) personnel and medical files and similar files the disclosure of which would constitute a clearly unwarranted invasion of personal privacy;

(7) records or information compiled for law enforcement purposes, but only to the extent that the production of such law enforcement records or information

(A) could reasonably be expected to interfere with enforcement proceedings,

(B) would deprive a person of a right to a fair trial or an impartial adjudication,

(C) could reasonably be expected to constitute an unwarranted invasion of personal privacy,

(D) could reasonably be expected to disclose the identity of a confidential source, including a State, local, or foreign agency or authority or any private institution which furnished information on a confidential basis, and, in the case of a record or information compiled by criminal law enforcement authority in the course of a criminal investigation or by an agency conducting a lawful national security intelligence investigation, information furnished by a confidential source,

(E) would disclose techniques and procedures for law enforcement investigations or prosecutions, or would disclose guidelines for law enforcement investigations or prosecutions if such disclosure could reasonably be expected to risk circumvention of the law, or

(F) could reasonably be expected to endanger the life or physical safety of any individual;

(8) contained in or related to examination, operating, or condition reports prepared by, on behalf of, or for the use of an agency responsible for the regulation or supervision of financial institutions; or

(9) geological and geophysical information and data, including maps, concerning wells. Any reasonably segregable portion of a record shall be provided to any person requesting such record after deletion of the portions which are exempt under this subsection. The amount of information deleted shall be indicated on the released portion of the record, unless including that indication would harm an interest protected by the exemption in this subsection under which the deletion is made. If technically feasible, the amount of the information deleted shall be indicated at the place in the record where such deletion is made.

(c)

(1) Whenever a request is made which involves access to records described in subsection (b)(7)(A) and—

(A) the investigation or proceeding involves a possible violation of criminal law; and

(B) there is reason to believe that

(i) the subject of the investigation or proceeding is not aware of its pendency, and

(ii) disclosure of the existence of the records could reasonably be expected to interfere with enforcement proceedings,

the agency may, during only such time as that circumstance continues, treat the records as not subject to the requirements of this section.

(2) Whenever informant records maintained by a criminal law enforcement agency under an informant's name or personal identifier are requested by a third party according to the informant's name or personal identifier, the agency may treat the records as not subject to the requirements of this section unless the informant's status as an informant has been officially confirmed.

(3) Whenever a request is made which involves access to records maintained by the Federal Bureau of Investigation pertaining to foreign intelligence or counterintelligence, or international terrorism, and the existence of the records is classified information as provided in subsection (b)(1), the Bureau may, as long as the existence of the records remains classified information, treat the records as not subject to the requirements of this section.

(d) This section does not authorize withholding of information or limit the availability of records to the public, except as specifically stated in this section. This section is not authority to withhold information from Congress.

(e)

(1) On or before February 1 of each year, each agency shall submit to the Attorney General of the United States a report which shall cover the preceding fiscal year and which shall include—

(A) the number of determinations made by the agency not to comply with requests for records made to such agency under subsection (a) and the reasons for each such determination;

(B)

(i) the number of appeals made by persons under subsection (a)(6), the result of such appeals, and the reason for the action upon each appeal that results in a denial of information; and

(ii) a complete list of all statutes that the agency relies upon to authorize the agency to withhold information under subsection (b)(3), a description of whether a court has upheld the decision of the agency to withhold information under each such statute, and a concise description of the scope of any information withheld;

(C) the number of requests for records pending before the agency as of September 30 of the preceding year, and the median number of days that such requests had been pending before the agency as of that date;

(D) the number of requests for records received by the agency and the number of requests which the agency processed;

(E) the median number of days taken by the agency to process different types of requests;

(F) the total amount of fees collected by the agency for processing requests; and

(G) the number of full-time staff of the agency devoted to processing requests for records under this section, and the total amount expended by the agency for processing such requests.

(2) Each agency shall make each such report available to the public including by computer telecommunications, or if computer telecommunications means have not been established by the agency, by other electronic means.

(3) The Attorney General of the United States shall make each report which has been made available by electronic means available at a single electronic access point. The Attorney General of the United States shall notify the Chairman and ranking minority member of the Committee on Government Reform and Oversight of the House of Representatives and the Chairman and ranking minority member of the Committees on Governmental Affairs and the Judiciary of the Senate, no later than April 1 of the year in which each such report is issued, that such reports are available by electronic means.

(4) The Attorney General of the United States, in consultation with the Director of the Office of Management and Budget, shall develop reporting and performance guidelines in connection with reports required by this subsection by October 1, 1997, and may establish additional requirements for such reports as the Attorney General determines may be useful.

(5) The Attorney General of the United States shall submit an annual report on or before April 1 of each calendar year which shall include for the prior calendar year a listing of the number of cases arising under this section, the exemption involved in each case, the disposition of such case, and the cost, fees, and penalties assessed under subparagraphs (E), (F), and (G) of subsection (a)(4). Such report shall also include a description of the efforts undertaken by the Department of Justice to encourage agency compliance with this section.

(f) For purposes of this section, the term—

(1) 'agency' as defined in section 551 (1) of this title includes any executive department, military department, Government corporation, Government controlled corporation, or other establishment in the executive branch of the Government (including the Executive Office of the President), or any independent regulatory agency; and

(2) 'record' and any other term used in this section in reference to information includes any information that would be an agency record subject to the requirements of this section when maintained by an agency in any format, including an electronic format.

(g) The head of each agency shall prepare and make publicly available upon request, reference material or a guide for requesting records or information from the agency, subject to the exemptions in subsection (b), including—

(1) an index of all major information systems of the agency;

(2) a description of major information and record locator systems maintained by the agency; and

(3) a handbook for obtaining various types and categories of public information from the agency pursuant to chapter 35 of title 44, and under this section.

Chapter 12

Between Obscurity and Clarity in Nigerian Legal Discourse: Aspects of Language Use in Selected Written Texts

Tunde Opeibi

Introduction

Studies of the intersection between language and law have generated a lot of interest in either disciplines in both the civil law and common law jurisdictions (Wagner and Cacciaguidi-Fahy 2006; Schane 2007). Efforts at making the language of legal instruments accessible to the ordinary person appear to be receiving increasing attention. This is because legal communication is central to peaceful social interactions. If the law and its system are to discharge its social functions, legal instruments must be accessible to those that they are meant to serve. Unfortunately, it is often not the case and many legal documents across the world remain unclear and obscure to the average reader.

This chapter examines features of legal language used in selected legal documents in Nigeria; namely deeds of assignments, wills, court summons, and charge sheets collected from a selected Magistrate court, legal firms and lawyers in Lagos. The overall purpose of my analysis is to describe and analyse the linguistic and discourse features that differentiate language use in the law conceived as a social institution from that of other fields. To what extent can legal documents be described as simple? Has the complexity of legal language in these documents any implication for the average person? Can English effectively function as a legal language in non-native speakers' communities?

Although scholars such as Tiersma (1999) claim that the language of the law promotes clear and concise communication through a specific legal vocabulary, it is obvious that the lexico-syntactic features of legal documents juxtapose this assertion. This is because, to a large extent, legal documents are particularly complex and difficult to read and understand. Others argue that the so-called obfuscation found in legal documents stem from the traditional view that law consists of conduct and power conferring norms that are often prescriptive in nature (O'Barr 1982). Hence, to make it sacrosanct, the language must retain its esoteric nature. Linguists, communication experts and more recently plain language campaigners, however, disagree with this view. To them, simplicity and clarity in any form of communication where human interests lie takes precedence over other considerations and must be pursued.

Negotiation of meaning in legal discourse is particularly significant because of the social implications of linguistic interactions that take place in this sociolinguistic domain. Scholars such as MacCormick and Weinberger (1986) and Ruiter (1993) have proposed frameworks to account for legal facts that emerge from human activities within the legal system. In almost every culture, the legal system is instituted to regulate human behaviour within the society and to apply sanctions when norms are disregarded. Regardless of where linguistic exchanges occur – in the courtroom, law chambers, and/or private residence of clients, legal documents play a significant role in dictating the scope of communicative exchanges that must occur.

In than sense, it is true that the application of legal statements usually leads to the creation of a new experience, affecting the existing state of affairs. The successful enactment of legal pronouncements such as 'I hereby bequeath my car to [...]', 'the assignee covenanted that [...]' usually engender a corresponding behaviour or action. Thus legal terminology plays a crucial role in our social life. Van Schooten (2007, 6) states that

> Law as a linguistic phenomenon and its relationship with social practices can be divided into three subsystems:
> 1. The legitimate legal rule (the formal dimension), which comprises a message (the material dimension)
> 2. The acts of the application of the rule by an official, and, in the case of a conflict, a judge
> 3. A degree of rule-conforming patterns of behaviour in social practice.

The legal context possesses a stylistic and discursive distinctiveness that sets it apart from language use in other domains. Law is particularly notorious for encoding meanings in a way that is different from everyday language use. Law is perceived as including different activities which either impose obligations and/or confer rights which is why legal texts, by and large, should be as drafted in a clear and comprehensible language.

Legal discourse: Obscurity versus clarity

Since the 1960s, many legal researchers have been interested in investigating and analysing the language of law. It has variously been categorised as an argot, a dialect, a register, a style or even a separate language. Some describe it as a complex collection of linguistic habits that have developed over many centuries and that lawyers have learned to use strategically (Tiersma 1999). Others have examined the historical and social reasons for the way Legal English has evolved (Melinkoff 1963; Danet 1980; Goodrich 1987; Baker 1990).

Linguists such as Crystal (1997) argue that it is probably the overriding concern for precise and consistent linguistic interpretation that has been responsible for the highly distinctive style with its obvious complexity in the written versions of legal communication. Although simplicity, clarity and conciseness are central to communication in any universe of discourse, legal documents demonstrate features of communication that are diametrically opposed to clear language. Among all the uses of language, it is in fact the least communicative (Crystal and Davy 1969, 193). Some of these features include archaism (Melinkoff 1963), wordiness (Butt 2002; Langton 2006), lack of clarity (Macdonald 2006b), use of complex sentences (Butt and Castle 2006), pomposity and dullness (Levi 2001; Sacco 2002) etc. Yet the opinion of many legal commentators weighs heavily in favour of using complex and technical legal language to ensure accuracy, precision in communication and specifically in legal interpretation (Wagner, Werner and Cao 2007).

Crystal and Davy (1969, 193) establish the historical link between the growth of the legal profession and Greek Civilisation and philosophy as accounting for archaic and Latinate expressions found in English legal texts. Words that are in everyday language use that will be regarded as out of fashion such as 'heretofore', 'herein', 'aforementioned', 'pursuant' etc. are assigned special functions in legal texts. The structure of written legal texts, which they describe as unconventional, particularly engages their attention. The layout and other visual devices are designed to reveal the content and logical progression and are used as a barrier against the insertion of 'unwanted' material which may negate the original intent of the drafter (for a further discussion, see Lötscher, Chapter Seven). Legal texts do not therefore generally follow the normal pattern of indentation and paragraphing found in conventional texts in other fields.

The language of law is also said to overuse passive constructions that depersonalise legal communication (Foley 2002; Williams 2006). This creates distance between the user of the language and the content of his utterance. For example, 'the accused is to be remanded in prison custody pending the determination of the suit' is preferred to 'I hereby remand you in custody'. This may be a result of the institutional nature of legal discourse in which the speaker functions as the agent of the State and does not take responsibility for the actions of his utterance. The presiding judge is often referred to as the 'Court' symbolising the agentive status.

In sum, legal texts can be categorised as discourses which over and above their formulation are 'said definitely', 'remain said', and 'are to be said again'. In that sense, they are formulae texts and ritualised sets of discourses recited in well-defined circumstances, 'things said once and preserved or documented to be acted upon now or in future (Foucault 1982).' Legal texts are rule-governed texts, indicating systems of restrictions or rituals that define the behaviour, circumstances, gestures and the whole set of signs which must accompany the discourse. Part of the nature of the discourse is that it also fixes the supposed or imposed efficacy of the words (for example the illocutionary force, see Schane 2007, 108-124), their effects (perlocutionary act, see Schane 2007, 108-124) on those to whom they are addressed and the limits of their constraining.

It was the concern for effective performance of the social roles of legal discourse that first precipitated the campaign for greater clarity in legal language. Since language is central to the enforcement of rules and law which the legal system bears, the people for whom the laws are made should be able to understand the words and expressions employed in the communication of legal meaning. As Hart (1958, 607) stated,

> If we are to communicate with each other at all, and if, as in the most elementary form of law, we are to express our intentions that a certain type of behaviour be regulated by rules, then the general words we use [...] must have some standard instance in which no doubts are felt about its application. There must be a core settled meaning [...].

Language should not be the barrier to exclude any group of people from enjoying the provisions of the legal system. Equality before the law which supposedly forms the basis of the judicial system must be entrenched in the language used in drafting legal documents. This is to allow every citizen to understand or have access to the contents of the law. No group or individuals should be given undue advantage over others by virtue of their professional training, social status or educational background. As Hart (1997, 124) again pointed out,

> In any large group, general rules, standards, and principles must be the main instrument of social control, and not particular directions given to each individual separately. If it were not possible to communicate general standards of conduct, which multitudes of individuals could understand, without further direction as requiring from them certain conduct when occasion arose, nothing that we now recognise as law could exist.

Plain language and the law

Advocates of plain language in law have been very active since the latter part of the twentieth century (Adler 1990; Serafin 1998; Asprey 2003; Butt and Castle 2006). They argue that 'plain language is concerned with all the techniques for clear communication' (Butt 2002) from clearer use of language to document design, better organised content and clearer visual design (see Cacciaguidi-Fahy and Wagner 2006, 21).

To the general public (the reader of the text), plain language is best described by Cutts (1997, 56) as

> the writing and setting out of essential information in a way that gives a co-operative, motivated person a good chance of understanding the document at first reading, and in the same sense that the writer meant it to be understood.

Plain English is generally understood as a clear and straightforward way of writing legal and administrative documents. It aims to avoid 'obscurity, inflated vocabulary and convoluted sentence construction' (Eaglson as cited in Sudrin 1998, 3).

As pointed by Williams (2007) 'the development and objectives of [the plain language] movement as it spread to [...] English-speaking countries have been well documented'. Yet, few scholars have debated the use of plain English or directly assessed the impact of plain language on the law on the African continent; albeit a few studies focusing on the case of South Africa (see for example Knight 1996) and the use of 'plain or simplified language in the formulation or use of law in multicultural societies with pluralist legal regimes' (Gutto 1995).

Plain language and the law in Africa

In Africa legal language is often viewed within its socio-historical context. It is embedded in the history of its colonial and imperialist past. It is considered by many as a tool used to impose the cultural values of the colonisers imposing subordination of the local /indigenous cultures. As a result, plain legal language aims primarily to 'maximise the popularity of law by improving the human values in the law as well as making the procedures more accessible and participatory' (Gutto 1995, 311). It is in fact viewed by many as a means of developing a certain consciousness of rights highlighting the need to make legal institutions and processes more accessible and participatory.

The hegemony of English in Nigeria: Implications for legal communication

English as a 'domesticated', 'indigenised', or 'nativised' language in Nigeria has been widely discussed (see Adegbija 1998, 2004; Bamgbose 1982, 1991; Banjo 1996; Adamo 2007). As 'a foreign-nationalised language', it remains an imposing force despite the multitude of local indigenous languages (Awonusi 2004, 3). Before and after independence from colonial administration, Nigeria was and remains a multilingual country *par excellence*. The reasons for this are not far-fetched. As pointed out by Awonusi (2007), they are primarily due to (i) the phenomenal growth of English and its global spread and importance over the last four centuries; (ii) English was the language of the British Empire that ruled Nigeria (iii) English has remained the official language since 1946; (iv) the complex linguistic terrain in Nigeria that has made it difficult to evolve a single national language out of the hundreds of languages in existence; and (v) the heavy functional loads that English is carrying via the medium of instruction at almost all the educational levels except the first three years of primary education, the language of politics, language of government administration, language of the mass media, and language of the law among others. The indices such as power, control, legitimacy and influence that show the hegemonic status of English in Nigeria remain (Awonusi 2004, 85-102).

The three local languages (Hausa, Igbo and Yoruba) that are now designated as national languages merely perform some cultural functions and also serve as regional lingua franca of the three major socio-political regions (Hausa in the North; Igbo in the East; and Yoruba in the South-West, see Awonusi 2007, 2). While efforts are being made to promote the use of local languages in some areas in Nigeria, English still imposes itself as a linguistic superstructure over the local languages (Awonusi 2007, 4).

As the language of the law, all laws statutes, agreements, bills, and bye-laws are written and interpreted in English. In addition, legal documents such as wills, tenancy agreements, certificates of occupancy, and affidavits are written and/or sworn in English. English is the language of legal proceedings in Nigerian Superior law courts (for example the Supreme, Appeal, High and Magistrate Courts) at the federal and state levels. The only exceptions where local languages are sometimes used are in the customary courts (in Southwest and East) where Yoruba and Igbo are used respectively, and Alkali or Sharia Courts (in the North) where Hausa or

Arabic is the primary medium of legal communication. In other instances, the local language (lingua franca) of the area over which these courts have jurisdiction may be employed for court proceedings, depending on the level of education of the litigants. In sum, all activities in the legal system in Nigeria, both training and practice, are conducted in English (Awonusi 2004, 67-82). By implication, legislative drafting, legal writing and thus many legal documents retain the complex, formulaic and sometimes obscure structure inherited from the English common law system.

However, given the current trend in society and the changes in the style of Nigerian English, a move is being advocated for a shift from the old, archaic style of legal language to the more everyday Nigerian English whereby legal drafts can be understood by the common man. It is seen, like in South Africa, as a necessity in view of the demands of society for legal language that is comprehensive yet in tune with every day English. While, unlike South Africa, it cannot be said that there is an official policy with respect to the use of plain legal language in legislative drafting/legal writing, it must be noted that in practice, the style of legal language is moving away from the archaic to the use of plain, clear and simple, modern style legal writing. In fact, some Court Chambers encourage their lawyers (especially young/junior counsels) to use plain language in drafting legal documents. This has given credence to the efforts made by the Council of Legal Education, Nigerian Law School – a body which is responsible for the legal education of students interested in studying law in Nigeria.[1]

The data: description and discussion

At the outset, it is important to note that some Nigerian legal texts exhibit syntactic and semantic features that are similar to those that exist in other common law jurisdictions. What is interesting, however, is that most Nigerian legal documents retain some 'traditional' features of 'obfuscation' that are today gradually disappearing in legal documents in many other countries.

Stability in the linguistic structure and meaning of Nigerian legal documents can be particularly noticeable in documents such as wills, deeds and statutes, which is the reason why I will focus on deed of assignment,[2] charge sheets, court summons[3] and wills.[4] I have selected these types of documents because they are socially-relevant legal documents and as such, if unclear and difficult to comprehend, directly affect the lives of the ordinary citizens. In my analysis, I classified these documents in two categories: (i) court-related legal texts: summons and charge sheets extracted from judicial proceedings, and (ii) individual-related legal texts such deeds and wills.

---

1 See <http://www.nigeria-law.org/Legal%20Education.htm>.

2 Deed of Assignment between Mr Taofik Olatona and Mr Nsidibe Inyang Akata sourced for research purposes only from Funmi Adams Esq. Chambers, Ikeja, Lagos, Nigeria.

3 Charge Sheets: (a) *Commissioner of Police v. Elizabeth Anolaje 'F' Aged 32 Years*, Chief Magistrate Court, Yaba, Lagos, Nigeria; (b) *Commissioner of Police v. Adewale Adeshina 'M' Aged 24 years*, ibid.

4 Will - (iv) *Last Will and Testament of Waidi Salami*, Funmi Adams Esq. Chambers, Ikeja, Lagos, Nigeria.

Lexico-syntactic features

Lexically and syntactically, the documents I analysed exhibit linguistic features that project the institutional setting that originally gave rise to the texts. At the lexical level, I identified the following features:

Registers/Technical words   Registerial items that specifically label each of the documents as belonging to the constitutive discourse genre include:

> WILL – 'will', 'testament', 'bequeath testamentary', 'dispositions', 'beneficiaries', 'devises', 'residue executors', 'direct', 'devises', 'bequests' etc.
> DEED of Assignment – 'deed', 'assign', 'assignee', 'assignor', 'transfer', 'occupancy', 'land', 'sold', 'guarantees', 'covenants', 'estate' etc.
> CHARGE SHEET – 'conspire', 'now at large', 'commit', 'felony', 'committed', 'offence', 'punishable', 'count I', 'count II', 'under section 390(a) of criminal code […]','Lagos Magisterial District', etc.
> SUMMONS – 'plaintiff', 'defendant', 'plaintiff's case', 'summoned to appear', 'before the court', 'to answer', 'on the grounds', 'if you dispute', etc.

Archaic words   Several words that exhibit features of Old English are still present in many of the documents examined especially wills and deeds. Examples from the corpus include, 'hereinafter', 'thereon', 'witnesseth', 'aforesaid', 'whereof', 'to wit', 'pursuant to', 'aforesaid', 'thereto'.

Although many legal professionals continue to defend the use of archaic expressions in legal documents, arguing that they are more precise that every day ordinary expressions, plain English advocates have described this argument as baseless and unfounded (Kimble 2003). For my part, I doubt that there is any idea, opinion or issue that cannot be expressed in contemporary English. One of the virtues of language is that it is dynamic. The vocabulary of English is large enough to accommodate any word or find an appropriate replacement for any old word. Besides, new words and new expressions come into the language daily to express new ideas and concepts. Both the lexical and syntactic structures of old legal documents can therefore be simplified. It is worth mentioning though that most Nigerian legal documents remain heavily influenced by the traditional complex linguistic features as illustrated above.

At the syntactic level, the study shows that the documents I examined do not deviate from the structural features found in similar documents in other countries. It appears that most of the texts studied conform to the universal features associated with such legal documents. They exhibited syntactic features such as complex sentence structure, redundant expressions, legalese, passive and impersonal constructions, use of conjunctions prepositional phrase in unusual position.

Complex sentence structure

Single passages consisting of several modified clauses in a single sentence are common occurrence:

Pursuant to the above recited agreement and in consideration of the sum of N150,000 (One Hundred and Fifty Thousand Naira only) paid by the Assignee to the Assignor before the execution of these

Presents (the receipt whereof of the Assignor hereby expressly acknowledges), the Assignor subject to the CONSENT of the Governor of Lagos State HEREBY SELLS, ASSIGNS AND TRANSFERS unto the Assignee ALL AND SINGULAR the Statutory Right of Occupancy in and over ALL THAT piece of land lying, situated and being at Plot 17 in Block 6, Ikorodu G.R.A. II, in Ikorodu Local Government Area of Lagos, State, and which piece of land measuring an Area of 853.354 Square Metres is more particularly described, delineated and shown verged "RED" on the Survey Plan No. LS/D/KD 164A dated 22:1:99 and signed by A.O. Somoye (Surveyor General of Lagos State) TO HOLD the same unto the Assignee for Assignee's absolute use and benefit subject to the provisions of the Land Use Act No. 6 of 1978 (Deed of Assignment).

The central message, that the seller has sold the piece of land to the buyer, is expressed in a long winding, complex single sentence made of one hundred and sixty words, and about ten clauses. Several redundant lexical items such as 'sells', 'assigns' and 'transfers' which could be replaced with a single word contribute to making the paragraph unnecessarily wordy and complex. The over-precision in the specification of detail is responsible for the use of long lists of lexical items connected by conjunctions such as 'and', 'or' 'with' or without any punctuation device.

Wordiness/Redundant expressions Legal texts are noted for their verbosity that is the presence of wordy and redundant phraseology. Examples found in the texts examined include:

> persons claiming for and on behalf/in trust for him;
> quiet, peaceful and undisturbed possession and ownership of the [...];
> hereby gives, conveys, and transfers
> This is the last Will and Testament of me [...]
> hereinafter referred to as "VENDOR" [...] which expression shall, where the context so admits, include his heirs, assigns, executors, successors in title, legal and personal representatives and other persons claiming for and on behalf or in trust for him
> more particularly described, delineated and show
> for the Donee's absolute use and benefit
> the donor hereby covenants, assures, undertakes and guarantees unto the Donee
> peaceful and quiet enjoyment
> the gift, conveyance and transfer of interest
> without interruption or disturbance
> hereby sold, conveyed and transferred in trust.

The above examples clearly demonstrate an overzealous tendency to be specific and place undue emphasis on details. Such wordy and redundant expressions can frustrate the reader, dull the text and weaken the essence of clear communication.

Legalese/Argots/Technical Jargons Riley (1991) describes legalese as a complex, intricate, even bizarre discourse genre, springing as it does from the authoritative role of the institution itself, which turns judges into legislators and makes the text central for the purposes of interpretation and its subsequent application. Although they could help to contextualise and distinguish a text as a particular discourse type, they have the disadvantage of obscuring plain meaning and a clear message. They weaken the process of communication by slowing down comprehension. Examples include:

> In pursuance, abuttals, indemnify, did conspire with others at large to commit, felony to with stealing of a vehicle, forenoon, the year first above written.[5]

Excessive use of conjunctions to link Words / Phrases To avoid misinterpretation and achieve emphasis and specificity, lawyers tends to multiply the use of conjunctions in legal drafting. However, the use of conjunctions often leads to unusual sentence structures which may obscure the meaning of the text. As an example,

> The Vendor covenants to indemnify *and* keep indemnified the Purchaser to the full value *and* interest at the current lending rate of the aforesaid plot of land including *but* not limited to interest thereon against any *and* all losses, costs, adverse claims *and* expenses in consequence of any act done by any rival claimant to the said plot of land *and* damages whatsoever arising from this land transaction.

> The Assignor covenants to indemnify *and* keep indemnified the Assignee to the full value *and* the interest at the prevailing rate of the aforesaid piece of land including *but* not limited to any *and* all adverse claims *and* expenses in consequence of any act done by any rival claimant to the said piece of land *and* damages whatsoever arising from any misdescription *or* misrepresentation in connection *with* this land transaction.[6]

The extracts above clearly demonstrate that the heavy use of conjunctions affect the text by making it unduly unwieldy and dull. Excerpted from a single document, they exhibit conjoined phrases with several subordinate phrases/clauses. The first paragraph contains six conjunctions (five additives, 'and'; one adversative, 'but'), while the second paragraph contains eight conjunctions (six additives, two adversatives). The preponderance of the use of conjunctions in legal documents is further confirmed by taking a closer look at the entire document which evidences the use of forty-four conjunctive words in a ten-paragraph document.

Impersonal and Passive Constructions

Generally speaking, passives and impersonal constructions weaken an utterance by shifting the focus of the action on the agent. The passive voice indicates that the actor (the subject of the action) is obscured which allows for its distanciation and makes the statement lose its force and appeal. In the deed examined, for instance, the expression 'NOW THE DEED WITNESS THAT:' will elicit from lay readers such

---

5 (i) Summons suit No RT/Y/1658/04, RT/Y/2536/04 (ii) Charge Sheets – (a) *Commissioner of Police v. Adewale A. 'M' Aged 24 yrs* – Yaba Magistrate Court, Lagos CA2 Yaba, 17/1/05; (b) *Commissioner of Police v. Elizabeth A. 'F' Aged 32 years* (ii) Motion ex-parte Suit No FHC/L/CS 862/2003.

6 See *supra* note 2.

a question as 'is it the deed that witness? Or the people involved in the agreement?' Such a confusing statement has a lot of implication for non-legal experts.

> *The Vendor* has agreed with *the Purchaser* in consideration of the sum of N52,000 (Fifty-two thousand Naira only) for the sale, conveyance and transfer of the plot of land hereinafter described to *the Purchaser* together with *the Vendor's* rights and interests in and over the land free from all encumbrances.
>
> In this connection, I direct *the Executors* to exclude any child from *my benefits* herein provided if any of *the beneficiaries* herein challenges *the devises* made in *these presents.*

Tiersma (1999) observes that a legitimate function of nominalisations is that they allow the law to be stated as generally and objectively as possible. They are, however, used by lawyers when they wish to be deliberately imprecise. Examples of nominalisations drawn from the texts include, 'quiet enjoyment and ownership', 'the sale', 'conveyance', 'without interruption or disturbance' etc.

Prepositional phrase in unusual position In the written communication of other disciplines, it is unusual to find prepositional phrases beginning a sentence. In deeds especially, prepositional phrases occur in unusual positions. Legal language thus violates the rules of grammar in order to communicate their messages in an unambiguous manner:

> By a Letter of Allocation dated 18th March, 1988, and a Letter of Confirmation dated 6th September 1999, the Lagos State Government transferred interest in the said piece of land to the Assignor.
>
> By virtue of a certificate of Occupancy dated the 17th day of January 2003, and registered as No. 73 at Page 73 in Volume 2002Q of the Lagos State of Nigeria Land Registry Office, Alausa, Ikeja, the said Assignor became the Holder of the Statutory Right of Occupancy in and over the said piece of land hereinafter described.

Besides the fronting of the prepositional phrase which can be confusing to the reader, the paragraphs above also contain a complex subordinate clause. Lawyers defend the use of such grammatical structure by arguing that they provide the reader with much needed information at first glance and reduce the possibility of misinterpretation, specifically pointing to the authenticity of the document and the claim of ownership to the property in this instance.

Between obscurity and clarity: resolving the dilemma

It is believed that 'the fewer the words that can be made to convey an idea, the clearer and the more forceful that idea' (Lambuth 1976). Most legal documents I describe above are crafted in expressions that contradict clarity and certainty. The pervasiveness of obscure expressions and fuzzy lexico-grammatical items has been identified in the documents. In the tables below, some selected legal words and expressions are presented in their original version while, for each, a clearer version is suggested.

Table 12.1 Word from obscurity to clarity

Obscure	Clear
Quiet, peaceful and undisturbed	Peaceful
Covenants, undertakes, guarantees	Undertakes
Give, devise and bequeath	Give
Sells, conveys, transfers	Sells
Shall	Will/may
Forenoon	Before 12:00 pm
Did steal	Stole
To wit	Which is/that is
Abuttals	attachments
Indemnify	Compensate
Verged	Marked
Assignor	Seller
Assignee	Buyer
Sale, Assignment and transfer	Sale

Table 12.2 Meaning from obscurity to clarity

Obscure	Clear
In this connection, I direct that such funeral expense and, or debts shall be met from whatever cash may be available in my house and or form my current account, in poverty over any other devise.	You should pay all funeral expenses and debts from money found in my house or current account before any other expenses.
I am also sole owner of a bungalow building of four rooms at Mobil Estate Satellite Town, Lagos, Nigeria. I give and desire the said building to my two daughters to share equally between them as joint tenants and remain there forever.	My four-room bungalow at Mobil Estate, Satellite Town, Lagos, Nigeria must be shared equally by my two daughters.
In this connection, I direct the Executors to exclude any child from my benefits herein provided if any of the beneficiaries herein challenges the devises made in these presents.	The executors must not give any property to any of my children or beneficiaries that expresses dissatisfaction with the procedures for sharing the property.
The Vendor has agreed with the purchase in consideration of the sum of ₦52,000 (fifty-two thousand naira only) for the sale, conveyance and transfer of the plot of land hereinafter described to the purchaser with the Vendor's rights and interests in and over the land free from all encumbrance.	The Vendor (Mr.....) has sold the land to the purchaser (Mr.....) for the sum of Fifty-two thousand naira (52,000:00k) only.

Written legal communication in Nigeria still contains peculiar features that often create difficulties for non-legal professionals. In the course of my research, I observed that the following factors explain the present state of Nigerian legal English:

(i) There is a general low awareness on the use of plain language among Nigerian legal experts

(ii) Linguistic continuity and permanence are especially strong because the law courts and legal experts still rely on a non-native language in which these documents have been drafted since the period of the colonial administration

(iii) Nigerian lawyers, especially the younger ones, learned their legal English from conservative senior lawyers that still believe in the preservation of the old tradition of legal drafting with lots of legalese and complex structures

(iv) The multilingual nature of the Nigerian society; the difficulty in adopting a common national language from over 400 competing local languages; and the hegemonic status of English over the indigenous languages have made it politically impossible to use simple language familiar to all citizens.

The social roles of legal texts in Nigeria are too important for them to be worded in a manner that is made the exclusive preserve of only lawyers, judges and members of the legal professions. Members of a society, especially those whose lives are directly affected by the provisions of legal documents, should be able to reasonably understand and interpret the legal English used in the texts. The situation is even more worrisome if we consider that beside the complex nature of the language of these documents, their being drafted in English makes them even more obscure and incomprehensible to many Nigerians who still use indigenous languages such as Yoruba, Igbo and Hausa. It is a fact that English is still understood and used by less than 30% of Nigerian citizens. The majority (for example about 70%) are thus cut off from the linguistic frequency of the transactions enacted in documents and legal proceedings that directly affect them. It is also important to point out that the present legal apparatus under which the documents are drafted does not give any room for flexibility in terms of amendments to any of the documents. Additions or corrections to the text (especially authoritative texts) can only be made through equally torturous, formal processes leading to loss of valuable time and assets (Opeibi 2005).

Concluding remarks

In Nigeria, some of these legal documents especially those that affect the public e.g. bills, statutes, ordinances, etc. will have to go through a very long road of constitutional amendments at the legislative houses at the local, state, or federal level as the case may be. Even in private documents such as Wills, or Deeds, legal requirements are expected to be fulfilled before any section can be amended. The need to draft legal documents in plain language may hinge on the following: (i) English is not the language of communication for most Nigerians; (ii) when the documents are written in simple, straightforward language, they become accessible to the average citizens; (iii) it will enable them make rational judgments or informed decisions on the basis of what they could understand from the documents; and (iv) if they are expected to respond positively to decisions that affect them directly, then the language of those documents should not be complex or obscure.

On a final note, it is worth noting that the drafting of the legal documents (especially the Deeds and Wills) demonstrates a high level of proficiency in the English language which is also required to comprehend them. It thus confirms our findings elsewhere (Opeibi forthcoming) that legal experts in Nigeria may be categorised among speakers who have near-native competence in English.

Bibliography

Adler, M. (1990), *Clarity for Lawyers: The Use of Plain English in Legal Writing* (UK: Law Society of England and Wales).

Adler, M. (2006), *Clarity for Lawyers* (London: Law Society).

Adamo, G.E. (2007), 'Nigerian English', *English Today*, 23:1, 42-47.

Adegbija, E. (2004), 'The Domestication of English in Nigeria', in Awonusi, S. and Babalola, E.A. (eds), *A Festschrift in Honour of Abiodun Adetugbo* (Lagos: University of Lagos Press).

Ahava, I. (1929), 'Lainsäädännöllisiä susia', *Lakimies* 219-228.

Ames, K. (1980), 'Material Cultural as Non-verbal Communication: A Historical Case Study', *Journal of American Culture* 3, 619-641.

Anon. (1974), *Ymmärrettävää virkakieltä* [Intelligible Administrative Language] (Helsinki: Valtion Painatuskeskus / Karisto Oy).

Anon. (1981), *Kieli ja virkakoneisto. Virkakielikomitean mietintö* [the *Language and the Machinery of Administration*] (Helsinki: Valtion Painatuskeskus / Karisto Oy).

Anon. (1997), *Lainlaatijan opas* [the *Legal Drafter's Manual*] (Helsinki: Edita).

Anon. (2004), 'Language Barriers: Can a Concept Exist Without Words to Describe It?', *The Economist* 19 August 2004, 66-67.

Anon. (2007), *Finlandssvenskarna 2005 – en statistisk rapport. Finlandssvensk rapport nr 43* (Helsingfors: Universitetstryckeriet).

Arendt, H. (2005), *The Promise of Politics*, tr. J. Kohn (New York: Schocken Books).

Arnaud, A.-J. (1998), 'La régulation par le droit en contexte globalisé', in Commaille and Jobert (eds), *Les métamorphoses de la régulation politique* (Paris: LGDJ), pp.147-176.

Asprey, M.M. (1991), *Plain Language for Lawyers* (Leichhardt, NSW: The Federation Press).

Asprey, M. (2003), *Plain Language for Lawyers*, 3rd Edition (Sydney: The Federation Press).

Augustine (1961), *Confessions*, tr. R.S. Pine-Coffin (London: Penguin Books).

Awonusi, V.O. (2004), 'The Functions of Nigerian English in Relation to other Nigerian Languages', in Dadzie, A.B.K. and Awonusi, S. (eds), *Nigerian English: Influences and Characteristics* (Lagos: Concept Publication), pp.62-82.

Azard, P. (1965), 'La Cour suprême du Canada et l'application du droit civil de la province de Québec', *Canadian Bar Review* 65, 553-60.

Bacon, F. (1877), *The Works of Francis Bacon,* vol. V, translation of De Augmentis Scientiarum, Book VIII (London: Routledge/Thoemmes Press, reprinted Edition. published 1996).

Baker, J.H. (1990), *An Introduction to Legal English History* (London Butterworths).

Bamgbose, A. (1982), 'Standard Nigerian English: Issues of Identification', in Kachru, B.B. (ed.), *The Other Tongue: English Across Cultures* (Oxford: Pergamon Press), pp.148-164.

Bamgbose, A. (1991), *Language and the Nation* (Edinburgh: Edinburgh University Press).

Banjo, A. (1996), *Making a Virtue of Necessity: An Overview of The English Language in Nigeria* (Idaban: University of Idaban Press).

Barnes, J. (June 2004), 'Shining examples', *The Loophole* 1, 8-24.

Barnes, G. (2006), 'The Continuing Debate About "Plain Language" Legislation: A Law Reform Conundrum', *Statute Law Review* 27:2, 83-132.

Barr, J. (1961), *The Semantics of Biblical Language* (Oxford: Oxford University Press).

Bartolini, F. and Delconte, R.C. (eds) (2001), *Il Codice dell'Arbitrato* [The Arbitration Code] (Piacenza: La Tribuna).

Baudouin, J.-L. (1975), 'L'interprétation du Code civil québécois par la Cour suprême du Canada', *Canadian Bar Review* 53, 715-37.

Baudouin, J.-L. (1986), 'La Cour suprême et le droit civil québécois: un bilan, un constat, une prospective', in Baudouin (ed.), *La Cour suprême du Canada – The Supreme Court of Canada* (Cowansville: Yvon Blais), pp.125-134.

Baudry-Lacantinerie, G. and Chauveau, A. (1905), *Traité théorique et pratique de droit civil, IV, Des Biens*, 6 vol. (Paris: Larose et Forcel).

Bekink, B. and Botha, C. (2007), 'Aspects of Legislative Drafting: Some South African Realities (or Plain Language is Not Always Plain Sailing)', *Statute Law Review* 28:1, 34-67.

Belkin, I. (2000), 'China's Criminal Justice System: A Work in Progress', *Washington Journal of Modern China* 6:2, 61-84.

Bell, J. and Engle, Sir G. (1995), *Cross on Statutory Interpretation*. 3rd Edition (London: Butterworths).

Belotti, U. (2002), 'The Language of Italian Arbitration Rules in English: Some Measurable Aspects', *Linguistica e Filologia* 15, 113-141.

Belotti, U. (2003), 'Generic Integrity in Italian Arbitration Rules', in Bhatia, Candlin and Gotti (eds), pp.19-40.

Bennion, F.A.R. (2002), *Statutory Interpretation*, 4th Edition (London: Butterworths).

Bennion, F.A.R. (2007), *Statutory Interpretation*, 5th Edition (London: Butterworths).

Bentham, J. (1830), *Traité de législation civile et pénale,* vol. III, 3rd Edition (Paris: E. Dumont).

Bergeal, C. (2001), *Savoir Rédiger un Texte Normatif: Loi, Décret, Arrêté, Circulaire* (Paris: Berger-Levrault).

Bergeal, C. (2006), 'La qualité de la réglementation en France: question politique ou juridique', in Wagner and Cacciaguidi-Fahy (eds), pp.203-236.

Bernini, G. (1998), 'Is There a Growing International Arbitration Culture?', *ICCA Congress Series* 8, 41-46.

Bernstein, R. and Wood, D. (1993), *Handbook of Arbitration Practice* (London: Sweet and Maxwell).

Berriat-Saint-Prix (1835), *Discours sur les vices du langage judiciaire* (Paris: Imprimerie et Fonderie de Fain).

Bertagnollo, F. and Laurent, C. (2005), 'Unkraut vergeht nicht: la corédaction dans l'administration fédérale suisse', in Gémar and Kasirer (eds), pp.119-126.

Bhatia, V.K. (1993), *Analysing Genre: Language Use in Professional Settings* (London: Longman).

Bhatia, V.K., Candlin, C. and Wei, S. (2001), *Legal Discourse in Multilingual and Multicultural Contexts: A Preliminary Study, Research Group Report* (Hong Kong: City University of Hong Kong).

Bhatia, V.K., Candlin, C. and Gotti, M. (eds) (2003), *Legal Discourse in Multilingual and Multicultural Contexts: Arbitration Texts in Europe* (Bern: Peter Lang).

Bhatia, V.K., Candlin, C., Engberg, J. and Trosborg, A. (eds) (2003), *Multilingual and Multicultural Contexts of Legislation* (Frankfurt am Main: Peter Lang).

Bhatia, V., Engberg, J., Gotti, M. and Heller, D. (eds), (2005), *Vagueness in Normative Texts* (Bern: Peter Lang).

Bhatia, V.K., Candlin, C. and Engberg, J. (eds) (forthcoming), *Legal Discourse across Cultures and Systems* (Hong Kong: Hong Kong University Press).

Bhatia, V.K., Candlin, C. and Evangelisti Allori, P. (eds) (forthcoming), *The Formulation of Legal Concepts across Systems and Cultures* (Bern: Peter Lang).

Bierce, A. (2001), *The Enlarged Devil's Dictionary* (London: Penguin Books Ltd).

Bix, B. (1993), *Law, Language and Legal Determinacy* (Oxford: Clarendon).

Blomquist, L. (2006), 'One Little Word...', in Wagner and Cacciaguidi-Fahy (eds), pp.301-327.

Borris, C. (1994), 'Common Law and Civil Law: Fundamental Differences and their Impact on Arbitration', *Arbitration* 60:2, 78-85.

Bowers, F. (1989), *Linguistic Aspects of Legislative Expression* (Vancouver: University of British Columbia Press).

Bredin, J.-D. (1963), 'Note sous Cass. civ. 1ère, 10 juillet 1962', *Revue Trimestrielle de Droit civil*, 121.

Brierley, J.E.C. and MacDonald, R.A. (1993), *Québec Civil Law: An Introduction to Québec Private Law* (Toronto: Emmond Montgomery).

Brodie, D. (1997), *Writing Changes Everything* (New York: St. Martin's Press).

Burtt, E. (ed.) (1939), *The English Philosophers from Bacon to Mill* (New York: Modern Library).

Butt, P. and Castle, R. (2001), *Modern Legal Drafting: A Guide to Using Clearer Language* (Cambridge: Cambridge University Press).

Butt, P. (2002), 'Modern Legal Drafting', *Statute Law Review* 23, 12-23.

Butt, P. and Castle, R. (2006), *Modern Legal Drafting: A Guide to Using Clearer Language* (Cambridge: Cambridge University Press).

Cacciaguidi-Fahy and Wagner (2006), in Wagner and Cacciaguidi-Fahy (eds), pp.19-32.

Candlin, C.N. and Gotti, M. (2004a), *Intercultural Discourse in Domain-Specific English. Special issue of Textus* 17:1.

Candlin, C.N. and Gotti, M. (eds) (2004b), *Intercultural Aspects of Specialised Communication* (Bern: Peter Lang).

Cao, D. (2004), *Chinese Law: A Language Perspective* (Aldershot: Ashgate).

Cao, D. (2007a), *Translating Law – with Foreword by Justice Michael Kirby of the High Court of Australia* (Clevedon: Multilingual Matters).

Cao, D. (2007b), 'Inter-lingual Uncertainty in Bilingual and Multilingual Law', *Journal of Pragmatics* 39, 69-83.

Capitant, H. (1917), 'Comment on fait les lois aujourd'hui', *Revue politique et parlementaire* 91.

Caron, C. (2002), 'Empiétement de 0.5 centimètre sur le terrain d'autrui: sévérité de la Cour de Cassation – Note sous Cass. civ. 3ème, 20 mars 2002', *Dalloz*, jur. 2075.

Carter, R. and Green, M. (2007), 'The Enactment is Self-Explanatory ... or is it?' – Explanatory Provisions in New Zealand Legislation', *Statute Law Review* 28:1, 1-33.

Champeil-Desplats, (2006), 'Les clairs-obscurs de la clarté juridique', in Wagner and Cacciaguidi-Fahy (eds), pp.35-64.

Charnock, R. (2006), 'Clear Ambiguity', in Wagner and Cacciaguidi-Fahy (eds), pp.65-103.

Chevallier, J. (2003), *L'Etat post-moderne*, Collection Droit et société / Série politique (Paris: LGDJ/MSH).

Commaille, J. and Jobert, B. (eds) (1998), *Les métamorphoses de la régulation politique* (Paris: LGDJ).

Coombe, R.J. (1989), '"Same as it Ever Was": Rethinking the Politics of Statutory Interpretation', *McGill Law Journal* 34:3, 603-51.

Cornu, G. (1988), *Droit civil: Introduction. Les personnes. Les biens* (Paris: Montchrestien).

Cornu, G. (2000), *Linguistique Juridique* (Paris: Montchrestien-EJA).

Cortese, G. (2005), 'Indeterminacy in "Rainbow" Legislation: The Convention on the Rights of the Child', in Bhatia, Engberg, Gotti and Heller (eds), pp.255-286.

Côté, P.-A. (1997), 'L'interprétation de la loi en droit civil et en droit statutaire: communauté de langue et différence d'accents', *Revue Juridique Thémis* 31, 45-85.

Côté, P.-A. (1999), *L'Interprétation des Lois*, 3rd Edition (Cowansville: Yvon Blais).

Courant, R. and Robbins, H. (1996), *What is Mathematics?* (Oxford: Oxford University Press).

Cremades, B.M. (1998), 'Overcoming the Clash of Legal Cultures: The Role of Interactive Arbitration', *Arbitration International* 14:2, 157-172.

Crystal, D. and Davy, D. (1969), *Investigating English Style* (London: Longman).

Crystal, D. (1997), *The Cambridge Encyclopedia of Language*, 2nd Edition (London: Cambridge University Press).

Cutts, M. (1997), 'Plain English in The Law', *Statute Law Review* 17:1, 50-61.

Cutts, M. (2000), 'Clarity in EC Legislation', *Clarity* 45, 11-12.

Cutts, M. (2001), *Clarifying Eurolaw* (Stockport: The Plain Language Commission Peak Press).

Cutts, M. and Wagner, E. (2002), *Clarifying EC Regulations. How European Community Regulations Could be Written More Clearly so that Citizens of*

Member States, Including Lawyers, Would Understand Them Better (Stockport: The Plain Language Commission).

D'Amato, A. (1989), 'Can Legislatures Constrain Judicial Interpretation of Statutes?', *Virginia Law Review* 75, 561-603.

D'Amato, A. (ed.) (1996), *Analytic Jurisprudence Anthology* (Cincinnati: Anderson Publishing).

Dan-Cohen, M. (1984), 'Decision Rules and Conduct Rules: On Acoustic Separation in Criminal Law'. *Harvard Law* Review 97:3, 625-634.

Danet, B. (1980), 'Language in the Legal Process', *Law and Society* 14:3, 445-564.

de Sousa Santos, B. (2002), *Towards a New Legal Common Sense*, 2nd Edition (London: Butterworths).

Debruche, A.-F. (forthcoming 2007), *Equité du juge et territoires du droit privé – Le paradoxe de l'emprise immobilière dans les systèmes romanistes et de common law* (Bruxelles / Cowansville: Bruylant / Yvon Blais).

Demolombe, C. (1854), *Cours de code Napoléon: Traité de la distinction des biens*, vol. 9. (Paris: Durand, etc.)

Derrida, J. (1990), *Du droit à la philosophie* (Paris: Galilée).

Descartes, R. (2006), *Descartes's Theory of Action* (Herndon: Brill Academic Publishers).

DeWolfe Howe, M. (ed.) (1961), *Holmes-Pollock Letters. The Correspondence of Mr. Justice Holmes and Sir Frederick Pollock, 1874-1932*, 2nd Edition (Cambridge, Mass.: Harvard University Press).

Dickerson, R. (1964), 'The Diseases of Legislative Language', *Harvard Journal of Legislation* 1, 5.

Drago, R. (ed.) (2005), *La confection de la loi* (Paris: PUF).

Duprat, J.-P. (2005), 'Genèse et développement de la légistique', in Drago (ed.), *La confection de la loi* (Paris: PUF), pp.10-25.

Dworkin, R. (1986), *Law's Empire* (Cambridge: Harvard University Press).

Economy, E.C. (2004), *The River Runs Black: The Environmental Challenge to China's Future* (Ithaca and London: Cornell University Press).

Ehrenberg-Sundin, B. (2000), 'Internationellt klarspråksarbete – en grund för bättre EU-texter?' [International Plain Language Work – A Basis for Better EU Texts?], in Melander, B. (ed.), *Svenskan som EU-språk* [Swedish as a European Union Language] (Uppsala: Hallgren and Fallgren), pp.144-178.

Ehrenberg-Sundin, B. (2002), 'The Swedish Government Promotes Clear Drafting', *Clarity* 47, 3-9.

Ehrenberg-Sundin, B. (2004), 'Med myrsteg eller jättekliv mot klarare EU-texter?' [Ant Steps or Giant Steps Towards Clearer EU Texts?], in Hellsten, U. and Ingerlund, B., *Språkets vård och värden – en festskrift till Catharina Grünbaum* [Language Cultivation and The Values of Language? – Essays in honour of Catharina Grünbaum] (Stockholm: Norstedts Ordbok), pp.176-187.

Ekerot, L-J (2000), 'Klar komplexitet' [Clear complexity], in Melander, B. (ed), *Svenskan som EU-språk* [Swedish as a European Union Language] (Uppsala: Hallgren and Fallgren), pp.46-77.

Endicott, T. (2000), *Vagueness in Law* (Oxford: Oxford University Press).

Endicott, T. (2003), 'Raz on Gaps: The Surprising Part', in Meyer, L.H., Paulson, S.L., and Pogge, T.W. (eds), *Rights, Culture, and the Law: Themes from the Legal and Political Philosophy of Joseph Raz* (Oxford: Oxford University Press), pp.99-115.

Endicott, T. (2005), 'The Value of Vagueness', in Bhatia, Engberg, Gotti and Heller (eds), pp.27-48.

Eve J. (1941), *Law Notes* 60, 26-31.

Faralli, C. and Pattaro, E. (eds) (1988), *Reason in Law* (Milan: Guiffrè).

Fernbach, N. (2005), 'Le mouvement pour la simplification des communications officielles', in Gémar and Kasirer (eds), pp.161-177.

Ferrari, V. and Faralli, C. (eds) (1993), *Laws and Rights* (Milan: Guiffrè).

Fish, S. (1989), *Doing What Comes Naturally: Change, Rhetoric, and the Practice of Theory in Literary and Legal Studies* (Durham: Duke University Press).

Fish, S. (1991), 'Almost Pragmatism: The Jurisprudence of Richard Posner, Richard Rorty, and Ronald Dworkin', in Brint and Weave (eds), *Pragmatism in Law and Society* (Boulder: Westview), pp.47-81.

Fjeld, R.V. (2001), 'Interpretation of Indefinite Adjectives in Legislative Language', in Mayer, F. (ed.), *Languages for Special Purposes: Perspectives for the New Millennium* (Tübingen: Narr), pp.643-650.

Fleiner, T. et al. (2005), *Swiss Constitutional Law* (The Hague, London and Boston: Kluwer).

Flückiger, A. (2005), 'Le multilinguisme de l'Union européenne: un défi pour la qualité de la législation', in Gémar and Kasirer (eds), pp.339-361.

Foley, R. (2002), 'Legislative Language in the EU: The Crucible', *International Journal for The Semiotics of Law* 15:4, 361-374.

Foucault, M. (1982), *Power/Knowledge: Selected Interviews and Other Writings by Michael Foucault, 1972-1977* (New York: Pantheon).

Fredrickson, K.M. (1996), 'Contrasting Genre Systems: Court Documents from the United States and Sweden, *Multilingua* 15, 275-304.

Freeman, M.D.A. (ed. 1998), *Legal Theory at the End of the Millennium* (Oxford: Oxford University Press).

Frenette, F. (1999), 'La problématique de l'empiétement', *Revue du Notariat* 101, 93-113.

Frommel, S.N. and Rider, B.A.K. (eds) (1999), *Conflicting Legal Cultures in Commercial Arbitration: Old Issues and New Trends* (The Hague: Kluwer Law International).

Gallas, T. (2001), 'La rédaction législative multilingue dans l'Union européenne: bilan et perspective', *LeGes – Législation and Evaluation* 12:3, 115-129.

Garzone, G. (2003), 'Arbitration Rules across Legal Cultures: An Intercultural Approach', in Bhatia, Candlin and Gotti (eds), pp.177-220.

Gaudemet, E. (1904), *Le Code civil 1804-1904, livre du centenaire* (Paris: [n.p.]).

Gémar, J.-C. and Kasirer, N. (eds) (2005), *Jurilinguistique: entre langues et droits / Jurilinguistics: Between Law and Language* (Brussels and Montreal: Bruylant/ Thémis).

Gény, F. (1904), 'La technique législative dans la codification civile moderne', in Gaudemet (ed.).

Gény, F. (1919), *Méthodes d'interprétation et sources en droit privé positif. Essai critique* (Paris: L.G.D.J.).

Gény, F. (1922), *Sciences et Techniques en Droit Privé Positif* (Paris: Recueil Sirey).

Gerbe, R-M. (2006), 'Le Présent de l'Indicatif dans le Discours Juridique', in Wagner and Cacciaguidi (eds), pp.265-302.

Gibbons, J. (2003), *Forensic Linguistics: An Introduction to Language in the Justice System* (Oxford: Blackwell).

Glenn, H.P. (2001), 'La Cour suprême du Canada et la tradition du droit civil', *Canadian Bar Review* 80, 151-70.

Gmür, R. (1965), *Das Schweizerische Zivilgesetzbuch* (Zurich: [n.p.]).

Goodrich, P. (1987), *Legal Discourses: Studies in Linguistics, Rhetoric and Legal Analysis* (London: Macmillan Press).

Goodrich, P. (1990), *Languages of The Law: From Logics of Memory to Nomadic Masks* (London: Weindfeld and Nicolson).

Gotti, M. and Dossena, M. (eds) (2001), *Modality in Specialised Texts* (Bern: Peter Lang).

Gotti, M. (2005), *Investigating Specialised Discourse* (Bern: Peter Lang).

Gotti, M. and Giannoni, D.S. (eds) (2006), *New Trends in Specialised Discourse Analysis* (Bern: Peter Lang).

Goubeaux, G. (1969), *La règle de l'accessoire en droit privé* (Paris: L.G.D.J.-Montchrestien).

Goubeaux, G. (1975), 'Note sous Cass. civ. 3ème, 8 octobre 1974', *Répertoire Defrénois* I, 30913.

Graham, R.N. (2001), *Statutory Interpretation – Theory and Practice* (Toronto: Emond Montgomery).

Green, M.K. (1993), 'Forms of Life and Pluralistic Paradigms in Law', in Kevelson (ed.).

Grice, H.P. (1975), 'Logic and Conversation', in Cole and Morgan (eds).

Grossfeld, B. (1990), *The Strength and Weakness of Comparative Law*, tr. T. Weir (Oxford: Clarendon Press).

Gustafsson, M. (1975), *Some Syntactic Properties of English Law Language* (Turku: University of Turku, Department of English).

Gustafsson, M. (1984), 'Syntactic Features of Binomial Expressions in Legal English', *Text* 4:1-3,123-142.

Gutto, S.B.O. (1995), 'Plain Language and the Law in The Context of Cultural and Legal Pluralism', *South Africa Journal on Human Rights* 11, 311-317.

Habermas, J. (2003), *Truth and Justification*, tr. B. Fultner (Cambridge: MIT Press).

Hansenne, J. (1996), *Les biens*, vol. 2, 2ème Edition (Liège: Collection Scientifique de la Faculté de Droit de Liège).

Hanson, N. (1959), *Patterns of Discovery: An Inquiry into the Conceptual Foundations of Science* (Cambridge: Cambridge University Press).

Hart, H.L.A. (1958), 'Positivism and the Separation of Law and Morals', *Harvard Law Review* 71:4, 593-629.

Hart, H.L.A. (1961), *The Concept of Law* (Oxford: Oxford University Press).

Hart, H.L.A. (1994), *The Concept of Law*, 2nd Edition (Oxford: Clarendon Press).

Hart, H.L.A. (1997), *The Concept of Law*, 2nd Edition (Oxford: Oxford University Press).

Hawkins, V.F. (1860), *On the Principles of Legal Interpretation*, reprinted in Thayer, J.B. (1898) *A Preliminary Treatise on Evidence at the Common Law* (London: [n.p.]).

Heidegger, M. (1962), *Being and Time*, tr. J. Macquarrie and E. Robinson (New York: Harper and Row).

Heidegger, M., and Fink, E. (1993), *The Heraclitus Seminar*, tr. C. Seibert (Evanston: Northwestern University Press).

Heidegger, M. (2004), *The Phenomenology of Religious Life*, tr. M. Fritsch and J. Gosetti-Ferencei (Bloomington: Indiana University Press).

Hennion-Moreau, S. (1983), 'L'empiétement', *Revue de droit immobilier*, 303-18.

Hiltunen, R. (1990), *Chapters on Legal English: Aspects Past and Present of the Language of the Law* (Helsinki: Suomalainen Tiedeakatemia).

Hjort-Pedersen, M. and Faber, D. (2001), 'Lexical Ambiguity and Legal Translation: A Discussion', *Multilingua* 20:4, 379-392.

Hobbes, T. (1651), *Leviathan*, Rep. 1985 (London: Penguin).

Hofman, G. (2003), *Har det hänt något på klarspråksfronten? En synkron och diakron jämförelse av svenska EU-direktiv* [Has anything happened regarding plain language? A Synchronic and Diachronic Comparison of EC Directives in Swedish] (Belgium: University of Gent).

Holland, J.A. and Weeb, J.S. (2003), *Learning Legal Rules*, 5th Edition (Oxford: Oxford University Press).

Holmes, J. (1984), 'Modifying Illocutionary Force', *Journal of Pragmatics* 8, 345-365.

Hopkins, E.R. (1937), 'The Literal Canon and the Golden Rule', *Canadian Bar Review* 15, 689-92.

Hoye, L. (1997), *Adverbs and Modality in English* (London: Longman).

Huber, E. (1901), *Code civil suisse: exposé des motifs* (Berne: [n.p.]).

Hume, D. (1882), *A Treatise on Human Nature* (London: Longmans).

Hunt, A. and Wickham, G. (1994), *Foucault and Law: Towards A Sociology of Law as Governance* (London: Pluto Press).

Hurlburt, W.H. (1978), 'Case Comments and Notes: Improvements under Mistake of Ownership: Section 183 of the Land Titles Act', *Alberta Law Review* 16, 107-16.

Iisa, K. and Piehl, A. (1992), *Virkakielestä kaikkien kieleen* (Helsinki: VAPK-kustannus).

Isidorus, H. (2004), *Etymologiae XIII: De Mundo et Partibus*, tr. G. Gasparatto (Paris: Les Belles Lettres).

Jackson, B. (1987), 'Can Legal Semiotics Contribute to Natural Law Studies?' *Vera Lex* 7, 9-18.

Jackson, B. (1992), 'Pour un modèle sémiotique de l'analogie du jeu en théorie du droit', *International Journal for the Semiotics of Law* 5:13, 55-90.

Jackson, B. (1993), 'Piaget, Kohlberg and Habermas: Psychological and Communicational Approaches to Legal Theory', in Ferrari, V. and Faralli, C. (eds), *Laws and Rights* (Milan: Guiffrè), pp.571-592.

Jarvin, S. (1999), 'Leading Arbitration Seats: A (Mostly European) Comparative View', in Frommel and Rider (eds), pp.39-61.

Ji, W. (2004), *Space of Choice and Judicial Discretion in China: A Perspective of Comparative Legal Culture, CDAMS Discussion Paper* (Kobe: Kobe University).

Kant, I. (1998), *Critique of Pure Reason*, tr. P. Guyer and A. Wood (Cambridge: Cambridge University Press).

Kant, I. (2003), *Critique of Pure Reason* (London: Palgrave-Macmillan).

Kayman, M. (2004), 'A Memorial for Jeremy Bentham: Memory, Fiction, and Writing the Law', *Law and Critique* 15:3, 207-29.

Keller, P. (1994), 'Sources of Order in Chinese Law', *The American Journal of Comparative Law* 42:4, 711-759.

Kerridge, R. (2000), *Hawkins on the Construction of Wills*, 5th Edition (London: Sweet and Maxwell).

Kessler, J. (2006), *Drafting Trusts and Will Trusts*, 8th Edition (London: Sweet and Maxwell).

Kevelson, R. (ed.) (1993), *Flux, Complexity, and Illusion*, vol. 6 (New York: Peter Lang).

Kimble, J. (1992), 'Plain English: A Charter for Clear Writing', *Thomas M Cooley Law Review* 9:1, 25-26.

Kimble, J. (1996-97), 'Writing for Dollars, Writing to Please', *Scribes Journal of Legal Writing* 6, 1-38.

Kimble, J. (2003), 'The Elements of Plain Language', *Clarity* 50, 22-23.

Kimble, J. (2004) 'You be the Judge', *Michigan Bar Journal* 83:12, 40-41.

Kimble, J. (2006), *Lifting the Fog of Legalese: Essays on Plain Language* (Carolina: Carolina Academic Press).

Kindermann, H. (1986), 'Gesetzessprache und Akzeptanz der Norm', in Öhlinger (ed.), *Recht und Sprache* (Wien, Manz), pp.53-68.

Kirby, M. Hon. J. (2003), 'Towards a Grand Theory of Interpretation: The Case of Statutes and Contracts', *Statute Law Review* 24:2, 95-111.

Klinge, A. (1995), 'On the Linguistic Interpretation of Contractual Modalities', *Journal of Pragmatics* 23:5, 649-675.

Knaack, J.A. (1993), 'Is Law the Least Bad Bet? Rationality, Rhetoric and Rules of Law', in Kevelson (ed.), pp.251-267.

Knight, P. (1996), *Clearly Better Drafting: A Report to the Plain English Campaign on Testing Two Versions of the South Africa Human Rights Commission Act 1995* (Stockport: Plain English Campaign).

Kooij, J.G. (1971), *Ambiguity in Natural Language: An Investigation of Certain Problems in its Linguistic Description* (Amsterdam/London: North-Holland Publishing Company).

Kramer, A. (2003), 'Common Sense Principles of Contract Interpretation', *Oxford Journal of Legal Studies* 23:2, 173-196.

Kripke, S. (1982), *Wittgenstein on Rules and Private Language* (Cambridge: Harvard University Press).

Kuner, C.B. (1991), 'The Interpretation for Multilingual Treaties: Comparison of Texts versus the Presumption of Similar Meaning', *The International and Comparative Law Quarterly* 40:4, 953-964.

Lafond, P.-C. (1991), *Droit des biens* (Montréal: Thémis).

Lalive, P. (1992), 'On Communication in International Arbitration', *The American Review of International Arbitration* 3:1-4, 79-82.

Lambuth, D. (1976), *The Golden Book on Writing* (London; Penguin).

Lang, J. (1994), *Urban Design: The American Experience* (London: Wiley).

Langan, P.S.J. (1969), *Maxwell on the Interpretation of Statutes*, 12th Edition (London: Sweet and Maxwell).

Langton, N. (2006), 'Cleaning Up the Act: Using Plain Language in Legislation', in Wagner and Cacciaguidi-Fahy (eds), pp.361-390.

Lasser, M. de S.-O.-l'E. (1994-1995), 'Judicial (Self-)Portraits: Judicial Discourse in the French Legal System', *Yale Law Journal* 104, 1326-410.

Lasserre-Kiesow, V. (2005), 'Comment faire les lois? L'éternel retour d'un défi', in Drago (ed.).

Lazareff, S. (1999), 'International Arbitration: Towards a Common Procedural Approach', in Frommel and Rider (eds), *Conflicting Legal Cultures in Commercial Arbitration: Old Issues and New Trends* (The Hague: Kluwer Law International), pp.31-38.

Leeds-Hurwitz, W. (1993), *Semiotics and Communication: Signs, Codes, Cultures* (New-Jersey Hove, London: Lawrence Erlbaum Associates).

Lerch, K (ed.) (2004), *Recht Verstehen. Verständlichkeit, Missverständlichkeit und Unverständlichkeit von Recht* (Berlin and New York: de Gruyter).

Levi, J.N. and Walker, A.G. (1990), *Language in the Judicial Process* (The Hague: Springer).

Lévis, M. (1989), *L'opposabilité du droit réel: De la sanction judiciaire des droits* (Paris: Economica).

Lewis, C. (1988), *Sylvie and Bruno* (New York: Dover).

Lewis, C.S. (1960), *Studies in Words* (*Canto*) (Cambridge: Cambridge University Press).

Lewison, K. (2004), *The Interpretation of Contracts*, 3rd Edition (London: Sweet and Maxwell).

Linday, P. (2003), 'The Ambiguity of GATT Article XXI: Subtle Success or Rampant Failure?', *Duke Law Journal* 52:5, 12777-1313.

Lindgren, B. (ed.) (2000), *Bättre språk i EU*, Rapport från en konferens den 29 november-1 december 1998 i Bryssel. (Stockholm: Nordiska språkrådet).

Locke, J. (1632-1704), *An Essay concerning Human Understanding* (London: Collier-MacMillan).

Lupu, M. (2003), 'Concepts vagues et catégorisation', *Cahiers de Linguistique Française* 25, 291-304.

MacCormick, N. and Weinberger, O. (1986), *An Institutional Theory of Law* (Dordrecht: D. Reidel).

Macdonald, R. (2006a), 'Legal Language as A Trauma of Law and The Road to Rehabilitation', *Journal of Commonwealth Law and Legal Education* 4:1, 5-33.1

Macdonald, R. (2006b), 'Writing Better Decisions: Plain English in Decision Making', in Wagner and Cacciaguidi-Fahy (eds), pp.331-360.

MacKinnon, C. (1983), 'Feminism, Marxism, Method, and State: Toward Feminist Jurisprudence', *Signs: Journal of Women in Culture and Society* 8:4, 635-58.

Mäkitalo, L. (1970), *1920-luvun suomalaisen lakikielen virkerakenteesta* (A Master's Thesis, University of Turku).

Maley, Y. (1994), 'The Language of the Law', in Gibbons (ed.), pp.11-50.

Martin, R. (1971), 'La construction sur le fonds voisin', *Annales des Loyers*, 1199-209.

Martineau, P. (1979), *Les biens*, 5ème Edition (Montréal: Thémis).

Mathieu, B. (2004), *La loi*, 2ème Edition (Paris: Dalloz).

Mattila, H.S.E (2006), *Comparative Legal Linguistics*, tr. C. Goddard (Aldershot: Ashgate).

McKendrick, E. (2003), 'The Interpretation of Contracts: Lord Hoffmann's Re-Statement', in Worthington, S. (ed.) *Commercial Law and Commercial Practice* (London: Hart).

McMeel, G.P. (2003), 'Prior Negotiations and Subsequent Conduct – The next Step forward for Contractual Interpretation', *Law Quarterly Review* 119, 272-297.

Megarry, R.E. (1955) *Miscellany at Law* (London: Stevens and Sons Ltd).

Mellinkoff, D. (1963), *The Language of the Law* (Boston: Little, Brown and Co).

Mertens, B. (2004), *Gesetzgebungskunst im Zeitalter der Kodifikationen* (Tübingen: Mohr Siebeck).

Merz, H. (1962), '50 Jahre schweizerisches Zivilgesetzbuch', *Juristenzeitung* 17, 585-9.

Mignault, P.-B. (1896), *Le droit civil canadien*, vol. 2 (Montréal: Théoret).

Mignault, P.-B. (1922-1923), 'L'avenir de notre droit civil', *Revue du Droit* 1, 54-65; 104-16.

Mignault, P.-B. (1935-1936), 'Le Code civil de la province de Québec et son interprétation', *University of Toronto Law Journal* 1, 104-36.

Mignault, P.-B. (1936-1937), 'L'appel au Conseil privé', *Revue du Droit* 15, 133-55.

Ministry of Justice Publications (2006), *Bill Drafting Instructions* (Helsinki: Edita Prima).

Montalivet, P. de (2005), 'La 'juridicisation' de la légistique', in Drago (ed.).

Montesquieu, C. (1914), *The Spirit of Laws*, tr. T. Nugent, rev. J.V. Prichard (London: G. Bell and Sons).

Montesquieu, C. (1964), *Œuvres complètes: L'Esprit des Lois* (Paris: Éditions du Seuil).

Moor, P. (1994), *Droit administratif*, 2ème Edition (Berne: Stämpfli).

Moor, P. (2005), *Pour une théorie micropolitique du droit* (Paris: PUF).

Morand, C.A. (1999a), *Le droit néo-moderne des politiques publiques* (Paris: L.G.D.J.).

Morand, C.A. (1999b), 'Eléments de légistique formelle et matérielle', in Morand (ed.).

Morand, C.A. (ed.) (1999c), *Légistique formelle et matérielle / Formal and Material Legistic* (Aix-en-Provence: Presses Universitaires d'Aix-Marseille).

Moreau-Margrève, I. and Delnoy, P. (1978), 'Rapport belge sur l'interprétation par le juge des règles écrites en droits civil et commercial belge', in *Travaux de l'Association Henri Capitant*, vol. XXIX (Journées Louisianaises) (Paris: Economica), pp.31-33.

Müller, F. (1996), *Discours de la méthode juridique* (Paris: PUF).

Müller, G. (2003), 'Rechtsbereinigung — Rechtsverbesserung', *Schweizerisches Zentralblatt für Staats- und Verwaltungsrecht* 104:11, 561-583.

Munz, P. (2004), *Beyond Wittgenstein's Poker* (Aldershot: Ashgate).

Murphy, J.B. (2006), 'The Lawyer and the Layman: Two Perspectives on the Rule of Law', *The Review of Politics* 68, 101-131.

[n.a.] (2000), *Pensée politique et loi,* colloque AFHIP 1999 (Aix-en-Provence: Presses Universitaires d'Aix-Marseille).

[n.a.] (2001), *Law, Prospect and Retrospect, Levi Conference Proceedings* (Finland: University of Rovaniemei).

Naskali, P. (1992), *Laki on niin kuin se kirjoitetaan*, Master Thesis (Turku: University of Turku).

Newman, P. (2006), 'Archaeology and Construction: The Use of Predecessors to Ascertain the Meaning of a Contract', *Trust Law International* 20, 115-121.

Nicholls, D. Lord (2005), 'My Kingdom for a Horse: The Meaning of Words', *Law Quarterly Review* 121, 577-591.

Niemikorpi, A. (1991), *Suomen kielen sanaston dynamiikkaa*, Acta Wasaensia No 26 (Vaasa: Vaasan yliopisto).

Nietzsche, F. (1927), *The Philosophy of Nietzsche*, tr. H. Zimmern (New York: Modern Library).

Nilsson, S. (2004), *Att översätta ett förslag till en EG-förordning ur klarspråksperspektiv - möjligheter och begränsningar* [Translating a Proposed EC Directive From a Plain Language Perspective – Possibilities and Restrictions]. (Stockholm: University of Stockholm).

Nivet, F. (1998), 'Equité et légalité', *Justices* 9, 157-93.

Normand, S. (1986-1987), 'Un thème dominant de la pensée juridique traditionnelle au Québec: la sauvegarde de l'intégrité du droit civil', *McGill Law Journal* 32, 559-601.

Norton, R.F. (1928), *A Treatise on Deeds*, 2nd Edition (London: Sweet and Maxwell).

Opeibi, T. (Forthcoming) 'Investigating Aspects of Language Use in a Nigerian Courtroom Proceeding', *Pragmatics*.

O'Barr, W. (1982), *Linguistic Evidence: Language, Power and Strategy in the Courtroom* (New York: Academic Press).

O'Brien, P. (2005), 'Use and misuse of examples', *The Loophole* 1, 47-54.

Olmsted, W.R. (1991), 'The Uses of Rhetoric: Indeterminacy in Legal Reasoning, Political Thinking and the Interpretation of Literary Figures', *Philosophy and Rhetoric* 24:1, 1-24.

Oosterhoff, A.H. and Rayner, W.B. (1985), *Anger and Honsberger Law of Real Property*, vol. 2, 2nd Edition (Aurora (Ontario): Canada Law Book).

Ost, F. and Van de Kerchove, M. (1989), *Entre la lettre et l'esprit. Les directives d'interprétation en droit* (Bruxelles: Bruylant).

Ost, F. and Van de Kerchove, M. (1992), *Le jeu: un paradigme pour le* droit (Paris: LGDJ).

Ost, F. and Van de Kerchove, M. (2002), *De la pyramide au réseau? Pour une théorie dialectique du droit* (Brussels: Facultés Universitaires Saint-Louis).

Pajula, P. (1960), *Suomalaisen lakikielen historia pääpiirteittäin* (Porvoo: Werner Söderström Osakeyhtiö).

Palmer, F.R. (1986, 2001), *Mood and Modality* (Cambridge: Cambridge University Press).

Papadopoulos, Y. (1995), *Complexité sociale et politiques publiques* (Paris: Montchrestien).

Papaux, A. (2003), *Essai philosophique sur la qualification juridique: de la subsomption à l'abduction: l'exemple du droit international privé* (Bruxelles, Paris and Zurich: Bruylant/LGDJ/Schulthess Médias Juridiques).

Parés, N. (2002), *Är beUrakratspråket lag? Undersökning av en EG-förordning ur klarspråksperspektiv* [Is EU Legalise Law? An EC Regulation From a Plain Language Perspective] (Stockholm: University of Stockholm).

Pathak, R.S., Justice (1998), 'When and Where Do National Courts Reflect an International Culture When Deciding Issues Relating to International Arbitration?', in *ICCA Congress Series* 8, 173-186.

Paulsson, J. (1981), 'Arbitration Unbound: Award Detached from the Law of its Country of Origin', *International and Comparative Law Quarterly* 30, 358-387.

Pearce, D.C. and Geddes, R.S (2001), *Statutory Interpretation in Australia*, 5th Edition (Sydney: Butterworths).

Peerenboom, R. (2002), *China's Long March toward Rule of Law* (Cambridge: Cambridge University Press).

Phillips, D.Z. and Ruhr, M. von der (eds) (2005), *Religion and Wittgenstein's Legacy* (Aldershot: Ashgate).

Piehl, A. (2000), 'Finska EU-tjänstemäns syn på EU-texter', in Lindgren (ed.).

Piehl, A. (2006), 'The Influence of EU Legislation on Finnish Legal Discourse', in Gotti and Giannoni (eds).

Planiol, M. (1904), 'Inutilité d'une révision générale du Code civil', in Gaudemet (ed.).

Planiol, M. and Ripert, G. (1932), *Cours de droit civil français*, vol. 1, 12ème Edition (Paris: L.G.D.J.).

Plato (tr. D. Lee) (1955), *The Republic*, Rev 2nd Rp Edition (London: Penguin Classics).

Poirier, D. and Debruche, A.-F. (2005), *Introduction générale à la common law*, 3rd Edition (Cowansville: Yvon Blais).

Portalis, J.-E.-M. (1988), *Ecrits et discours juridiques et politiques* (Aix-en-Provence: Presses Universitaires d'Aix-Marseille).

Potter, P.B. (2001), *The Chinese Legal System: Globalization and Local Legal Culture* (London: Routledge Curzon).

Raynal, M. (1976), 'L'empiétement matériel sur le terrain d'autrui en droit privé', *Juris-Classeur Périodique*, I, 2800.

Raz, J. (1979), *The Authority of Law* (Oxford: Clarendon Press).

Rickheit, G and Strohner, H. (1999), 'Textverarbeitung; Von der Proposition zur Situation', in Friederici, A.D. (ed.), *Sprachrezeption* (Göttingen: Hogrefe), pp.271-306.

Riley, A. (1991), *English for the Law* (London: Macmillan).

Robertson, D. (1998), *Judicial Discretion in the House of Lords* (Oxford: Clarendon Press).

Robertson, R. (1992), *Globalization: Social Theory and Global Culture* (Sage: London).

Robinson, W. (2005), 'How the European Commission Drafts Legislation in 20 Languages', *Clarity* 53.

Rontu, H. (1974), *Ymmärrettävää virastokieltä* (Oikeusministeriön tiedote n:o 37).

Rontu, H. (1977), *Ymmärrettävää virastokieltä* (Oikeusministeriön lainsäädäntöosasto).

Rorvig, M. (1999), 'A Visual Exploration of the Orderliness of TREC Relevance Judgments', *Journal of the American Society for Information Science* 50:8, 652-660.

Ross, C. and Ross, L. (2000), 'Language and Law: Sources of Systemic Vagueness and Ambiguous Authority in Chinese Statutory Language', in Turner, K., Feinerman, J.V., and Guy, R.K, (eds), *The Limits of the Rule of Law in China* (Washington: The University of Washington Press), pp.221-270.

Ruiter, D.W.P. (1993), *Institutional Legal Facts: Legal Powers and Their Effects* (Dordrecht: Kluwer).

Sacco, R. ed. (2002), *L'Interprétation des textes juridiques rédigés dans plus d'une langue* (Torino: L'Harmattan Italy).

Saleh, S. (1992), 'La perception de l'arbitrage au Machrek et dans les pays du Golfe', *Revue de l'Arbitrage* 4, 549.

Saleilles, R. (1904), *Le Code civil et la méthode historique* ([n.p.]:[n.p]).

Salmi-Tolonen, T. (2003), 'Arbitration Law as Action: An Analysis of the Finnish Arbitration Act', in Bhatia, Candlin and Gotti (eds), pp.313-332.

Salmi-Tolonen, T. (2004), 'Legal Linguistic Knowledge and Creating and Interpreting Law in Multilingual Environments', *Brooklyn Journal of International Law* 29:3, 1167-1191.

Sanders, P. (1999), *Quo Vadis Arbitration? Sixty Years of Arbitration Practice* (The Hague: Kluwer Law International).

Schane, S. (2002), 'Ambiguity and Misunderstanding in the Law', *Thomas Jefferson Law Review* 25:1, 167-194.

Schane, S. (2007), *Language and The Law* (London: Continuum).

Schopenhauer, A. (1969), *The World as Will and Representation*, tr. E.F.J. Payne, 2 vols. (New York: Dover Books).

Seneca, L.A. (1938), *Ad Lucilium epistularum moralium quae supersunt*, iterum edidit, supplementum Quirinianum adiecit Otto Hense (Leipzig: Teubner).

Serafin, A. 1998), 'Kicking The Legalese Habit: The SEC's "Plain English Disclosure" Proposal', *Loyola University Chicago School of Law* 28, 681.

Shanker, S.G. (1987), *Wittgenstein and the Turning-Point in the Philosophy of Mathematics* (Albany: State University of New York Press).

Sheikhi, K. (1998), *Offentligt språk i Sverige och i EU – en jämförelse* [Language in Public Documents in Sweden and in The EU] (Mälardalen: Mälardalen University).

Smith, H. (2003), 'The Language of Property: Form, Context, and Audience', *Stanford Law Review*, 55, 1105-1191.

Smith, N. (1902), *Studies in the Cartesian Philosophy* (London: Macmillan).

Solan, L.M. (1993), *The Language of Judges* (Chicago: The University of Chicago Press).

Solan, L. (2004), 'Law and Language: Pernicious Ambiguity in Contracts and Statutes', *Chicago-Kent Law Review* 79, 859-877.

Spinoza, B. (1955), *Ethics*, tr. J. Gutmann (New York: Hafner Publishing).

Staughton, Sir, C. (1999), 'How do Courts Interpret Commercial Contracts', *The Cambridge Law Journal* 58:2, 303-313.

Stenqvist, U. (2000), 'Krav och förutsättningar för lagspråk i Europeiska unionen att använda det nationella språket internationellt', in Lindgren (ed.).

Stevens, W. (1997), *The Collected Poems of Wallace Stevens* (New York: Vintage Books).

Stevenson, D. (2003), 'To Whom is the Law Addressed?' *Yale Law and Policy Review*, 21, 105.

Stone, J. (1964), *Legal System and Lawyers' Reasonings* (Stanford: Stanford University Press).

Stora, C. (1982), 'Les empiétements sur le terrain d'autrui', *Revue administrer* Mai, 11-3.

Stratman, J.F. (2004), 'How Legal analysts Negotiate Indeterminacy of Meaning in Common Law rules: Towards a Synthesis of Linguistic and Cognitive Approaches to Investigations', *Language and Communication* 24, 23-57.

Sullivan, R. (1994), *Driedger on the Construction of Statutes*, 3rd Edition (Toronto: Butterworths).

Sullivan, R. (2001), 'Some Implications of Plain Language Drafting', *Statute Law Review* 22, 145-180.

Tanner, E. (2006), 'Clear, Simple, and Precise Legislative Drafting: How Does a European Community Directive Fare?' *Statute Law Review* 27:3, 150-175.

Tercier, P. (1991), *La recherche et la rédaction en droit suisse* (Fribourg: Editions Universitaires).

Terré, F. and Simler, P. (1998), *Droit civil. Les biens*, 5ème Edition (Paris: Dalloz).

Thuronyi, V. (1996), 'Drafting Tax Legislation', in Thuronyi, V. (ed.), *Tax Law Design and Drafting*, vol. 1 (Washington DC: IMF).

Tiersma, P. (1999), *Legal Language* (Chicago: The University of Chicago Press).

Touffait, A. and Tunc, A. (1974), 'Pour une motivation plus explicite des décisions de justice et en notamment de celles de la Cour de Cassation', *Revue Trimestrielle de Droit civil* 72, 487-508.

Trosborg, A. (1997), *Rhetorical Strategies in Legal Language* (Tübingen: Gunter Narr).

Tucker, E. (1985), 'The Gospel of Statutory Rules of Interpretation Requiring Liberal Interpretation according to St.-Peters', *University of Toronto Law Journal* 35, 113-53.

Tyynilä, M. (1984), *Lainvalmistelukunta 1884–1964* (Vammala: Vammalan kirjapaino Oy).

Van den Berg, J. (ed.) (1998), *International Dispute Resolution: Towards an International Arbitration Culture* (Dordrecht: Kluwer Law International).

Van Schooten, H. (2007), 'Law as Fact, Law as Fiction A Tripartite Model of Legal Communication', in Wagner, A., Werner, W. and Cao, D (eds), *Interpretation, Law and the Construction of Meaning* (Aldershot: Ashgate), pp.3-20.

Várady, T. (2006), *Language and Translation in International Commercial Arbitration: From the Constitution of the Arbitration Tribunal Through the Recognition and Enforcement Proceedings* (The Hague: T.M.C. Asser Press).

Viandier, A. (1986), 'La crise de la technique législative', *Droits* 4, 75.

Virtaniemi, A. (1992), *Säädöskielen virkerakenne*, Master Thesis (Jyväskylä: University of Jyväskylä).

Wagner, A. (2005a), 'Les apports de l'analyse linguistique dans la conception du flou et de la sécurité juridique', *La Semaine Juridique, Edition. Générale* 51, 2355-2359.

Wagner, A. (2005b), 'Semiotic Analysis of the Multistage Dynamic at the Core of Indeterminacy in Legal Language', in Bhatia, Engberg, Gotti and Heller (eds), 173-200.

Wagner, A. and Cacciaguidi-Fahy, S. (eds 2006), *Legal Language and The Search for Clarity* (Bern: Peter Lang).

Wagner, E. and Cutts, M. (2002), 'European Initiatives in the Use of Plain Legal Language', *Clarity* 47, 1-30.

Waismann, F. (1979), *Wittgenstein and the Vienna Circle: Conversations Recorded by Friedrich Waismann*, tr. J. Schulte and B. McGuiness (Oxford: Basil Blackwell).

Wallin, S. (2004), *Klarspråk inom EU. Om kvaliteten på dagens EU-texter och originalens betydelse för översättningarna* [About The Quality of Today's EU Texts and The Source Text's Influence on The Translated Text] (Gotheburg: University of Gothenburg).

Walton, F.P. (1980), *Le domaine et l'interprétation du Code civil du Bas-Canada*, tr. M. Tancelin (Toronto: Butterworths).

Wang, S. (1995), 'The Judicial Explanation in Chinese Criminal Law', *The American Journal of Comparative Law* 43:4, 569-579.

Wang, S. (2004), 'Environmental Crime and Environmental Criminal Law in the People's Republic of China', *European Journal of Crime, Criminal Law and Criminal Justice* 12:2, 150-165.

Warren, B. (1988), 'Ambiguity and Vagueness in Adjectives', *Studia Linguistica* 42:2, 122-172.

Weisflog, W.E. (1987), 'Problems of Legal Translation', *Swiss Reports presented at the XIIth International Congress of Comparative Law* (Schulthess, Zürich), pp.179-218.

Welle, D.W. and Farber, F.D. (1981), *Making the Unreadable Readable: From "Legalese" to Plain Language*: a paper presented at the annual conference of the College Reading Association, Louisville, Kentucky, October 31, 1981, unpublished.

Wheat, D. (1980), 'Disposition of Civil Law Appeals by the Supreme Court of Canada', *Supreme Court Law Review* 1, 425-55.

Williams, C. (2006), 'Fuzziness in Legal English: What Shall We Do with Shall?', in Wagner and Cacciaguidi-Fahy (eds), pp.237-264.

Williams, C. (2007), 'Crossovers in Legal Cultures in Westminster and Edinburgh: Some Recent Changes in The Language of The Law', *ESP Across Culture* 4.

Williamson, T. (2001), 'Vagueness, Indeterminacy and Social Meaning', *Critical Studies* 16, 61-76.

Willke, H. (1997), *Supervision des Staates* (Frankfurt am Main: Suhrkamp).

Wimsatt, W.K. and Beardsley, M. (1954), 'The Intentional Fallacy', in *The Verbal Icon: Studies in the Meaning of Poetry* (Lexington; University of Kentucky Press; reprinted in 1970, New York: Noonday Press):

Wittgenstein, L. (1958), *Philosophical Investigations*, tr. G.E.M. Anscombe, 3rd Edition (New York: Macmillan).

Wittgenstein, L. (1960), *The Blue and Brown Books* (New York: Harper and Row).

Wittgenstein, L. (1969), *Philosophische Grammatik* (Oxford: Basil Blackwell).

Wittgenstein, L. (1974), *Tractatus Logico-Philosophicus*, tr. D.F. Pears and B.F. McGuinness (Atlantic Highlands: Humanities Press International).

Wittgenstein, L. (1975), *Philosophical Remarks*, tr. R. Hargreaves and R. White (Chicago: University of Chicago Press).

Wittgenstein, L. (1976), *Lectures on the Foundations of Mathematics: Cambridge 1939*, Diamond, C. (ed.) (Chicago: University of Chicago Press).

Wittgenstein, L. (1978), *Philosophical Grammar*, tr. R. Rhees and A. Kenny (Berkeley: University of California Press).

Wittgenstein, L. (1979), *Wittgenstein's Lectures: Cambridge, 1932–1935*, Ambrose, A. (ed.) (Chicago: University of Chicago Press).

Wittgenstein, L. (1980), *Culture and Value*, tr. P. Winch (Chicago: University of Chicago Press).

Wittgenstein, L. (1983), *Remarks on the Foundation of Mathematics*, tr. G.E.M. Anscombe (Cambridge: MIT Press).

Wittgenstein, L. (1984), *Notebooks 1914–1916*, tr. G.E.M. Anscombe, 2nd Edition (Chicago: University of Chicago Press).

Wittgenstein, L. (1988), *Wittgenstein's Lectures on Philosophical Psychology, 1946–47*, Geach P.T. (ed.) (Chicago: University of Chicago Press).

Wittgenstein, L. (1994), *Wiener Ausgabe* (Vienna: Springer).

Wittgenstein, L. (1995), *Cambridge Letters*, McGuinness, B. and von Wright, G.H. (eds) (Oxford: Blackwell).

Wittgenstein, L. (2003), *Public and Private Occasions*, Klagge, J. and Nordmann, A. (ed.) (Lanham, MD: Rowman and Littlefield).

Wittgenstein, L., and Waismann, F. (2003), *The Voices of the Vienna Circle*, Baker, G. (ed.) (London: Routledge).

Wright, S. (2000), *Community and Communication: The Role of Language in Nation State Building and European Integration* (Clevedon: Multilingual Matters).

Wu, D., Ren, Y. and Li, L. (1992), *Bijiao lifa zhidu* [A Comparative Study of Legislative Systems] (Beijing: Qunzhong chubanshe).

Yang, S. and Huang, Y.Y. (2004), 'The Impact of the Absence of Grammatical Tense in L1 on the Acquisition of the Tense-Aspect System in L2', *International Review of Applied Linguistics* 42: 49-70.

Zimmerman, R. (1997), '"Statuta Sunt Stricte Interpretanda"? Statutes and the Common Law: A Continental Perspective', *Cambridge Law Journal* 315-28.

Online sources

Arbitration Institute of the Stockholm Chamber of Commerce (2004), *Rules of the Arbitration Institute of The Stockholm Chamber of Commerce* <http://www. sccinstitute.com/_upload/shared_files/regler/web_A4_vanliga_2004_eng.pdf>, accessed 25 February 2007.

Aristotle (350BC), *Nicomachean Ethics*, tr. W.D. Ross <http://www.constitution. org/ari/ethic_00.htm>, accessed 12 March 2007.

Awonusi, S. (2007), *Linguistic Hegemony and the Plight of Minority Languages in Nigeria* <http://www.reseau-amerique-latine.fr/ceisal-bruxelles/ESE/ESE-7-AWONUSI.pdf>, accessed 5 December, 2007.

Baedecke, B. and Sundin, M. (2002), 'Plain Language in Sweden: a Progress Report', *Fourth Biennial Conference Proceedings Plain Language Association International* (Toronto September 26 – 29, 2002) <http://www.plainlanguagenetwork.org/ conferences/2002/sweden/>, accessed on 6 September 2007.

Bergamo Arbitration Chamber (BAC) <http://www.bg.camcom.it/>, accessed 1 March 2007.

Bill Drafting Instructions (English version) <http://www.om.fi/uploads/ 7b3b69oecmj2dy2.pdf>, accessed 4 September 2007.

Campbell, L. (1996), 'Drafting Styles: Fuzzy or Fussy?' *E Law - Murdoch University* Electronic Journal of Law 3:2 (published online 4 August 1996) <http://www. murdoch.edu.au/elaw/issues/v3n2/campbell.html>, accessed 30 December 2006.

Chartre de la qualité de la réglementation du Ministère de la défense (2004) <http:// www.thematiques.modernisation.gouv.fr/UserFiles/File/C42-2%20doc%202b %20Processus%20labellisation%20VF%2016%2005%2007.pdf>, accessed 24 August 2007.

Confédération Suisse. *Recueil systématique du droit fédéral* <www.admin.ch>, accessed 2 March 2007.

Corpus Iuris Civilis [The Body of Civil Law] <http://www.thelatinlibrary.com/ justinian.html>, accessed 13 March 2007.

Cutts, M. (1994), *Lucid Law*, 1st Edition. <http://www.clearest.co.uk/>, accessed 21 February 2007.

Cutts, M. (1994), *Lucid Law*, 2nd Edition. <http://www.clearest.co.uk/index. php?id=22>, accessed 21 February 2007.

Dave, S. (2002), *Plain Language in Law* <http://www.llrx.com/features/ plainlanguage.htm#Table%20of%20Contents>, accessed in 5 December 2007.

European Union (1999) 'Interinstitutional Agreement of 22 December 1998 on Common Guidelines for the Quality of Drafting of Community Legisla*tion* (OJ C 073 17/3/1999: 0001-0004)' *Official Journal of the European Union* <http://eur-lex.europa.eu/LexUriServ/LexUriServ.do?uri=CELEX:31999Y0317(01):EN: HTML>, accessed 13 March 2003.

European Union (1999), 'Interinstitutional Agreement of 22 December 1998 on Common Guidelines for the Quality of Drafting of Community Legisla*tion* (OJ C 073 17/3/1999: 0001-0004)', *Official Journal of the European Union* <http://eur-lex.europa.eu/LexUriServ/LexUriServ.do?uri=CELEX:31999Y0317(01):EN: HTML>, accessed 24 August 2007.

European Union (2002), 'Euroopan parlamentin ja neuvoston direktiivi 2002/20/ EY, annettu 7 päivänä maaliskuuta 2002, sähköisiä viestintäverkkoja ja -palveluja koskevista valtuutuksista' (EYVL nro L 108 , 24/4/2002 0021 - 0032) <http:// eur-lex.europa.eu/LexUriServ/LexUriServ.do?uri=CELEX:32002L0020:FI: HTML>, accessed 4 September 2007.

European Union (2003), 'Interinstitutional Agreement on Better Law-Making (2003/ C 321/01)', *Official Journal of the European Union* <http://eur-lex.europa.eu/ LexUriServ/site/en/oj/2003/c_321/c_32120031231en00010005.pdf>, accessed 13 March 2003.

European Union (2003), *Joint Practical Guide of the European Parliament, the Council and the Commission or persons involved in the drafting of legislation within the Community institutions* <http://eur-lex.europa.eu/en/techleg/index. htm>, accessed 21 February 2007.

EU-språkvården [EU Language Service] <www.regeringen.se/sb/d/2750>, accessed 2 March 2007.

General Rules of Interpretation, Article 5.101 (Ex art. 7.101/ 101A) (1998), *The Principles of European Contract Law* <http://www.jus.uio.no/lm/eu.contract. principles.1998/doc.html>, accessed 14 December 2006.

Generic Integrity in Legislative Discourse in Multilingual and Multicultural Contexts <http://gild.mmc.cityu.edu.hk/>, accessed 1 March 2007.

Giscard d'Estaing V. (2003), 'La Convention européenne à mi-parcours' <http:// www.aidh.org/Europe/Conv_pdv03.htm>, accessed 13 March 2007.

Hallintolaki (2003) <http://www.finlex.fi/en/laki/kaannokset/1982/en19820598. pdf> (English translation), accessed 24 August 2007.

Horne, N. (2005), Legislative Drafting in Australia, New Zealand and Ontario: Notes on An Informal Survey. *The Loophole – Journal of the Commonwealth Association of Legislative Counsel*, 1: 55-102. Available at <http://www.opc.gov. au/calc/docs/LOOPHOLE2005v7.pdf>, accessed 13 September 2007.

Institutet för språk och folkminnen [Institute for Dialectology, Onomastics and Folklore Research in Uppsala] <www.sofi.se>, accessed 2 March 2007.

Intercultural Discourse in Domain-specific English <http://www.unibg.it/cerlis>, accessed 1 March 2007.

International Court of arbitration (2004), *Rules of Arbitration of the International Chamber of Commerce* <http://www.iccwbo.org/court/english/arbitration/pdf_ documents/rules/rules_arb_english.pdf>, accessed 25 February 2007.

Klarspråksgruppens enkätresultat [Result of Surveys] <www.sprakradet.se/2067>, accessed 2 March 2007.

Klarspråkstestet [plain language test] <www.sprakradet.se/2065>, accessed 2 March 2007.

Lainlaatijan EU-opas [the *Legal Drafter's Guide to the European Union*] (Helsinki: Edita) <http://www.om.fi/25714.htm>, accessed 4 September 2007.

London Court of International Arbitration (1998), *Rules of The London Court of International Arbitration* <http://www.lcia.org/ARB_folder/ARB_DOWNLOADS/ENGLISH/rules.pdf>, accessed 25 February 2007.

Milan Arbitration Chamber (MAC) <http://www.mi.camcom.it/show.jsp?page=327160>, accessed 1 March 2007.

Office of the Chief Parliamentary Counsel Victoria (March 2006), Notes on the PreparationofStatutoryRules<http://www.vcec.vic.gov.au/CA256EAF001C7B21/WebObj/NotesfortheGuidanceofLegislationOfficers2006/$File/Notes%20for%20the%20Guidance%20of%20Legislation%20Officers%202006.pdf>, accessed 13 September 2007.

På väg mot ett bättre myndighetsspråk (2001:18) [Towards better Swedish in public authorities] <www.sprakradet.se/2067>, accessed 2 March 2007.

Plain Swedish Group (2002), *Klarspråksbulletinen* [The Plain Swedish Bulletin] Special Edition. in English <http://www.sweden.gov.se/content/1/c6/04/01/75/aa294215.pdf>, accessed 2 March 2007.

Paremman sääntelyn toimintaohjelma - Valtioneuvoston kanslian julkaisusarja [the Better Regulation Programme] (2006) (Edita: Valtioneuvoston kanslia) <http://www.vnk.fi/julkaisukansio/2006/j08-paremman-saantelyn-toimintaohjelma-osa-1/pdf/fi.pdf>, accessed 4 September 2007.

Quiggin, P. (2007), Training and Development of Legislative Drafters. *The Loophole – Journal of the Commonwealth Association of Legislative Counsel*, 2: 14-30 <http://www.opc.gov.au/calc/docs/calc_loophole_july_2007.pdf>, accessed 13 September 2007.

Redaktionella och språkliga frågor i EU-arbetet (SB PM 2005:3) [Editorial and linguistic issues on implementing EU legislation] <www.regeringen.se/sb/d/2750>, accessed 2 March 2007.

Scott, A and Zuleeg, F. (2005), *Clarity and Transparency: Impact of Existing EU Legislation on Business in Member States* <http://www.scotland.gov.uk/Resource/Doc/917/0022212.pdf>, accessed 6 March 2007.

Secrétariat général du Gouvernement and Conseil d'Etat (2005), *Guide pour l'élaboration des textes législatifs et réglementaires* (Paris: La documentation française) <http://www.legifrance.gouv.fr/html/Guide_legistique/guide_leg.pdf>, accessed 13 March 2007.

Skatteverket [Central Tax Authority] <www.skatteverket.se>, accessed 2 March 2007.

Språkrådet [Language Council] <http://www.sprakradet.se/plain_language>, accessed 2 March 2007.

Statskontoret [Swedish Agency for Public Management] <www.sprakradet.se/2067>, accessed 2 March 2007.

Stuart, G. (2004), 'Few have read draft but already are rushing into Yes or No camp' *Daily Telegraph* (published on line 29 April 2004) <http://www.telegraph.co.uk/news/main.jhtml;jsessionid=SJ5NFO03J210HQFIQMGSFF4AVCBQWIV0?xml=/news/2004/04/29/neu129.xml>, accessed 13 March 2007.

Sundrin, M. (1998), *Plain English and Swedish Klasprak: A Comparison between Plain Language Movements, Style Guides and Practice* <http://www.textfixarna.se/include/arbete/plain_english.pdf>, accessed 29 March, 2007.

Svarta listan [black list] <http://www.regeringen.se/content/1/c6/01/97/75/e28ebb27.pdf>, accessed 2 March 2007.

Switzerland, Federal Office of Justice (2002), *Guide de législation: guide pour l'élaboration de la législation fédérale* (Berne: [n.p.]) <http://www.bj.admin.ch/bj/fr/home/themen/staat_und_buerger/legistik/gesetzgebungsleitfaden.html>, accessed 5 December 2007.

Tiersma, P. (1999), *The Creation, Structure, and Interpretation of The Legal Text* <http://www.languageandlaw.org/LEGALTEXT.HTM>, accessed 5 December 2007.

Translation Centre for the European Union Bodies <www.cdt.europa.eu>, accessed 2 March 2007.

UNCITRAL Arbitration Rules <http://www.uncitral.org/pdf/english/texts/arbitration/arb-rules/arb-rules.pdf>, accessed 4 February 2007.

UNCITRAL Model Law on International Commercial Arbitration <http://www.uncitral.org/pdf/english/texts/arbitration/ml-arb/06-54671_Ebook.pdf>, accessed 4 February 2007.

Venice Court of National and International Arbitration (VENCA) <http://www.venca.it/index.html>, accessed 1 March 2007.

WTO Dispute Settlement Body Special Session (25 October 2005), *Negotiations on Improvements and Clarifications of the Dispute Settlement Understanding. Further Contribution of the United States on Improving Flexibility and Member Control in WTO Dispute Settlement – Communication from the United States* TN/DS/W/82/Add.1 <http://www.law.georgetown.edu/iiel/research/projects/dsureview/documents/W82A1.doc>, accessed 4 February 2007.

Zhai, J. (2002), 'Judicial Information of the People's Republic of China: A Survey' (published on line 1 October 2002) <http://www.llrx.com/features/chinajudicial.htm>, accessed 24 August 2007.

Conference Papers

Adegbija, E. (1998), 'Nigerian Englishes: Towards A Standard Variety', Keynote Address Presented at the *5th Conference of the International Association of World Englishes* (IAWE) (Urbana: University of Illinois).

Battistoni, E. (2005), Opacité dans le langage juridique et dans les écrits juridiques en Belgique: Des Problèmes de lisibilité. Les présages d'un changement possible. Synthèse de quelques initiatives. Prospectives. Paper presented at the International Conference on Clarity and Obscurity in Legal Language / Transparence et opacité du discours juridique (Boulogne sur Mer: Université du Littoral Côte d'Opale, 5- 9 July), pp.1-46. On file with author.

Opeibi, T. (2005) 'Between Clarity and Obscurity: A Study of Selected Legal Texts in Nigeria', Paper presented at the *Colloque International sur la Transparence et Opacité du Discours Juridique 2005* (France: Université du Littoral, Côte d'Opale). On file with author.

Reports

Law Reform Commission (2000), *The Report on Statutory Drafting and Interpretation: Plain Language and the Law in Ireland LRC 61 – 2000* (Dublin: LRC).

Mål i mun (SOU 2002:27) [State Commission Report: Speech – Draft Action Programme for the Swedish Language].

New Zealand Law Commission (1995), *Legislation Manual: Structure and Style (Report 35)*.

OECD (2002), 'Regulatory Policies in OECD Countries, From interventionism to regulatory governance', *OECD Reviews of Regulatory Reform* (Paris: OECD).

Office de Révision du Code Civil (1978), *Rapport sur le Code civil du Québec*, vol. I, livre IV (Montréal: Editeur officiel du Québec).

Svenskan i EU (SOU 1998:14) [Swedish in the EU].

Socialförsäkringsbalk (SOU 2005:114) [Social Insurance Code].

Index